The Secular Outlook

Blackwell Public Philosophy
Edited by Michael Boylan, Marymount University

In a world of 24-hour news cycles and increasingly specialized knowledge, the Blackwell Public Philosophy series takes seriously the idea that there is a need and demand for engaging and thoughtful discussion of topics of broad public importance. Philosophy itself is historically grounded in the public square, bringing people together to try to understand the various issues that shape their lives and give them meaning. This "love of wisdom" – the essence of philosophy – lies at the heart of the series. Written in an accessible, jargon-free manner by internationally renowned authors, each book is an invitation to the world beyond newsflashes and soundbites and into public wisdom.

Forthcoming:

For further information about individual titles in the series, supplementary material, and regular updates, visit www.blackwellpublishing.com/publicphilosophy

The Secular Outlook
In Defense of Moral and Political Secularism

Paul Cliteur

A John Wiley & Sons, Ltd., Publication

This edition first published 2010
© 2010 Paul Cliteur

Blackwell Publishing was acquired by John Wiley & Sons in February 2007. Blackwell's publishing program has been merged with Wiley's global Scientific, Technical, and Medical business to form Wiley-Blackwell.

Registered Office
John Wiley & Sons Ltd, The Atrium, Southern Gate, Chichester, West Sussex, PO19 8SQ, United Kingdom

Editorial Offices
350 Main Street, Malden, MA 02148-5020, USA
9600 Garsington Road, Oxford, OX4 2DQ, UK
The Atrium, Southern Gate, Chichester, West Sussex, PO19 8SQ, UK

For details of our global editorial offices, for customer services, and for information about how to apply for permission to reuse the copyright material in this book please see our website at www.wiley.com/wiley-blackwell.

The right of Paul Cliteur to be identified as the author of this work has been asserted in accordance with the UK Copyright, Designs and Patents Act 1988.

Library of Congress Cataloging-in-Publication Data
Cliteur, P. B.
    The secular outlook : in defense of moral and political secularism / Paul Cliteur.
      p. cm. – (Blackwell public philosophy ; 10)
    Includes bibliographical references and index.
    ISBN 978-1-4443-3520-0 (hardcover : alk. paper) – ISBN 978-1-4443-3521-7 (pbk. : alk. paper) 1. Secularism. 2. Free thought. 3. Religion and ethics. 4. Religion and politics. I. Title.
    BL2747.8.C58 2010
    211'.6–dc22

                                             2010006499

Hardback ISBN: 9781444335200

A catalogue record for this book is available from the British Library.

Set in 10 on 12 pt Sabon by Toppan Best-set Premedia Limited
Printed and bound in Malaysia by Vivar Printing Sdn Bhd

01   2010

Contents

Acknowledgments

I should like to add a word of acknowledgment to my colleague Professor Afshin Ellian, who coordinates the activities of the work group "Social Cohesion, Multiculturalism, and Globalization" at the Law School of the University of Leiden in the Netherlands. I have greatly benefited from discussions with him and other members of the research group on secularism and the role of religion in public life. Needless to say, I am solely responsible for any conclusions reached in the book.

And finally, as always, I should like to thank my wife Carla. She has read all the chapters time and again and provided me with some extremely helpful suggestions for their improvement.

Introduction:
The Secular Outlook

What nobody would have thought possible in the 1960s and 1970s actually happened in the following decades: a widening of the gulf between religious believers and unbelievers. Christianity is growing modestly, Islam is growing exponentially, but atheism also has more adherents than ever before.

A lively debate on religion is also taking place. Books like Richard Dawkins' *The God Delusion* (2006)[1] are being sold in huge numbers, but so are books written from an explicitly Christian or other religious point of view (e.g. those by Karen Amstrong).

At the same time, the world is being confronted with a relatively new phenomenon: religious violence – in particular, religious terrorism. Governments are suddenly facing religious leaders who issue death sentences for writers, and they are struggling with the demands of religious minorities in the midst of their liberal democracies.

This book addresses some of these issues and makes a case for a "secular outlook" on life. That implies that it is not primarily concerned with defending atheism, nor does it defend theism – its central concern is to show how religious believers and unbelievers can live peacefully together and what principles the state should try to stimulate in its citizenry to achieve social harmony and social cohesion. The underlying idea is that the basic principles of secularism are important for the time in which we live.

*   *   *

In recent decades we have, according to many people, witnessed an upsurge of religion. Among scholars there seems to be a nearly universal consensus that the so-called "secularization thesis" has failed. The secularization thesis, advocated by seminal social thinkers in the nineteenth and twentieth centuries, held that religion would gradually fade in importance and even

---

[1] Dawkins, Richard, *The God Delusion*, Black Swan, Transworld Publishers, London 2006.

cease to be significant with the advent of modern society. Emile Durkheim, Max Weber, Karl Marx, and Sigmund Freud, amongst others, all subscribed to this vision of the future course of events. However, in 2000, the sociologists of religion Rodney Stark (1934–) and Roger Finke (1954–) suggested that it was time to bury the secularization thesis.[2]

Up until the 1970s and '80s secularization seemed to be on the march in Europe, especially in the Netherlands and the Scandinavian countries. But this, some scholars say, all changed 10 to 20 years later. A number of them referred to a "revanche of God,"[3] or a "return of the sacred."[4] Even so notorious a secularist philosopher as Jürgen Habermas (1929–) seemed to have second thoughts.[5] Secularization was not an irreversible process, many scholars now write. Theodore Dalrymple (1949–) captures the mood rather well:

> In my naive, historicist way, I assumed that secularization was an irreversible process, like the breaking of eggs: that once people had seen the glory of life without compulsory obeisance to the men of God, they would never turn back to them as the sole guides to their lives and politics.[6]

Whether this reversal of the climate of opinion is real or superficial, whether it is temporary or permanent, remains to be seen. But what can be said is that ideas of secularism and the secular state no longer go unchallenged. This challenge comes from two sides. On the one hand, it comes from those advocating a greater influence of religion on the state and the public domain *on religious grounds*. On the other hand, it comes from those who, on *non-religious grounds*, claim that we should give more attention to religion.

---

[2]   Stark, Rodney, and Finke, Roger, *Acts of Faith*, University of California Press, Berkeley 2000, p. 79. For the opposite view, see: Paul, Gregory S., "Cross-National Correlations of Quantifiable Social Health with Popular Religiosity and Secularism in the Prosperous Democracies," *Journal of Religion and Society*, 7 2005, pp. 1–17.

[3]   Kepel, Gilles, *La Revanche de Dieu: Chrétiens, juifs et musulmans à la reconquête du monde* [The Revenge of God: Christians, Jews, and Muslims Out to Reconquer the World], Le Seuil, Paris 1991.

[4]   Bell, Daniel, "The Return of the Sacred," in: Daniel Bell, *The Winding Passage. Essays and Sociological Journeys 1960–1980*, Basic Books, New York 1980, pp. 324–355.

[5]   See on this: Habermas, Jürgen, and Ratzinger, Joseph, *The Dialectics of Secularization: On Reason and Religion*, Ignatius Press, San Francisco 2005, and for an analysis of this exchange of views: Bowman, Jonathan, "Extending Habermas and Ratzinger's *Dialectics of Secularization*: Eastern Discursive Influences on Faith and Reason in a PostsecularAge," *Forum Philosophicum*, 14 2009, pp. 39–55, p. 29: "Jurgen Habermas and Joseph Ratzinger agree that we have entered a postsecular age (2006)."

[6]   Dalrymple, Theodore, "When Islam Breaks Down," in: Theodore Dalrymple, *Our Culture, What's Left of It: The Mandarins and the Masses*, Ivan R. Dee, Chicago 2005, pp. 283–296, p. 283.

The latter approach is defended under the banner of "multiculturalism."[7] Those two positions, although leading to the same end, must be carefully distinguished.

Moreover, there is another distinction that we have to honor.

On the one hand, we have the discussion among sociologists of religion about the validity of the secularization thesis. Does it hold? Is it true that modernization is pushing religion to the margins of existence? Or should we follow Stark and Finke in burying that thesis?

This "secularization debate" is to be distinguished from a debate among constitutional scholars, moral philosophers, and political theorists on the question of how the state and society should react to the presumed comeback of religion in the public arena.[8] This second debate is not about the process of secularization but about the value of secularism in both ethics and politics. We should carefully distinguish secularization from secularism.

First: what is *secularization*? Daniel Philpott (1967–) avers that:

> Secularization is a rather descriptive statement, holding that the political ends of citizens, organizations, and societies themselves are no longer as explicitly religious as they once were or are no longer explicitly religious at all.[9]

In the words of the American sociologist Peter L. Berger (1929–) secularization is the "process by which sectors of society and culture are removed from the domination of religious institutions and symbols."[10]

In contrast to secularization, "secularism," in the sense in which I will use the term, is a normative or ethical creed. The secularist contends that the best way to deal with religious differences is a morally neutral vocabulary that we all share and a morality that is not based on religion. The

---

[7]   See: Baber, H.E., *The Multicultural Mystique: The Liberal Case against Diversity*, Prometheus Books, Amherst, NY 2008, p. 26 ff. Severe criticism of multiculturalism is also found in: Rooy, Wim van, *De Malaise van de Multiculturaliteit* [The Malaise of Multiculturalism], Acco, Leuven/Voorburg 2008; a defense in: Parekh, Bhikhu, *Rethinking Multiculturalism: Cultural Diversity and Political Theory*, Macmillan Press, Basingstoke 2000; Parekh, Bhikhu, *A New Politics of Identity: Political Principles for an Interdependent World*, Palgrave Macmillan, Basingstoke 2008.

[8]   See on this: Sajó, András, "Preliminaries to a Concept of Constitutional Secularism," *International Journal of Constitutional Law*, July 29, 2008, pp. 1–25; Sajó, András, "A Reply," *International Journal of Constitutional Law*, June 15, 2009, pp. 515–528; Zucca, Lorenzo, "The Crisis of the Secular State – A Reply to Professor Sajó," *International Journal of Constitutional Law*, June 15, 2009, pp. 494–514.

[9]   Philpott, Daniel, "The Challenge of September 11 to Secularism in International Relations," *World Politics*, 55 2002, pp. 66–95, p. 69.

[10]   Berger, Peter L., *The Social Reality of Religion*, Allen Lane, London 1973, p. 113; for a commentary see: Madan, T.N., "Secularism in Its Place," *The Journal of Asian Studies*, 46, no. 4 1987, pp. 747–759, p. 748.

words "secular" and "secularism," in the sense that I use them, do not entail any negative attitude to religion.[11] Although George Holyoake (1817– 1906) coined the term "secularism" as a "policy of life for those who do not accept theology," I will not subscribe to his semantics.[12]

Secularism should also be clearly distinguished from the position of those who predict the demise of religion (i.e. "secularization"). In her book *The Case for God* (2009) Karen Armstrong (1944–) writes: "Contrary to the confident secularist predictions of the mid twentieth century, religion is not going to disappear."[13] My point is that Armstrong, like some other authors writing on religion and secularism, mixes up "secularism" and the "secularization thesis." A secularist to her is someone who believes in the secularization thesis. This book is mainly devoted to secularism, not to secularization. Armstrong and others may, of course, gleefully criticize the secularization thesis, but that is flogging a dead horse. Their argumentation has no consequence whatsoever for the viability of secularism as a moral and political philosophy or a vision of how the state should relate to religion. On the contrary.

This subject is topical. It has been said that "In spite of the critiques of religion put forward by scientists and atheists, the number of people professing some kind of religious belief is actually increasing worldwide."[14] The approximate numbers of adherents to the largest faiths as percentages of the world's total population are as follows: Christianity 32%, Islam, 21%, Non-religious 15%, Hinduism 12.5%, Primal religions 5.5%, Chinese traditional 5.5%, Buddhism 5.5%, Sikhism 0.35%, Judaism 0.25%, other 2.4%.[15]

What makes this rising trend for religions even more important is that, according to perspicacious observers, we are not only witnessing the return

---

[11] See on this: Davison, David, "Turkey, a 'Secular' State? The Challenge of Description," *The South Alantic Quarterly*, 102, no. 2/3 2003, pp. 333–350, p. 334: "*Secular* may thus convey a negative translation to religion and religiosity." Although it is widespread, I will not follow this use of the term "secular." Karen Armstrong contends that "in the Muslim world, secularism has often consisted of a brutal attack upon religion and the religions." See: Armstrong, Karen, *Islam: A Short History*, Random House, Toronto 2002, p. 158. It is not clear what she means by that and she does not give examples, but, whatever the case may be, secularism is not necessarily anti-religious, as I will try to make clear in this book. Secularism has nothing to do with a "brutal attack upon religion" but with fostering a moral attitude and developing political institutions that make it possible for people from different religious and non-religious persuasions to live together.

[12] Holyoake, George Jacob, *The Principles of Secularism*, third edition, Austin and Company, London 1870, p. 6.

[13] Armstrong, Karen, *The Case for God: What Religion Really Means*, The Bodley Head, London 2009, p. 9.

[14] Wilkinson, Philip, *Religions*, Dorley Kindersley Limited, London 2008, p. 338.

[15] Ibid.

of religion in general, but that of violent, fundamentalist, or even terrorist varieties of religious belief. In 2007 the United Nations published a report with the shocking (although not unexpected) conclusion that religious tolerance (in the sense of tolerance exerted by religions)[16] is on the wane everywhere.[17] The special reporter for the UN, Asma Jahangir (1952–), noted that religious groups in general are tending to be less and less tolerant toward criticism of their beliefs. This religious intolerance manifests itself not only in Islam, but also in Christianity, and even in Buddhism.

This intolerance can be discerned in the increasing number of complaints from people who feel they have been offended in their religious convictions. More and more people are protesting about what they read and hear from others.[18] As you can see if you carefully study what these people complain about, the complaints, in many cases, relate to trivial matters. Nevertheless, the grievances arise, and for those affected they seem to be terribly real.

That brings us to the subject of "religious violence," a notion that is central to this book. In the words of Mark Juergensmeyer (1940–) there seems to be a "global rebellion" against the secular state.[19] Catholic theologian and leading public intellectual George Weigel (1951–) formulates the significance of the religious upsurge referring to 9/11:

> Viewed through history's wide-angle lens, the events of September 11, 2001, were one lethal expression of the fact that, contrary to secularization theory and the widespread assumptions of the world's elites (including governmental elites), the twenty-first century will be one in which rapidly advancing modernization coincides with an explosion of religious conviction and passion.[20]

Recent decades have witnessed not only an upsurge of religious feelings, but also an increasing willingness by people to perpetrate violence or threaten violence if they are offended in those feelings. We have, for instance, seen an increasing amount of religious violence and even terrorism directed

---

[16]   So this is about tolerance as *practiced by* religions, not tolerance *toward* religions. Although both forms of tolerance are important, the first issue is a blind spot in the literature on this subject, the latter a sole preoccupation.

[17]   Jahangir, Asma, *Promotion and Protection of all Human Rights, Civil, Political, Economic, Social and Cultural Rights, including the Right to Development*, Report by the Special Rapporteur on Freedom of Religion or Belief, A/HRC/6/5, 20 July 2007.

[18]   An impressive analysis of this process is also to be found in: Malik, Kenan, *From Fatwa to Jihad: The Rushdie Affair and Its Legacy*, Atlantic Books, London 2009, especially p. 142 ff.

[19]   Juergensmeyer, Mark, *Global Rebellion: Religious Challenges to the Secular State, from Christian Militias to Al Qaeda*, University of California Press, Berkeley 2008.

[20]   Weigel, George, *Faith, Reason, and the War against Jihadism: A Call to Action*, Doubleday, New York 2007, p. 3.

against public intellectuals, comedians, cabaret performers, cartoonists, playwrights, and others who use the spoken and written word.[21] The fatwa against Salman Rushdie (1947–) issued in 1989 is a notorious case in point. In 2002 American Islamic scholar Daniel Pipes (1949–) wrote: "Khomeini himself passed from the scene just weeks after issuing his edict, but the spirit it engendered very much lives on. Since 1989, militant Islamic efforts to silence those who critique Islam or Muslims have had impressive results."[22] Unfortunately, Pipes was not being unduly pessimistic in 2002, and he seems even more right today. Since that time threats against writers have proliferated.[23] In 2004 the Dutch filmmaker and writer Theo van Gogh (1957–2004) was murdered by a jihadist who claimed to be following a "law" that commanded him to chop the head off of everyone who calls Allah and his Prophet names.[24] In 2006 the Danish cartoon affair caused much havoc in Europe and the Middle East.[25] Perhaps less well known to the general public is the fact that on March 27, 2008 the Dutch Parliamentarian Geert Wilders (1963–) put a movie on the Internet under the title *Fitna*. The movie is a 16-minute succession of images connecting Islam with violence and oppression.

From an artistic point of view the film is not very interesting,[26] but the reactions certainly were. As probably never before, representatives of the international community considered it their task to publicly comment on a

[21]   See on this: Murray, Douglas, and Verwey, Johan Pieter, *Victims of Intimidation: Freedom of Speech within Europe's Muslim Communities*, The Centre for Social Cohesion, London 2008; Murray, Douglas, "Think Tank: Betrayal of Muslim Reformers," *Timesonline*, November 23, 2008.

[22]   Pipes, Daniel, *Militant Islam Reaches America*, W.W. Norton & Company, New York, London 2002, p. 172.

[23]   See: King, Anna, "Islam, Women and Violence," *Feminist Theology*, 17 no. 3 2009, pp. 292–328, p. 296.

[24]   Declared by B. during his trial at 12 July 2005 and to be found (in Dutch) at: http://www.nos.nl/nosjournaal/dossiers/terreurinnederland/verklaringbtekst.html. Two weeks later, at 26 July 2005, B. was sentenced to a life imprisonment for the murder of Van Gogh. For a succinct presentation of some of the facts of the case, see: Berg, Floris van den, "Zero Tolerance," *Free Inquiry*, January/February 2005, p. 1.

[25]   See on this: Sifaoui, Mohamed, *L'affaire des caricatures de Mahomet: dessins et manipulations* [The Affair of the Cartoons of Mohammed: Drawings and Manipulations], Éditions Privé, Paris 2006; Jespersen, Karen, and Pittelkow, Ralf, *Islamisten en naïvisten. Een aanklacht* [Islamists and Naivists. An Accusation], Nieuw Amsterdam, Amsterdam 2007.

[26]   This distinguishes Wilders' film from that of the Dutch politician Ehsan Jami (1985–) who posted on the internet on December 9, 2008 a sometimes ironic, sometimes comic dialogue with the founder of the Islamic faith with the title "An Interview with Muhammed." On behalf of the Dutch government, the Ministry of Foreign Affairs published a "declaration" in response to Jami's film ("Verklaring van de Nederlandse regering inzake de film van Jami," at: www.minbuza.nl) stating that the Netherlands has a tradition of freedom of worship but also of freedom of speech. Hurting the feelings of others is not part of that tradition.

film. Wilders' film set the precedent.[27] In a joint statement all the ministers of foreign affairs of European countries distanced themselves from *Fitna*. They emphatically rejected the idea that there was a connection between Islam and violence. In itself this is not a surprising comment and there may even be good reasons for this point of view, but what *was* surprising was that official representatives of European states felt inclined to comment on a film that was – in the opinion of the ministers themselves as well, because nobody declared the film illegal – made under the protection of the European principle of free speech.

Even the United Nations went so far as to comment on the film. On March 28 the Secretary General of the United Nations, Ban Ki-moon (1944–), criticized the film for being "offensively anti-Islamic."[28] "I condemn in the strongest terms, the airing of Geert Wilders' offensively anti-Islamic film," Mr. Ban said in a statement. "The right to free expression is not at stake here," he added. "Freedom must always be accompanied by social responsibility." The EU's Slovenian presidency said the film served no purpose other than "inflaming hatred." The irony was, of course, that this film was meant as a *protest* against hatred and violence grounded in religion. Apparently, Ban Ki-moon and Wilders have a different opinion of the nature of a world religion, which is perfectly legitimate. But what was new was that the Secretary General of the United Nations felt compelled to take a stance in a criminological and theological debate about the connection between religion and violence. I refer to the science of criminology because this is the discipline that takes a stance on what the causes of crime are (and perpetrating violence is a crime). Is this judgment by the Secretary General based on scientific research? And if so, what research? The Secretary General also takes a stance on the proper interpretation of a religious tradition. This is a new development in the history of the UN, something that is usually left to theologians. Is the UN the proper institution to proclaim official stances on criminology and theology? This is certainly not something that has a basis in the founding documents of the UN.

And how could the Secretary General contend that "the right of free expression is not at stake here?" If freedom of expression is not at stake *here*, then when is it exactly?

There were hardly any voices that proclaimed the principle of tolerance (in the sense of tolerating religious criticism, not in the sense of abolishing religious criticism), the principle of free speech (as enshrined in the European Convention on Human Rights and Fundamental Freedoms) or the freedom of religion (including the right to criticize religion or apostatize, as article

[27]   See on this: Ellian, Afshin, "Criticism and Islam," *The Wall Street Journal*, March 31, 2008.
[28]   BBC, "UN chief condemns anti-Islam film," *BBC News*, March 28, 2008.

18 of the Universal Declaration of Human Rights proclaims). The Dutch prime minister J.P. Balkenende (1956–), apparently also an expert on theology, said shortly before (!) the release of the film: "We reject this interpretation."[29]

Perhaps these highly unusual comments by high-ranking politicians are justified against the backdrop of a terrorist threat.[30] But, if that is the case, there should at least be a coherent analysis of the situation, and a subsequent balancing of the threats with the loss of values and rights that seems imminent. In 1859 the British philosopher John Stuart Mill (1806–1873) wrote: "If all mankind minus one, were of one opinion, and only one person were of the contrary opinion, mankind would be no more justified in silencing that one person, than he, if he had the power, would be justified in silencing mankind."[31] This seems like an echo from a past era. This sentence voices the same worldview as the famous words often attributed to Voltaire (1694–1778): "I may disagree with what you have to say, but I shall defend, to the death, your right to say it."[32] The values espoused by Voltaire, Mill, and many other important authors are not eclipsed – but they are surely challenged – by violent religious fanaticism.

What is particularly disturbing is the awkward reaction by official institutions to the challenge that religious fanatics make to the values of free speech, tolerance, freedom of religion and freedom of conscience. We may say with Friedrich Hayek (1899–1992) that "the basic principles on which this civilization was built have been falling into increasing disregard and oblivion."[33]

What I want to do in *The Secular Outlook* is to present what I call a "secular outlook"[34] on life and society as clearly and consistently as I can.

---

[29]   Ibid.

[30]   An attempt to analyze the reactions of Europe's political elite is made by: Caldwell, Christopher, *Reflections on the Revolution in Europe: Immigration, Islam and the West*, Allen Lane, Penguin Books, London 2009; Jenkins, Philip, *God's Continent: Christianity, Islam, and Europe's Religious Crisis*, Oxford University Press, Oxford 2007; Bawer, Bruce, "Heirs to Fortuyn," *The Wall Street Journal*, April 23, 2009; Bawer, Bruce, *Surrender: Appeasing Islam, Sacrificing Freedom*, Doubleday, New York 2009.

[31]   Mill, John Stuart, *On Liberty*, 1859, ed. Stefan Collini, Cambridge University Press, Cambridge 1989, p. 20.

[32]   These actual words are not to be found in Voltaire's works, but they are certainly in harmony with the spirit of his ideas. See: Baggini, Julian, "I may disagree with what you have to say, but I shall defend to the death your right to say it," in: Julian Baggini, *Should You Judge this Book by its Cover? 100 Fresh Takes on Familiar Sayings and Quotations*, Granta, London 2009, pp. 35–36.

[33]   Hayek, F.A., *Law, Legislation and Liberty*, Routledge and Kegan Paul, London 1982, p. 2.

[34]   When I use the words *The Secular Outlook* (in italics) I refer to this book. If I refer to "the secular outlook," I have in mind the composite traditions of (private) atheism (non-

It may be possible that those values that were once the pride of Europe no longer reflect its actual priorities. But in order to gauge whether the classical foundations have any validity in these times, we should at least make those principles explicit. That is my aim. My purpose is to present a moral vision that is not based on the worldview of one of the world religions and that favors the importance of criticism, individual moral autonomy, and the separation of religion from politics.

Characteristic of my approach is that I will try not to speculate about the future course of secularization in Europe and the world in general (so I will not enter into the secularization debate). Whether Europe will stay secular or whether the process of secularization will be reversed, is a matter of scholarly research and, in part, of speculation. It is difficult to prophesy, especially about the future, it has been said. But I will assume that the critics of the secularization thesis (Stark and others) who predict that more and more religious groups will try to force their worldview on secular European societies may be right. The next question then is: how should we react to that? *The Secular Outlook* sketches such a possible reaction.

My answer will not be that we need more multiculturalism, more "openness" to religious worldviews, more "dialogue" with religious groups, and, least of all, more appeasement of religious terrorists. That is not because I am against "openness" and "dialogue," but because I think these seemingly innocuous concepts are misused to squander one of the great traditions of the West. That great tradition is the tradition of critique, also religious critique, of moral autonomy, and of the religiously neutral or secular state.

The development of Europe is intimately connected with the spirit of religious criticism. This is the tradition of Socrates, condemned to death for criticizing the religious ideas of his fellow Athenians; of Lucretius, Spinoza, Voltaire, Diderot, T.H. Huxley, Nietzsche, and Russell – to name only a few.[35]

More particularly, I will try to demonstrate in *The Secular Outlook* that the religiously neutral state is based on certain traditions such as a predilection for moral autonomy (or moral secularism)[36] and on secularist movements, such as atheism (or better non-theism) and freethought (i.e. the combination of religious criticism and an emphasis on the importance of

---

theism), freethought, moral secularism, and political secularism, which are portrayed in this book.

[35] See on them: Joshi, S.T., ed., *Icons of Unbelief: Atheists, Agnostics, and Secularists*, Greenwoord Press, Westport, CT 2008.

[36] The terms "moral secularism" and "political secularism" were coined by the Dutch humanist and freethinker Floris van den Berg. See: Berg, Floris van den, *Hoe komen we van religie af? Een ongemakkelijke liberale paradox* [How Do We Get Away from Religion? An Uncomfortable Liberal Paradox], Houtekiet/Atlas, Antwerpen 2009, pp. 24 and 28.

free speech). *The Secular Outlook* is meant to be a "revindication" of this tradition.

The argument developed here is predicated on the notion of values as essential for the identity of a civilization. This may be contested, of course, but it is not arbitrary. The American political scientist Leslie Lipson (1912–2000) makes a similar point in his book *The Ethical Crises of Civilization* (1993) when he asks whether the significance of Athens is primarily due to its technology, which extracted silver from the mines at Laurium, or whether it is rather Socrates questioning the Athenians in the *agora* and questing for truth? Lipson refers to John Ruskin (1819–1900) who wrote: "Great nations write their autobiographies in three manuscripts, the book of their deeds, the book of their words and the book of their art." Ruskin was on the right track, Lipson continues, but he proposes to add yet another book: the book of their values.[37] The prime distinguishing feature of a civilization is the values that it espouses. By whatever values it selects, a civilization defines itself, and thus resembles, or differs from, others.[38]

Here I side with Bassam Tibi (1944–) who writes that the civilizational identity of Europe is secular. And, precisely for that reason, it is inclusive as well.[39]

Western civilization is to a considerable degree defined by what I call "the secular outlook" or that specific combination of values that make it possible for people of different religious persuasion to live together in a peaceful and respectful way. T.S. Eliot (1888–1965) famously quipped that if Christianity goes, Western civilization goes (I will comment on his work more elaborately later in this book).[40] I think this is untrue. With all due respect for Christianity, I do not think that Western civilization is doomed if cultural and religious pluralism becomes more common than it is now, not even if Christianity develops into a minority position. Europe and the Western world certainly can survive religious pluralism, but if we destroy

---

[37] Lipson, Leslie, *The Ethical Crises of Civilization: Moral Meltdown or Advance?*, Sage Publications, London 1993, p. 9.

[38] Ibid.

[39] Tibi, Bassam, *Euro-Islam: Die Lösung eines Zivilisationskonfliktes* [Euro-Islam: The Solution to a Conflict of Civilizations], Primus Verlag, Darmstadt 2009, p. 10: "Die säkulare zivilisatorische Identität Europas ist dem Modell nach inklusiv, und sie kann einen offenen Islam aufnehmen sowie europäisieren, aber nur, wenn dieser von Schari'a und Djhad abgekoppelt wird. [Europe's secular civilizational identity is constructed on an inclusive model, and it is able to take in, and Europeanize, an open Islam, but only if the latter is uncoupled from sharia and jihad.]"

[40] See: Eliot, T.S., *Notes towards the Definition of Culture*, 1948, in: T.S. Eliot, *Christianity and Culture*, Harcourt, Inc., San Diego 1976, pp. 79–202, p. 200: "If Christianity goes, the whole of our culture goes. Then you must start painfully again, and you cannot put on a new culture ready made. You must wait for the grass to grow to feed the sheep to give the wool out of which your new coat will be made."

the principles and values that make pluralism possible, Western civilization is moribund indeed.

Although Eliot may be wrong, those critics who proclaim that Western civilization is intimately bound up with the secular outlook are right. Only within the framework of democracy, the rule of law, the secular state, and human rights, as expounded in European constitutions and Human Rights declarations, is it possible to develop a framework for religious and cultural pluralism. Therefore revindicating the secular outlook is essential to European civilization's chances of surviving and flourishing, and those of wider Western civilization as well.[41]

Is this a needlessly provocative thesis with regard to religion? I believe it is not. It would be a serious mistake to consider the values espoused in the secular outlook as in any way inimical to religion or the rights of religious believers. On the contrary, secularism is the only perspective under which people of different religious persuasions can live together. It is an essential precondition for the free development of religion, although, *mirabile dictu*, many serious believers do not seem to be interested in its free development.

Nowadays, many people argue that *because* the secularization thesis is obsolete, secularism is at the end of its tether. In *The Secular Outlook* the reverse will be defended. *Especially* if it is true that the secularization thesis no longer holds, the traditions brought together under the heading of the secular outlook are of paramount importance.

*   *   *

The secular outlook is usually associated with four traditions. Each of these traditions is the focus of a chapter in this book. The first chapter is dedicated to atheism. The second and third chapters deal with religious criticism and free speech (two aspects of freethought). Chapter 4 expounds the element of moral autonomy (moral secularism).

Central to my argument is a separation between private and public. One of my aims is to show that atheism can best be regarded as a private doctrine and not as public policy. That means that atheism is primarily important as a *personal* conviction. Freethought and secularism, for their part, are important elements of Western civilization that, although highly contested, have an indispensable *public function* in contemporary society.

Finally, a note about the character of this book and what the reader may expect. If anything, this book is primarily an exercise in practical ethics, political and legal philosophy, and the philosophy of religion. Its main orientation is discursive. I try to advocate some approaches in the fields indicated above, and I will do this as clearly as I can.

---

[41] See also: Tibi, *Euro-Islam*, p. 41.

The Secular Outlook is not meant as a "polemical" treatise in the sense that I have looked for the most provocative ways of formulating my points. On the contrary, I have tried as best as I can to suppress a polemical tone. Nevertheless, I am well aware that some of my conclusions may be experienced as controversial, but this is because they deviate from what is most commonly accepted. I am referring here not only to the content of my book, but also to its form. In this book I set out to take sides. I try to explain why it is reasonable to choose atheism, or rather non-theism (and not agnosticism); why moral autonomy is better than moral heteronomy. I do not simply analyze and describe the different points of view and then say to the reader at the end of every chapter "now you have to choose for yourself" (the reader will do that anyway, notwithstanding this somewhat paternalistic advice). Instead, I try to show why some choices are morally preferable to others from the standpoint of individual freedom and the ideal of an open society. This is more or less in agreement with a method of working employed in the field of practical ethics.[42] It differs from a common practice nowadays, that of not choosing. There are many "discourse analyses" available that will give you all the viewpoints, but do not themselves make a choice in favor of one perspective or the other. I find this disappointing. What I expect from a book is not only that the author guides me through the subject, expounding all the relevant theories and arguments, but also that he presents me with his personal, although well argued, view as to which perspective he considers best. But I am often disappointed. This has to do, I believe, with the popularity of post-modern relativism; the notion that all the different perspectives are of equal value. Authors cannot choose anymore, probably because they do not find one perspective preferable (let alone "superior") to another. All ideologies, political views, and religions are equally true – and hence also equally false. Therefore, contemporary analysis is often cynical and offers no prospect for a solution of our problems.

This book is peculiar in yet another way: it is written for an Anglophone public by someone born and raised in Europe, more specifically in Holland. My personal background has left its mark on some of my examples and my choice of literature, but it also reflects some of the experiences my country has gone through lately. Those experiences, in particular the

---

[42]   See on this: LaFollette, Hugh, "Theorizing about Ethics," in: Hugh LaFollette, ed., *Ethics in Practice: An Anthology*, second edition, Blackwell, Cambridge, MA 2002 (1997), pp. 3–11; Singer, Peter, *Practical Ethics*, second edition, Cambridge University Press, Cambridge 1993 (1979); Singer, Peter, *The President of Good and Evil. Taking George W. Bush Seriously*, Granta Books, London 2004; Rachels, James, "Introduction," in: James Rachels, ed., *Ethical Theory, I, The Question of Objectivity*, Oxford University Press, Oxford 1998, pp. 1–19; Rachels, James, "Morality and Moral Philosophy," in: James Rachels, *The Right Thing To Do. Basic Readings in Moral Philosophy*, McGraw-Hill, New York etc. 1989, pp. 3–32.

encounter with religious terrorism, are relevant to the subject of free speech and civil liberties in general. In an age when religious terrorism seems an important challenge, the adoption of the secular outlook is even more necessary than in times when religion manifests itself through its gentler side.

This book also draws upon other sources of inspiration from Dutch culture. The Netherlands is the country of Spinoza (1632–1677), a key figure in the "Radical Enlightenment." Spinoza advocated a radical *libertas philosophandi*, freedom to philosophize (see Chapter 3). It is also the country of Hugo de Groot (Grotius, 1583–1645) who was one of the first thinkers to consider the moral law as not dependent on the will of God. He also wanted international public law to be put on a firm secular footing (see Chapter 4). Holland is also a country with a Calvinist past, where in the 1960s secularization was carried out at an unprecedented pace.

Finally, in the twenty-first century these developments clashed severely with a new upsurge of radical religiosity from some of the country's minorities, leading to the tragic murder of Theo van Gogh, an "unsparing critic of European passivity in the face of fundamentalist Islam," as the American journalist and writer Bruce Bawer (1956–) characterized him.[43] Van Gogh was an icon of free speech; a principle that integrally includes the right to "shock, disturb and offend," in the words of the European Court of Human Rights, Strasbourg, in the Handyside case of 1976. These words are now almost forgotten by most of the representatives of European institutions, by the heads of state of European countries and by the United Nations, as we have seen before.

All these influences, to some extent, reverberate in this book.

---

[43]   Bawer, Bruce, *While Europe Slept: How Radical Islam Is Destroying the West From Within*, Doubleday, New York 2006, p. 2.

1

Atheism, Agnosticism, and Theism

Non-Religious Ethics is at a very early stage. We cannot yet predict whether, as in Mathematics, we will all reach agreement. Since we cannot know how Ethics will develop, it is not irrational to have high hopes. (Derek Parfit, 1984)[1]

He has told you, O man, what is good; and what does the Lord require of you but to do justice, and to love kindness, and to walk humbly with your God? (Micah 6:8)

Let us start with what people most often associate with "the secular outlook." If with anything at all, they associate it with atheism. But what is atheism? Sometimes atheism is presented as a coherent worldview, encompassing all the other traditions supposedly associated with the secular outlook. On this basis the Christian theologian and physicist Alister McGrath (1953–) writes: "Atheism is the religion of the autonomous and rational human being, who believes that reason is able to uncover and express the deepest truths of the universe, from the mechanics of the rising sun to the nature and final destiny of humanity."[2] The first thing that strikes us is that atheism is presented here as a "religion." A second point that is remarkable is that McGrath depicts as "atheism" beliefs that most people would associate with "rationalism." In clarifying his definition the author even introduces other elements, such as optimism. Atheism, so McGrath writes, "was a powerful, self-confident, and aggressive worldview. Possessed of a boundless confidence, it proclaimed that the world could be fully

[1] Parfit, Derek, *Reasons and Persons*, Clarendon Press, Oxford 1984, p. 454.
[2] McGrath, Alister E., *The Twilight of Atheism: The Rise and Fall of Disbelief in the Modern World*, Doubleday, New York 2004, p. 220.

understood and subsequently mastered."[3] Often these definitions seem animated by an aversion to the denial of God. This also seems true in the case
of McGrath. McGrath wrote a history of atheism based on a claim that its
significance was declining.

A similar thesis is defended by the prolific Catholic historian Paul Johnson
(1928–). "Atheism as a positive set of beliefs, including a code of moral
behavior, has failed to flourish," Johnson writes.[4] It may be that fewer and
fewer people in Western countries practice religion, Johnson tells us, but
the number of those prepared to state their disbelief in God openly and
specifically is extremely small. There is only a small minority that does that,
whose numbers are probably no greater today than in the time of Percy
Bysshe Shelley (1792–1822), who was expelled from Oxford University for
his atheism. Shelley's *Queen Mab: A Philosophical Poem* (1813) was a
forceful attack on organized religion. It takes the form of a dream-vision
allegory in which the fairy Queen Mab takes the mortal maiden Ianthe on
an extraterrestrial excursion in order to show her the past, present, and
future states of the human world. According to Shelley, the past is irrational. It is the record of one mistake after another. The present is irrevers-
ibly corrupted by kings, priests, and statesmen. But the future will be a
supremely glorious affair.[5] Several atheistic passages were removed from
the first edition, but they were restored in the second. The poem's publisher,
Edward Moxon (1801–1858), was prosecuted and convicted of blasphemous libel. In the 1820s the British intellectual and bookseller Richard
Carlile (1790–1843) issued a new edition of the poem.

That the development of atheism is still at the same stage as Shelley left
it at the beginning of the nineteenth century, as Paul Johnson contended in
1996, is not very convincing given the vast quantity of literature that has
appeared on atheism recently. But maybe this has to do with the fact that
it is far from clear what Johnson means when he uses the term "atheism."

More attention is given to this matter in monographs explicitly devoted
to the subject. According to Julian Baggini (1968–) atheism is "extremely
simple to define," because "it is the belief that there is no God or gods."[6]

In other definitions atheism is contrasted with theism. Robin Le Poidevin
(1962–) writes: "An *atheist* is one who denies the existence of a personal,
transcendent creator of the universe rather than one who simply lives life

---

[3]   Ibid., p. 220. McGrath writes "was" because the thesis of his book is that atheism is no
longer something that people subscribe to. It is a thing of the past.
[4]   Johnson, Paul, *The Quest for God: A Personal Pilgrimage*, Weidenfeld and Nicolson,
London 1996, p. 2.
[5]   McGrath, Alister E., *A Brief History of Heaven*, Blackwell Publishing, Oxford 2003,
p. 73.
[6]   Baggini, Julian, *Atheism: A Very Short Introduction*, Oxford University Press, Oxford
2003, p. 3.

without reference to such a being. A *theist* is one who asserts the existence of such a creator. Any discussion of atheism, then, is necessarily a discussion of theism."[7] So, in contrast to Baggini, Le Poidevin asserts that atheism is related to a *specific concept* of god: god as a personal and transcendent creator of the universe. According to Le Poidevin, atheism also implies a conscious and explicit position in the sense that simply living a life without God is not sufficient to call someone an "atheist."

We find the same contrast between theism and atheism in Daniel Harbour who writes: "Atheism is the plausible and probably correct belief that God does not exist. Opposed to atheism, there is theism, the implausible and probably incorrect view that God does exist."[8]

Atheism is generally considered to be an integral part of the tradition of the secular outlook. In what follows I will delineate what seems to me a defensible approach to atheism. Nevertheless, as I will try to show, few people approach atheism the way I do. Atheism has negative overtones. That does not make it necessarily untrue, of course, but the forces united against atheism as a creed, voiced by McGrath, Johnson, and many other detractors, are so formidable, and the misunderstandings about atheism so widespread, that it seems advisable to be somewhat cautious in using the term. In any case one should not identify the secular outlook entirely with atheism.[9] It would surely be wrong to say that if atheism goes, the secular outlook goes. That, at least, will be my conclusion. Secularism is not atheism. Most atheists are secularists.[10] Not all secularists are atheists. Atheism is about the existence of God. Secularism is about the role of religion in public life and about the way we should legitimize our moral commitments. But let us start with a defensible approach to atheism.

The Alpha Privative

I recommend the terminology used by Le Poidevin and Harbour. Atheism is a-theism. So: "a," hyphen, "theism." An atheist is someone who does not subscribe to the central tenets of theism. The "a" is an alpha privative, it denies what follows. So an atheist denies what a theist tries to assert.

---

[7]   Le Poidevin, Robin, *Arguing for Atheism: An Introduction to the Philosophy of Religion*, Routledge, London 1996, p. xvii.

[8]   Harbour, Daniel, *An Intelligent Person's Guide to Atheism*, Duckworth, London 2001, p. 1.

[9]   See also: Grayling, A.C., *Ideas that Matter: A Personal Guide for the 21st Century*, Weidenfeld & Nicholson, London 2009, p. 334: "Secularism should be distinguished from both atheism and humanism."

[10]   As Grayling, ibid., writes: it would be "odd to find an atheist who was an anti-secularist."

Someone who is a-religious is simply what it says: not religious. It is not the case that by denying a religion you, by some magic trick, invent a religion of your own: the religion of irreligious or a-religious people. Atheism is no more a religion than not playing chess is a hobby. Perhaps this sounds like a commonplace, nevertheless it is necessary to state it. Atheists are often considered to be driven by a religious impulse: the religious impulse to deny religion. Denying religion is in itself a religion, it is said. As a matter of fact, we have seen this with McGrath. I consider this form of reasoning to be a strange rhetorical trick.

Because atheism is the denial of theism, every tract on atheism should also address the question "what is theism?" Theism is the same as – monotheism, which is the more current term. Theists are adherents of one of the three theistic religions: Judaism, Christianity and Islam. Theists believe in one god. That makes the word "monotheism," strictly speaking, a pleonasm. But theism is more than belief in one god; it also requires a conception of a *specific* god. God, according to theists, is good. And not only "good" in the sense you and I can be good, but *perfectly* good. Someone who identifies God with evil ("the supreme evil, God"), as the great Victorian poet Algernon Charles Swinburne (1837–1909) did,[11] cannot be a theist. The god of Jews, Christians and Muslims is *eo ipso* good.

Goodness is not the only attribute of the theistic god. He is eternal, the creator of the universe, almighty, transcendent, omniscient, holy, and personal. Western theology has tried to reflect on those characteristics and construe a concept of God that is consistent (I will elaborate on these attributes in the first section of Chapter 4, Pope Benedict XVI on the Apostles' Creed).[12]

Atheism and Liberal Concepts of God

Theism as outlined above is something different from religious belief in general. So atheism in the sense outlined here is not opposed to religion as such. Atheism is concerned with *one specific concept* of god: the theistic god. The theistic god has a name and this is written with a capital: God.[13] At face value it may be strange to limit atheism so that it is opposed only

---

[11] Swinburne quoted in: Bury, *A History of the Freedom of Thought*, Thornton Butterworth, London 1932 (1913), p. 208. See also: Hargreaves, H.A., "Swinburne's Greek Plays and God, 'The Supreme Evil,'" *Modern Language Notes*, 76, no. 7 (1961), pp. 607–616.

[12] See also: McGrath, Alister E., *Christian Theology: An Introduction*, Blackwell, Oxford 1994. And for the way the theistic conception of god has developed: Tilghman, B.R., *An Introduction to the Philosophy of Religion*, Blackwell, Oxford 1994, pp. 10–46.

[13] See: Wright, Robert, *The Evolution of God*, Little, Brown and Company, New York, Boston, London 2009, p. 209: "God with a Capital G."

to the theistic concept of god and not to all the other gods that have been venerated by man. Buddhists or Hindus subscribe to polytheistic apprehensions of the divine. Should not they be included in the atheist rejection of the divine, as they are in Baggini's definition of atheism, mentioned above? I think not and I will now spell out my reasons for using the narrow definition.

The best way to make my position clear is by means of an example. There are people who are in awe of, or even venerate, vague and wide dimensions of reality that they identify as "the totally other" (*das ganz Andere*).[14] Or who refer to a particular mystical experience.[15] There are people and theologians who claim to worship "the absolute" or "ultimate reality" or the "unsearchable region out of which all phenomena spring."[16] C.S. Lewis (1898–1963), who was not particularly fond of this approach, called it "Christianity-and-water."[17] Take the theologian Paul Tillich (1886–1965). In his book *Dynamics of Faith* (1958) Tillich tells us: "The fundamental symbol of our ultimate concern is God."[18] Here God is not a person, not a father, not a creator, but a symbol. You cannot pray to a symbol, so it would seem. A symbol does not lead the Jewish people through the desert. A symbol does not reveal the Ten Commandments to Moses on Mount Sinai, and symbols do not have sons to be sent to the earth to atone for our sins. The concept of God advocated by Tillich is completely different from the one that theistic religions proclaim. Should an atheist also be opposed to (or deny) the reality of such symbols? My answer is "no."

Another theologian, J.A.T. Robinson (1919–1983), in his book *Honest to God* (1963) criticizes the conception of God as a supernatural being "out there" or the "old man in the sky." God, so Robinson proclaims is, by definition, "ultimate reality." Robinson adds that it is meaningless to ask whether God exists. The only question we can fruitfully pose is: what does that ultimate reality look like?[19]

We also find ideas like those of Robinson and Tillich in the work of the German theologian and philosopher of religion Rudolf Otto (1869–1937)[20]

---

[14] As is the case with the German philosopher Max Horkheimer. See: Horkheimer, Max, *Die Sehnsucht nach dem ganz Anderen, Ein Interview mit Kommentar von Helmut Gumnior* [Longing for the Totally Other, an Interview with Commentary by Helmut Gumnior], Furche Verlag, Hamburg 1975 (1970).

[15] For several approaches see: Happold, F.C. (ed.), *Mysticism, A Study and an Anthology*, Penguin Books, Harmondsworth 1979 (1963).

[16] Caird, John, *An Introduction to the Philosophy of Religion*, James Maclehose and Sons, Glasgow 1894, p. 8.

[17] See: McGrath, *A Brief History of Heaven*, p. 132.

[18] Tillich, Paul, *Dynamics of Faith*, Harper Torchbooks, New York 1958, p. 45.

[19] Robinson, John A.T., *Honest to God*, The Westminster Press, Philadelphia 1963, p. 29.

[20] Otto, Rudolf, *The Idea of the Holy: An Inquiry into the Non-rational Factor in the Idea of the Divine*, second edition, Oxford University Press, New York 1958.

and Friedrich Daniel Ernst Schleiermacher (1768–1834).[21] I will not be concerned with conceptions of the divine as advocated by those liberal theologians (although Schleiermacher's hermeneutics will be discussed in Chapter 4). Why not?

First: a possible discussion with Robinson and Tillich would probably not deal with theism or atheism but with logic, methodology, or the philosophy of science. The discussion would focus on the question of whether it is fruitful to discuss such vague concepts as "ultimate reality." What is "reality"? Is the love for my daughter "reality" or "a reality"? Is the dream I had last night part of "reality"? These are all difficult problems that have to be solved first if one is to discuss whether God is "reality" (or "a reality"). And what characteristics should reality have if it is to be "ultimate"? And what justification do we have for identifying such vague concepts with "God"? Would not that be a kind of verbal inflation? Is what Tillich and Robinson do, not to present a kind of sophisticated atheism?[22] Philosopher Paul Kurtz (1925–) coined the word "igtheism" to denote what he thinks underlies the theism of many theologians. The prefix "ig" is derived from the word ignorant. Kurtz argues that when theologians speak in woolly abstractions about the "ground of being" they are really employing murky language as a dodge to cover up our ignorance of how the universe actually operates.[23]

Suppose someone is so completely immersed in fishing that his "ultimate concern" lies in his hobby. During Sunday service this person sits at the side of the lake enjoying his favorite sport. Would this make fishing his "religion"? Of course not. Following that semantic strategy would amount to enormous verbal inflation. The eighteenth-century freethinker and sexual debaucher the Marquis de Sade (1740–1814) would have sadistic sex as his "religion." Youngsters who idolize Justin Timberlake (1981–) would be the members of a new "religious" sect.

Perhaps for sociologists of religion, trying to be as neutral as they can towards the different manifestations of "God," "religion," and the "divine," this may be an interesting approach. But should it therefore be our leading perspective in every other context? This may be doubted, and this doubt is

---

[21] Schleiermacher, Friedrich, *On Religion: Speeches to its Cultured Despisers*, Cambridge University Press, Cambridge 1996.

[22] One of the most severe criticisms of the father of liberal theology, Schleiermacher, stems from J.M. Robertson who writes that the work of Schleiermacher "did little harm save insofar as it fostered the German proclivity to the nebulous in thought and language, and partly encouraged the normal resistance to critical thought." See: Robertson, J.M., *A History of Freethought in the Nineteenth Century*, Vol. I, Watts & Co., London 1929, p. 49.

[23] In: Kurtz, Paul, *The New Skepticism: Inquiry and Reliable Knowledge*, Prometheus Books, Amherst, NY 1992 and: Cooke, Bill, *Dictionary of Atheism, Skepticism, and Humanism*, Prometheus Books, Amherst, NY 2006, p. 277.

highly relevant for atheism. An atheist, so it may be safely contended, is primarily concerned with one specific religious tradition. He is concerned with the idea of a personal, almighty, omniscient, and perfectly benevolent god. The concept of "atheism" I try to defend in this book acknowledges that it is difficult, if not impossible, and also useless to develop an argument against *all the different concepts of god and religion* that are sometimes defended. The only thing an atheist can do is to oppose the kind of discourse that makes it impossible to discern under what circumstances one can legitimately say "I am not religious." If everybody is "religious" but only the content of that religion varies, the word "religion" has lost all meaning.

Philosopher Roger Scruton (1944–) contributes to the inflation of the word "religion" when he writes: "We have cults like football, sacrificial offerings like Princess Diana and improvised saints like Linda McCartney."[24] He also speaks about "the new secular religion of human rights" and continues: "I call it a religion because it seems to occupy the place vacated by faith. It tells us that we are the centre of the universe, that we are under no call to obedience, but that the world is ordered in accordance with our rights."[25] Such language can draw our attention to certain similarities between football and religion in the sense of one of the world's religions, but we should be careful not to identify those phenomena as "religion."

To illustrate this, let me present a last example in the form of a dialogue. Suppose someone says "God is love" and the subsequent dialogue evolves:

"Do you mean love is one aspect of the divine being?"
"No, I mean God *is* love; God is identical with love."
"But in that case God can not be a person."
"No, indeed."

When an atheist opposes the statement "God is love" this is not because he wants to deny the importance of love, but because he deems it inappropriate to mix up this human emotion with the divine being that Judaism, Christianity, and Islam traditionally refer to as the transcendent, personal, almighty and perfectly good god, *viz.* God. In other words there are good reasons for maintaining the limited conception of "atheism." "Atheism" is nothing more than the denial of the claims of theism.

Atheism as an Unpopular Position

Atheism has always been a very unpopular position, to say the least. Theologian and classics scholar Richard Bentley (1662–1742) wrote in 1724

---

[24]   Scruton, Roger, *Gentle Regrets: Thoughts from a Life*, Continuum, London 2005, p. 232.
[25]   Ibid., p. 238.

in *Eight Sermons* that an atheist can never be a loyal friend.[26] He also proclaimed that an affective relation is impossible with an atheist and that an atheist can never be a loyal citizen. The Protestant theologian Robert Flint (1838–1910) asserted that in every country where atheism became dominant, "national decay and disaster" would be the result. In France, it was impossible to publish books defending atheism until the French Revolution. That is why famous atheist philosophers, such as the Baron d'Holbach (1723–1789) and Denis Diderot (1713–1784), wrote anonymously.[27]

In classical antiquity the attitude towards unbelievers was more tolerant, but in Greek society too there was no complete freedom of religion (including the possibility of rejecting a religion). Plato (*c.* 428–347 BCE) discerned four categories of "atheists," but all deserved the punishment of death.[28]

The attitude towards atheism in the middle ages was, as one would expect, even more severe. Thomas Aquinas (*c.* 1225–1274), like Plato, proposed the death penalty for atheists.[29] Even John Locke (1632–1704), the writer of several treatises defending tolerance, was vehemently opposed to atheists. One of the reasons he put forward was that promises made by atheists would not be kept. When d'Holbach's *Le système de la nature* [The System of Nature] (1770) was published, the hangman complained that only the book could be burned and not the author.

Obviously, past atheists had to be cautious. And Joseph McCabe (1867–1955) rightly censured the Danish philologist A.B. Drachmann (1860–1935), writer of a book entitled *Atheism in Pagan Antiquity* (1922), for not having taken this sufficiently into account.[30] According to Drachmann, only ten known Greek and Roman thinkers, and few others, had been

---

[26]   In this overview of reactions towards atheism I am indebted to: Edwards, Paul, "Atheism," in: *The Encyclopedia of Philosophy*, Paul Edwards, ed., Vol. I, MacMillan & The Free Press, New York 1967, pp. 174–189; Edwards, Paul, "God and the Philosophers. Part I: From Aristotle to Locke," *Free Inquiry*, 18, no. 3, 1998; Edwards, Paul, "God and the Philosophers. Part II: From Fideism to Pragmatism," *Free Inquiry*, 18, no. 4, 1998; Edwards, Paul, *God and the Philosophers*, Introduction by Timothy J. Madigan, Prometheus Books, Amherst, NY 2009; Nagel, Ernest, "A Defense of Atheism," in: Paul Edwards and Arthur Pap, eds., *A Modern Introduction to Philosophy*, revised edition, The Free Press, Collier-MacMillan, New York 1967, pp. 460–473.

[27]   Paul-Henri Thiry, Baron d'Holbach was the pre-eminent eighteenth-century theoretician of atheism and the author of, among other works, a *Critical History of Jesus Christ* and *The Sacred Contagion, a Natural History of Superstition*. For other authors, see: Graille, Patrick, & Kozul, Mladen, *Discours anti-religieux français du dix-huitième siècle. Du curé Meslier au Marquis de Sade* [French Eighteenth-Century Anti-Religious Texts. From the Curé Meslier to the Marquis de Sade], Les Presses de l'Université Laval, Paris 2003.

[28]   Plato, *The Laws*, Book X, and: Schofield, Malcolm, *Plato: Political Philosophy*, Oxford University Press, Oxford 2006, p. 313.

[29]   *Summa Theologica*, 2-2. I-16.

[30]   Drachmann, A.B., *Atheism in Pagan Antiquity*, Kessinger Publishing, Whitefish 2005 (1922).

atheists over a period of more than a thousand years. McCabe calls such a remark misleading: "Professor Drachmann means that very few stood out in the cities of Greece and said that the gods did not exist." But what can you expect after Socrates had been condemned to drink the hemlock?[31]

What McCabe wrote about the Greek philosophers in particular could be said about other philosophers as well. A case in point is that of Spinoza (1632–1677), nowadays considered to be one of the most important influences on the European Enlightenment.[32] Because of his unorthodox views he was excommunicated from the Jewish community in 1656, and he changed his name from Baruch to Benedict. In 1670 his *Tractatus Theologico-Politicus* was published – anonymously. His *Ethica* (1677) was only published after his death. The *Ethics* rejected the idea of a personal creator, free will, and personal immortality. On the criteria outlined before, Spinoza should be characterized as an atheist.

Like Kant and Hume,[33] Spinoza was extremely careful not to offend the authorities. He was well aware that freedom of speech (or freedom of expression) was far from accepted even in a relatively free country such as the Dutch Republic. The most vehement reactions to Spinozistic doctrines were directed at disciples of Spinoza, such as Adriaan Koerbagh.

Adriaan Koerbagh (1632–1669) is regarded as one of the most radical thinkers of the early Enlightenment.[34] During the early 1660s Adriaan and his brother Johannes Koerbagh (1634–1672) became strongly involved with the heterodox Spinozistic circles in Amsterdam, and eventually with Spinoza himself. In 1668 Adriaan published two books, *Bloemhof* and *Ligt*, which struck at the very roots of Christianity. Adriaan, however, did what Spinoza himself was always too cautious to do: he published in the vernacular language. The reason for this was that he wanted to enlighten not only the

---

[31]   McCabe, Joseph, *The Existence of God*, Watts & Co., London 1933, p. 31.

[32]   See: Israel, Jonathan I., *Radical Enlightenment. Philosophy and the Making of Modernity 1650–1750*, Oxford University Press, Oxford 2001; Israel, Jonathan I., *Enlightenment Contested. Philosophy, Modernity, and the Emancipation of Man 1670–1752*, Oxford University Press, Oxford 2006.

[33]   See on this: Mossner, Ernest C., "The Enigma of Hume," *Mind*, New Series, 45, no. 179 1936, pp. 334–349; Mossner, Ernest C., "The Religion of David Hume," *Journal of the History of Ideas*, 39, no. 4 1970, pp. 653–663. But, for all his cautiousness, Hume could not avoid a reputation for being a radical. "Throughout his life he would be dogged with the unfair accusation of atheism," writes Roderick Graham in *The Great Infidel: A Life of David Hume*, John Donald, Edinburgh 2004, p. 27. See also: Ross, J.M., "Introduction," in: Cicero, *The Nature of the Gods*, translated by Horace C.P. McGregor, Penguin Books, London 1972, pp. 7–63, p. 60: "Hume was a complete sceptic in religion but felt he had to cast his work in dialogue form and pay verbal respect to current religious beliefs because otherwise he could never have got a hearing in eighteenth-century Scotland."

[34]   Wielema, M.R., "Adriaan Koerbagh," in: Wiep van Bunge, et al. (eds.), *The Dictionary of Seventeenth and Eighteenth-Century Dutch Philosophers*, Thoemmes Press, Bristol 2003, pp. 571–574.

academic elite, but the common people as well. He was sentenced to ten years' imprisonment in the Rasphuis (a prison) in 1668 and subsequent banishment from Holland. He died in prison three months later due to the harsh conditions.

Although severe punishments such as those inflicted upon Koerbagh are unheard of in the modern Western world, that should not make us forget that atheism, or even changing one's religion for another religion, is sometimes still not possible without fear of death or serious reprisals. If the stake could still be invoked as the *ultima ratio theologorum* [theologians' final argument] it certainly would be, Schopenhauer remarked cynically.[35]

It is difficult to understand how atheism can ignite so much hatred in many people. Recent rebuttals of atheism usually try to credit it with colossal pretensions. This is, for instance, the case with a recent wave of criticism directed against the so-called "New Atheism" of Richard Dawkins,[36] Daniel Dennett,[37] Sam Harris,[38] Victor Stenger[39] and Christopher Hitchens.[40] One of those criticisms contains the following sentence:

> Those who believe they know how to bring about a conclusion to life seek to eradicate all other schemes for human perfection. These competing visions, in their eyes, pollute society, lead people astray, and stymie the ultimate possibilities of human happiness. The new atheists, like all true believers, want these competing visions destroyed.[41]

Destroyed? These are very strange ideas. The average atheist, like Spinoza or Hume, is far removed from the fanatic frame of mind that this author associates with atheism. Apparently, atheists are not only feared but hated.

Atheism – or rather charges of atheism – can still pose great problems for the writers involved. The most serious recent attack on the principle of freedom of thought and religion was perpetrated by the Iranian cleric Ayatollah Khomeini (1902–1989). If Khomeini had had his way, the British writer Salman Rushdie would have been killed for writing a novel.[42]

---

[35] Schopenhauer, Arthur, *Die Welt als Wille und Vorstellung* [The World as Will and Representation], II, Cotta-Verlag/Insel-Verlag, Stuttgart/Frankfurt am Main 1976, p. 212.

[36] Dawkins, Richard, *The God Delusion*, Black Swan, Transworld Publishers, London 2006.

[37] Dennett, Daniel C., *Breaking the Spell. Religion as a Natural Phenomenon*, Allen Lane, Penguin Books, New York 2006.

[38] Harris, Sam, *Letter to a Christian Nation*, Alfred A. Knopf, New York 2006; Harris, Sam, *The End of Faith: Religion, Terror, and the Future of Reason*, The Free Press, London 2005.

[39] Stenger, Victor J., *The New Atheism: Taking a Stand for Science and Reason*, Prometheus Books, Amherst, NY 2009.

[40] Hitchens, Christopher, *god is not Great*.

[41] Hedges, Chris, *I Don't Believe in Atheists*, The Free Press, New York 2008, p. 99.

[42] Pipes, Daniel, *The Rushdie Affair: The Novel, the Ayatollah, and the West*, second edition with a postscript by Koenraad Elst, Transaction Publishers, New Brunswick (USA) and London (UK) 2003.

The same fate might have befallen the Bengali novelist Taslima Nasreen (1962–), who had to flee India for criticizing religion and openly advocating atheism. In the Middle East several people have, in fact, been killed by religious fanatics, for example, the Egyptian thinker Farag Foda (1946–1992).[43] So, although atheism is not legally prohibited in many parts of the world, and is even protected by the clauses on freedom of speech, freedom of thought, freedom of religion and freedom of worship in declarations of human rights and national constitutions, this situation is far from effective in securing freedom of conscience and the right to free discussion. What these examples make clear is that those favoring free speech, freedom of conscience, and the right to critique (including criticism of religious ideas) have more to refer to than the well-known historical examples of religious violence against Giordano Bruno (1548–1600), burned at the stake in 1600, or Galileo Galilei (1564–1642), intimidated by the Church and placed under house arrest in 1633.

It is rather odd that even in the twenty-first century atheism is highly unpopular: "would you confess to atheism in Texas, let alone Jeddah?" two writers of a recent overview of the comeback of religion in the public arena ask us.[44] It seems that the nature of the rejection of atheism has changed, but there still is, so it seems, a widespread condemnation of it. In the eighteenth and nineteenth centuries the atheist was criticized because his worldview was said to undermine sound morals and deprive life of meaning. The contemporary complaints are that atheists show no "respect" for other people's religion or do not want to enter into "dialogue" with believers. Other complaints frequently voiced are that atheists are "polarizing" society or are "just as dogmatic" as religious fundamentalists.

These complaints are hardly convincing. Philosopher A.C. Grayling (1949–) seems right when he says: "Religious apologists charge the non-religious with being 'fundamentalist' if they attack religion too robustly."[45] He continues with the contention that "it is time to reverse the prevailing notion that religious commitment is intrinsically deserving of respect, and that it should be handled with kid gloves and protected by custom and in some cases law against criticism and ridicule."[46] His point of view regarding religious criticism is that "nothing that people choose in the way of politics, lifestyle or religion should be immune from criticism and (when, as so often

[43]   See on this: Jansen, Johannes J.G., *The Dual Nature of Islamic Fundamentalism*, Cornell University Press, Ithaca, New York 1997, pp. 113–116.

[44]   Micklethwait, John, and Wooldridge, Adrian, *God Is Back: How the Global Rise of Faith Is Changing the World*, Allen Lane, Penguin Books, London 2009, p. 26.

[45]   Grayling, A.C., *Against All Gods: Six Polemics on Religion and an Essay on Kindness*, Oberon Books, London 2007, p. 7.

[46]   Ibid. p. 15.

it does, it merits it) ridicule."[47] Dawkins makes the same point. He casti-gates the view that "religious faith is particularly vulnerable to offence and should be protected by an abnormally thick wall of respect, in a different class from the respect that any human being should pay to any other."[48] He goes on:

> I am not in favor of offending or hurting anyone just for the sake of it. But I am intrigued and mystified by the disproportionate privileging of religion in our otherwise secular societies. All politicians must be used to disrespectful cartoons of their faces, and nobody riots in their defense. What is so special about religion that we grant it such uniquely privileged respect?[49]

But Dawkins' attitude is far from common nowadays.

Against the background of the universal unpopularity of atheism it is hardly surprising that the epithet is usually rejected and seldom vindicated. Only a few philosophers have insisted on being called "atheists."[50] Most people, Hume being one example, have been labeled "atheists" by their opponents, often with unfortunate consequences. Lady Mary Wortley Montagu (1689–1762) confided that the philosophy of Hume could be characterized as follows: "Take the 'not' out of the Decalogue and put it in the Creed."[51]

A Definition of Atheism

Atheism as a-theism

So far I have been mainly concerned with what atheism is *not*. Yet it is equally important to specify some of the implications of what atheism *is*. First we have to emphasize its intimate relation with theism. Philosopher Ernest Nagel (1901–1985) puts it as follows in his *A Defense of Atheism* (1957): "I shall understand by 'atheism' a critique and a denial of the major claims of all varieties of theism."[52] And theism is the view that holds that

---

[47] Ibid., p. 19.
[48] Dawkins, *The God Delusion*, p. 42.
[49] Ibid., p. 50.
[50] Edwards, "Atheism," p. 175.
[51] Quoted in Beck, Lewis White, "Hume," in: Lewis White Beck, *Six Secular Philosophers. Religious Thought of Spinoza, Hume, Kant, Nietzsche, William James and Santayana*, Thoemmes Press, Bristol 1997, pp. 41–63, p. 41.
[52] Nagel, Ernest, "A Defense of Atheism," in: Paul Edwards and Arthur Pap, eds., *A Modern Introduction to Philosophy*, revised edition, The Free Press, Collier-MacMillan, New York 1967 (1957), p. 460.

the "heavens and the earth and all that they contain owe their existence and continuance in existence to the wisdom and will of a supreme, self-consistent, omnipotent, omniscient, righteous, and benevolent being, who is distinct from, and independent of, what he has created," as one author has stipulated.[53]

In this quote we encounter the elements of theism that were introduced before: omnipotence, omniscience, perfect righteousness, benevolence. So an atheist is someone who denies the existence of a god *with characteristics as set out above*. In other words: he denies the existence of "God."

This is the approach we find in Le Poidevin, Harbour, Nagel, and also Paul Edwards (1923–2004). Edwards writes: "On our definition an 'atheist' is a person who *rejects* belief in God."[54] So an atheist (as a-theist) is *not* someone who rejects belief in *gods* (without further specification) but only belief in the existence of God; God being a god with certain characteristics. What are those characteristics? Edwards states: "All the believers in the question have characterized God as a supreme personal being who is the creator or the ground of the universe and who, whatever his other attributes may be, is at the very least immensely powerful, highly intelligent and very good, loving, and just."[55]

Often atheism is characterized as a broader position. Michael Martin (1932–), one of the most important contemporary authors on atheism, writes: "In its broader sense *atheism*, from the Greek *a* ('without') and *theos* ('deity'), standardly refers to the denial of the existence of any god or gods."[56] This is also the way Bill Cooke (1956–) defines the concept: "Atheism: an attitude of skepticism toward claims of the existence of any sort of God or gods."[57] The broader definition is also adopted by George H. Smith (1949–), a passionate atheist himself, who writes: "An atheist is a person who does not believe in any god or number of gods."[58] Nevertheless Smith adds that "some theists" have been called "atheists" for disbelieving

---

[53]   That author was Robert Flint, Professor of Divinity at the University of Edinburgh; see: ibid., p. 461.
[54]   Edwards, "Atheism," p. 175.
[55]   Ibid.
[56]   Martin, Michael, "Atheism," in: Tom Flynn, ed., *The New Encyclopedia of Unbelief*, Prometheus Books, Amherst, NY 2007, pp. 89–96, p. 88. See also: Martin, Michael, "Atheism Defined and Contrasted," in: Michael Martin, *Atheism: A Philosophical Justification*, Temple University Press, Philadelphia 1990, pp. 463–476.
[57]   Cooke, Bill, "Atheism," in: Bill Cooke, *Dictionary of Atheism, Skepticism, & Humanism*, Prometheus Books, Amherst, NY 2006, pp. 49–50, p. 49. See also: Geisler, Norman L., and Turek, Frank, *I Don't Have Enough Faith to Be an Atheist*, Crossway Books, Wheaton, Illinois 2004, p. 22: "An *atheist*, of course, is someone who does not believe in any type of God."
[58]   Smith, George H., *Why Atheism?*, Prometheus Books, Amherst, NY 2000, p. 19. "Theism" is defined by Smith as: "belief in god or gods." See: Smith, George H., *Atheism: The Case Against God*, Prometheus Books, Buffalo, NY, 1989 (1979), p. 7.

in the god (or gods) of the "orthodox majority."[59] With that last qualification, the god of the orthodox majority, the more narrow definition of
atheism comes into focus. This is also the case when Martin notes that:

> in Western society the term atheism has most frequently been used to refer
> to the denial of theism, in particular Judeo-Christian theism. This is the posi-
> tion that a being that is all-powerful, all-knowing, and all-good exists who is
> the creator of the universe and who takes an active interest in human con-
> cerns, and guides his creatures by revelation.[60]

That more limited or narrow definition of atheism ("atheism" as the
term has most frequently been used in Western society, according to
Martin)[61] or, what I have called, atheism as a-theism, has some advantages
but also some disadvantages vis-à-vis the broader sense (atheism as the
rejection of *any* god or gods). Although I prefer the narrow definition of
atheism, let's start with the disadvantages.

One obvious disadvantage of the limited definition is that it has some
counter-intuitive effects. These are as follows.

On the basis of the more limited definition of atheism, polytheist concep-
tions are "atheist." From the perspective of atheism as a-theism, Greek and
Roman polytheism, for instance, would have to be classified as "atheist."
The depiction of ultimate reality as impersonal (which we find in the earlier
Upanishads) would also be categorized "atheist." Theravada Buddhism and
Jainism, which also reject a theistic creator god, would fall into the same
category.[62] Pantheism, being a rejection of a personal god, is "atheistic"
from the perspective of atheism as a-theism as well. Spinoza was an atheist,
from this point of view.

Many people find this puzzling.

An even more unacceptable consequence of the definition of atheism as
a-theism is that liberal conceptions of the divine would have to be qualified
as "atheist." Spinoza would not be alone in being characterized as an
atheist. The religious convictions of modern theologians such as John A.T.

---

[59] Smith, *Why Atheism?*, p. 19. See also: "The term theism usually refers to the belief in a
personal god or gods such as found in Judaism, Christianity, Islam, and Hinduism. Technically
then, an atheist is someone who does not believe in the gods of these religions." In: Stenger,
Victor J., *The New Atheism: Taking a Stand for Science and Reason*, Prometheus Books,
Amherst NY 2009. p. 21. This is a somewhat eccentric definition of both theism and atheism
because Stenger includes a polytheistic religion, Hinduism, under the heading of (mono)theism.
[60] Martin, "Atheism," p. 88.
[61] See also: "General Introduction," in: Martin, Michael, ed., *The Cambridge Companion
to Atheism*, Cambridge University Press, Cambridge 2007, p. 1: "In modern times 'theism'
has usually come to mean a belief in a personal God who takes an active interest in the world
and who has given a special revelation to humans."
[62] Martin, "Atheism," p. 88.

Robinson and Paul Tillich, whose work was mentioned before, would put them in the same camp. Some people find this deeply counterintuitive. From the perspective of liberal theology it is repugnant, for it would imply that only – what they like to call – the most orthodox and "fundamentalist" positions would be accepted as "theistic" and more liberal positions would become "atheist." That gives much too much ground to the fundamentalists, is a common objection.

This type of criticism might be illustrated by reference to the work of one of the most well-known representatives of the analytical tradition in the philosophy of religion: the Oxford philosopher Anthony John Patrick Kenny (1931–).

Kenny gives a lucid summary of his views on religion in his book *What I Believe* (2006).[63] Kenny was ordained a priest in 1955, but he did not think that the existence of God could be demonstrated. This was a problem because pontifical doctoral candidates had to take an oath rejecting various modern heresies. The oath also included the statement that it was possible to demonstrate the existence of God.[64] After two years of priesthood he decided that he could no longer continue as a teacher of doctrines and moral precepts about whose validity he was increasingly doubtful.[65] That is why he obtained leave from the Pope to return to the lay state and had several academic posts in Oxford.

From 1969 to 1972 Kenny lectured on Natural Religion. He analyzed the relationship between the divine attributes: omniscience, omnipotence, benevolence. His view was this:

> I argued that these three attributes were incompatible with one another, as could be seen by reflection on the relationship between divine power and human freedom. If God is to be omniscient about future human actions, then determinism must be true. If God is to escape responsibility for human wickedness, then determinism must be false. So there cannot be an omniscient, omnipotent, all good being.[66]

Kenny writes that he concluded from this that there cannot be such a thing as the God *of scholastic or rationalist philosophy*. Nevertheless, this did not bring him to the atheist position. Why not? Kenny answers: "I left the question open whether it is possible to conceive, and believe in, a God defined in less absolute terms."[67]

---

[63]   Kenny, Anthony, *What I Believe*, Continuum, London 2006.
[64]   Ibid., p. 5.
[65]   Ibid., p. 6.
[66]   Ibid., p. 8.
[67]   Ibid. Perhaps Kenny's position is somewhat similar to that of the humanist as defined by Corliss Lamont (1902–1995). Lamont writes: "Speakers of the Moral Majority insist that all Humanists are pernicious atheists, although Humanists have more and more tended to call

Is that a reasonable position to take? From the perspective of atheism as a-theism it is not.[68] Kenny seems to think that he has only rejected the "God of scholastic or rationalist philosophy," but is that true? Hasn't he done much more? I think he has. He has rejected the idea of God as defended through the ages by the Church and also, I am inclined to think, God as He appears to us in some important passages in Holy Scripture.

Whether that last contention is true depends, of course, on the question of whether the attributes of God as defended by the Church have a firm basis in Scripture. In other words: is it true that Scripture presents us with an omniscient, benevolent, and omnipotent person? Or is the personal, omniscient, benevolent, and omnipotent God an invention of scholastic and rationalist philosophy, as Kenny seems to presuppose?

My impression is that the Church is on much firmer ground than liberal theologians like to acknowledge. In other words: I think the characteristics that the Church, the Church fathers and the scholastic philosophers have attributed to God, have a firm basis in Scripture. Scripture does not present us with a God who is limited in power, for instance.

A person who believes in the existence of a god with the characteristics described before is generally considered to be a "theist." That is not very controversial. The controversy centers on the other position: the atheistic one. How do we qualify the person who does *not* believe in that specific concept of god? A reasonable answer, so it seems to me (following Harbour, Nagel and Le Poidevin), is "atheist." So Kenny, so it seems to me, is an "atheist" in the sense outlined above.

Nevertheless, he is adamant about *not* adopting that epithet. Kenny himself is not a "theist," as he explains in chapters 4 and 5 of his book (those chapters are titled "Why I am Not a Theist I" and "Why I am Not a Theist II"), but in chapter 3 of his book he claims not to be an "atheist" either (chapter 3 is called "Why I am Not an Atheist").

What is the reason for his not wanting to adopt the term "atheism" as a designation for his position? That appears to be, as we have seen in the passage quoted above, that he "left the question open whether it is possible to conceive, and believe in, a God defined in less absolute terms."[69]

---

themselves nontheists or agnostics. Humanists find no adequate proof of a supernatural God functioning upon this earth and guiding the human race to a divine destiny; but the immensity of the universe makes them cautious about absolutely denying the existence of God among the billions of stars, many of which might have planets where some form of life could have developed." See: Lamont, Corliss, *The Philosophy of Humanism*, eighth edition, Humanist Press, Amherst, NY 1997 (1949), p. xxv.

[68] Although some scholars defend the view that one can adhere to theism and yet reject the belief that an omnipotent God exists. See on this: Bishop, John, "Can There Be Alternative Concepts of God?" *Noûs*, 32, no. 2 (1998), pp. 174–188.

[69] Kenny, *What I Believe*, p. 8.

Kenny does not elaborate on what that "less absolute god" would look like. This question is literally "left open" in the sense that Kenny does not make the slightest attempt to provide us with any information about *his* conception of god, although the fact that he has this conception is the reason why he rejects the epithet "atheist."[70]

What he does, though, is to leave the reader with the expectation that there is research that could be done – as if that research might reveal that it is indeed possible to arrive at a god-conception on less absolutist terms. But is not that a little misleading? I am inclined to think it is. I say this because, in my opinion, no further research or deeper reflection is required to defend the position that a less absolutist conception of God is perfectly possible. One might remove, for instance, omnipotence from the characteristics of the theistic god. Or one might leave out benevolence. Either strategy would annul the difficulty of explaining the evil in the world and reconciling this with the idea of an omnipotent creator. As long as Kenny does not give us an idea of what his less absolutist conception of God looks like, we are not in a position to affirm or deny the existence of such a god or tell whether that god ought to be an object of veneration.

This implies that, as long as Kenny does not present a less absolute god-conception of his own, we cannot adopt an a-theistic stance towards it. This is precisely my problem with the broader definition of atheism that some authors favor. As long as we do not have an idea what someone means when he or she refers to "god," there is no need to deny this god.

People can entertain some very curious notions of "god." The Marquis de Sade (1740–1814) could have said "sadistic sex is my god." Leopold von Sacher Masoch (1836–1895), whose name gives us the word "masochism," could have pointed to the divine experience of sexual submission to his mistress. After all, submissive sex was exactly where his ultimate commitment lay, and modern theologians use that as a definition of god or "religion." If we follow Paul Tillich's definition of faith as a state of being grasped by an ultimate concern,[71] there is no reason to deny the Marquis de Sade or Leopold von Sacher Masoch the status of "religious" persons. Their gods are very different from the gods of most other people, but they are gods nonetheless, because they were the *ultimate concern* of their adherents. The relevant question seems to be this: "Is there some threshold for 'godliness' that one cannot transgress?" We may suppose that many people will reject definitions such as "god is sex," but on what grounds

---

[70] Neither does he tell us what his definition of "atheism" is, by the way. Probably Kenny sees the atheist as someone who rejects belief in the existence of *all* gods (whatever their nature), as many other writers on the subject do.

[71] See on this: Braaten, Carl E., "Paul Tillich and the Classical Christian Tradition," in: Paul Tillich, *A History of Christian Thought From Its Judaic and Hellenistic Origins to Existentialism*, A Touchstone Book, Simon and Schuster 1967, pp. xiii–xxxiv, p. xxviii.

do they do this? Definitions like "god is love" are less unusual. Why? Is it because sex is considered less worthy than love? Or is it, perhaps, because the idea of God as presented in Holy Scripture manifests more love than sex?

Anyhow, in principle we can take the attitude that everybody is free to present and venerate his or her own conception of "god." We may even proclaim this to be the essence of religious freedom as enshrined in national constitutions and human rights declarations. One could say, for instance, "god is love" and because there is love in this world reject the epithet "atheist." One might say "god is truth." One might also say: "I believe in love" or "I believe in truth" and in doing so one might have presented conceptions of god in – to quote Kenny – "less absolute terms." But the question is, of course, should someone who denies the existence of "truth" or "love" be called an "atheist"? The answer is clearly "no." Someone who denies the existence of "truth" is a relativist or a nihilist, perhaps, but not an "atheist." The atheist does not deny *everything* that people may choose to call "god," but only "God."

One thing is clear. From the position of atheism as a-theism, the position taken by Nagel, Le Poidevin and others, Kenny is an "atheist."[72] On the basis of the broader definition of atheism (rejection of God *and* gods, whatever the nature of the god or gods may be) he obviously is not. But who would be?

Everybody is free to use his or her own definitions, but it does seem fair to say is that the limited definition of atheism is the more useful one because it seems appropriate to have a shorthand label for the position of someone who does not accept the central claims of theism as made by the Church on the basis of Holy Scripture.[73]

A Dictionary of Philosophy (1979), edited by Antony Flew (1923–2010), gives a succinct argument for the narrow definition of atheism as "the rejection of belief in God." It states:

[72] See also: Kenny, Anthony, *The Unknown God: Agnostic Essays*, Continuum, London 2004.

[73] See also: Smith, George H., *Why Atheism?*, Prometheus Books, Amherst, NY 2000, p. 28: "Given the wide diversity of religious opinions, I have chosen to discuss Christianity throughout this book in order to focus my arguments. But most of my arguments also pertain to any religion (e.g. Islam and some forms of Judaism) that contains the following elements: (1) a doctrine of personal immortality, (2) a promise of salvation for those with orthodox (i.e. correct) belief, and (3) a belief that a least some knowledge necessary for salvation requires faith in divine revelation, knowledge that cannot otherwise be justified through reason alone. These elements constitute what is generally called a 'salvation religion' or a 'personal religion', so I shall use these labels interchangeably." What this all amounts to, in my view, is that, although Smith presents a broad definition of atheism (see the previous pages), his focus is on atheism in the narrow sense of the word, *viz.* the denial of the existence of the theistic god: God.

It can be said with some point that atheism exists only in relation to some conception of deity, that the professed atheist can always reasonably be asked what God he denies, and that "God" covers so many different conceptions, from crude anthropomorphism to sophisticated ideas of an Infinite Substance or Ground of all Being, that everyone is perforce an atheist in relation to some of them. However, the label "atheist" is ordinarily, though probably not invariably, applied without qualification only to someone who denies God in any of the senses that current uses of the term allow.[74]

One may object that this narrow definition of "god" (god as God) was not the preoccupation of the majority of the philosophers and theologians of the Western tradition. So atheists focusing on the narrow definition of "god" are fighting a straw man, it is often said. But that is certainly not true. There is a long discussion of the nature of the *theistic* god in Western culture. Great philosophers and theologians like Plato, Aristotle, Cicero, Augustine, Boethius, Saadia, Avicenna, Anselm, Ghazali, Averroes, Maimonides, Thomas Aquinas, John Duns Scotus, William of Ockham, Martin Luther, Luis de Molina, Francisco Suárez, Thomas Hobbes, René Descartes, Blaise Pascal, Spinoza, Malebranche, Leibniz, Bayle, Berkeley, Voltaire, Paley, Hume, Kant, Hegel, Feuerbach, Darwin, Marx, Kierkegaard, Nietzsche, William James, Freud, Bertrand Russell, Alfred North Whitehead, C.S. Lewis, Alvin Plantinga, George Mavrodes, John Hick, Richard Swinburne, Daniel Dennett, and Richard Dawkins have all participated in a discussion on the existence of the *theistic* god, i.e. "God," with the characteristics as defined by the Church and based on the interpretation of Holy Scripture (Qur'an and Bible). That discussion through the ages was not a conversation about the different attitudes people had with regard to the ultimate ideals of life, but about the characteristics of the theistic god and in what sense these were compatible with each other and with other human ideals. If God knows the future, how can we have free will (Cicero)? What was God doing *before* He created the world (Augustine)? Must God, if he exists in the mind, also exist in reality (Anselm)? Can an omnipotent being be constrained by justice and goodness (Ghazali)? As the author of a recent overview of these arguments says:

thinkers from all three faiths [Judaism, Christianity and Islam] grappled with the general philosophical problems that needed solving if the great monotheism they were jointly constructing was to be viable, developing not merely sophisticated proofs of God's existence but also detailed conceptions of God's

---

[74] Flew, Antony, ed., *A Dictionary of Philosophy*, Pan Books, Macmillan, London 1979, p. 28. See also: Jean Montenot, *Encyclopédie de la Philosophie* [Encyclopedia of Philosophy], La Pochothèque, Livre de Poche, Paris 2002, p. 106 using "atheism" as a term signifying the denial of the existence of God.

various key attributes: omnipotence (or power), omniscience (or knowledge), perfect goodness, eternality, immutability, and so on.[75]

What this all amounts to is that discussions on the existence of God very often were discussions about the compatibility of the characteristics that in the theistic tradition are ascribed to God. Those who held those characteristics to be compatible were called "theists," those who did not "atheists." Discussing the existence of a god with no characteristics or characteristics too vague or undetermined to know much about seems a senseless activity. That implies that *affirming* the existence of such a "god" would be senseless and *denying* it would be equally so. Leslie Stephen (1832–1904) writes: "Dogmatic Atheism – the doctrine that there is no God, whatever may be meant by God – is, to say the least, a rare phase of opinion."[76] Whether it is indeed "rare," as Stephen suggests, is difficult to say, but that it is senseless is true. As I have said, that also has consequences for the affirmative position. It is similarly senseless to affirm the position of a "god" that we do not know anything about. So the liberal theologian who leaves the existence of such a god "open" is naturally allowed to do so, but this position is more problematic and also a little bit more trivial than it appears – or so the adherent of the conception of atheism as a-theism may contend. The atheistic approach, in the sense of the denial of the theistic conception of god (God), is also different from the approach of those atheists who see atheism as the rejection of all things supernatural. As we have seen, Julian Baggini (1968–) defines atheism as "the belief that there is no God or gods."[77] But he goes further:

> The atheist's rejection of belief in God is usually accompanied by a broader rejection of any supernatural or transcendental reality. For example an atheist does not usually believe in the existence of immortal souls, life after death, ghosts, or supernatural powers.[78]

Baggini acknowledges that "strictly speaking" an atheist could believe in any of these things and still remain an atheist, but, so he contends, "the arguments and ideas that sustain atheism tend naturally to rule out other beliefs in the supernatural or transcendental."[79]

---

[75] Pessin, Andrew, *The God Question: What Famous Thinkers from Plato to Dawkins Have Said about the Divine*, Oneworld, Oxford 2009, p. 20.

[76] Stephen, Leslie, "An Agnostic's Apology," *Fortnightly Review*, Vol. XXV, 1876, pp. 840–860, also in: Andrew Pyle, ed., *Agnosticism: Contemporary Responses to Spencer and Huxley*, Thoemmes Press, Bristol 1995, pp. 48–72, p. 48.

[77] Baggini, Julian, *Atheism: A Very Short Introduction*, p. 3.

[78] Ibid., p. 4.

[79] Ibid.

We find the same approach in the Dutch atheist Floris van den Berg (1973–). Atheists do not believe in "god, in gods, not in dwarfs, elves, Martians, tarot cards, astrology."[80] He makes a useful distinction between "narrow atheism" (which focuses on the three monotheist faiths) and "broad atheism" (rejecting all things supernatural) and considers himself to be a broad atheist. Broad atheism rejects all gods, all religions, and all forms of transcendentalism.[81]

The negative character of atheism as a-theism

So far I have been concerned with atheism as the denial of theism. The nature of that denial requires some comment though. Many rational nineteenth-century atheists were adamant that their doctrine was "negative" in the sense that they did no more than deny the claims of others. This "negative atheism" was, for instance, the focus of the most important advocate of atheism in the nineteenth century: Charles Bradlaugh (1833–1891). Besides being an atheist, Bradlaugh was a campaigner for progressive causes such as birth control, republicanism, the alleviation of poverty and the separation of Church and State. In his *A Plea for Atheism* (1864) he defined the essence of atheism thus:

> The atheist does not say "There is no God," but he says: "I know not what you mean by God; I am without idea of God; the word 'God' is to me a sound conveying no clear or distinct affirmation. I do not deny God, because I cannot deny that of which, I have no conception, and the conception of which by its affirmer, is so imperfect that he is unable to define it to me."[82]

Another classic thinker in the atheist tradition was G.W. Foote (1850–1915), editor of the *Freethinker* and also the author of many books and

---

[80]   Berg, Floris van den, *Hoe komen we van religie af? Een ongemakkelijke liberale paradox* [How Do We Get Away from Religion? An Uncomfortable Liberal Paradox], Houtekiet/Atlas, Antwerpen 2009, p. 9.

[81]   Berg, Ibid., p. 9. See also: Thiselton, Anthony C., *A Concise Encyclopedia of the Philosophy of Religion*, Oneworld Publications, Oxford 2002, p. 18: "In the broadest terms, atheism denotes the denial of the existence of God." The distinction between small and broad atheism is also made by William Rowe. See: Rowe, William L., *Philosophy of Religion: An Introduction*, second edition, Wadsworth Publishing Company, Belmont, California 1993, pp. 14–15: "In the broader sense, a theist is someone who believes in the existence of a divine being or beings, even if his idea of the divine is quite different from the idea of God we have been describing. Similarly, in the broader sense of the term, an atheist is someone who rejects belief in every form of deity, not just the God of the traditional theologians."

[82]   Bradlaugh, Charles, "A Plea for Atheism" (1864) at: http://www.infidels.org/library/historical/charles_bradlaugh/plea_for_atheism.html (accessed 2/19/10), also in: *Champion of Liberty: Charles Bradlaugh*, Watts & Co. and Pioneer Press, London 1933, and: Stein, Gordon, ed., *An Anthology of Atheism and Rationalism*, Prometheus Books, Buffalo, NY 1980, pp. 9–19, p. 10.

articles on atheism. Foote was convicted of blasphemy and even sent to prison for his convictions.[83] He insisted that atheism is properly defined as the *absence* (or lack) of theistic belief, and not as the positive denial of God's existence.[84] He said: "The atheist is a person who is *without* belief in a god; that is all the 'A' before 'Theist' really means."[85] According to the New Zealand historian and humanist Bill Cooke (1956–) the philosophy of atheism was helped tremendously by the distinction between negative and positive atheism. "This had done a lot to clear up very old misconceptions about what atheism is really saying."[86] So when Mel Thompson writes "belief in the existence of God ... is theism" and "the conviction that there is no such being is atheism," he exaggerates the ambitions of the atheist.

So far this "reasonable definition of atheism" or atheism as a-theism has two elements. On the one hand it is limited to a stance vis-à-vis the *theistic* god (and not the "less absolute" conceptions of the theistic god; we may call this, with Van den Berg, "narrow atheism"). On the other hand the nature of that stance is *not subscribing to the position of his existence* (in contrast to the pretension that you can disprove his existence).

This negative character of atheism is easily misunderstood, and that has to do with the ambiguities in the word "negative." "Negative," as used in connection with atheism, simply means "not affirmative." The atheist does not affirm the position of theism. But the word "negative" has all sorts of other meanings. A fact, situation, or experience that is "negative" is unpleasant, depressing, or harmful. If someone is "negative" or has a "negative" attitude, they consider only the bad aspects of a situation, rather than the good ones. Negative people are people who moan.

Critics of atheism usually capitalize on the second meaning of the word and reproach atheists for being "only negative." This is, for example, the case in a critique of secularism by the American scholar Brendan Sweetman. In *Why Politics Needs Religion: The Place of Religious Arguments in the Public Square* (2006), Sweetman argues that secularism is itself a kind of religion.[87] It has its own morality and its own vision of the good life. He

---

[83] Herrick, Jim, "Foote, George William," in: Tom Flynn, ed., *The New Encyclopedia of Unbelief*, Prometheus Books, Amherst, NY 2007, pp. 332–333; Royle, Edward, "Foote, George William," in: Gordon Stein, ed., *The Encyclopedia of Unbelief*, Vol. I, Prometheus Books, Buffalo, NY 1985, pp. 224–226; Levy, Leonard W., *Blasphemy: Verbal Offense against the Sacred from Moses to Salman Rushdie*, The University of North Carolina Press, Chapel Hill 1993, pp. 481–485.

[84] Smith, *Why Atheism?*, p. 23.

[85] Quoted ibid., p. 23.

[86] Cooke, Bill, *Dictionary of Atheism, Skepticism, and Humanism*, Prometheus Books, Amherst, NY 2006, p. 49. Cooke's book is an invaluable source of material for those interested in the secular tradition.

[87] Sweetman, Brendan, *Why Politics Needs Religion: The Place of Religious Arguments in the Public Square*, Interversity Press, Downers Grove 2006.

opposes the claim by secularists that only secular arguments should count in the public square. If Christians want to make a case against abortion or euthanasia, so Sweetman argues, they should be free to refer to the Judeo-Christian tradition as something that motivates their commitment.

It is important at this point to comment on Sweetman's ideas, expounded in his book *Religion* (2007),[88] on what he calls "an important distinction between *negative atheism* and *positive atheism*."[89] Up until the twentieth century, Sweetman argues, atheism was almost always presented as a "negative thesis" or position. It was negative in three ways.

First, the atheist defined his view in terms of what it was not, rather than in terms of what it was. "So in the past an atheist might say, when asked what he believed, that he did not think that God existed, or that he rejected religious morality, or that he did not follow his church's teaching, all claims about what he doesn't believe, not about what he does believe."[90]

Second, the atheist often regarded himself negatively from a psychological point of view: belonging to a minority he couldn't avoid understanding his identity in terms of what he was not.

Third, the atheist defended his view negatively, *viz.* by "attacking religion and religious arguments for religious belief."[91]

In the twentieth century "all this has changed," according to Sweetman, because atheists realized that a more "cultivated approach" was necessary. Subsequently, Sweetman formulates what "positive atheism" would look like, and in doing this he identifies "positive atheism" with "secularism."

> Nowadays, a secularist is much more likely to present secularism as a positive thesis, one that identifies what he believes, rather than what he does not believe. As noted above, secularists will say they believe that human life is the outcome of a purely random, naturalistic process (evolution), and that all reality is physical. And, very important, their defense of these claims will not now consist simply of attacking the arguments for religious belief: they will try to offer positive arguments to support these views.[92]

I do not think this proposal in the field of terminology is much of an improvement. What Sweetman proposes is, first, to blur the distinction between atheism, secularism, and materialism. One may do this, of course, but the result is to introduce vagueness whereas clarity would be obtained by clearly distinguishing between these concepts. He also mixes up the two senses of "negativity": negative in the sense of "not affirmative" and nega-

---

[88] Sweetman, Brendan, *Religion*, Continuum, London 2007.
[89] Ibid., p. 9.
[90] Ibid.
[91] Ibid.
[92] Ibid.

tive in the sense of "unpleasant" or "harmful." There is nothing wrong with simply not affirming a certain position. A pacifist is against war. Now, it is possible that pacifists have ideas about how a society without war would look, but what binds them is that they reject war. It seems idle to expect them to argue in favor of peace or to require them to tell us what additional "positive things" they aspire to besides absence of war. The meaning of a word is its use. Sweetman may propose all kinds of semantic distinctions, but I think it would be unfortunate if a clear semantic distinction that was held "up until the twentieth century" should fall into oblivion. If this sounds "conservative," so be it.

Atheism does not have the burden of proof

That brings us to an important consequence. This "negative approach" to atheism (defining atheism in terms of what it is not) has serious consequences for the burden of proof. Atheism in the sense outlined above simply denies the claims of theism. "Theists believe in God, while atheists do not have such a belief," as one author succinctly formulates it.[93] Atheists do not pretend that they are able to prove that God does not exist. The atheist George H. Smith (1949–) puts it as follows: "Atheism, in its basic form, is not a belief: it is the absence of belief."[94] That implies that the atheist does not defend the claim that he can prove God's non-existence, neither does he need to. "An atheist is not primarily a person who *believes* that a god does *not* exist; rather, he does *not believe* in the existence of a god."[95]

I quote the claims of a self-confessed atheist at some length because his words contradict what is often alleged about atheists. Atheism is commonly presented as a special kind of "belief" that God does not exist. We find this in the definition of atheism offered by the philosopher of religion John Hick (1922–). Hick writes: "atheism (not-God-ism) is the belief that there is no God of any kind."[96] By attributing to atheism the pretension to reject gods *of any kind*, Hick advances claims that a more cautious atheist would be inclined to deny.[97] He also deviates from the approach of Nagel and

---

[93] Johnson, B.C., *The Atheist Debater's Handbook*, Prometheus Books, Buffalo 1981, p. 11.
[94] Smith, George H., *Atheism. The Case against God*, Prometheus Books, Buffalo, NY, 1989 (1979), p. 7.
[95] Smith, Atheism, p. 7. The French atheist Paul Desalmand writes that the atheist does not try to demonstrate the non-existence of God because he knows this is an idle undertaking. He only wants to show the inconsistencies in the theist position. See: Desalmand, Paul, *L'athéisme expliqué aux croyants* [Atheism Explained to Believers], Le Navire en Pleine Ville, Paris 2007, p. 38.
[96] Hick, John, *Philosophy of Religion*, fourth edition, Prentice Hall International, Inc., London 1990 (1963), p. 5.
[97] Baggini, whose definition of atheism was quoted before, is the exception here.

Bradlaugh inasmuch as he suggests that the atheist must prove that God *does not exist*. This puts the atheist in a disadvantageous position, because if the atheist is not successful in this undertaking (and how can he ever achieve such an ambitious goal?), it will be commonly supposed that he has failed to substantiate his position. According to Smith, Nagel and other defenders of the "negative" approach, Hick's claim is an impossible claim to make. From their point of view, the only thing the atheist has to do is to wait until the theist has made his position clear. At that point the atheist can judge whether he is convinced by the theist's arguments. If he is not convinced, then atheism is the stronger position vis-à-vis theism.

Is that not the way we normally operate? I cannot *prove* that the world is not created by an elephant standing on the back of a tortoise, but why should I? It is up to the speaker who makes such a claim to prove his case.

The atheist's position may be summarized thus: atheism is a negative doctrine. The atheist is not convinced by the proofs of theism. This being the case, he does what every sensible person would do. He says "I am not a theist."

This falls far short of what Alister McGrath expects atheists to defend. McGrath gleefully ascribes colossal pretensions to atheists: "Atheism is the religion of the autonomous and rational human being, who believes that reason is able to uncover and express the deepest truths of the universe, from the mechanics of the rising sun to the nature and final destiny of humanity."[98] So an atheist should have pretensions to solve the riddle of the universe. He should be able to express its "deepest truths." That kind of vocabulary does not make sense to atheists – at least not to the "reasonable" kind I have introduced. What special properties must a truth possess to be "deep" or even "the deepest"? Why should the atheist commit himself to speculations about the "final destiny of the universe"? McGrath mistakes atheism for a religion, in his case the religion of Christianity. Christianity claims to provide deep truths about the universe, for example that Jesus is the Son of God.[99] Christianity also pretends to know what the final destiny of the universe is. The atheist does not profess to have any knowledge of this kind.[100] Because McGrath thinks that atheism is the exact antithesis of Christian belief, he supposes that the atheist must also have certain opinions on these matters, but this is not the case. In reality we never hear atheists boasting about the discovery of deep truths and ideas about the final destiny of the universe. McGrath is probably confusing atheism with the worldview

---

[98]   McGrath, *The Twilight of Atheism*, p. 220.
[99]   See: Evans, Stephen C., *The Historical Christ and The Jesus of Faith. The Incarnational Narrative as History*, Clarendon Press, Oxford 1996.
[100]   See: Kirsch, Jonathan, *A History of the End of the World: How the Most Controversial Book in the Bible Changed the Course of Western Civilization*, HarperCollins, New York 2007.

of Marxism-Leninism, of which a denial of God was one part.[101] But no sane atheist would have such pretensions. The British philosopher Antony Flew (1923–2010) made this clear when he coined the expression: the *presumption of atheism*.[102] Another way of putting it is that we should regard atheism as the default position. The theist has to prove his case. The historian J.B. Bury (1861–1927) presents this idea with a funny example:

> If you were told that on a certain planet revolving round Sirius there is a race of donkeys who talk the English language and spend their time in discussing eugenics, you could not disprove the statement, but would it, on that account, have any claim to be believed?[103]

That brings us to a fourth and final element of the concept of atheism.

Atheism is an examined choice

A fourth element of the atheist position is the psychological attitude of the atheist himself: atheism is considered to be an explicit intellectual choice. I hinted at this before when discussing Le Poidevin's thesis: simply living a life without God is not sufficient grounds for calling someone an "atheist."

Let me illustrate this with an example. Suppose someone tells us: "God? I don't know what that means. I've never thought about it." How should we characterize this view? Is the person expressing this view an "atheist"? Many of us would waver, and rightly so. What this person lacks is a conscious intellectual commitment. It would be strange to characterize this person as an "atheist." That is why children, by definition, cannot be "atheists" as d'Holbach once proclaimed they were. People who have never thought about God are pagans perhaps, not atheists.

This does not mean that atheism has to be what it is nowadays called "strident" or "militant."[104] One of the most frequently made comments on atheism is that atheists are "militant." This is also the reason why many people are reluctant to call themselves "atheists," fearing that they will be

---

[101] See on this: Froese, Paul, "Forced Secularization in Soviet Russia: Why an Atheistic Monopoly Failed," in: *Journal for the Scientific Study of Religion*, 43:1 (2004), pp. 35–40. For the ideology of Marxism-Leninism in general: Acton, H.B., *The Illusion of the Epoch: Marxism-Leninism as a Philosophical Creed*, Routledge & Kegan Paul, London 1962 (1955).

[102] Flew, Antony, *The Presumption of Atheism, and Other Philosophical Essays on God, Freedom and Immortality*, Elek/Pemberton, London 1976. Flew caused some controversy because of a new development of his thinking in: Flew, Antony (with Roy Abraham Varghese), *There Is a God: How the World's Most Notorious Atheist Changed His Mind*, HarperCollins, New York 2007.

[103] Bury, *A History of the Freedom of Thought*, p. 20.

[104] See on this: Berman, David, *A History of Atheism in Britain: From Hobbes to Russell*, Routledge, London 1988, pp. 212–235: "Militant and Academic Atheism."

considered impolite, unfriendly, and disrespectful. Some atheists are, indeed, straightforward in their opinions. The most well-known example is Richard Dawkins (1941–). Dawkins advocates "actively disbelieving in God's existence."[105] One passage from his bestselling book *The God Delusion* (2006) that is often referred to is this:

> Imagine, with John Lennon, a world with no religion. Imagine no suicide bombers, no 9/11, no 7/7, no Crusades, no witch-hunts, no Gunpowder Plot, no Indian partition, no Israeli/Palestinian wars, no Serb/Croat/Muslim massacres, no persecution of Jews as "Christ-killer," no Northern Ireland "troubles," no "honor killings," no shiny-suited bouffant-haired televangelists fleecing gullible people of their money ("God wants you to give till it hurts"). Imagine no Taliban to blow up ancient statues, no public beheadings of blasphemers, no flogging of female skin for the crime of showing an inch of it.[106]

Another proponent of what is often referred to as "militant atheism" is Christopher Hitchens (1949–). Hitchens formulates the following four objections to religious faith in *god is not Great* (2007):

> That it wholly misrepresents the origins of man and the cosmos, that because of this original error it manages to combine the maximum of servility with the maximum of solipsism, that it is both the result and the cause of dangerous sexual repression, and that it is ultimately grounded on wish-thinking.[107]

The New Atheism does not only have adherents in the anglophone world. The Dutch atheist Floris van den Berg (1973–) is a representative of the new current in the Netherlands. Van den Berg adopts the term "moral atheist," because he thinks religion is an impediment to individual freedom and autonomy.[108] In a liberal democracy the state should not forbid, but discourage, religion. The attitude towards religion should be the same as towards smoking: you do not forbid it, but you do try to discourage people from associating themselves with it. In any case parents should not be in a position to cripple the minds of their children with their own religious preoccupations.[109] Religious privileges should be abolished.[110] "Where reli-

---

[105]   Dawkins, *The God Delusion*, p. 99.

[106]   Ibid., p. 24.

[107]   Hitchens, Christopher, *god is not Great: How Religion Poisons Everything*, Twelve, New York, Boston 2007, p. 4. In my terminology the title of this book should be: "God is not Great"; "god" with a capital "g." The reason is that the Hitchens's criticism is directed at a particular conception of "god": the theistic god.

[108]   Berg, *Hoe komen we van religie af?*, p. 16.

[109]   Ibid., p. 21.

[110]   Ibid., p. 24.

gion is empowered, society transforms into a prison."[111] Not believing is "normal," believing is "abnormal."[112] Atheists should raise their voices, van den Berg advocates; they should wear T-shirts with atheist texts. He organized the Dutch equivalent of the London buses that drove through the streets with the slogan:

> There's probably no god,
> Now stop worrying
> And enjoy your life.

Another representative of the New Atheism is the American author Sam Harris (1967–), whose *The End of Faith* (2004) emphasizes the destructive power of religious belief. He writes:

> There seems ... to be a problem with some of our most cherished beliefs about the world: they are leading us, inexorably, to kill one another. A glance at history, or at the pages of any newspaper, reveals that ideas which divide one group of human beings from another, only to unite them in slaughter generally have their roots in religion. It seems that if our species ever eradicates itself through war, it will not be because it was written in the stars but because it was written in our books; it is what we do with words like "God" and "paradise" and "sin" in the present that will determine our future.[113]

This is all strong language and many people associate "atheism" with *advocating* atheism or with confrontational language. Is that right?

I do not think so. Atheism can be defended forcefully, as is the case in the work of the New Atheists, but Christianity can be as well. People like Martin Luther (1483–1546) or the contemporary Christian apologist Dinesh D'Souza[114] (1961–) defend Christianity in much the same way as Dawkins and Hitchens defend their atheism, and we should not mix up the way a point of view is defended with what is defended in itself. As long as there is a reasonable exchange of arguments (as there certainly is between people like Dawkins, Hitchens, Harris, and Dennett on the one hand and Alister McGrath and Dinesh D'Souza on the other) there is nothing wrong with a debate along these lines. On the contrary, I think philosopher of religion Charles Taliaferro is right when he says that the books by Dawkins and Dennett "have done a great deal of good by bringing the topic of religion to the fore of public discourse."[115] That compliment can be extended

---

[111] Ibid., p. 30.

[112] Ibid., p. 34.

[113] Harris, Sam, *The End of Faith: Religion, Terror, and the Future of Reason*, The Free Press, London 2005 (2004), p. 12.

[114] D'Souza, Dinesh, *What's so Great about Christianity*, Regnery Publishing, Inc., Washington, DC 2007.

[115] Taliaferro, Charles, *Philosophy of Religion*, Oneworld, Oxford 2009, p. ix.

to the work of Hitchens and Harris as well. The New Atheists have stimulated an enormous debate on the merits of theism that contrasts favorably with the woolly self-complacent abstractions of the liberal theologians that set the tone in the 1960s and 1970s.

This overview would not be complete without another allegation that is often voiced about atheism. Atheists, so some authors say, *despise* religion or religious believers. This is insinuated in the following words by philosopher of religion John D. Caputo (1940–) who writes that he does not want to be "accused of behaving like an *Aufklärer*, like one more learned despiser of religion."[116]

These words imply a highly negative and rhetorical vision of the Enlightenment as a movement that *despises* religion. But why should an *Aufklärer* [rationalist (from the Enlightenment)] despise religion? If you carefully analyze the arguments of the protagonists of religion and politely tell them you are not convinced, does that testify to a negative attitude?[117] And if you do not locate the source of moral norms in God but in the nature of man, as Enlightenment philosophers did,[118] are you then a "despiser" of religion? I do not think so and this rhetorical device should be unmasked for what it is: a cheap trick to intimidate critics into swallowing things that should not be swallowed.

Motives for Atheism

In this section I wish to conclude my reflections on the *definition* of atheism. The characteristics presented in the previous section are, basically, what the concept is all about. An atheist simply denies the claims of theism. As we have seen, we should not mix this up with the ways in which atheism can be defended. Nor should we fail to distinguish between *what atheism is* and the *motives* for atheism.

---

[116]   Caputo, John D., *On Religion*, Routledge, London 2001, p. 94.

[117]   Caputo continues with the remark that he does not "want to dismiss fundamentalist spirituality as so much nonsense." He says: "I want to settle inside this passion for the impossible, to rock with the rhythms of its divine madness, to sway with the joyous pulsations of the Word of God as it shakes the bodily frames of mortal coils of these whole-hearted believers. I want to dance and sing, not sneer!" Ibid., p. 95. What this means and if it means anything at all is difficult to say. Should we read this as a Dionysian glorification of irrationality? Is not dancing and singing an irresponsible reaction in this time of religious violence?

[118]   See: Larmore, Charles, "Beyond Religion and Enlightenment," *San Diego Law Review*, 30 (1993), pp. 799–815, p. 803: "Despite the obvious danger in defining a movement so complex as the Enlightenment, I believe we may consider as one of its most important legacies the project of locating the source of moral norms, no longer in God, but in the nature of Man."

This is – to my mind – what is neglected in the attempt to define atheism by the Irish philosopher and sociologist Patrick Masterson (1936–). Masterson writes in his book *Atheism and Alienation* (1971) that the emphasis of contemporary atheists has shifted from a critique of the proofs for the *existence* of God to the rejection of the *properties* traditionally attributed to Him. The atheism of his day, so he continues, consists chiefly in asserting the impossibility of the coexistence of finite and infinite being. What contemporary atheists object to is that "the affirmation of God as infinite being necessarily implies the devaluation of finite being and, in particular, the dehumanization of man."[119] This is all very well, but isn't this more about the motives of contemporary atheists?

Many people are motivated not to subscribe to the belief in an omnipotent, perfectly good, personal god because this would conflict with important values they would prefer to uphold. It is also perfectly possible to say that one can be a "non-believer" in the existence of God (and so an atheist) and a "believer" in human freedom, human dignity, progress, and many other things. As a matter of fact, this is a combination that one often encounters. People's motives for developing an atheist position are often grounded in a laudable type of engagement and not in disillusion. So, in most atheists we find a combination of "belief" and "unbelief," but what they believe in is not God and is sometimes deemed to be irreconcilable with God. That is manifested clearly in a kind of "profession of faith" by the great American infidel Robert Ingersoll (1833–1899). Ingersoll wrote:

> I am an unbeliever, and I am a believer .... I do not believe in the "Mosaic" account of creation, or in the flood, or the Tower of Babel, or that General Joshua turned back the sun or stopped the earth. I do not believe in the Jonah story ... and I have my doubts about the broiled quails furnished in the wilderness. Neither do I believe that man is wholly depraved. I have not the least faith in the Eden, snake and apple story. Neither do I believe that God is an eternal jailer; that he is going to be the warden of an everlasting penitentiary in which the most of men are to be eternally tormented. I do not believe that any man can be justly punished or rewarded on account of his belief.
>
> But I do believe in the nobility of human nature; I believe in love and home, and kindness and humanity; I believe in good fellowship and cheerfulness, in making wife and children happy. I believe in good nature, in giving to others all the rights that you claim for yourself. I believe in free thought, in reason, observation and experience. I believe in self-reliance and in expressing your honest thoughts. I have hope for the whole human race. What will happen to one, will, I hope, happen to all, and that, I hope, will be good. Above all, I believe in Liberty.[120]

[119] Masterson, Patrick, *Atheism and Alienation: A Study of the Philosophical Sources of Contemporary Atheism*, Penguin Books, Harmondsworth 1973 (1971), p. 13.
[120] Quoted in: Williams, David Allen, *A Celebration of Humanism and Freethought*, Prometheus Books, Amherst, NY 1995, p. 67.

Ingersoll was a very successful public speaker, as everyone who reads this passage will understand, and this probably has to do with the fact that he, like no other, understood how to ride the moral high ground. He competed with the religious orators in the sense that he used some of their imagery, e.g. when he writes: "I believe in the religion of reason – the gospel of this world; in the development of the mind, in the accumulation of intellectual wealth, to the end that man may free himself from superstitious fear, to the end that he may take advantage of the forces of nature to feed and clothe the world."[121]

It is difficult to cast somebody who writes and speaks like this as a cynic or as someone without firm beliefs and ideals.

As we might expect on the basis of the last sentence from the passage by Ingersoll, one of the most important values that animates much of atheist writing is the attempt to safeguard human freedom. This we encounter in the work of the German philosopher Eduard von Hartmann (1842–1906). In 1874 von Hartmann wrote a small book under the title *Die Selbstzersetzung des Christenthums und die Religion der Zukunft* [The Self-Annihilation of Christianity and the Religion of the Future]. In that book von Hartmann distinguished between the traditional religious position, based on moral heteronomy, and his own position, which was based on moral autonomy (see Chapter 4). It was the Protestant tradition in Christianity in particular that brought human autonomy to the fore, but, so von Hartmann argued, the principle of moral autonomy, although generated within the Christian worldview, will ultimately destroy Christianity. And he would have been pleased with that. Once one gives primacy to human reason and moral autonomy, the authority of the divine will and scripture have to be rejected: "For the absolute moral principle of Christianity is obedience to the divine will as expressed in Holy Scripture."[122] This is – and here comes my point – irreconcilable with human freedom, according to von Hartmann. As long as we believe in the theistic god who has created us and the rest of the world we have to conclude that we are nothing, he claims. Our true morality, von Hartmann tells us, can be nothing other than strict submission to

---

[121]   See: Ingersoll, R.G., "Why Am I an Agnostic?" *North American Review*, December 1889, Part I, pp. 1–14, p. 6. See also: Ingersoll, R.G., "Mistakes of Moses," in: R.G. Ingersoll, *Complete Lectures of Col. R.G. Ingersoll*, M.A. Donogue & Company, Chicago 1900, pp. 7–19, p. 7: "Now and then someone asks me why I am endeavoring to interfere with the religious faith of others, and why I try to take from the world the consolation naturally arising from a belief in eternal fire. And I answer: I want to do what little I can to make my country truly free. I want to broaden the horizon of our people."

[122]   Von Hartmann, Eduard, *Die Selbstzersetzung des Christenthums und die Religion der Zukunft* [The Self-Annihilation of Christianity and the Religion of the Future], Zweite Auflage, Carl Ducker Verlag, Berlin 1874, p. 12.

the almighty will of this transcendent god. In that situation morality is heteronomous.[123]

True morality, so von Hartmann contended, will always start with human autonomy, and, like Ingersoll, he also spelled out what this implies for the theistic worldview: "then all theistic morality will be necessarily unethical."[124] This implies that the "Christian idea has run its full course."[125] We have to find a new moral perspective for the modern world. As long as we believe in the idea of the theistic God we are nothing but an object, a material object made by a divine creator and, accordingly, limited in our freedom.

A similar argument to von Hartmann's is used by another German philosopher, Nicolai Hartmann (1882–1950). In his *Ethics* (1926)[126] Hartmann developed a theory of values that, though objective, have ideal being, affecting the world insofar as men act on them.

It has been rightly said that "the absence of religious thought in Hartmann's philosophy is conspicuous."[127] For the history of atheism Hartmann is important because he denies the existence of a providential God. God's providence would annihilate human freedom. Hartmann, in his "postulatory atheism," teaches the opposite of Kant with regard to God: human freedom does not necessitate us to postulate God, but the reverse. God's nature and human freedom stand in a contradictory relation as "thesis" and "anti-thesis."

Atheist Values

A similar point was made by the twentieth-century French philosopher Jean-Paul Sartre (1905–1980) in *L'existentialisme est un humanisme* [Existentialism is a Humanism] (1946). If we try to imagine a world created by a divine creator, a supernatural craftsman, we, humans, are not free. We can only play the role He has written for us, and this completely destroys human freedom. So Sartre developed what he called an "atheistic

---

[123] Ibid., p. 30.
[124] Ibid.
[125] Ibid., p. 91.
[126] Reissued in English as: Hartmann, Nicolai, *Moral Phenomena*, Vol. I of *Ethics*, With a new introduction by Andreas A.M. Kinneging, Transaction Publishers, New Brunswick, 2002; Hartmann, Nicolai, *Moral Values*, Vol. II of *Ethics*, Transaction Publishers, New Brunswick 2003; Hartmann, Nicolai, *Moral Freedom*, Vol. III of *Ethics*, Transaction Publishers, New Brunswick 2004.
[127] Cerf, Walter, "Nicolai Hartmann," in: Paul Edwards, ed., *The Encyclopedia of Philosophy*, Vol. III, Macmillan & The Free Press, New York 1967, pp. 421–426, p. 426.

existentialism," in contrast with Christian varieties of existentialism that had been developed by Christian philosophers like Gabriel Marcel (1889–1973). Human freedom demands that we proclaim that man has no "essence," but only "existence." Only within the confines of such an ontology is human freedom secured.[128]

So far we have seen that some thinkers consider that the theistic worldview contradicts human freedom. That has to do with the field of meta-ethics. But it is also possible to present a critique of the Christian worldview because the values it espouses conflict with our own ethical values. This is the focus of one of the most elegant books on moral and political philosophy from an explicitly atheist point of view: *An Atheist's Values* (1964) by Richard Robinson.[129]

Robinson (1902–1996) studied philosophy at Oxford and Marburg, taught philosophy at Cornell University for nearly 20 years and then back at Oriel College, Oxford for more than 20 years.[130] He wrote on ancient Greek philosophy (in particular Plato and Aristotle) and logic.[131]

What Robinson tried to do in *An Atheist's Values* is to establish a counterpoint to the "Christian values" that we hear people talk about. He made a distinction between "personal goods" and "political goods." The things that he described as personal goods were beauty, truth, reason, love, conscientiousness, and religion. His treatment of religion was, as one might expect, very critical. Religion is more of an evil than a good because it is gravely inimical to truth and reason.[132] Faith is a vice. There is no God or afterlife and religion provides no good reason for behaving morally. But Robinson also gave an introduction to political philosophy with his treatment of the "political goods": the state, equality, freedom, tolerance, peace and justice, and democracy.

An Atheist's Values is in many ways a brilliant book, but I fear that its title is somewhat misleading. Many people will be scared off because they expect a long diatribe against religious faith, against Christianity in particular. This is not the case. What Robinson shows is that it is perfectly possible

---

[128] See: Sartre, Jean-Paul, *L'être et le néant, Essai d'ontologie phénoménologique* [Being and Nothingness, an Essay in Phenomenological Ontology], Gallimard, Paris 1943, pp. 485 ff. and Sartre, Jean-Paul, *L'existentialisme est un humanisme* [Existentialism Is a Humanism], Les Éditions de Nagel, Paris 1970, p. 17, where he states that all forms of existentialism have in common that "existence precedes essence, or, if you like, that one has to take subjectivity as a point of departure."

[129] Robinson, Richard, *An Atheist's Values*, The Clarendon Press, Oxford 1964.

[130] Walter, Nicolas, "Obituary: Richard Robinson," *The Independent*, June 14, 1996.

[131] See Robinson, Richard, *The Province of Logic: An Interpretation of Certain Parts of Cook Wilson's "Statement and Inference,"* George Routledge, London 1931 and Robinson, Richard, *Definition*, Oxford University Press, Oxford 1962 (1954).

[132] Robinson, *An Atheist's Values*, p. 113.

to write about ethics and politics from a purely secular perspective. In other words, a secular life stance is perfectly suited to moral and political reflection.

Spiritual Excellences and the Liberal Decalogue

Another author who is, in a certain sense, similar to Robinson is L. Susan Stebbing (1885–1943). Stebbing was the first female professor of philosophy in Britain, and what Bill Cooke (1956–) calls a "formidable smiter of humbug."[133] She came down strongly against pretentious woolly thought, as may be gathered from her *Thinking to Some Purpose* (1939)[134] and her *Philosophy and the Physicists* (1937)[135] where she targets Sir James Jeans (1877–1946) and Sir Arthur Eddington (1882–1944), two theistic astronomers who, according to Stebbing, strayed from their area of expertise into Christian apologetics.

Stebbing wrote at a time during which British universities were becoming strongholds of analytical philosophy. The attitude of this philosophical movement to values was not altogether appreciative. It associated them with the metaphysical and absolutist philosophy of Plato (*c.* 428–347 BCE) and his acolytes. So Thomas Dewar Weldon (1896–1958)[136] wrote somewhat dismissively about

> Plato and his modern disciples who suppose that philosophy leads to the discovery of eternal Ideas and Values and that anyone who is acquainted with these must know beyond any possibility of doubt how all States ought to be organized and what the relation of States to one another and to their own members ought to be. This special insight into the nature of reality makes the philosopher the final court of appeal of all kinds of important practical problems such as education, birth-control and the proper use of atomic bombs.[137]

---

[133] Cooke, Bill, *Dictionary of Atheism, Skepticism, and Humanism*, p. 505.
[134] Stebbing, L. Susan, *Thinking to Some Purpose*, Penguin Books, Harmondsworth 1952 (1939).
[135] Stebbing, L. Susan, *Philosophy and the Physicists*, Dover Books, New York 1958 (1937).
[136] Well known for his analytical approach to political philosophy in Weldon, T.D. *The Vocabulary of Politics*, Penguin Books, Harmondsworth 1953. The main contribution of this book was, according to Robert Goodin and Phillip Pettit, "to pour cold water on the aspiration of political philosophy to say something important." See: Pettit, Philip, "Analytical Philosophy," in: Robert E. Goodin and Philip Pettit, eds., A *Companion to Contemporary Political Philosophy*, Blackwell, Oxford 1993, pp. 7–39, p. 9.
[137] Weldon, T.D., *States and Morals: A Study in Political Values*, John Murray, London 1946, preface.

It is a funny statement, of course, and in the mind's eye the image arises of a pretentious philosopher-cleric who has no practical experience whatsoever and still tries to tell us how "beyond any possibility of doubt" we have to deal with the great political problems of our time. And yet, we may ask ourselves whether a curious and modest philosopher who engages in the analyzing and weighing of values, and subsequently advocates some of these values, necessarily has to cut such a pompous figure. In any case, this is not the impression we get from the work of such intellectually conscientious philosophers as John Stuart Mill, Bertrand Russell, Richard Robinson, and Susan Stebbing.[138] It seems possible to engage in an analysis of values and still avoid the pretentious claims of the Hegelians that T.D. Weldon and his fellow analytical philosophers revolted against.

Stebbing formulated a different vision from Weldon's. In 1943 she wrote:

> Moral philosophers, I contend, must be concerned with the ways in which men live – their ways of life which embody their ideals. I conceive that it falls within the proper province of moral philosophers to formulate ideals worth living for and the attempt to make clear principles which may afford guides for action. This is a task difficult to fulfil.[139]

In *Ideals and Illusions* (1941)[140] Stebbing listed "spiritual excellences" that were not based on any religious conviction:

- love for other human beings;
- delight in creative activities of all kinds;
- respect for truth and the satisfaction in learning to know what is true about the world and about ourselves;
- loyalty to other human beings;
- generosity of thought and sympathy with those who suffer, and hatred of cruelty and other evils;
- delight in the beauty of nature and in art; and
- to have experience of pain and of forgoing what would be good for oneself in order that the needs of others may be met.[141]

---

[138]   Or a contemporary moral philosopher such as Peter Singer. See, for example: Singer, Peter, *Practical Ethics*, second edition, Cambridge University Press, Cambridge. 1993 (1979); Singer, Peter, *The President of Good and Evil. Taking George W. Bush seriously*, Granta Books, London 2004. Both books combine critical acumen with a firm choice of values.
[139]   Stebbing, L. Susan, "Men and Moral Principles," Oxford University Press, London 1944, also in: *Hobhouse Memorial Lectures 1941–1950*, Oxford University Press, London 1952, pp. 3–27, p. 4.
[140]   Stebbing, L. Susan, *Ideals and Illusions*, with an introduction by A.E. Heath, Watts & C., London 1948 (1941).
[141]   Stebbing, *Ideals and Illusions*, pp. 29–30.

Like Robinson, she did not shy away from presenting values, and even wanted to use the word "spiritual" for her "goods" or "values."[142]

The last philosopher I want to mention in this context is the most well known, Bertrand Russell (1872–1970). Russell had a tremendous influence on the whole tradition of secularist thought in the twentieth century, of course. To borrow a phrase from Noel Annan (1916–2000), Russell wrote "in a prose whose lucidity was equalled by its elegance."[143] With books like *The Scientific Outlook* (1931), *Religion and Science* (1936), *Why I am Not a Christian and Other Essays* (1957)[144] and many others, he proved to be a paragon of liberal and secular thought in the twentieth century, comparable only with John Stuart Mill in the nineteenth. Russell also wrote an influential history of philosophy, in which his worldview is expressed in sometimes hilarious comments on his fellow philosophers, ancient and modern.[145] One of his lesser-known pieces, but relevant for our topic, is his "Liberal Decalogue" as part of what he called the "Liberal outlook." He presented this Liberal Decalogue not as a "substitute" for the Ten Commandments but as a supplement to them. "Perhaps the essence of the Liberal outlook could be summed up in a new Decalogue, not intended to replace the old one but only to supplement it," Russell writes.[146] But whoever takes cognizance of his "Liberal Decalogue" can hardly fail to notice that it looks more like a devastating criticism of the work of Moses than a "supplement." This is what Russell, as a twentieth-century liberal-secular legislator, presents us with:

1. Do not feel absolutely certain of anything.
2. Do not think it worth while to proceed by concealing evidence, for the evidence is sure to come to light.

---

[142] In her attempt to combine secular ideals with a certain input of *spiritualité* Stebbing is somewhat similar to the French philosopher André Comte-Sponville whose atheism was characterized by the atheist Michel Onfray as "Christian atheism." Comte-Sponville, André, *L'esprit de l'athéisme. Introduction à une spiritualité sans Dieu* [The Spirit of Atheism. Introduction to a Godless Spirituality], Albin Michel, Paris 2006.

[143] Annan, Noel, *Our Age: The Generation that Made Post-War Britain*, Fontana, London 1990, p. 101.

[144] Russell, Bertrand, *The Scientific Outlook*, Routledge, London 2001 (1931); Russell, Bertrand, *Religion and Science*, Oxford University Press, London 1935; Russell, Bertrand, *Why I Am Not a Christian: And Other Essays on Religion and Related Subjects*, Routledge, London 2004 (1957).

[145] Russell, Bertrand, *History of Western Philosophy And Its Connection with Political and Social Circumstances from the Earliest Times to the Present Day*, George Allen & Unwin, London 1974 (1946).

[146] Under the title "The Best Answer to Fanaticism – Liberalism" published in *The New York Times*, December 16, 1951, and subsequently included in: Russell, Bertrand, *The Autobiography of Bertrand Russell*, Unwin Paperbacks, London 1975, pp. 553–554.

3. Never try to discourage thinking for you are sure to succeed.
4. When you meet opposition, even if it should be from your husband or your children, endeavour to overcome it by argument and not by authority, for a victory dependent upon authority is unreal and illusory.
5. Have no respect for the authority of others, for there are always contrary authorities to be found.
6. Do not use power to suppress opinions you think pernicious, for if you do the opinions will suppress you.
7. Do not fear to be eccentric in opinion, for every opinion now accepted was once eccentric.
8. Find more pleasure in intelligent dissent than in passive agreement, for, if you value intelligence as you should, the former implies deeper agreement than the latter.
9. Be scrupulously truthful, even if the truth is inconvenient, for it is more inconvenient when you try to conceal it.
10. Do not feel envious of the happiness of those who live in a fool's paradise, for only a fool will think that is happiness.

These examples could be augmented *ad libitum*, but that is not necessary within the confines of this book. My primary purpose is analytical – in particular, to distinguish the *concept* of atheism (limited or "negative") from the *motives* that atheists have for subscribing to this position (a predilection for human freedom, as we see in the work of Sartre and von Hartmann, or other specific liberal values, as expounded by Stebbing, Robinson, and Russell).

So, now we have discerned two options. On the one hand we have the theist position, on the other, the atheist perspective. But is the whole spectrum adequately covered by this dichotomy?

Agnosticism

Many people have the feeling that these two positions do not adequately cover the field. Should we not distinguish a third position, they say, to wit: *that we cannot know* whether God exists or not? This view is commonly designated as "agnosticism." The agnostic usually claims "to leave open" the question of whether or not God exists. Agnosticism is the theory according to which things within a specified realm cannot be known.[147] Although that "specified realm" is not necessarily religion, the term is usually applied

---

[147] See: Mautner, Thomas, *The Penguin Dictionary of Philosophy*, Penguin Books, London 2000 (1996), p. 9.

in a religious context, more particularly with reference to the existence of God. In that sense the agnostic claims that we cannot know whether or not God exists.[148] Is this a viable position? Many people are convinced it is. "In all rigour, agnosticism is the only defensible position, and it does not advance anybody one step on the road to atheism or one step on the road to theism," the humanist H.J. Blackham (1903–2009) wrote in 1963.

One of the first questions with regard to the agnostic position is this: what is the agnostic really agnostic about? Does he or she also "leave open" the position that Zeus may exist? Or Allah?

Usually the agnostic does not seriously uphold the idea that the Greek gods may exist. But what exactly is being left unanswered? The agnostic may say: "That's the question, stupid, I do not know. I have no idea about the nature of God, that's exactly the reason why I do not want to affirm or deny his existence." But is that a fruitful position to take? You leave open the existence of something you cannot say anything about.

Probably the agnostic does not leave open the existence of *all* the gods that humans have venerated from the Stone Age to the twenty-first century, but only the existence of the god that is held in high esteem in the culture in which he or she lives, that is, the theistic god (or God). But in order to leave open the existence of the theistic god, you should at least distinguish some of his characteristics. And once you have done that, why not specify your reasons for holding these characteristics to be compatible or not? Is it impossible to say anything about the likelihood of the existence of a personal, eternal, omnipotent, and perfectly good being? The atheist deems his existence unlikely. The atheist thinks – and here he sides with the theist – that you can *argue* about those things. The atheist will point out that the existence of evil does not fit in easily with divine omnipotence and perfect goodness. This is adumbrated in a poem by Samuel Porter Putnam (1838–1896).

Putnam was an American atheist and lecturer on freethought whose most important work was a massive history of the freethought movement: *Four Hundred Years of Freethought*.[149] Putnam's greatest political success was his effort to defeat a proposal to alter the US Constitution by inserting God into it in 1896. Putnam made a speech before the Joint Judiciary Committee of the US House of Representatives on March 11 and helped to kill the bill. He also wrote poetry.[150] In "Why Don't He Lend a Hand" from 1890 Putnam presents a mild critique of the idea that God's omnipotence can be reconciled with perfect goodness.

---

[148] Ibid., p. 10.

[149] Putnam, Samuel Porter, *Four Hundred Years of Freethought*, The Truthseeker Company, New York 1894.

[150] Cooke, Bill, "Samuel Porter Putnam," in: Tom Flynn, ed., *The New Encyclopedia of Unbelief*, Prometheus Books, Amherst, NY 2007, pp. 624–625.

You say there is a God
Above the boundless sky,
A wise and wondrous deity
Whose strength none can defy.
You say that he is seated
Upon a throne most grand,
Millions of angels at his beck –
Why don't he lend a hand?

See how the earth is groaning,
What countless tears are shed,
See how the plague stalks forward
And brave and sweet lie dead.
Homes burn and hearts are breaking,
Grim murder stains the land;
You say he is omnipotent –
Why don't he lend a hand?

Behold, injustice conquers;
Pain curses every hour;
The good and true and beautiful
Are trampled like the flower.
You say he is our father,
That what he wills doth stand;
If he is thus almighty
Why don't he lend a hand?

What is this monarch doing
Upon his golden throne,
To right the wrong stupendous,
Give joy instead of moan?
With his resistless majesty,
Each force at his command,
Each law his own creation –
Why don't he lend a hand?

Alas! I fear he's sleeping,
Or is himself a dream,
A bubble on thought's ocean,
Our fancy's fading dream.
We look in vain to find him
Upon his throne so grand,
Then turn your vision earthward –

'Tis we must lend a hand.
'Tis we must grasp the lightning,

And plough the rugged soil;
'Tis we must beat back suffering,
And plague and murder foil;
'Tis we must build the paradise
And bravely right the wrong;
The god above us faileth,
The god *within* is strong.[151]

Theodicy, or the reconciliation of evil in the world with God's omnipotence and goodness, has inspired countless debates between theists and atheists.[152] There is a well-known treatment of this theme in the satirical story, *Candide* (1759), by Voltaire (1694–1778). Voltaire mocks Leibniz's thesis that it is all for the best in the best of all possible worlds.[153] James Mill (1773–1836), John Stuart Mill's father, had similar problems with the theistic conception of God. In his *Autobiography* (1873) John Stuart (1806–1873) wrote about his father: "He found it impossible to believe that a world so full of evil was the work of an Author combining infinite power with perfect goodness and rightness."[154]

Richard Robinson (1902–1996) wrote that in the Christian religion, though perhaps not in any other, we frequently find a conception of god that is self-contradictory and therefore corresponds to nothing. That is the conception formed by the following three propositions together:

1. God is all-powerful.
2. God is all-benevolent.
3. There is much misery in the world.

Robinson contended that a god who was all-powerful but left much misery in the world could not be all-benevolent. An all-benevolent god in a world containing much misery would not be all-powerful. A world containing a god who was both all-powerful and all-benevolent would contain no misery. That means that anyone who is confident that he frequently comes across misery in the world may conclude with confidence that there is no such thing as an all-powerful and all-benevolent god. "And this mathematically disposes of official Christianity," Robinson implacably wrote.[155]

---

[151] Quoted in: Stein, Gordon, *A Second Anthology of Atheism and Rationalism*, Prometheus Books, Buffalo, NY 1987, pp. 180–81.
[152] See: Larrimore, Mark, ed., *The Problem of Evil: A Reader*, Blackwell Publishing, Malden, MA 2008.
[153] Voltaire, *Candide ou l'Optimisme* [Candide or Optimism], Conte philosophique, Éditions Larousse, Paris 2007 (1759).
[154] Mill, John Stuart, *Autobiography of John Stuart Mill*. Published from the original manuscript in the Columbia University Library, with a preface by John Jacob Coss, Columbia University Press, New York 1924 (1873), p. 28.
[155] Robinson, *An Atheist's Values*, p. 124.

Sometimes apologists of religion respond to this dilemma by declaring the whole affair a "mystery." Or they refer to God's wisdom as being higher than our wisdom. Nevertheless, that would be begging the question. We are still considering *whether there is a god*, in the sense that he is portrayed in Christian doctrine.

These debates are inconclusive, as so many other philosophical debates are, but they are not meaningless or impossible. Nor are the other discussions of the theistic god. For instance, the question what is the source of morality? Is morality grounded in the will of God? Does the fact that God wills something make that thing *eo ipso* good? Or is it good in and of itself and therefore willed by God? I will treat some of these problems in Chapter 4 of this book.[156]

These are all important and interesting debates, and the agnostic seems to evade his responsibility as a critical thinker by not participating. By doing this, the agnostic poses as "modest" or "not arrogant," as someone who does not overestimate the capacity of the human mind. But is that pretence justified? Anthony Thiselton (1937–) writes: "At first sight agnosticism is often perceived as being less dogmatic and more open than either theism or atheism when applied to belief-systems of religions. It appears to suspend the acceptance or rejection of belief." That this pretence is unfounded Thiselton substantiates by referring to the "paradox of skepticism": "How do I know that I cannot know, if I cannot know whether I know?"[157]

It seems not unreasonable to first ask the agnostic what he understands by "God" before entering into a discussion of whether we can know whether God exists. And one thing is sure. The theistic god as "He" appears to us in the Bible and Qur'an has some definite characteristics we can talk and argue about. If the agnostic does not want to join this debate, fine, but that is more a manifestation of his aversion to the philosophy of religion than an interesting religious or quasi-religious position in itself.

Theists and atheists are discussing *the theistic concept* of god. They are not discussing some kind of unknowable entity. That implies, of course, that the claims of atheism should be limited, as I have expounded before. George I. Mavrodes seems right when he reminds us: "Atheism is ostensibly the doctrine that there is no God. Some atheists support this claim by arguments. But these arguments are usually directed against the Christian concept of God, and are largely irrelevant to other possible gods. Thus

---

[156]   See on this: Rachels, James, "God and Human Attitudes," in: *Religious Studies*, 7 (1971), pp. 325–37, also in: Rachels, James, *Can Ethics Provide Answers? And Other Essays in Moral Philosophy*, Rowman & Littlefield Publishers, Lanham 1997, pp. 109–125.
[157]   Thiselton, Anthony C., *A Concise Encyclopedia of the Philosophy of Religion*, Oneworld Publications, Oxford 2002, p. 4.

much Western atheism may be better understood as the doctrine that the Christian God does not exist."[158]

This is partly true. Mavrodes is right that most of the books on the philosophy of religion that have been published in the Western world discuss the characteristics of the theistic God as presented by *Christian* theologians and philosophers. But because the Christian god is a theistic god and Islam and the Jewish religion subscribe to the theistic concept of god as well, this discussion also has implications for the *Islamic* and the *Jewish* concepts of god.

Another question for agnostics is why they do not apply this position to the other dimensions of life. Why be reluctant to choose between the different positions that can be taken with regard to the theistic concept of God and not between those that relate to the other spheres of life? Politics is a difficult business as well. Yet most committed citizens vote. Who has all the available information about politics, international relations, psychology and all the other areas of knowledge where full expertise would be necessary to make a well-considered choice in favor of this government or the other?

The History of Agnosticism

The intellectual father of agnosticism is the Greek philosopher Protagoras (*c.* 481–411 BCE), considered to be the "most gifted and original brain among the sophists."[159] He is supposed to have written a book "On the Gods" as a result of which he was prosecuted for blasphemy.[160] Protagoras is well-known for the sentence "man is the measure of all things, of those that are that they are, of those that are not that they are not."[161] He regarded all morals and laws as only relatively valid, and binding only in the human community which formulated them.[162] According to Protagoras there is no absolute religion, no absolute morality, and no absolute justice. His agnosticism appears in his conviction that certain matters are too lofty

[158] Mavrodes, George I., "Atheism and Agnosticism," in: Ted Honderich, ed., *The Oxford Companion to Philosophy*, Oxford University Press, Oxford New York 1995, pp. 63.
[159] Zeller, Eduard, *Outlines of the History of Greek Philosophy*, thirteenth edition, revised by Wilhelm Nestle, Dover Publications, New York 1980 (1883), p. 81.
[160] Ibid. Although this may be apocryphal, see: Dillon, John, and Gergel, Tania, eds., *The Greek Sophists*, Penguin Books, London 2003, p. 2.
[161] See: Dillon and Gergel, *The Greek Sophists*, p. 13.
[162] Plato, *Theaetetus*, 167c, in: Plato, *Complete Works*, ed. John M. Cooper, Hackett Publishing Company, Indianapolis 1997, p. 186.

for human beings to form a valid opinion about.[163] The agnostic attitude is well illustrated by another of Protagoras' sayings:

> I am unable to reach knowledge about the gods, either that they exist, or do not exist, or of their essential nature. Among the many factors which prevent me from knowing are the obscurity of the subject and the shortness of human life.[164]

Like agnosticism, atheism was also a well-known position in antiquity. Atheism was associated with Diagoras of Melos. He was surnamed "the godless" and convicted on a charge of impiety. The arguments that Diagoras used are unknown.

Other classical philosophers standing in the agnostic or atheist tradition are Prodicus of Ceos (dates uncertain) and the Athenian Critias (c. 460–403 BCE). In one of his plays Critias made a character argue that the notion of an all-seeing, all-knowing deity was simply a fiction invented by some clever statesman to put the fear of god into wrong-doers.[165]

Because we do not have more than fragments from the pre-Socratic philosophers we can only guess what they thought exactly. Did Protagoras, for instance, referring to the "shortness of human life," think that if human life would have been longer or even infinite we would be able to acquire more knowledge about the gods? If that were the case, this would presuppose that in this life we are able to gather at least *some* information about the nature of the gods. And if this is possible it might follow that we could bequeath this information to succeeding generations. So why should not our knowledge of the gods grow, just as scientific knowledge grows? Or is the agnostic doomed to be and stay "agnostic"?

Although this remark by Protagoras about the shortness of human life frustrating our knowledge of the gods is intriguing, most self-confessed agnostics seem to consider their agnosticism to be something that is founded in the limited capacity of the human mind. Man is inherently unable to gauge the depth of the divine mind.

The Oxford philosopher Anthony Kenny (1931–) discusses agnosticism in his autobiography *A Life in Oxford*. He comments on the work of the poet Arthur Hugh Clough (1819–1861). Clough was an agnostic poet struggling with language to say something about God in his poetry. In a poem from 1851, "Hymnos, Aumnos" ("a hymn, yet not a hymn"), Clough started with the statement that we should search for God in the inner

---

[163]   Luce, J.V., *An Introduction to Greek Philosophy*, Thames and Hudson, London 1992, p. 82.
[164]   Quoted ibid., p. 82.
[165]   See: ibid., p. 85.

dimension of our soul. But we should never presume that we can gauge his qualities.

> O thou, in that mysterious shrine
> Enthroned, as we must say, divine!
> I will not frame one thought of what
> Thou mayest either be or not.
> I will not prate of "thus" and "so"
> And be profane with "yes" and "no."
> Enough that in our soul and heart
> Thou, whatso'er thou may'st be, art.

This is the agnostic position as formulated by a poet. Kenny, who wrote a monograph on Clough, characterizes agnosticism as follows: "Not only can we not say of God what he is, we are equally impotent to say what he is not."[166]

Kenny and Clough fail to notice, however, that presupposed in this question are at least two – highly controversial – characteristics. Apparently God is a "he" (so male) and a "person." But the question arises, what exactly is the difference between agnosticism and atheism for practical purposes? Does the agnostic "sometimes pray," for instance? Just to be sure?

Huxley and Russell

It was T.H. Huxley (1825–1895) who actually coined the term "agnosticism." He may be familiar to the public at large nowadays as the grandfather of the novelist Aldous Huxley (1894–1963) and the biologist and broadcaster Julian Huxley (1887–1975). "T.H." was an important character in nineteenth-century Britain, engaged in the struggle for the supremacy of the evolutionist point of view (which brought him the nickname "Darwin's bulldog").[167] But a third contribution "T.H." made to Western cultural heritage is less well known. He was the father of "agnosticism."

Huxley coined the concept in 1869. He used it to designate his own stance toward knowledge of the transcendental realm. Huxley said: "Agnosticism is not a creed but a method." The essence of this method was characterized as follows: it is "the vigorous application of a single principle." This principle has a positive and a negative side. "Positively," Huxley

---

[166]   Kenny, Anthony, *A Life in Oxford*, John Murray, London 1997, p. 230.
[167]   Desmond, Adrian, *Huxley: From Devil's Disciple to Evolution's High Priest*, Helix Books, Reading, MA 1994, pp. 195 ff. Karen Armstrong calls Huxley a "crusader." See: Armstrong, Karen, *A Short History of Myth*, Canongate, Edinburgh 2005, p. 132.

said, "the principle may be expressed in matters of intellect, follow your reason as far as it can take you without other considerations." And negatively: "do not pretend conclusions are certain that are not demonstrated or demonstrable."[168]

Twenty years later he characterized agnosticism in more or less the same way in his essay *Agnosticism and Christianity* (1889). He wrote: "That it is wrong for a man to say he is certain of the objective truth of a proposition unless he can produce evidence which logically justifies that certainty. This is what agnosticism asserts and, in my opinion, is all that is essential to agnosticism."

As I have said, agnosticism is widely popular nowadays. It can boast great adherence in intellectual circles. About the cause of this popularity one can only speculate. Perhaps agnosticism is considered attractive because it scorns dogmatism. Agnosticism has an air of liberal-mindedness, of tolerance about it.

Agnosticism also exerted a great attraction on one of the most anticlerical minds of the twentieth century, Bertrand Russell. In his long life, which encompassed almost a century (1872–1970), Russell wrote many articles on religious matters. His discussion with Father Copleston (1907–1994), author of a monumental *History of Philosophy*, on the BBC in 1948 is well known. His essay *Why I am not a Christian* (1927), published twenty years earlier, also caused much controversy. Russell gained the reputation of a freethinker and an atheist mainly on the basis of these two publications.[169] But although he wrote disparagingly about God, he did *not* adopt the term "atheist" to designate his own position. Russell called himself an "agnostic."[170]

---

[168]   *Agnosticism* (1869) is included in: Huxley, Thomas Henry, *Agnosticism and Christianity and other Essays*, Prometheus Books, Buffalo, NY 1992. Commentaries on Huxley in: Pyle, Andrew, ed., *Agnosticism. Contemporary Responses to Spencer and Huxley*, Thoemmes Press, Bristol 1995. Huxley's *Agnosticism* is also included in: Stein, Gordon, ed., *An Anthology of Atheism and Rationalism*, Prometheus Books, Buffalo, NY 1980. On agnosticism see further: Stein, Gordon, "Agnosticism," in: Gordon Stein, ed., *The Encyclopedia of Unbelief*, Vol. I, Prometheus Books, Buffalo, NY 1985, pp. 3–4 and the excellent introduction by Pyle to the volume mentioned before.

[169]   See: Copleston, F.C., *A History of Philosophy*, Vol. VIII, Part II, Image Books Edition, New York 1967, p. 241: "Technically speaking ... he is an agnostic. At the same time he does not believe that there is any real evidence for the existence of God" and Berman, David, *A History of Atheism in Britain. From Hobbes to Russell*, Routledge, London 1988, p. 230: "For many people Bertrand Russell is the most formidable British atheist, if not *the* atheist." But, so Berman writes, Russell's criticism on religious matters is not "straightforwardly atheistic."

[170]   On the question of what his religion was, Russell answered: "I never know whether I should say "Agnostic" or whether I should say "Atheist." See: Russell, Bertrand, *Bertrand Russell on God and Religion*, ed. Al Seckel, Prometheus Books, Buffalo, NY 1986, p. 85.

In 1953 he gave a clear indication of what he thought was the essence of the agnostic position. He responded to the question of whether an agnostic was an atheist, and said: "No. An atheist, like a Christian, holds that we *can* know whether or not there is a God. The Christian holds that we can know there is a God; the atheist, that we can know there is not. The agnostic suspends judgment, saying that there are not sufficient grounds for affirmation or for denial."[171]

From these words it appears that Russell and Huxley were in agreement. Theism and atheism are rejected for the same reasons. Theists and atheists alike pretend to have knowledge about matters one cannot have knowledge of.

It is clear that when two of the most critical minds in the history of freethought – or what is presented here as the secular outlook – prefer the position of the agnostic above that of the atheist, this is cause for serious concern. Agnosticism has always attracted people who scorn the straightforwardness of the atheist position.

Paradoxically, this can again be the basis for a reaffirmation of the theistic position on professed pragmatic grounds. A notorious argument in this direction was presented by the great French seventeenth-century thinker Blaise Pascal.

Pascal's Wager

Pascal (1623–1662) was many things: a brilliant mathematician, philosopher, and scientist, but also a Christian apologist. Mathematicians recognize him as the inventor of Pascal's Triangle and the calculating machine. Physicists and historians of science acknowledge his pioneering work on the vacuum. In his *Provincial Letters* (1657) we get to know him as a brilliant theological polemicist.[172] The word "Jesuitical" owes its pejorative sense to Pascal's satirical attack on the Society of Jesus.[173] Here I only want to address his ideas on the existence of God. A striking feature of the argument developed in his *Pensées* [Thoughts] (1669)[174] is that, just like Huxley and Russell, Pascal denied that we can know for certain whether God exists or not. That does not lead to a position of permanent agnosticism, however, because, he argued, we should *bet on God*.

---

[171] Ibid., p. 73.

[172] Pascal, Blaise, *The Provincial Letters*, 1657, translated with an introduction by A.J. Krailsheimer, Penguin Books, Harmondsworth 1982 (1967).

[173] Hammond, Nicholas, "Introduction," in: Nicholas Hammond, ed., *The Cambridge Companion to Pascal*, Cambridge University Press, Cambridge 2003, pp. 1–3, p. 1.

[174] Published posthumously. See: Pascal, Blaise, *Pensées*, 1669, translated by A.J. Krailsheimer, Penguin Books, London 1966.

Pascal's argument is included in almost every anthology of the philosophy of religion.[175] It is designated as "The Wager."

Somewhat shortened it can be presented thus. According to Pascal, we can never know for certain whether God exists or not.

> If there is a God, He is infinitely incomprehensible, since, having neither parts nor limits, He has no affinity to us. We are then incapable of knowing either what He is or if He is. This being so, who will dare to undertake decision of the question? Not we, who have no affinity to Him.

So far Pascal seems inclined towards agnosticism, just like Huxley and Russell. But his argument takes a different turn when he introduces the idea that we have to wager. We cannot avoid the choice for or against God. "We are embarked," Pascal wrote. In this situation the choice for God is the most reasonable. Because what do we have to lose and what do we have to gain in making a choice for God? If we gain, we gain all. If we lose, we lose nothing.

Is Pascal convincing? This argument, it would seem, could be contested on several grounds. Many people will retort that we cannot simply start believing – on command – and merely because this will have favorable consequences. Either you believe or you do not. Belief can be compared with love. You cannot love someone because this would have favorable results. Love, like the choice for God, is not possible on the basis of a utilitarian calculus.

Another criticism of Pascal's idea focuses on the moral viability of his pragmatic approach. This matter has also been discussed with regard to the question of whether religious belief is useful for upholding the moral order. We find this in the following contention by Richard Neuhaus (1936–2009): "Religious belief was seen as reinforcement, a backstop, if you will, to the public ethic. Religion, especially in its insistence upon ultimate rewards and punishments, was the motivating force for good behavior."[176] Shouldn't this be an important argument for accepting religious belief?

This is Richard Robinson's answer to this question. After dissecting the proposition that religion is an important *reason* for moral behavior, Robinson treats the question of whether religion can be a *cause* that does in fact makes people obey moral laws. His answer is straightforwardly this:

---

[175] Pascal, "The Wager," in: Louis Pojman, ed., *Philosophy of Religion. An Anthology*, Wadworth Publishing Company, Belmont, CA 1994, pp. 420–422; Pascal, "The Wager," in: Michael Peterson, *et al.*, ed., *Philosophy of Religion. Selected Readings*, Oxford University Press, New York 1996, pp. 63–65.

[176] Neuhaus, Richard John, *The Naked Public Square: Religion and Democracy in America*, second edition, William B. Eerdmans, Publishing Company, Grand Rapids, MI 1997 (1984), p. 22.

The first and most important point to make about this proposition is that, whether it is true or false, to use it as an argument in favor of religious belief is a disgraceful thing to do. To do that is to commit the pragmatic dishonesty of arguing that a creed is true because it is useful that people should believe it. I know that this argument *is* used extremely frequently, and in the most respected quarters. Nevertheless, it is self evidently null both in logical effectiveness and in common decency.[177]

In short: "To preach a false doctrine, or to preach a doctrine without considering whether it is false or true, is base and beneath human dignity."[178]

But let us leave these moral objections for a moment and concentrate on the question of whether Pascal's argument is convincing purely on a factual basis. According to Pascal, we miss out on something that we would otherwise acquire: eternal happiness. The idea is familiar. He who believes in God (and makes the right choice) will earn heaven. He who does not believe (and makes the wrong choice) will be punished.

Like many modern believers, Pascal did not much emphasize the last aspect. He avoided speaking about the bad news and concentrated on the good news. But it is clear that as important a religious authority as Jesus Christ pointed out the punishments for those who do not believe. Nonbelievers will be thrown "into the furnace of fire" where "men will weep and gnash their teeth," just as "the weeds are gathered and burned with fire" (Matthew 13:40–42). For Ezekiel, the people of Jerusalem had brought their destruction and exile upon themselves by profaning the temple of the Lord, and failing to live up to their obligations as God's people.[179] Under these circumstances the choice for God seems reasonable.

Yet there is a fundamental flaw in Pascal's Wager that was not very obvious in his time, but invalidates his argument in ours. The problem with Pascal's argument is that he only includes the *Christian* God in his wager. This may have been comprehensible and excusable in the seventeenth century, but in the twentieth century it is not. We live, in contrast to Pascal, in a religiously pluralistic society. Many gods compete for our attention. We not only have to wager for or against the *Christian* God, but we have knowledge of the gods of the Greeks, the Romans, the Vikings, the Huns, the Hindus, the Muslims, and all kinds of new gods.

When we further speculate about the character of these gods, we might perhaps presume that the other gods, just like the theist god, are jealous and in a state of competition with their divine rivals.

Under these circumstances betting on one specific god is tricky business. *First*, we do not have a 50% chance of making the right choice, but a much

177 Robinson, *An Atheist's Values*, p. 133.
178 Ibid., p. 134.
179 McGrath, *A Brief History of Heaven*, p. 45.

lower percentage. And *second*, the wrong choice may cause heavy penalties from the gods who are offended by our wrong choice. (Perhaps Pascal currently lives in the hereafter as a Christian Prometheus, being eternally punished by the gods of the Vikings for the wrong choice he made.)

So what would be the most reasonable choice under the circumstance of religious pluralism? It seems to me, the most reasonable choice would be not betting on any god at all. And would that not bring us close to "atheism" in the sense outlined before? That is the concept of "negative atheism" as defended by Ernest Nagel, Charles Bradlaugh, and other authors. The atheist in that sense does not prove that God does not exist but simply does not engage in believing in Him because the evidence is not convincing.

Pascal's Insight

So far, I have been critical of Pascal's argument as developed in his Wager. I have also dwelled on Pascal's mistake in neglecting the non-Christian religions. But there is something appealing about his approach as well, and this point has great relevance for the viability of agnosticism. The strong point in the argument of Pascal's Wager is *that we cannot suspend judgment on the transcendental realm*. "Il faut parier" – we have to bet, Pascal wrote. This "we have to" can be seen as an exhortation to bet, but also as the proclamation of the inevitability of a choice.

That last element is the one that is most important to emphasize. As living beings, acting in this world, we all make choices, every day, every moment. We either pray or we do not. We either thank God for our dinner or we do not. We either listen to his moral councils or we do not. We either give sense to life by reference to the religious tradition or we find meaning in life without recourse to the religious dimension. *We simply cannot avoid these choices.* What we can do, is *say* that we suspend judgment. But every time that we do *not* pray, do *not* give thanks for our dinner, we make a choice. So every human being is a living manifesto of what he or she believes in or not. This is the first dimension of "we have to choose." It is for this reason that I concluded the section on the history of agnosticism with the question: does the agnostic pray *sometimes*? Choosing is inevitable and is what we actually do.

But Pascal's Wager also (and perhaps mainly) stresses that we should make the choice consciously. Make the leap. Take your stance deliberately. Of course, for Pascal this was an exhortation to make the theistic choice. But what he says about the choice for God and therefore for theism can also be employed for the atheistic choice. Live consciously and rationally "for the unexamined life is not worth living for men," as Socrates told us.[180] Try to give a justification, as well as you can, for the choices you implicitly make, every day, every hour.

This is what both theists and atheists do. Theists try to explain why they believe in God, atheists try to explain why they do *not* believe in God. Between theism and atheism there is – given the fact that we have to act – no middle ground, at least not an attractive intermediary position, so it seems to me.

The agnostic *says* he suspends judgment while in every act he chooses in favor of or against God. As Ferdinand Canning Scott Schiller (1864–1937) says: "the emotional value of 'no answer' is equivalent to an answer in the negative."[181] So the agnostic can be adequately defined as the man "who does not know," but his lack of knowledge is not some superior position that goes back to the *docta ignorantia* of Socrates (470–399 BCE) or Montaigne (1533–1592), but the ignorance of someone who is unable or unwilling to take intellectual responsibility for a philosophical outlook that he honors in his deeds. There surely is some ignorance here. But this is not ignorance of a sophisticated kind, as the agnostic himself considers it to be. This is the ignorance of the unexamined life. As the nineteenth-century lawyer and public intellectual Frederic Harrison (1831–1923) writes in his critique of agnosticism: what the religion of the agnostic comes to is "the belief that there is a sort of something, about which we can know nothing."[182] Agnosticism is not a religion, nor the shadow of a religion; it is "the mere disembodied spirit of dead religion," so Harrison writes in criticizing the work of some nineteenth-century agnostics who wanted to present agnosticism as a *remplaçant* for traditional religion.

Atheism or Non-Theism?

In other words, atheism seems to be superior to agnosticism. Does that mean that atheism is the best position? In a certain sense it is. Atheism *in the sense defined before* is highly defensible. The only problem is, hardly anybody follows the semantic convention that I, following Nagel and others, have proposed. In popular parlance atheism is associated with all kinds of negative ideas and attitudes, especially due to the way it *can* be defended (and undoubtedly *has been* defended). Atheists have a reputation

---

[180]   Plato, *Apology*, 38a. Plato, *Complete Works*, p. 33.

[181]   Schiller, F.C.S., "Pessimism in Philosophy," in: F.C.S. Schiller, *Humanism: Philosophical Essays*, second edition, Greenwood Press, Westport, CT 1970 (1912), pp. 157–165, p. 162.

[182]   Harrison, Frederic, "The Ghost of Religion," *The Nineteenth Century*, Vol. XV, March 1884, pp. 494–506, also in: Andrew Pyle, ed., *Agnosticism: Contemporary Responses to Spencer and Huxley*, Thoemmes Press, Bristol 1995, pp. 109–124, p. 111.

for being arrogant, militant, missionary, zealous, and also impolite if not rude. For that very reason George Jacob Holyoake coined the word "secularism."

George Jacob Holyoake (1817–1906) is most famous nowadays for his trial on the grounds of "blasphemy."[183] During one of his lectures in Cheltenham he was confronted with a question from the audience about man's duty to God. Holyoake's response was that England was too poor to have a God. So it would not be a bad idea to put Him on "half pay." For this remark he was convicted of blasphemy and sentenced to six months in jail. After his release he returned to Cheltenham. There he reiterated the exact words that had gotten him into trouble the first time.

Less well known is the fact that Holyoake coined the word "secularism." He did this because he was convinced that "atheism" was in bad repute. He defined secularism as concern with the problems of *this* world. He summarized his position in the following words:

> (1) Secularism maintains the sufficiency of Secular reason for guidance in human duties. (2) The adequacy of the Utilitarian rule which makes the good of others, the law of duty. (3) That the duty nearest at hand and most reliable in results is the use of material means, tempered by human sympathy for the attainment of social improvement. (4) The sinlessness of well-informed sincerity. (5) That the sign and condition of such sincerity are – Freethought – expository speech – the practice of personal conviction within the limits of neither outraging nor harming others.[184]

Holyoake may have been a learned man but he did not possess the gift of making snappy phrases. Nevertheless, in one respect he was right: the concept of "atheism" is hopelessly tainted with negative images, and any author who wants to put this epithet on the banner advertising his lifestyle is confronted with almost insurmountable difficulties. He is constantly obliged to explain his use of the term "atheism" while his audience reacts by saying: "All right, but is not atheism also …?" And then the whole litany against atheism starts all over again: isn't it a bit arrogant to pretend to know that God does not exist? (Answer: the atheist does not proclaim that God does not exist, he affirms that the reasons to believe in his existence

---

[183] Levy, Leonard W., *Blasphemy: Verbal Offense against the Sacred from Moses to Salman Rushdie*, The University of North Carolina Press, Chapel Hill 1993, pp. 453–7; Bradlaugh Bonner, Hypatia, *Penalties Upon Opinion: Some Records of the Laws of Heresy and Blasphemy*, third edition, Watts & Co., London 1934, pp. 71–75.

[184] Holyoake, George Jacob, and Bradlaugh, Charles, "Is Secularism Atheism?" in: Gordon Stein, *A Second Anthology of Atheism and Rationalism*, Prometheus Books, Buffalo, NY 1987, pp. 345–369, p. 348.

are inadequate.) Why are people not allowed to believe in God? (Answer: atheists are not against free speech or against freedom of conscience or freedom of religion; they only claim the right to disagree with anyone who affirms the existence of God.) Isn't atheism a bit arrogant? (Answer: atheism is no more arrogant than agnosticism or theism. The "arrogance" is not in the position itself, but in the way that people hold their opinions: that is, if people are dogmatic or not willing to discuss their views. Atheists are usually fond of discussions.)[185]

That means that although atheism is a defensible position, the odds appear very much against it. This has brought many people to the conclusion that it may be better to keep the position but to change the name. We find this with A.C. Grayling (1949–), for instance. He avoids the term "atheism" when he writes: "I subscribe to a non-religious outlook, and criticize religions both as belief systems and as institutional phenomena which, as the dismal record of history and the present both testify, have done and continue to do much harm to the world, whatever good can be claimed for them besides."[186] So Grayling speaks of a "non-religious outlook." He also writes: "As it happens, no atheist should call himself or herself one. The term already sells a pass to theists, because it invites debate on their ground. A more appropriate term is 'naturalist,' denoting one who takes it that the universe is a natural realm, governed by nature's laws."[187]

Another author who avoids the term "atheism" as a designation for his own position is Paul Kurtz (1925–). Kurtz favors the term "humanism" and speaks of humanism as *eupraxophy* (good wisdom and practice). By this he means "that humanism expresses a distinctive nonreligious life-stance."[188]

> Specifically, it advocates a cosmic outlook based upon science and philosophy and a practical ethical approach to the good life. Unlike theoretical science, which seeks to explain how nature operates, or pure philosophy, which is concerned with analysis, eupraxophy attempts to apply knowledge to practical normative issues. I especially wish to contrast humanistic eupraxophy with

[185] Although there is a tendency among some liberals not to discuss religion. They mistakenly consider this reluctance to be part of the liberal attitude. See on this: Dacey, Austin, *The Secular Conscience: Why Belief Belongs in Public Life*, Prometheus Books, Amherst, NY 2008.
[186] Grayling, A.C., *Against All Gods: Six Polemics on Religion and an Essay on Kindness*, Oberon Books, London 2000, p. 9.
[187] Ibid., p. 28. See also: Kors, Alan, *Atheism in France, 1650–1729*, Vol. I, *The orthodox sources of disbelief*, Princeton University Press, Princeton, NJ 1990, p. 7. Kors writes that Calvin, Luther, Zwingli and also Erasmus were all decried as "atheists" in the debates on their work.
[188] Kurtz, Paul, *The Courage to Become: The Virtues of Humanism*, Praeger, Westport, CT 1997, p. 2.

both transcendental theistic religion, which often considers the highest moral virtues to be faith, hope, and charity, and the skeptical nihilistic attitude, which denies that there are any objective grounds for the moral virtues.[189]

Holyoake (in countering the atheist Bradlaugh)[190] seems to be animated by similar concerns. He proposed the term "secularism" as an adequate formula for the convictions outlined above. This is possible, but I will argue that it would be better if the term "secularism" were reserved for the position that I will discuss in Chapter 4 of *The Secular Outlook*. Perhaps it is better to use the term "non-theism" for the position of a conscious rejection of the thesis that God exists. And if one wants to retain the word "atheism" for its respectable historical lineage it might also be possible to add "private" to the term. In sum, atheism as an integral part of the secular outlook should be "private atheism."

There is some risk involved in using the word "private" in this context, though. Private atheism in the sense expounded above ought *not* to mean that the atheist should refrain from voicing his or her worldview in a public context.[191] Nor ought it to mean watering down the claim that the position is better defensible than the theistic one (an atheist is not a relativist). It only means that the atheist should not commit to the view that all people have to subscribe to his or her view of life in order to live peacefully together. Atheists and theists can live together under a constitutional framework that recognizes the "right to read"[192] or freedom of speech and freedom of religion for all the citizens of the state. In that sense there is no need for an atheist to be "missionary" or "militant."

Perhaps the following example can serve as a clarification. A man, let's call him David, does not believe in the existence of God. And not only does David not believe in the existence of God as a kind of gut feeling of the secularized non-reflective individual, but he has read about the topic. He has studied books on the philosophy of religion, has read about the proofs for the existence of God, but, all things considered, he claims to have good reasons not to believe. Nevertheless, he does not make a great point of his unbelief. He specifies the reasons for his unbelief only when his position is challenged. That happens when someone, let's call him Peter, says:

---

[189]   Ibid., p. 2. See also: Kurtz, Paul, *Eupraxophy: Living without Religion*, Prometheus Books, Amherst NY 1998; Kurtz, Paul, *Forbidden Fruit: The Ethics of Humanism*, Prometheus Books, Amherst NY 1988; Kurtz, Paul, *What is Secular Humanism?*, Center For Free Inquiry, Prometheus Books, Amherst, NY 2006.

[190]   Holyoake and Bradlaugh, "Is Secularism Atheism?"

[191]   This is the trap warned against by Austin Dacey in *The Secular Conscience*.

[192]   Blanshard, Paul, *The Right to Read: The Battle Against Censorship*, The Beacon Press, Boston 1955.

"What, you are an atheist? How can you find meaning in life?"
"You do not believe in God? How come you behave like a responsible moral
   agent?"
"No belief in God? How can you raise your children without the idea of an
   objective moral law?"

David is not only surprised by so much arrogance and lack of knowledge
about the topics he has read about but also annoyed. He answers:

"You believe in the existence of a perfectly good, omnipotent and all-seeing
   God? How can you give meaning to your life if – on the basis of your own
   suppositions – you are nothing more than an automaton that plays a part
   in a play predestined by His script? What about human freedom?"
"What? You simply execute the will of God as revealed in His Scripture? So
   you are going to kill simply because that is written down in an ancient text
   the origin of which you know hardly anything about?" Or:
"How do you raise your children in a morally justified manner if you do not
   clearly spell out that the moral law has primacy over all other considerations, religious considerations included? Should you not teach your children
   that their religious choices have to be made on moral grounds instead of
   vice versa?"

And let us now ask how David's position should be qualified. Is he an
ordinary unbeliever? Not quite perhaps. Is he an atheist? In a certain way
he is. One may also qualify him, perhaps, as a "contextual atheist." It is
only in certain contexts that he will specify the reasons for his unbelief, for
instance in the context of a conversation, as mentioned before. But the most
important is that it would be quite unjust if Peter were to react with this:
"You're a bit of a dogmatic, stubborn, fundamentalist zealot, aren't you?
Member of the Church of Dawkins, are you?" This would be unjust because
what David does, is what may be expected from every self-conscious citizen
and moral agent. David follows Socrates and reminds us that only the
examined life is worth living. He tries to give reasons for his moral choices
and he takes his discussion partner seriously. He does not hide behind
"personal choices."[193] He does not shy away from addressing the great
questions of life. He does not consider it an intrusion of his privacy when
asked about his ultimate commitments. On the contrary, as a non-believer
he tries to take his believing friends seriously.

It is often said that the debate between theists and atheists is senseless
because both positions cannot be proved in any conclusive way. Here is a
comment on the debate by the American sociologist Rodney Stark (1934–),
whose thoughts on the secularization thesis I have already discussed in my

---

[193]   See on this: Dacey, *The Secular Conscience.*

foreword: "It is entirely impossible for science to discover the existence or non-existence of Gods. Therefore, atheistic *and* theistic assumptions are equally unscientific, and work based on either is equally deficient."[194]

This seems to me a not very satisfying approach. It may be true that *science* cannot establish whether God exists or not. But that does not mean that we cannot sensibly *argue* about the matter. This is particularly the case when the concept of "god" is sufficiently specific to make a rational debate possible. The theistic god, "God," is sufficiently specific.

Finally we should clearly proclaim that atheism in the sense of private atheism or non-theism does *not* imply that atheism should be some kind of state doctrine as was the case in the former Soviet Union. So that brings us to three kinds of atheism, or rather three positions an atheist can take towards his own view of life. First, there is "private atheism" or what I will call "non-theism": the view of someone who rejects the theistic worldview and proclaims to do this on good grounds. This is the position of David expounded before. Second, there is "public atheism." Here the atheist creed is perceived to be something that we have to share with fellow citizens, because otherwise no decent society is possible. Here some "missionary" element is involved: the atheist actively wants to "convert" his fellow citizens to his personal conviction. Third, there is "political atheism"; the conviction that the state has to eradicate all kinds of religious belief, as was done in the Soviet Union and in Albania.

Atheism as part of the secular outlook should primarily be private atheism or non-theism: skeptical towards public atheism, and downright dismissive of political atheism. But because using the term "atheism," even in the first sense, has overtones of atheism in the second and third senses it may be advisable to refrain from using the term altogether and rather refer to "non-theism." By doing this, atheists acknowledge that they have won the intellectual battle, but have lost the debate when it comes to public perception.

[194] Stark, Rodney, *One True God: Historical Consequences of Monotheism*, Princeton University Press, Princeton 2001, p. 5.

2

Freethought I: Criticism of Religion

Test everything; hold fast to what is good. (1 Thessalonians 5:21)

It is wrong always, everywhere, and for anyone, to believe anything upon insufficient evidence. (W.K. Clifford, 1877)[1]

In Chapter 1 I was mainly concerned with atheism as an element of the secular outlook. But there is a second position that we immediately think of as being associated with secularist ideas. That is the tradition of freethought. In Chapter 1 I presented atheism as a private matter. Freethought, in contrast, has an important public function to fulfill. In Chapters 2 and 3 I will be concerned with freethought and the significance of that tradition for our contemporary world.

The English word "freethinker" turns up for the first time in Kehl's edition of Voltaire's *Traité sur la tolérance* (1763).[2] The idea was to become more common, however, in the nineteenth century. In an anthology of the *Classics of Free Thought* (1977) by the philosopher Paul Blanshard (1892–1980),[3] freethinkers are described as follows: "Isolated iconoclasts aim[ing] their verbal weapons at the primary enemy, organized religion."[4] So freethought aims to criticize religion. Although this is an important element of freethought, and perhaps the element that freethinkers are most notoriously

---

[1] Clifford, W.K., "The Ethics of Belief," 1877, in: W.K. Clifford, *The Ethics of Belief and Other Essays*, Introduction by Timothy J. Madigan, Prometheus Books, Amherst, NY 1999, pp. 70–96, p. 70, p. 77. See on Clifford: Madigan, Timothy J., *W.K. Clifford and "The Ethics of Belief,"* Cambridge Scholars Publishing, Cambridge 2009.

[2] See Lalouette, Jacqueline, *La libre pensée en France 1848–1940* [Freethought in France 1848–1940], Albin Michel, Paris 2001 (1997), p. 15.

[3] Not to be confused with his twin brother Brand Blanshard (1892–1987).

[4] Blanshard, Paul, "The Capricious Cannonade," in: Paul Blanshard, ed., *Classics of Free Thought*, Prometheus, Buffalo, NY 1977, pp. ix–xi, p. ix.

associated with, we should never forget the *reason* for their critical attitude towards organized religion. This reason was presented by the twentieth-century freethinker Chapman Cohen (1868–1954). Freethought is first of all free thought, he told us, that is, the free development of thought. And, because thought and the expression of thoughts are intimately connected, the tradition of freethought is also the movement favoring freedom of speech. Cohen spelled out his motivations for this: "Speech is, in fact, one of the great factors in human progress. It is that which enables one genera-tion to hand on to another the discoveries made, the inventions produced, the thoughts achieved, and so gives a degree of fixity to the progress attained."[5]

So freethought is intimately connected with critique of religion (Blanshard) and with free speech (Cohen). How do these two ideas come together? Cohen provided the answer to this question: "Freethought is that form of thinking that proceeds along lines of its own determining, rather than along lines that are laid down by authority."[6] And because that authority was often claimed by religious institutions, freethought was also directed at precisely this pretension: "merely as a matter of history, the first active manifestation of Freethought should have occurred in connection with a revolt against religious teaching and authority."[7]

The intricate relationship between criticism of religion on the one hand and the principle of free speech on the other is also emphasized by Joseph Martin McCabe (1867–1955), a freethinker already introduced in Chapter 1.[8] In his book *The Existence of God* (1933) McCabe presents at the outset "a historical truth that no religious writer ever notices." What is that truth? "It is that during the last four thousand years disbelief in God or gods has spread always in exact proportion to the growth of knowledge and of freedom to express one's belief."[9]

These two elements (critique of religion and predilection for free speech) adequately sum up the movement for freethought. Nevertheless, many of the definitions of freethought are loaded with ideals and convictions that go much further than my own minimalist account. Freethought is also frequently connected with belief in progress. Blanshard is a case in point. In his anthology of writings derived from the tradition of freethought he assures us that the "pulpit is losing its once-magic power. Science and philosophic realism have replaced Christian orthodoxy as the standard

[5]   Cohen, Chapman, *A Grammar of Freethought*, The Pioneer Press, London 1921, p. 35.
[6]   Ibid., p. 40.
[7]   Ibid., p. 42.
[8]   See on McCabe: Cooke, Bill, *A Rebel to his Last Breath: Joseph McCabe and Rationalism*, Prometheus Books, Amherst, NY 2001.
[9]   McCabe, *The Existence of God*, p. 4.

guides of moral behavior."[10] Here freethought comes close to an outspoken confidence that the world will increasingly be directed by science and rationality. Apparently, Blanshard subscribed to the secularization thesis. This kind of optimism is also voiced in his contention that "although ours is not yet a secular state – let no professed atheist try for public office! – it is rapidly becoming a true exemplar of religious freedom."[11]

Although it should be acknowledged that in the work of individual freethinkers we encounter a broader range of convictions than the necessity of free speech and religious criticism, I nevertheless think that these elements are the core of the tradition. With regard to freethought we have to follow the same semantic strategy as in the case of atheism and free the concept from unfruitful associations. Belief in progress is one of these. I do not think contemporary freethinkers would exhibit the same kind of optimism as Blanshard with regard to secularization.

Every book on freethought seems to bear the marks of the time in which it was written. Susan Jacoby's (1954–) book *Freethinkers* (2004) was published during the Bush administration and voiced concern precisely about the increasing influence of religious groups on public policy.[12] The situation in the year 1921 (Cohen) was different from that in 1977 (Blanshard), which was different again from the situation in 2004 (Jacoby). Nevertheless there is a common core, and I will concentrate on this commonality. One can stick to the ideals of freethought without the sanguine confidence that those ideals will materialize within the foreseeable future.

In *The Secular Outlook* I will be concerned with freethought as defined by the two ideals formulated by Blanshard and Cohen, that is: first, the legitimacy and even necessity of critique of religion and, second, an affirmation of the importance of freedom of thought and speech, independent of all political and ecclesiastical authority. We could call these the "two pillars of freethought."

Arguably, freethought comes close to the Victorian idea of agnosticism as developed by T.H. Huxley, W.K. Clifford, and Leslie Stephen. This is what I would like to call "robust agnosticism," stipulating that we should always be critical and not accept anything on grounds of authority. Applied to religion it leads to a critical attitude towards religious creeds.

But this original "Victorian agnosticism" (Huxley, Clifford, and Stephen) soon degenerated into another type of agnosticism (even in Victorian times). If our reason is limited and cannot prove the existence of God then surely reason cannot *disprove* the existence of God either. This opened up new possibilities for the religionists. It opened the option of "maybe." Maybe

---

[10] Blanshard, "The Capricious Cannonade," p. x.
[11] Ibid.
[12] Jacoby, Susan, *Freethinkers. A History of American Secularism*, Henry Holt and Company, New York 2004.

there is an afterlife. Who can say? The rationalist surely cannot *disprove* such a possibility. Unfortunately, the "maybe" variety of agnosticism proved to be more popular than the stern creed of Huxley and Clifford. The concept of "agnosticism" quickly acquired a totally different meaning. The agnostic party became the party of those who flirted with the transcendent dimension of existence without feeling obliged to present substantive reasons for it. Here we will concentrate on classical agnosticism, Victorian agnosticism, "robust" agnosticism, or on freethought as outlined above.

An advantage of this minimalist concept of freethought is that its contemporary significance clearly comes to the fore. It is on this contemporary importance of freethought that I will focus in Chapters 2 and 3 of *The Secular Outlook*.

Let us first dwell a little longer on the first pillar of freethought: the critique of religion. The first thing we have to explain is in what sense the critical position of freethought differs from atheism. This may be illustrated with references to two of the most important icons of the secular outlook.

"Écrasez l'Infâme"

First, Voltaire. For many people Voltaire is the archetype of the mocking atheist, as can be clearly read from William Blake's (1757–1827) famous lines.

> Mock on, mock on, Voltaire, Rousseau;
> Mock on, mock on, 'Tis all in vain.
> You throw the sand against the wind.
> And the wind blows it back again.[13]

Mocking he was, but atheism was something Voltaire rejected. Voltaire's reputation for being a religious radical is undeserved. It would be better to say that he was vehemently anticlerical. That is to say, he subjected organized religion to rigorous analysis and criticism. He did not accept the Church as the one and only interpreter of religion, as was the norm in Catholic circles. And he expected religion to be purified as a result of analysis and criticism.[14] In particular, he opposed the organized religion of the Catholic Church and other – in his eyes – intolerant institutions. But, as indicated before, he was neither opposed to religion in general nor to theism

---

[13] Quoted in: Williams, David Allen, *A Celebration of Humanism and Freethought*, Prometheus Books, Amherst, NY 1995, p. 215.

[14] This appears clearly from: Voltaire, *Examen important de Milord Bolingbroke ou le tombeau du fanatisme* [An Important Examination of Lord Bolingbroke or the Tomb of Fanaticism], (1736), in: Voltaire, *Mélanges* [Miscellaneous Writings], Texte établi et annoté par Jacques van den Heuvel, Gallimard, Paris 1961, pp. 1001–1099.

in particular. He even dubbed his own position "theist."[15] He proclaimed that we should favor the idea of an almighty, vengeful god to deter villains from breaking the law and tyrants from exploiting their citizens. Abolish the idea of such a god, and chaos and disorder would ensue. If God did not exist we should have to invent him.[16] So Voltaire was a freethinker without being an atheist.[17]

The Baron d'Holbach on the other hand, was quite a different character. Although sharing Voltaire's predilection for religious criticism, d'Holbach was an atheist *tout court*.[18] D'Holbach's attitude can best be summarized by saying that if God did exist, we should have to abolish him. This was also the attitude of the Russian anarchist Michael Bakunin (1814–1876).[19]

I do not want to elaborate on these differences between important thinkers from the secular tradition but expand on what they have in common: their critical stance towards the dark sides of religion. They are freethinkers in the sense that they are critics of religion, although with a different emphasis and motivation.

But, as I indicated before, freethinkers not only have a critical attitude towards religion in common. Their stance is also identified by a certain attitude towards free speech. What characterizes the freethinker is the fact that he combines his critical stance towards religion with high expectations about freedom of speech. The British agnostic and freethinker[20] Leslie Stephen (1832–1904) wrote: "I hold the pleasant old doctrine that truth has a tendency to prevail."[21] For many Victorians this doctrine was blended with an evolutionist philosophy. Stephen again: "I believe

[15] Voltaire, "Théiste" [Theist], in: *Dictionnaire Philosophique* [Philosophical Dictionary], avec introduction, variantes et notes par Julien Benda, texte établi par Raymond Naves, Éditions Garnier Frères, Paris n.d. (1764), pp. 399–400.

[16] This quote is to be found in: Voltaire, *Epître à l'auteur du livre des Trois Imposteurs* [Epistle to the Author of the Book of the Three Impostors], in: *Œuvres complètes de Voltaire*, ed. Louis Moland, Garnier, Paris 1877–1885, tome 10, pp. 402–405.

[17] Although perhaps there will always remain an element of doubt because Voltaire, like Hume, does not seem inclined to put all his cards on the table. See: Arnold, Ages, "Voltaire and the Problem of Atheism: the Testimony of the Correspondence," in: *Neophilologus*, 68 1984, pp. 504–512.

[18] D'Holbach Paul Henri Dietrich Baron, *Histoire critique de Jésus-Christ* [Critical History of Jesus Christ], in: D'Holbach, *Premières œuvres* [Early Works], Préface et notes Paulette Charbonnel, Les Classiques du Peuple, Éditions Sociales, Paris 1971, pp. 176–198, p. 179.

[19] Bakunin turned Voltaire's words upside down in the motto of his book on religion and the state: "If God really existed it would be necessary to abolish him." See: Bakunin, Michael, *God and the State*, 1916, ed. Paul Avrich, Dover Publications, New York 1970, p. 3 and 17.

[20] See in particular: Stephen, Leslie, *Essays on Freethinking and Plainspeaking*, Longmans, Green, London 1879 (republished 1969).

[21] Stephen, Leslie, "The Religion of All Sensible Men," in: Leslie Stephen, *An Agnostic's Apology and Other Essays*, Smith, Elder & Co., London 1893 (republished 1969), pp. 338–380, p. 343.

that we may discern in the past history of mankind a slow approximation toward truth."[22]

From these quotes by Blanshard, Leslie Stephen and others it is clear how we can easily slide from a predilection for free speech into a belief in progress. Stephen speaks of a "slow approximation toward truth," but it is clear that from here we can easily move forward to a more substantial conviction of an inexorable march of reason through the world. Contemporary freethought would doubtless be better advised to refrain from such evolutionist, Spencerian, Hegelian, or Comtian approaches. Perhaps we may put it in the following way. Freedom of thought does not give us the guarantee of progress,[23] but the *absence* of such freedom is surely a harbinger of stagnation.

According to freethinkers, religion has to be publicly criticized, because only if religion is subjected to rigorous criticism can it be purified of some unfortunate elements and tendencies inherent in it. Does that imply that a freethinker is necessarily convinced that religion should be eradicated root and branch? I do not think so. There are many praiseworthy exhortations in Holy Scripture that a freethinker might defend. Take this famous passage from the New Testament: "Test everything; hold fast to what is good" (1 Thessalonians 5:21). This is a beautiful quote. It is taken from the Bible. It may even be considered the essence of freethought. So not everything in the Bible is necessarily antiquated and to be rejected by modern thinkers. Here, in a nutshell, we find what has been called "the scientific outlook."[24] There is a kind of optimism inherent in such an attitude: by testing we can make progress. We have to be careful of a "revolution of rising expectations," but surely humanity can emancipate itself from some illusions and "poisonous opinions"[25] by critical discussion. The attitude of the freethinker was also aptly summarized by T.H. Huxley in the words:

> That it is wrong for a man to say that he is certain of the objective truth of any proposition unless he can produce evidence which logically justifies that certainty.[26]

The best-known formulation of the same idea was presented by W.K. Clifford in the famous sentence that is the motto of this chapter:

[22]   Stephen, "The Religion of All Sensible Men," p. 343.
[23]   Bury, J.B., *The Idea of Progress. An Inquiry into its Origin and Growth*, Macmillan, London 1920.
[24]   Russell, Bertrand, *The Scientific Outlook*, Routledge, London 2001 (1931).
[25]   Stephen, Leslie, "Poisonous opinions," in: Leslie Stephen, *An Agnostic's Apology and Other Essays*, Smith, Elder & Co., London 1898 (republished 1969), pp. 242–383.
[26]   Huxley, Thomas Henry, "Agnosticism and Christianity," in: Thomas Henry Huxley, *Agnosticism and Christianity and Other Essays*, Prometheus Books, Buffalo, NY 1992, pp. 193–232, p. 193.

It is wrong always, everywhere, and for anyone, to believe anything upon insufficient evidence.[27]

But reading Clifford (a real joy, because, as W.R. Sorley rightly remarks, "there was insight as well as courage in all he wrote, and it was conveyed in a brilliant style")[28] makes us also aware that no ideology, no book, no religion, no cultural practice may be exempt from criticism. That implies that, on the basis of "Test everything; hold fast to what is good" (1 Thessalonians 5:21), the *Bible itself* also has to be "tested." Some passages are good, some are bad. The testing that 1 Thessalonians 5:21 encourages us to do has also implications for Holy Scripture itself.

How can Holy Scripture be considered "holy" if it has to stand trial like everything else? That depends on the meaning we give to the term "holy." If "holy" means "elevated above all criticism," no book can claim "holy" status.

That also applies to ideologies, cultural practices, religions. As Grayling says: "Everyone is free to believe what they want, providing they do not bother (or coerce, or kill) others; but no one is entitled to claim privileges merely on the grounds that they are votaries of one or another of the world's many religions."[29]

This is also in harmony with the principles of the secular state (*laïcité*). All our ideas, our political and religious convictions, must be debated and tested in order to judge whether they can withstand criticism or have to be abandoned for others. This attitude is also to be found (with different shades of emphasis) in the work of Immanuel Kant (1724–1804),[30] John Stuart Mill (1806–1873),[31] and, among contemporary thinkers, Karl Popper (1902–1994).[32] A freethinker is, in other words, an advocate of critical discussion' and of freedom of thought and inquiry, freedom of conscience,

---

[27]   Clifford, W.K., "The Ethics of Belief," 1877, in: W.K. Clifford, *The Ethics of Belief and Other Essays*, Introduction by Timothy J. Madigan, Prometheus Books, Amherst, NY 1999, pp. 70–96, p. 70, p. 77.

[28]   Sorley, W.R., *A History of British Philosophy to 1900*, Cambridge University Press, London 1965 (1920), p. 145, p. 276.

[29]   Grayling, *Against all Gods*, p. 16.

[30]   In particular: Kant, Immanuel, *An Answer to the Question: What is Enlightenment?* 1784 see http://www.marxists.org/reference/subject/ethics/kant/enlightenment.htm.

[31]   Mill, John Stuart, *On Liberty*, 1859, *With the Subjection of Women and Chapters on Socialism*, ed. Stefan Collini, Cambridge University Press, Cambridge 1989.

[32]   Popper, K.R., "Immanuel Kant. Der Philosoph der Aufklärung" [Immanuel Kant. The Philosopher of the Enlightenment], in: Joachim Kopper und Rudolf Malter, eds., *Immanuel Kant zu ehren* [In Honor of Immanuel Kant], Suhrkamp, Frankfurt am Main 1974, pp. 335–347; Popper, Karl R., "Science: Conjecture and Refutations," A lecture given at Peterhouse, Cambridge, in Summer 1953, in: *Conjectures and Refutations*, Harper Torchbooks, Harper & Row, New York 1968 (1962).

and freedom of speech. As I indicated before, the freethinker is the Victorian agnostic.

The question is, is this merely stuffy old material from the eighteenth and nineteenth centuries or does it have some relevance for our contemporary predicament? What is the meaning of freethought today?

Religion and Evil

Let us first address the freethinker's critical stance towards religion: the thesis that religion not only has positive sides, it has darker sides as well. The second pillar of freethought will be the focus of Chapter 3.

The relevance of this first pillar of freethought is clear, and seems particularly important at a time when religions show their uglier faces. However, before elaborating on that contention let me first state clearly that religion has also inspired men to noble deeds.[33] It brought Albert Schweitzer (1875–1965) to his commitment to the sick and destitute in Africa.[34] Religion motivated Mother Teresa (1910–1997) in her work.[35] It led Mahatma Gandhi (1869–1948) to advocate that Hindus and Muslims should respect each others' right to exist.[36] Religion inspired J.S. Bach (1685–1750) to compose his perennial masterpieces, stimulated Chateaubriand (1768–1848) to write *Génie du Christianisme* [The Genius of Christianity],[37] and prompted Michaelangelo (1475–1564) to paint the Sistine Chapel ceiling. And so on and so forth.

Nobody can or has to deny this. It is equally true that the Bible and other holy books contain many laudable exhortations and precepts. One of the best is this: "Abstain from every form of evil" (1 Thessalonians 5:21). Or: "Abhor what is evil; hold fast to what is good" (Romans 12:4). The only thing is: this is only one side of the matter. There is also another story to tell about religion. That "alternative story," so to speak, was the source of inspiration for historical works like those written by W.E.H. Lecky (1838–1903) in his *History of European Morals from Augustus to Charlemagne* (1869)[38] or A.D. White (1832–1918) in *A History of the*

---

[33]   That point is stressed by: Wolterstorff, Nicholas, "An Engagement with Rorty," *Journal of Religious Ethics*, 2003, 31, no. 1, pp. 129–139, p. 135.

[34]   Schweitzer, Albert, *Out of My Life and Thought*, Johns Hopkins University Press, Baltimore 1998.

[35]   The nature of which is severely contested by: Hitchens, Christopher, *The Missionary Position: Mother Theresa in Theory and Practice*, Verso, London 1997.

[36]   Gandhi, M.K., *Ethical Religion*, translated by A. Rama Iyer, S. Ganesan Publisher, Triplicane, Madras 1922.

[37]   Chateaubriand, *Génie du Christianisme ou Beautés de la Religion Chrétienne* [Genius of Christianity or the Beauties of the Christian Religion], ed. Maurice Regard, Gallimard, Paris 1978 (1802).

[38]   Lecky, W.E.H., *History of European Morals from Augustus to Charlemagne*, Longmans, London 1869.

Warfare of Science with Theology in Christendom (1896)[39] or Bertrand Russell (1872–1970) in *Religion and Science* (1935).[40]

Russell published a remarkable essay in 1957 entitled: "Has Religion Made a Useful Contribution to Society?"[41] And his answer was negative.

That is, for a reader living in the twenty-first century, perhaps not such a very shocking idea, but it certainly was in the 1950s.[42] A forerunner of Russell in the nineteenth century, John Stuart Mill, presented a similar analysis of religion in a more moderate or restrained form.[43] Ultimately Mill's utilitarian assessment of religion (and Russell's as well) went back to the Greek philosopher Epicurus (342/41–271/70 BCE) and his Roman disciple Lucretius (96–55 BCE) who tried to free people from fear of death and what might happen in the afterlife.[44]

The dark sides of religion as exemplified by critical philosophers are manifold. Religion estranges us from our earthly life (Marx,[45] Nietzsche).[46] Religion presents us with an illusion (Freud).[47] Religion causes conflicts that cannot be decided in a rational way (Harris and Dawkins).[48] And there are many other problematic sides to religion, according to its critics.

I want to concentrate on one specific problem: religious violence, or as some would prefer to call it "violence in the name of religion."

Religious Violence

This choice of topic will hardly surprise the reader. There is a growing stack of literature on the topic of religious violence nowadays. It is not difficult

[39] White, A.D., *A History of the Warfare of Science with Theology in Christendom*, Dover Publications, New York 1960 (1896).

[40] Russell, Bertrand, *Religion and Science*, Oxford University Press, London 1935.

[41] Included in: Russell, *Why I Am Not a Christian. And Other Essays on Religion and Related Subjects*, Routledge, London 2004 (1957).

[42] See on the public role of religion in the US: Singer, Peter, *The President of Good and Evil. Taking George W. Bush Seriously*, Granta Books, London 2004.

[43] Mill, John Stuart, *Three Essays on Religion*, Prometheus Books, Amherst, NY 1998 (1874).

[44] See on Epicurus: Onfray, Michel, *Les Sagesses Antiques. Contre-histoire de la Philosophie, 1* [Wisdoms of Antiquity. Counter-history of Philosophy, 1], Bernard Grasset, Paris 2006, pp. 177–224.

[45] Marx, Karl, *Zur Kritik der Hegelschen Rechtsphilosophie* [Critique of Hegel's Philosophy of Right], 1843/44, in: Karl Marx, Friedrich Engels, *Ausgewählte Werke* [Selected Works], Dietz Verlag, Berlin 1977, pp. 9–25, p. 9.

[46] Nietzsche, Friedrich, *The Anti-Christ*, 1888–89, translated with an introduction by H.L. Mencken, See Sharp Press, Tucson, AZ 1999.

[47] Freud, Sigmund, *The Future of an Illusion*, W.W. Norton, New York 1989 (1927).

[48] Dawkins, Richard, *The God Delusion; Harris, Sam, The End of Faith: Religion, Terror, and the Future of Reason*, The Free Press, London 2005 (2004). See also: Stenger, Victor J., *The New Atheism: Taking a Stand for Science and Reason*, Prometheus Books, Amherst NY 2009, p. 15: "Faith is always foolish and leads to many of the evils of society."

to gauge where this literature finds its sources of inspiration. Many countries in the East and West find themselves under terrorist threat. Terrorists are prepared to use violence to realize their aims, intimidating the state and its citizens. With the attacks of September 11, 2001 in New York, of March 11, 2004 in Madrid, of July 7, 2005 in London and with the murder of the Dutch writer and filmmaker Theo van Gogh (1957–2004) on November 2, 2004, the association of religion with violence is less strange than it used to be in the 1990s. When a scholar like René Girard (1923–) in *La violence et le sacré* [Violence and the Sacred] (1972)[49] focused on the relationship between religion and violence his ideas might at the time of writing have been considered intriguing but a bit eccentric. Nowadays this is demonstrated before our very eyes.[50]

Nevertheless, the situation is ambivalent. Although there is a wide literary canon on religion and violence, at the same time there is a great reluctance among scholars and the public at large to acknowledge that relationship. The "friends of religion" (and these are not only believers themselves) simply cannot accept that religion also has a dark and violent side. To illustrate this let us see how they usually react to what is commonly called "religious terrorism."[51]

In earlier times violence and intimidation were regarded as necessary for the preservation of religion. A religious war or the torture of a heretic or an infidel was not considered to be morally outrageous, but necessary for the preservation of belief and ultimately the social order. This attitude is not very common nowadays, at least not in the Western world. Nevertheless, that does not mean that people take religion to task when it seems to be connected with violence. What the advocates of religion usually do, is simply deny that religion has anything to do with the violence perpetrated, for example, by religious terrorists. They say: "Religion is only *superficially* involved in this new type of violence. Terrorism is caused by exclusion,

---

[49]   Girard, René, *Violence and the Sacred*, translated by Patrick Gregory, The Johns Hopkins University Press, Baltimore 1977.
[50]   See on this: Selengut, Charles, *Sacred Fury. Understanding Religious Violence*, Rowman & Littlefield Publishers, Lanham, 2003; Haught, James A., *Holy Hatred. Religious Conflicts of the '90s*, Prometheus Books, Amherst, NY 1995; Haught, James, A., *Holy Horrors. An Illustrated History of Religious Murder and Madness*, Prometheus Books, Amherst, NY 1990.
[51]   Guiora, Amos N., *Fundamentals of Counterterrorism*, Wolters Kluwer, Austin, TX 2008, p. 8 defines terrorism as: "the killing, injuring, or intimidation of, or causing property damage to innocent civilians by an individual or group seeking to advance a social, political, economic, or religious cause." In most of the commentaries the "religious cause" is underestimated or even flatly denied. Not by Guiora, though, who states that "religion is certainly a primary motivator for modern terrorists" (p. 3). For the definition of terrorism, see also: Coady, C.A.J., "Defining Terrorism," in: Igor Primoratz, ed., *Terrorism. The Philosophical Issues*, Palgrave, Macmillan, Basingstoke 2004, pp. 3–15 and Primoratz, Igor, "Terrorism," in: *Stanford Encyclopedia of Philosophy*, http://plato.stanford, edu, 2007, pp. 1–31.

racism, personality disorders, social and economic inequality and lots of other things, but one thing is sure: this violence has nothing to do with religion." That means that the terms "religious violence" or "religious terrorism" are misnomers.[52]

When freethinkers point out what, according to their analysis, the relationship between religion and violence amounts to, the advocates of religion, in most cases, react with dismay and even indignation. How can anybody be so stupid as not to see that religion is only "superficially" connected with the behavior we all reject? How can we fail to understand that bad men and women "misuse" religion for their own petty ends?[53] If the freethinker persists in his indictments, the advocates of religion usually get more impatient. They accuse him of "insulting" believers and try to silence him through blasphemy laws. Terms like "religious terrorism" or "religious violence" are invented by the enemies of religion, they say, by the secularists, the atheists, people who want to scoff at religion – but religion itself is, by its very nature, pure and pristine. However, as the prominent Islamic scholar, political scientist, and professor of international relations Bassam Tibi (1944–) rightly stresses when referring to the sociologist Mark Juergensmeyer (1940–),[54] "Jihadism as 'terror in the mind of God' is based on 'ideals and ideas' which are 'authentically and thoroughly' religious."[55] Time and again Tibi warns us against the common mistake of underestimating the relationship between contemporary terrorism and its roots in Islamic doctrine, because the Islamist challenge can only be met if we first acknowledge that parts of the Islamic tradition are vitiated by Islamist ideology. Tibi contends this as a Muslim because it is necessary to separate violent tendencies from peaceful tendencies within the Islamic tradition.

Even stronger in her rejection of Islamist radicalism is Nonie Darwish (1948–), an Egyptian-born American who writes about her experiences in Egypt under sharia law. In her book *Cruel and Unusual* (2008) she writes:

---

[52] See for another approach: Phillips, Melanie, *Londonistan. How Britain is Creating a Terror State Within*, Gibson Square Books, London 2006; Laqueur, Walter, *Krieg dem Westen. Terrorismus im 21. Jahrhundert* [War on the West. Terrorism in the Twenty-First Century], Propyläen, München 2003; Tibi, Bassam, *Kreuzzug und Djihad: Der Islam und die christliche Welt* [Crusade and Jihad: Islam and the Christian World], Goldman, München 2001 (1999).

[53] An intermediate position is defended by: Steffen, Lloyd, *Holy War, Just War: Exploring the Moral Meaning of Religious Violence*, Rowman & Littlefield Publishers, Lanham 2007.

[54] See: Juergensmeyer, Mark, *Terror in the Mind of God. The Global Rise of Religious Violence*, third edition, University of California Press, Berkeley 2003; Juergensmeyer, Mark, *Global Rebellion: Religious Challenges to the Secular State, from Christian Militias to Al Qaeda*, University of California Press, Berkeley, 2008.

[55] Tibi, Bassam, *Political Islam, World Politics and Europe: Democratic Peace and Euro-Islam versus Global Jihad*, Routledge, London 2008, p. 98.

The West doesn't get it; they can't understand this kind of crime [religiously motivated murder]. They cannot call it "terrorism" because the individual Muslim is not linked to al Qaeda. But it is a special kind of terrorism that can be perpetrated under Islamic Sharia by just one individual who feels he is killing in the name of Allah.[56]

These kinds of comments on religion are as unpopular nowadays as the study of the Inquisition in relation to Catholic doctrine used to be. The pioneering work by Henry Charles Lea (1825–1909) was frustrated in this respect by the same opposition as critics and reformers of Islam have to deal with nowadays.[57]

It is one of the ambitions of *The Secular Outlook* to understand the nature and the implications of the opposition to what might be called an open attitude toward scrutinizing religion. A candid perusal of religion is often rejected as being "merely negative" or motivated by feelings of spite on the part of the researcher. Great pressure is exerted to portray religion only from its most positive side. And the analysis of religion is severely damaged by the reluctance of the general public and the scholarly community alike to treat religion as a phenomenon like any other. The aim of this chapter is to present an analysis of the theistic religions that is fair, which means that it has the ambition to avoid the pussyfooting attitude that is usually taken for granted.

Let us first cast a glance at some classic discussions of this theme in the past.

Father and Daughter

One of the most important historical documents on the subject of religion in relation to the autonomy of morals is a dialogue by Plato, the *Euthyphro*.[58] This starts with a dramatic scene. Euthyphro has just deposed murder charges against his own father for the death of a servant. Prosecuting your own father on such a charge is quite uncommon and Socrates seems very surprised: "Good heavens! ... Euthyphro, most men would not know how

---

[56]   Darwish, Nonie, *Cruel and Unusual*, Thomas Nelson, Nashville 2008, p. 146.
[57]   See on Lea: Tollebeek, Jo, *Writing the Inquisition in Europe and America: The Correspondence between Henry Charles Lea and Paul Fredericq (1888–1908)*, Koninklijke Academie van België, Brussel 2004.
[58]   See: Taylor, A.E., *Plato. The Man and his Work*, Methuen & Co, London 1977 (1926), p. 151 and Kretzmann, Norman, "Abraham, Isaac, and Euthyphro: God and the Basis of Morality," in: Eleonore Stump and Michael J. Murray, eds., *Philosophy of Religion: The Big Questions*, Blackwell Publishers, Malden 1999, pp. 417–427.

they could do this and be right."[59] Socrates further inquires: "Is then the man your father killed one of your relatives? Or is that obvious, for you would not prosecute your father for the murder of a stranger."[60] Now Euthyphro is shocked: "It is ridiculous, Socrates, for you to think that it makes any difference whether the victim is a stranger or a relative. One should only watch whether the killer acted justly or not; if he acted justly, let him go, but if not, one should prosecute, even if, that is to say, the killer shares your hearth and table."[61]

From a perspective of abstract justice Euthyphro may be right. But, at the same time, it seems realistic to suppose that not all of us would act in accordance with his high morals. Philosopher Brand Blanshard (1892–1987), the twin brother of Paul Blanshard whose definition of freethought was quoted at the beginning of this chapter, may have been more realistic when he wrote: "Mothers at murder trials are notorious witnesses that their sons are white souls incapable of such deeds; and the son whose mother has been insulted is not likely to pause for a reflective reply."[62] Not many people will react with the same witty detachment as Lord North (1732–1792) when confronted with deadly insults aimed at his wife and daughter. It is said that Lord North once, in a theatre, was addressed by someone who said: "Who is that plain-looking woman?" "That, sir," said the noble lord, "is my wife." "Oh, no," said the inquirer, "I mean the one next to her." "That sir," said Lord North, "is my daughter. And let me tell you, sir, that we are considered to be three of the ugliest people in London."[63]

This is superhuman. Most fathers (or husbands) would react differently. Imagine a father who has a lovely daughter, eighteen years old. (This is not particularly difficult to imagine, of course, because most daughters are lovely in their father's eyes.) One gloomy day the police arrive at this man's front door. "What's happened?" he asks. "Your daughter has committed a very serious crime," they inform him, "homicide." What is his reaction likely to be?

Every father's first reaction will be one of indignation and disbelief. This cannot be true. The people accusing his daughter (bystanders, the police, the whole world) must have made a terrible mistake. Why? Because his

---

[59] Plato, *Euthyphro*, 4a, in: Plato, *Complete Works*, ed. John M. Cooper, Hackett Publishing Company, Indianapolis 1997, pp. 1–17, p. 3.
[60] Plato, *Euthyphro*, 4b.
[61] Plato, *Euthyphro*, 4c.
[62] Blanshard, Brand, *Four Reasonable Men: Marcus Aurelius, John Stuart Mill, Ernest Renan, Henry Sidgwick*, Wesleyan University Press, Middletown, CT 1984, p. 259.
[63] Lucas, F.L., *The Art of Living: Four Eighteenth-Century Minds: Hume, Horace Walpole, Burke, Benjamin Franklin*, Cassell, London 1959, p. 139 n.

daughter is *no murderer,* of course. Every loving father knows that for sure. So his state of disbelief automatically transforms itself into a state of denial.

Now let us take the step over to religion. What do religions have in common with daughters? Every believer knows for sure that God is love, and that religion is the most holy thing in the world. That is the reason why the believer is a believer in the first place. Now here are some strange people who have suddenly come up with stories about the violent aspects of religion: scientists, scholars, free-thinkers, secularists, atheists, and other critics. Their accounts cannot be true. They must be prejudiced by their negative attitude towards the faith. "If my religion had a violent tendency then I myself would be a potential criminal," the believer will tell us. This is too absurd even to contemplate.

And so the loving father (or loving husband) and the true believer will never accept that their favorites are in any way implicated in gross violence or other atrocious acts. As philosopher Brand Blanshard put it: "Next to romantic love, religion is the area of human life where reason is most easily swept away. Against faith, reason has little chance with the great majority."[64]

Yet there are differences between fathers and true believers too. In the state of denial that both share, the father is in a less fortunate position than the true believer. That has to do with the nature of reality. Daughters are humans, that is, physical entities. So homicide, as punishable by law, is also something that can be empirically verified. And that means the loving father, however reluctantly, may have to face the dreadful fact of his daughter's guilt if the evidence is as strong as the police contend, and, in particular, if that evidence satisfies a judge and jury.

The situation of the true believer in a state of denial is more promising. That has to do with the nature of religion. Religion is not – as daughters are – something that can be empirically perceived. Religion is a mental, not a spatiotemporal thing. Religion is mental, because ideas are mental. So, whether the motives of religious terrorists are truly "religious" is a matter of interpretation. And for the true believer, so it seems, there are always escape routes. He or she can always (and will often) say: "it was not religion, it was someone's culture, social position, mental condition and or any one of a host of other things"; it was anything but religion that was the cause of the trouble.[65]

This attitude was aptly formulated by the philosopher Herbert Spencer (1820–1903), himself an agnostic, when he said:

---

[64]   Blanshard, *Four Reasonable Men,* p. 105.

[65]   This is clearly noticable e.g. in: Gresh, Alain, *L'Islam, la République et le Monde* [Islam, the Republic and the World], Fayard, Paris 2006, p. 54 and 59.

The truly religious element of Religion has always been good; that which has proved untenable in doctrine and vicious in practice, has been its irreligious element; and from this it has been undergoing purification.[66]

This is a revealing sentence. Religion is good, according to Spencer. What seems bad in religion is simply "irreligious."

What distinguishes a freethinker from the true believer – and also from the agnostic of the Spencerian[67] kind – is that he is not automatically prepared to do what Spencer proposes. Freethinkers take a different stance. They say: "What socially manifests itself as religion is part of that religion." In other words: if people who profess to subscribe to a religion commit violence and refer to their religion in legitimating that violence, we should at least make a serious effort to analyze whether there is a relationship between that violence and that religion.

Of course, numbers count. You cannot say a religion is violent because only a few believers make a totally unwarranted connection between their criminal behavior and their religion. But if, during the sixteenth and seventeenth centuries, witches, heretics, and infidels were burnt at the stake and religious and political leaders adduced theological reasons from scripture in support of such punishments, you cannot say: "that had nothing to do with religion."[68] In those days Christianity *was* a violent religion. Because nowadays witches, heretics, and infidels are no longer burned, we can say that contemporary Christianity is much less violent than its sixteenth- and seventeenth-century predecessor. But what we should *not* do – as the apologists of religion want us to do – is to say that because *nowadays* Christianity has lost many of its violent characteristics the violence perpetrated *in earlier times* had nothing to do with religion.

I personally think that freethinkers, adopting the critical attitude, are on firmer ground than the believers and those who have "belief in belief" (a phrase introduced by Daniel Dennett)[69] who categorically deny any relationship between religion and violence. A religion does not simply exist in the fantasy of some of its enlightened followers, it also manifests itself in the real world.

[66] Spencer, Herbert, "The Reconciliation," in: Andrew Pyle, ed., *Agnosticism. Contemporary Responses to Spencer and Huxley*, Thoemmes Press, Bristol 1995, pp. 1–19, p. 3.
[67] Spencer's agnosticism should be carefully distinguished from agnosticism as understood by Huxley. See Huxley, Thomas Henry, "Agnosticism."
[68] On witchcraft and its suppression see: Lecky, W.E.H., *History of the Rise and Influence of Rationalism in Europe*, Vol. I, Longman, Green, Longman, Roberts, & Green, London 1865, pp. 1–150.
[69] Dennett, Daniel C., *Breaking the Spell*, p. 200 ff. See also: Dawkins, Richard, *The God Delusion*, p. 20: "These people may not be religious themselves, but they love the idea that other people are religious."

How to Discover a Relationship between Religion and Violence

How can this dispute about the relationship between religion and violence be resolved? Can it be resolved at all? Or will this always remain a matter of opinion, reflecting the personal life stances of the disputants? It would appear that there are at least two ways to discover whether there is such a relationship and, if so, what its nature is. The first "research-strategy" is to examine whether a particular religion is based on a revealed holy book from which the adherents of that religion derive their moral ideas. This is indeed the case with the Jewish, Christian, and Muslim religions. The so-called "theistic beliefs" are "religions of the book."[70] Those religions have a special relationship with three books that reveal the truth about God's wishes with regard to mankind. Those books are: the Old Testament, the New Testament, and the Qur'an. The Old Testament is the most important book for the Jews. The New Testament is of paramount importance for Christians. The Qur'an, finally, is the Holy Book for Muslims.

Anyone who wants to verify whether religion (or a religion) condones or even incites violence should consult those books and try to ascertain whether (and under what circumstances) violence is permitted or even encouraged in the texts. Once this study is undertaken, perhaps backed up with the relevant literature on religion and violence, such as the books *Sacred Fury* (2003)[71] by Charles Selengut or the book with the ominous title *Is Religion Killing us?* (2003)[72] by the politician and academic Jack Nelson-Pallmeyer (1951–), every reader will see that there is much more in the holy writ than just the Sermon on the Mount.

I will not back up this contention with the many passages that are elaborately expounded on and analyzed in works by authors like Nelson-Pallmeyer, Selengut, Sam Harris,[73] Shadia B. Drury,[74] Joseph Hofmann,[75] Christopher Hitchens,[76] James Haught,[77] and many other commentators.

[70]   Fernández-Armesto, Felipe, "Books of Truth: the Idea of Infallible Holy Scriptures," in: Fernández-Armesto, Felipe, *Ideas That Changed the World*, Dorling Kindersley, London 2003, pp. 106–107.
[71]   Selengut, Charles, *Sacred Fury. Understanding Religious Violence*, Rowman & Littlefield Publishers, Lanham, 2003.
[72]   Nelson-Pallmeyer, Jack, *Is Religion Killing Us? Violence in the Bible and the Qur'an*, Trinity Press International, Harrisburg 2003.
[73]   Harris, Sam, *The End of Faith. Religion, Terror, and the Future of Reason*, The Free Press, London 2005.
[74]   Drury, Shadia B., *Terror and Civilization. Christianity, Politics, and the Western Psyche*, Palgrave MacMillan, Basingstoke 2004.
[75]   Hoffmann, Joseph R., ed., *The Just War and Jihad. Violence in Judaism, Christianity, and Islam*, Prometheus Books, Amherst, NY 2006.
[76]   Hitchens, Christopher, *god is not Great*.
[77]   Haught, James A., *Holy Hatred and Holy Horrors*.

It suffices to illustrate this point with some remarks on just two passages from holy books: one from the Qur'an, the other from the Bible. I will start with the youngest revelation: the Qur'an.

In the Qur'an (24:2) there is a passage on adultery and fornication. The passage runs as follows: "The woman and the man guilty of adultery or fornication, flog each of them with 100 stripes: Let no compassion move you in their case, in a matter prescribed by Allah, if you believe in Allah and the Last Day." This passage is quoted by Ayaan Hirsi Ali (1969–), a former Dutch politician and, at present, a fellow of the American Enterprise Institute, in an article on a 20-year-old woman from Qatif, Saudi Arabia, reported to have been abducted by several men and repeatedly raped. Judges found that the victim was, herself, guilty. Her crime is called "mingling." When she was abducted, the woman was sitting in a car with a man not related to her by blood or by marriage. This is illegal in Saudi Arabia. She was sentenced to 200 lashes with a bamboo cane.[78]

This sentence will be described by many people as draconian, outrageous, or unjust. Why was this women punished, and not the man? Why was this women given such a harsh sentence? Because Saudi law prescribes this sentence for this specific offence. But why is Saudi law so cruel in this matter? Judging from the fact that Hirsi Ali starts her article with a specific passage from the Qur'an her stance does not leave much room for speculation: she thinks that the passage in the Qur'an has something to do with the way people think, behave, and, in this case, judge in Saudi Arabia. What Hirsi Ali intends with her article, obviously, is to make people aware of the cruel passages in the holy book. She also argues that those passages inhibit the moral evolution of the people living under the guidance of the holy book. But she not only criticizes the book, the judges, and the Saudi penal system but also, as appears from her article, the so called "moderate" adherents of the religion. She criticizes them for two reasons.

The first is that the "moderates" do not speak out clearly against such atrocious acts. They "whisper" (my choice of words) something such as that they do not consider it a good idea to punish women so cruelly for petty crimes. But – and here comes Hirsi Ali's point – they do not speak out loudly.

The second reason for criticizing the "moderates" is because they obfuscate the relationship between the passage in the holy book and the social practice that is – according to Hirsi Ali – based on that book, or at least influenced by that book. She refers to one of the most vocal spokesmen for that moderate approach, the well-known Muslim preacher Tariq Ramadan (1962–).[79]

---

[78] Hirsi Ali, Ayaan, "Islam's Silent Moderates," *The New York Times*, December 7, 2007. As a result of a worldwide protest the woman was not punished in the way indicated.

[79] Ramadan is often criticized for an alleged "double agenda." I will not enter into this subject and only comment on what he writes in response to Hirsi Ali in the newspaper article

Ramadan v. Hirsi Ali

Ramadan is the grandson of Hassan al-Banna (1906–1949), the founder of the Muslim Brotherhood in Egypt, which is considered to be one of the sources of Islamist terrorism.[80] He was born in Switzerland and is a Swiss citizen.[81] He has appeared on countless television shows, taken part in public debates, and his messages on cassette have reached a wide audience. Although Ramadan's teaching has been widely dispersed, there is great confusion about its essence. For some he is a fundamentalist, for others, a Muslim reformer. His message is somewhat ambivalent. On the one hand Ramadan says that Muslims first and foremost belong to the *umma* (that is the community of believers). They should not do anything that would make them bad Muslims. On the other hand he also says that the allegiance of Muslims in the West should be to the state and country in which they live. The question is whether these two positions are compatible, and one can easily agree with Walter Laqueur's (1921–) balanced judgment in his *The Last Days of Europe* (2007):

> He could not very well remain the idol of the Muslim Paris *banlieues* and at the same time of liberal intellectuals: He had to adjust himself to his audience, giving different talks, often inconsistent and even contradictory. While basically he remained a fundamentalist (as shown in his attacks against Muslim liberals and reformers), he understood that reforms were necessary to some extent if European Islam wanted to keep the loyalty of a younger generation exposed to Western influences.[82]

Analyzing the work of Ramadan is beyond the confines of my topic, but what he writes in reaction to Ayaan Hirsi Ali's article on the Saudi woman

---

indicated before. See on this: Berman, Paul, "Who is Afraid of Tariq Ramadan? The Islamist, the Journalist, and the Defense of Liberalism," in: *The New Republic*, June 4, 2007, pp. 37–62. In the Netherlands in 2009 there was a vehement discussion of Ramadan's ideas on homosexuality, equality between the sexes and other topics. Many commentators considered him unfit to act as a mediator in the city of Rotterdam, although he received an assignment from the municipal authorities for precisely that purpose, a contract that was, despite vehement resistance, prolonged till 2011 (although it ended in 2009; see the subsequent notes).

[80]   See for different perspectives: Lo, Mbaye, "Seeking the Roots of Terrorism: An Islamic Traditional Perspective," *Journal of Religion and Popular Culture*, Vol. X, Summer 2005, pp. 1–13; Esposito, John L., *Unholy War: Terror in the Name of Islam*, Oxford University Press, New York 2002.

[81]   See: Laqueur, Walter, *The Last Days of Europe: Epitaph for an Old Continent*, Thomas Dunne Books/St. Martin's Griffin, New York 2007, pp. 88–95.

[82]   Ibid., p. 93. In August 2009 Ramadan was fired by the University of Rotterdam and the Rotterdam municipal authorities as well because of his ties to the Iranian regime. He worked for the Iranian-sponsored Press TV.

accused of mingling is pertinent to the theme of this book. Apparently he had read the article by Hirsi Ali and, ten days later, he answered her indictment in a rejoinder quoting the same passage from the Qur'an that she had used. In his reply Ramadan gave a defense of his position that seems to me characteristic of a widely dispersed attitude towards religious criticism among contemporary intellectuals. Ramadan writes:

> What kind of message does she [Hirsi Ali] exactly want to convey by quoting a verse referring to corporal punishment? That Islam, per se, is advocating violence? That violent Muslims or the so-called Islamic governments acting undemocratically are in fact genuinely implementing the Islamic message? Through her text, the message becomes clear: Islam is an archaic religion, the Qur'an is a violent text and the only way to reform Islam is simply to "deislamisize" the Muslims.[83]

This kind of response to critics of religion, of Islam in particular, has been repeated many times in recent discussions on this issue. Ramadan advances some consequences of Hirsi Ali's reasoning that seem to him (and with him many others) simply unacceptable or unwelcome. Let us analyze the most important aspects of Ramadan's answer.

First, Ramadan asks "what kind of message does she exactly want to convey by quoting a verse referring to corporal punishment?" A strange question. For the message conveyed by Hirsi Ali is crystal-clear: passages in the Holy Book do actually influence behavior. That is what she wants to say. This may be true or untrue (that has to be the subject of our analysis and should be the focus of Ramadan's answer as well), but Ramadan can hardly fail to understand, or feign not to understand, what issue is at stake. We can frame it like this: the issue is whether Sura 24:2 is indeed the *basis of* or, to put it more cautiously, *influential in* the Saudi penal system and the harsh punishments it inflicts on Saudi women. What (if any) is the direct or indirect impact of Sura 24:2 on the ideas of the Saudi judges and the Saudi law? Ramadan avoids addressing this question directly. He answers with a move that directs attention away from Islam. In an elaboration of the passage quoted before he writes:

> Would it not be possible to quote here tens of passages from the Bhagavad-Gita, the Torah, the Gospels and the Epistles that are violent without reaching the conclusion that Hinduism, Judaism or Christianity are violent per se? Is it difficult to understand that this is a question of interpretation and that to condemn in such a way a religion, by its very essence, is not only unjust but deeply counterproductive? It does not help the inner dynamic of reforms.

---

[83]   Ramadan, Tariq, "A Response to Ayaan Hirsi Ali: A Case of Selective Hearing," *The International Herald Tribune*, 17 December, 2007.

This answer is illuminating because it is characteristic of many other answers that are given to the indictment that violent scriptural passages have an influence on actual cruel behavior. Therefore, we should carefully analyze what Ramadan says explicitly and what suggestions are implicit in his answer.

The first explicit contention in this second quote from Ramadan's article is that he can produce violent passages from the holy books of other great religions. That necessitates two questions. First: is this true? Second: is it relevant?

Would it be possible, for instance, to quote from the Gospels, as Ramadan explicitly contends, passages from which it appears that Jesus Christ is in favor of the same harsh punishments as indicated in Sura 24:2?[84] On this point Ramadan does not provide examples but uncritically supposes this to be the case. I doubt whether he can provide examples from the Gospels that are similar to the one quoted from the Qur'an, but that he would be able to quote passages of that nature from the Old Testament seems clear enough, as will become evident later when we analyze a passage on freedom of religion (or rather the lack of it) derived from the book of Deuteronomy. The problem with this reasoning, however, is something else. It has to do with the relevance of his response. The main problem, so it seems, is that it is no answer to Hirsi Ali's indictment. The fact that *other religions* prescribe violent behavior as well as Islam, does not exonerate Islam. What Ramadan seems to do is to accuse Hirsi Ali of selective indignation. His message seems to be: "because other religions are violent you have to castigate them all before you have the moral right to criticize one specific religion, i.e. Islam." This is not a strong defense for the simple reason that the direct occasion for Hirsi Ali's criticism was the Saudi woman being convicted of "mingling." If the whole discussion had been ignited by the imminent flogging of a Jewish woman in Israel convicted in a Jewish Court, the focus ought rightly to have been on the Old Testament and whether the Israeli judges could have been influenced by a passage from Deuteronomy

---

[84]   One of the passages often quoted (e.g. by Frégosi, Franck, *Penser l'islam dans la laïcité* [Thinking Islam in the Secular State], Fayard, Paris 2008, p. 34) is John 15:6–7, where Jesus says: "If anyone does not abide in me he is thrown away like a branch and withers; and the branches are gathered, thrown into the fire, and burned." This could be interpreted as metaphorical perhaps. But that is more difficult with 2 Thessalonians 1:6–9: "This is evidence of the righteous judgement of God, that you may be considered worthy of the kingdom of God, for which you are also suffering – since indeed God considers it just to repay with affliction those who afflict you, and to grant relief to you who are afflicted as well as to us, when the Lord Jesus is revealed from heaven with his mighty angels in flaming fire, inflicting vengeance on those who do not know God and on those who do not obey the gospel of our Lord Jesus." That means the gospel is not something one can voluntarily subscribe to but should be "obeyed." Vengeance is justified even with regard to people who are of a different religious persuasion.

or any other notoriously violent texts from the Old Testament.[85] But this was not the case.

In other words: it is not the violent passages from the holy book that are the focus of our attention, it is the combination of scriptural authority with contemporary social practices. Scriptural passages advocating violence that are not heeded by believers in the twenty-first century because they are considered to be poetry of some kind give us less cause for concern.

Religion "per se"

There is a second point that Ramadan addresses. This second point is only made in passing in the first quote from his article, more by way of sugges-tion than as an explicit argument. He seems to insinuate that, although it may be possible to quote violent passages from holy books and holy tradi-tions, one is not justified in concluding from this that those religions are violent "per se." This may seem an insignificant distinction but, in fact, it is very important indeed. Ramadan suggests that we should distinguish between, first, the actual consequences that are drawn from a religion and some passages in its holy book and, second, that "religion per se." A "reli-gion per se," in his worldview, seems to be something that remains untouched by the social manifestations of that religion and the possibly violent pas-sages in the texts of revelation. I therefore propose to dub this the "meta-physical conception of religion" in contrast to what one might label the "empirical conception of religion." What worries Ramadan is that Hirsi Ali apparently refuses to subscribe to the metaphysical notion of religion, to the religion "per se." Hirsi Ali is indicted with playing a false game: she wants to judge and possibly reject a religion on the basis of its unwelcome manifestations, the contents of its holy books, and the attitude of its believ-ers, whereas, according to Ramadan, we have to judge a religion on what might be called its "per-se character" or its metaphysical dimension.

It seems Ramadan is under the same spell as Herbert Spencer in the passage I quoted before: "The truly religious element of Religion has always been good; that which has proved untenable in doctrine and vicious in practice, has been its irreligious element; and from this it has been undergo-ing purification."[86] This is also the case of the loving father who cannot

---

[85] Many examples are assembled in: Nelson-Pallmeyer, *Is Religion Killing Us?* Reading these is unlikely to lead us to the conclusion that T.H. Huxley was right when he wrote: "All that is best in the ethics of the modern world, in so far as it has not grown out of Greek thought, or Barbarian manhood, is the direct development of the ethics of old Israel. There is no code of legislation, ancient or modern, at once so just and so merciful, so tender to the weak and poor, as the Jewish law." (Huxley, "Agnosticism and Christianity," p. 187).

[86] Spencer, "The Reconciliation," p. 3.

believe that the apple of his eye has done something atrocious. The belief that religion is *in essence* good, whatever the social manifestations of that religion may be, is so tenacious that it resembles the religious position itself.

This phenomenon – or something similar to this – has also been analyzed by Theodore Dalrymple (1949–) in his book *Life at the Bottom* (2001)[87] with regard to people from the "underclass." Dalrymple was struck by the fact that people living on the lower rungs of society frequently share a common worldview. They are all determinists who think they are not responsible for their own lives and their own actions. "The murderer claims the knife went in or the gun went off."[88] Dalrymple noticed that criminals, when explaining their deeds, often use the expression "It wasn't me."[89]

> Here is the psychobabble of the slums, the doctrine of the "Real Me" as refracted through the lens of urban degradation. The Real Me has nothing to do with the phenomenal me, the me that snatches old ladies' bags, breaks into other people's houses, beats up my wife and children, or repeatedly drinks too much and gets involved in brawls. No, the Real Me is an immaculate conception, untouched by human conduct: it is that unassailable core of virtue that enables me to retain my self-respect whatever I do.[90]

This sounds familiar, does it not? We find this also in the work of Karen Armstrong (1944–). Her book *The Case for God* (2009) has an interesting subtitle: "What Religion Really Means."[91] The crucial word here is "really." What does it mean? Is there a difference between "what religion means" and "what religion really means"? I think there is. The word "really" tends to suggest that Armstrong will be not presenting us with *all* the manifestations of religion, but only with those which put religion in a favorable light. Those manifestations that do *not* put religion in a favorable light are seen as not "really" part of religion.

This is also the way Ramadan talks about his religion. In introducing this pristine and metaphysical "per se" notion of religion, always unaffected by the vicissitudes of religion in this empirical world, Ramadan makes several metaphysical claims that need to be studied and analyzed thoroughly. It is certainly not only Ramadan whose commentaries are based on this distinction. Although far more critical than Tariq Ramadan even as accomplished an Islamic scholar as Abdelwahab Meddeb (1946–) seems

---

[87]   Dalrymple, Theodore, *Life at the Bottom: The Worldview That Makes the Underclass*, Ivan R. Dee, Chicago 2001.
[88]   Ibid., p. ix.
[89]   Ibid., p. 10.
[90]   Ibid.
[91]   Armstrong, Karen, *The Case for God: What Religion Really Means*, The Bodley Head, London 2009.

to be under the spell of that dubious metaphysical idea that a religion has a pristine core (*l'islam en tant que tel* [Islam as such]) that remains uncorrupted by its social manifestations in this world.[92]

We should be on our guard with this distinction. In contrast to the "metaphysician of religion" (Ramadan), we may distinguish the "empiricist of religion" (the freethinker or in this discussion Hirsi Ali). The empiricist of religion will say: there is no "religion per se" apart from the manifestations of that religion. A religion *is* what is written about in the holy book and what the believers act upon. There is no mysterious entity "religion per se" distinct from the texts of the holy book and the behavior of its devotees. The metaphysical approach to religion must be rejected.

There is a famous quote attributed to Gandhi: "God has no religion." There are many interpretations of this paradoxical but also witty expression. The one I would favor is that what God means by "religion" we will never know.[93] We have to deal with the religion of man, not with the religion of God; with what man *has made* of religion. What we "see" of the Jewish religion, the Christian religion, the Muslim religion is all "man-made."

Perhaps these distinctions will strike the reader as overly subtle, scholastic or whatever you want to call them. The fact that I have to introduce them, though, is because that "per se" notion of religion is enormously influential. As a matter of fact, these distinctions are not specifically mine. They are made and held by writers like Ramadan himself, although unconsciously and with no idea of their dubious character. That there is a "religion per se" apart from the social manifestations of a religion is simply *presupposed* by many people active in this debate.

Textual Relativism

That brings me to a remark about the British historian and social critic Thomas Carlyle (1795–1881) made by the Catholic writer and essayist G.K. Chesterton (1874–1936). Chesterton wrote of Carlyle: "he startled men by attacking not arguments but assumptions." Chesterton continued: "He

---

[92]   Meddeb, Abdelwahab, "En terre d'islam" [On Islamic Soil], in: André Glucksmann, Nicole Bacharan, Abdelwahab Meddeb, *La plus belle histoire de la liberté* [The Most Beautiful History of Freedom], Éditions du Seuil, Paris 2009, pp. 123–167, p. 134: "les archaïsmes que l'on attribue à l'islam appartiennent bien plus souvent aux sociétés patriarcales dans lesquelles la religion opère ou s'invente qu'à l'islam en tant que tel" [The archaisms that are attributed to Islam more often belong to the patriarchal societies in which the religion operates or was made up rather than to Islam as such].

[93]   Which also finds some support with believers. See: McGrath, *A Brief History of Heaven*, p. 3: "Our knowledge of God is accommodated to our capacity."

simply brushed aside all the matter which the men of the nineteenth century held to be incontrovertible, and appealed directly to the very different class of matters which they knew to be true. He induced men to study less the truth of their reasoning and more the truth of the assumptions upon which they reasoned."[94]

This is an important observation because both Chesterton and Carlyle appear to have understood that people are deeply influenced by ideas that they do not explicitly argue for but that are presupposed in their reasoning. That is no different in the twenty-first century than in the nineteenth. One of the most widespread assumptions of the twenty-first century in the Western world, and one which pertains to our topic, is that Scripture has no authority over us in the sense that we are not forced into this or that interpretation of a text on the basis of the content of the text itself. In the Western world, under the aegis of postmodernism, we are almost all "textualist relativists," in the sense that we think that we can interpret texts any way we like. This textual relativism is intimately related to a more general form of relativism disseminated by intellectuals like Michel Foucault (1926–1984) and among the earlier thinkers Friedrich Nietzsche.[95] That Ramadan also writes under the spell of this typically post-modern conviction is clear from the rhetorical question that follows the introduction of his "per se" notion. "Is it difficult to understand," so he asks rhetorically with regard to the matter of the violent character of religion, "that this is a question of interpretation ...?"

At the end of the nineteenth century Nietzsche criticized positivism on the grounds that there were no "facts," as positivists supposed, only "interpretations."[96]

It may safely be said that these words had a disastrous influence on scholarly discourse in the twentieth century. Chiefly because Nietzsche added that we do not even have to try to establish facts.[97] This led people to believe that words can mean anything we want them to mean. It made the semantics of Humpty Dumpty current.

---

[94]   Chesterton, G.K., "Thomas Carlyle," 1902, in: *The Essential G.K. Chesterton*, introduced by P.J. Kanavagh, Oxford University Press, Oxford 1987, pp. 3–7, p. 5. See also: Searle, John R., "Rationality and Realism, What is at stake?" *Daedalus, Journal of the American Academy of Arts and Sciences*, 122, no. 4 1993, pp. 55–83, p. 60: "We cannot discover the essential elements of the Western Rationalistic Tradition just by studying the doctrines of the great philosophers. Often the important thing is not what the philosopher said but what he took for granted as too obvious to need saying."
[95]   See on this: Scruton, Roger, *Culture Counts: Faith and Feeling in a World Besieged*, Encounter Books, New York 2007, p. 75 ff.
[96]   Nietzsche, Friedrich, *Werke IV, Aus dem Nachlass der Achtzigerjahre, Briefe (1861–1889)* [Works Vol. IV, From the Remains of the Eighties, Letters (1861–1889)], ed. Karl Schlechta, Ullstein, Frankfurt am Main 1969, p. 495.
[97]   Ibid.

Humpty Dumpty is a character in Lewis Carroll's *Through the Looking Glass* (1871). Humpty Dumpty uses the word "glory" in a highly idiosyncratic manner.

"I don't know what you mean by 'glory'," Alice said.
Humpty Dumpty smiled contemptuously. "Of course you don't know – till I tell you. I meant 'there's a nice knock-down argument for you!' "
"But 'glory' doesn't mean 'a nice knock-down argument,' " Alice objected.
"When *I* use a word," Humpty Dumpty said, in rather a scornful tone, "it means just what I choose it to mean – neither more nor less."
"The question is," said Alice, "whether you *can* make words mean so many different things."
"The question is," said Humpty Dumpty, "which is to be master – that's all."
Alice was too much puzzled to say anything.[98]

So Alice was too puzzled to present an adequate reaction to semantic relativism. But should we all be too puzzled to say anything? Should semantic *laissez-faire* have the final word? The most straightforward answer to Ramadan would be that it is difficult to understand that it is all a matter of interpretation because this simply is not true. As human rights scholar Jack Donnelly says: "We need not – and should not – hold that all 'interpretations' are equally plausible or defensible. They are interpretations, not free associations or arbitrary stipulations."[99] Philosopher John Searle (1932–) is even more critical of semantic relativism. If, as Nietzsche says, "There are no facts, only interpretations," then what makes one interpretation better than another cannot be that one is true and the other false, but, for example, "that one interpretation might help overcome existing hegemonic, patriarchal structures and empower previously underrepresented minorities."[100] Nietzsche's "Humpty Dumptian" remark, endlessly repeated and ruminated by whole departments of literary studies,[101] is not

---

[98]   Carroll, Lewis, *Through the Looking-Glass*, in: Lewis Carroll, *Complete Works*, Vintage Books, Random House, New York 1976, pp. 138–277, p. 214.

[99]   Donnelly, Jack, "Cultural Relativism and Universal Human Rights," *Human Rights Quarterly*, 6 1984, pp. 400–419, p. 408. See also: Dundes Renteln, Alison, "The Unanswered Challenge of Relativism and the Consequences for Human Rights," *Human Rights Quarterly*, 7, no. 4 1985, pp. 514–540.

[100]   Searle, "Rationality and Realism, What is at stake?" p. 71. See for a good example of the kind of views that Searle had in mind in writing his critique: Goldstone, Brian, "Violence and the Profane: Islamism, Liberal Democracy, and the Limits of Secular Discipline," *Anthropological Quarterly*, 80 no. 1 2007, pp. 207–235.

[101]   See on this: Young, R.V., *At War with the Word. Literary Theory and Liberal Education*, ISI Books, Wilmington, DE 1999; Windschuttle, Keith, *The Killing of History. How Literary Criticism and Social Theorists Are Murdering our Past*, Encounter Books, San Francisco 1996; Kimball, Roger, *Tenured Radicals. How Politics Has Corrupted Our Higher Education*, Ivan R. Dee Publisher, Chicago 1998 (1991); Tallis, Raymond, *Enemies of Hope: A Critique of*

convincing. Nevertheless, it is hugely influential. According to the famous French philosopher Michel Foucault "Truth is a thing of this world. It is produced only by multiple forms of constraint and that includes the regular effects of power."[102] So Humpty Dumpty is right: the only question is "which is to be the master?" When you claim to have truth, you are trying to get power and control over other people, that is how Timothy Keller (1950–) summarizes this way of thinking is his book *The Reason for God* (2008).[103] "Foucault was a disciple of Nietzsche," as Keller says. And a disciple of Humpty Dumpty as well, as I would like to add.

Ramadan seems also to be under the spell of these postmodern convictions. Most often, these are not explicitly argued for, but are presupposed in every kind of discourse. People are under the spell of unarticulated presuppositions, like the people criticized by Carlyle in the nineteenth century. And these presuppositions are highly questionable. It is simply not true that we can interpret away all problematic texts.[104] The reason is that some texts are quite clear. There may be an element of ambiguity or vagueness in some texts,[105] but the unarticulated notion of postmodernism that Ramadan and many others bring to the conclusion that texts *can have* any meaning *we want them to have* is simply unconvincing.[106]

Can Translation Mitigate All Immoral Passages in Scripture?

The point that Ramadan makes with regard to interpretation is also made for translation. Everyone who has discussed scriptural authority with believers and unbelievers alike knows that many of them, if confronted with violent texts from their revealed sources, react by contending that the vio-

---

Contemporary Pessimism, Irrationalism, Anti-Humanism and Counter-Enlightenment, Macmillan, Basingstoke 1997 and Sokal, Alan and Bricmont, Jean, *Impostures Intellectuelles* [Intellectual Impostures], Éditions Odile Jacob, Paris 1997. In French postmodern studies the influence of Nietzsche is so pervasive that philosophers who do not enter the fold feel compelled to declare why. See: Boyer, Alain, ed., *Pourquoi nous ne sommes pas nietzschéens* [Why We Are Not Nietzscheans], Grasset, Paris 1991.
[102] Foucault, Michel, *Power/Knowledge: Selected Interviews and Other Writings 1972–1977,* ed. Colin Gordon, Pantheon, New York 1980, p. 131.
[103] Keller, Timothy, *The Reason for God: Belief in an Age of Skepticism,* Riverhead Books, New York 2008, p. 37.
[104] See on this issue also: Thatcher, Adrian, *The Savage Text: The Use and Abuse of the Bible,* Wiley-Blackwell, Malden 2008.
[105] See: Bix, Brian, *Law, Language, and Legal Determinacy,* Clarendon Press, Oxford 1993.
[106] See for a criticism of postmodern relativism: Gellner, Ernest, *Reason and Culture. The Historic Role of Rationality and Rationalism,* Blackwell, Oxford 1992; Searle, "Rationality and Realism, What is at stake?"

lence is only superficially there. It has to do with the "translation" of the text in question. Usually that remark is followed by good advice from the believer to look for a more reliable translation. And, of course, translations matter. This is not only underscored by those who have a rosy picture of religion. The American psychiatrist Wafa Sultan (1958–) writes in her book *A God who Hates* (2009): "When you read the Koran in English or in any other language, you are reading not a literal translation but, rather, the meaning that the translator wants to impart to the text."[107] The text Hirsi Ali and Ramadan refer to in their exchange of views can be translated in different ways. This notorious Sura 24:2 is translated by Majid Fakhry as follows:

> The adulteress and the adulterer, whip each one of them a hundred lashes; and let no pity move you in Allah's religion, regarding them; if you believe in Allah and the Hereafter. And let a group of believers witness their punishment.[108]

N.J. Dawood (1927–) translates as follows:

> The adulterer and the adulteress shall each be given a hundred lashes. Let no pity for them cause you to disobey God, if you truly believe in God and the Last Day; and let their punishment be witnessed by a number of believers.[109]

This translation is slightly different from the one quoted by Hirsi Ali. But does that help the apologists of religion? The answer is clearly negative. The differences between Dawood's translation and the one used by Hirsi Ali and Ramadan are marginal, as we can see, and that may be expected when we consider that many scholars will have thought carefully about how that passage should be translated.

So, if "translation" is no help to the apologist of religion with regard to Sura 24:2, perhaps "interpretation" will do better. It is for "interpretation" that Ramadan has high expectations, judging from his rhetorical exclamation: "Is it difficult to understand that this is a question of interpretation ...?"

But can "interpretation" do what Ramadan supposes it can? Is it possible to provide an "interpretation" of Sura 24:2 that makes the message

---

[107] Sultan, Wafa, *A God who Hates: The Courageous Woman Who Inflamed the Muslim World Speaks Out Against the Evils of Islam*, St. Martin's Press, New York 2009, p. 167.
[108] Fakhry, Majid, *An Interpretation of the Qur'an*, New York University Press, New York 2002, p. 349.
[109] *The Qur'an*, translated with notes by N.J. Dawood, Penguin Books, London 1999, p. 246.

acceptable by modern moral standards? And what would that interpretation look like?

If Nietzsche is right that there are no "facts," but only "interpretations," this should not be too difficult. That is the great challenge that has to be met by the "moderates" unwilling to confess openly that they get their guidance not from the holy text itself, but from moral considerations that are read into that text. The "moderate" believer must show that there is an interpretation of this specific passage that effaces its violent character. Is it likely that such an interpretation can be provided?

Even a provisional glance at the text makes that improbable. Nevertheless, let us start with the most promising element: an interpretation of what is meant by the terms "adulterer" and "adulteress." Why is the Saudi woman characterized as an "adulteress"? The only thing she has done is "mingling": sitting in a car with someone who is not her husband or a member of her direct family. Is that adultery?

Can Interpretation Mitigate All Immoral Passages in Scripture?

According to the *Concise Oxford Dictionary* "adultery" means: "Voluntary sexual intercourse of married person other than with spouse." Because in this case there is no mention of *sexual intercourse*, there is no adultery, so it seems. So the Saudi judges gave a wrong interpretation to Sura 24:2, the "moderate" could answer. Would that not help us out of the quandary?

Not quite. First, we have to remember that what we have done with the passage in Sura 24:2, is to force our contemporary idea of adultery onto a completely different situation. The *Concise Oxford Dictionary* simply follows the contemporary meaning. "Voluntary sexual relations with someone other than one's spouse" is roughly what most people in the language community nowadays mean when they use the word "adultery." But that is likely to be different from what people mean by "adultery" in Saudi Arabia. It is also very different from what people meant in the time and the culture from which the Qur'an stems. To give the word "adultery," as it is used in the Qur'an, the same meaning that it has in modern English is more a *revision* of the Qur'an than an "interpretation."

Nevertheless, if we follow the somewhat dubious approach of reading contemporary meanings into ancient texts there is *some* hope for modern "minglers." I stress "some," in contradistinction to "much." What I mean is this. Suppose the Saudi woman did indeed have sexual intercourse with the man in the car. In that case the punishment as described in Sura 24:2 had to be executed, *viz.* a hundred lashes. Would that make our opposition to the text less urgent? The answer is clear: even in the case of *actual sexual intercourse* we are not in favor of lashes. So the problem is not the "interpretation" of this text. The problem is *the text itself.*

Moderates are always reluctant to admit this. For them, as for Ramadan, the problems that arise are always perceived as problems of "interpretation." Therefore they never do what should be done to remedy our problems: to demystify the idea of scriptural authority itself. The problem is not that people give a "conservative interpretation" to a religion that is "per se" pristine and incorruptible, but that people think that they can make their modern conscience defer to ancient texts. We may also put it thus: the problem is (a) the *content* of the text itself and (b) the *attitude* of the people who think that they should follow ancient texts.

So far, I have concentrated on the concept of "adultery," as part of the text of Sura 24:2. But I think analogous remarks could be made about the other words in the text. We could also focus on the meaning of "flogging" or "lashes," as indicated in Sura 24:2, and pretend that these concepts have a different meaning now than they used to have in ancient Arabic culture. In that case we should proclaim that we interpret "lashing" as something less painful, let's say "criticizing." Is that a viable road to take?

I do not think so. There may be slight variations between what we, in the twenty-first century, understand by "flogging" and what people centuries ago understood by this term, but these variations are negligible.

Perhaps we could focus on the *number* of lashes? Sura 24:2 refers to *a hundred* lashes while the Saudi woman was sentenced to *two hundred* lashes. "You see, there are Qur'anic grounds for mitigating the sentence," the apologist of religion might say. But this would hardly be convincing. Critics like Hirsi Ali and many other contemporaries would say that they object to flogging or lashing *in general,* the number of lashes is immaterial. That brings us to the conclusion that even if it were possible to argue that the woman from Qatif was not an "adulteress" because the only crime she committed was "mingling," that might help *this woman* but not the *next* who behaves in a way that undoubtedly falls within the ordinary semantic meaning of the word "adulteress."

What is the result of all this? The upshot is that Ramadan should have said: "I am opposed to *all* punishment for *all* adulterers." This seems to be what Hirsi Ali requires him to do and what he is so manifestly reluctant to contemplate (as he was in a discussion with Sarkozy on a similar point that will be discussed in the next section).

Why is he not willing to do this? That a courageous stand can help sometimes is made clear by the Sudanese journalist Lubna Ahmed al-Hussein, whose situation came to international attention in July 2009 and soon became a test case for women's rights in Sudan. She was prosecuted for wearing trousers. The legal system of Sudan is based on sharia law and the criminal law includes a clause that threatens 40 lashes and a fine for anyone "who commits an indecent act which violates morality or wears indecent clothing."[110]

The police arrested Hussein and 12 other women wearing trousers at a Khartoum restaurant on July 3, 2009. Two days later 10 of the women accepted a punishment of 10 lashes, but Hussein appealed in a bid to eliminate such rough justice. "My main objective is to get rid of article 152" (the law that prescribes the punishment). Hussein contended that tens of thousands of women and girls have been whipped for their clothes over the last 20 years. Amnesty International released a statement asking the Sudanese government to repeal article 152 and drop the charges against her.

The "trousers case" was held before a court in Khartoum on September 7, 2009, Hussein still wearing her trousers. The verdict was remarkable. Hussein was spared a whipping, but the court instead fined her 500 Sudanese pounds (200 dollars). Hussein, still intransigent, said she would rather go to prison than pay the fine.

Why Are "Moderates" so Reluctant to Criticize Religion?

Why will Ramadan not take a stance on the harsh punishments prescribed by sharia law? His reasons seem to be multifarious. On the one hand there is the motive analyzed above. Ramadan seems to think that by means of "interpretation" we can achieve any result that seems acceptable. The relevance of this conviction is clear. If one is convinced that any desired social change can be effected by reading the prescripts in a way that is conducive to that end, one will be less enthusiastic about undermining scriptural authority. Why bother to demystify the notion of scriptural authority if you can read everything you wish into Holy Scripture? Why advocate adopting the Universal Declaration of Human Rights and other human rights documents if, without acknowledging them explicitly, you can always read those human rights clauses into every biblical or qur'anic passage? Many who have a reputation of being reformers of religion seem to be motivated by this relativist stance towards interpretation. It is also, as we have seen, presupposed in what Ramadan contends. His relativist theory convinces him that by means of interpretation we can achieve everything. In combination with, or rather based on, this he presents a strategic argument. Condemning a religion "by its very essence, is not only unjust but deeply counterproductive," Ramadan writes. He specifies: "It does not help the inner dynamic of reforms."

Again, like a modern Carlyle, we have to address the underlying presuppositions of these words. The presupposition in this case is that criticizing

[110] "Sudan women 'lashes for trousers,'" BBC News, August 13, 2009.

a religion directly is "counterproductive" or – as Ramadan says – "deeply counterproductive."[111] Ramadan makes allusions to an "inner dynamic of reforms." But what does "inner dynamic of reforms" mean? Does it mean that in criticizing objectionable cultural practices we can only expect to make minimal progress, step by step? Do we first have to advocate a *reduction* of the amount of lashes from 200 to 100 before we can advocate the *abolition* of lashing altogether?[112]

On this topic there was a notorious confrontation between Ramadan and the incumbent president of France, Nicolas Sarkozy (1955–). The subject of their discussion was the stoning of women accused of adultery. Ramadan did not clearly reject this practice. He proposed a "moratorium" on the stoning of women. Sarkozy, incensed, criticized him heavily for this, just as Hirsi Ali did in the case of the Saudi woman accused of mingling. There is a transcript of this debate between Sarkozy and Ramadan, made by Aziz Zemouri:

SARKOZY: A moratorium … Mr. Ramadan, are you serious?
RAMADAN: Wait, let me finish.
SARKOZY: A moratorium, that is to say, we should for a while hold back from stoning women?
RAMADAN: No, no, wait … What does a moratorium mean? A moratorium would mean that we absolutely end the application of all of those penalties, in order to have a true debate. And my position is that if we arrive at a consensus among Muslims, it will necessarily end. But you cannot, you know, when you are in a community … Today on television, I can please the French people who are watching by saying: "Me, my own position." But my own position doesn't count. What matters is to bring about an evolution in Muslim mentalities. Mr. Sarkozy, it's necessary that you understand …[113]

But Sarkozy remained implacable, as we can understand. "To stone a woman because she is an adulterer. That's monstrous!" Sarkozy exclaimed. He deemed it necessary to condemn the stoning outright.[114] But according to Ramadan this was "too easy."

[111]   One of the strong points of Timothy Keller's book *The Reason for God* is that he convincingly demonstrates that the dominant relativistic mindset is based on assumptions that are just as dubious as the mindset of the religious believer. See on this: ibid., pp. 5–21.

[112]   This seems to be the interpretation that Walter Laqueur gives to Ramadan's remarks on this subject. He writes about Ramadan's proposal to take a less strict attitude towards some religious precepts: "His suggestions were unanimously rejected. As one of the legal scholars put it, if we call for a moratorium on stoning women and the death penalty, tomorrow there will be the demand to abolish the Friday prayer. (Ramadan had not asked for the abolition of the old laws, only a moratorium.)" See: Laqueur, *The Last Days of Europe*, p. 92.

[113]   Quoted in: Berman, "Who is afraid of Tariq Ramadan?" p. 58.

[114]   This stance by Sarkozy is all the more remarkable because he cannot be accused of antireligious bias. About terrorists he says "Ces fous de Dieu n'ont rien à voir avec Lui" [These

Many commentators have censored Ramadan for this. Paul Berman writes: "Some six million French people watched that exchange. A huge number of Muslim immigrants must have been among them – the very people who might have benefited from hearing someone speak with absolute clarity about violence against women. Ramadan couldn't do it."[115]

But the question is *why* couldn't he do it?

There are three possible answers to this question. The *first* is the answer given by people who feel sympathetic to Ramadan's approach. They usually consider the exchange of views with Sarkozy as an unfortunate accident that does not manifest Ramadan's true opinion. He was a bit clumsy, perhaps, in answering the experienced debater Sarkozy, but, surely, Ramadan is against stoning. So, why all the fuss?

This answer does not seem very convincing to me, because the same point returns in the discussion with Hirsi Ali. In the discussion with Sarkozy Ramadan was disinclined to reject stoning outright; in the discussion with Hirsi Ali, he was not prepared to reject the flogging of the woman who "mingled" outright. There seems to be a pattern there. So the question still stands: why?

A *second* answer is that given by those who simply do not trust Ramadan. He has a double agenda, they say.[116] He poses as a reformer, but he is not one. Of course he will never reject stoning for adulterers; neither will he reject flogging for minglers. The reason is simple: he is not really opposed to those practices.

To evaluate this claim we would have to read all of Ramadan's work, as Caroline Fourest (1975–) and Paul Landau, two of Ramadan's most severe detractors, have done.[117] I have not read all of Ramadan's writings; only the books by Fourest and Landau. So I will not presume to present expert judgment on Ramadan's motives. But what I can do is to point out that there is a *third* explanation of his curious behavior. That is that Ramadan is under the spell of post-modern ideology. According to postmodernists, texts can mean everything. So "cruel and unusual punishments"

---

madmen for God have nothing to do with Him]. And further: "Ils détournent un message d'amour et de paix en instrument de guerre" [They distort a message of love and peace into an instrument of war]. See: Sarkozy, N., *La République, les religions, l'espérance. Entretiens avec Thibaud Collin et Philippe Verdin* [The Republic, Religions, Hope. Conversations with Thibaudet Collin and Philippe Verdin], Les Éditions du Cerf, Paris 2004, p. 9.

[115]   Berman, "Who is afraid of Tariq Ramadan?", p. 58.

[116]   See e.g.: Caldwell, Christopher, *Reflections on the Revolution in Europe: Immigration, Islam and the West*, Allen Lane, Penguin Books, London 2009, p. 237 ff.

[117]   Fourest, Caroline, *Brother Tariq: The Doublespeak of Tariq Ramadan*, Encounter Books, New York 2008; Landau, Paul, *Le Sabre et le Coran. Tariq Ramadan et les Frères Musulmans à la Conquête de l'Europe* [The Sabre and the Qur'an. Tariq Ramadan and the Muslim Brothers out to Conquer Europe], Éditions du Rocher, Paris 2005.

in Scripture, which are so disquieting for people who believe a text has a fixed meaning, do not worry the postmodernist in the least. The postmodernist is convinced that simply by reading the text differently, by "interpreting" it, he can achieve *any* result.

The upshot of all this is that we can have our cake and eat it too. We can stick to the idea of an eternal revealed text and at the same time make the text do the work we want it to do. From this perspective, any attack on the text, on scriptural authority, divine revelation, and other elements of the theistic way of thinking contradicts "the inner dynamic of reforms." It's all "deeply counterproductive." So we should never target "religion per se" as the cause of problems. It's after all only a matter of interpretation.

Ramadan seems completely confident about the superiority of his cautious way of operating if compared with the more straightforward approach of critics of the Islamic religion such as Hirsi Ali,[118] Taslima Nasreen,[119] Irshad Manji,[120] Mina Ahadi,[121] Wafa Sultan,[122] Necla Kelek,[123] Nonie Darwish,[124] and others. But his confidence is predicated on a spurious notion of relativism about the meaning of texts, and therefore ultimately not very convincing. Which approach is the most fruitful remains to be seen, but as long as the one favored by Ramadan has not been vindicated by spectacular results, I am inclined to be skeptical. In the light of the problems as sketched before, the outright rejection of the idea of scriptural authority seems to be more straightforward and intellectually promising than any alternative I am aware of. There will always be parts of Holy Scripture that pose a problem to our modern morality and politics. And the sooner we acknowledge this, the more effective we will be in fighting injustice in this world.

Although Tariq Ramadan uses the concept of "Euro-Islam" it is hard to see that the kind of Islam he envisages is very promising. Much more attractive seems the perspective of Euro-Islam as developed by Bassam Tibi (1944–). Tibi coined the concept "Euro-Islam" in 1998 in his book *Europa*

---

[118]   Hirsi Ali, Ayaan, *Infidel: My Life*, The Free Press, London 2007.

[119]   Nasreen, Taslima, *Selected Columns*, Translated by Debjani Sengupta, Srishti Publishers, New Dehli 2004.

[120]   Manji, Irshad, *The Trouble with Islam: A Muslim's Call for Reform in Her Faith*, St. Martin's Press, New York 2003.

[121]   Ahadi, Mina, (with Sina Vogt), *Ich habe abgeschworen: warum ich für die Freiheit und gegen den Islam kämpfe* [I have Apostatized: Why I Fight for Freedom and against Islam], Heyne, München 2008.

[122]   Sultan, Wafa, *A God who Hates: The Courageous Woman Who Inflamed the Muslim World Speaks Out Against the Evils of Islam*, St. Martin's Press, New York 2009.

[123]   Kelek, Necla, *Die fremde Braut: Ein Bericht aus dem inneren des türkischen Lebens in Deutschland* [The Foreign Bride: A Report from inside Turkish Life in Germany], Kiepenheuer & Witsch 2005.

[124]   Darwish, Nonie, *Cruel and Unusual*, Thomas Nelson, Nashville 2008.

ohne Identiät [Europe without Identity] (1998)[125] and further developed this idea in *Euro-Islam* (2009).[126] The difference between Ramadan and Tibi is that Tibi presents a kind of Islam that is really in harmony with democracy, human rights, and the European concept of freedom of the individual. Tibi defends Islam against Islamism, but he also defends European culture against erosion and he warns against the concessions that are being made by the politically correct European elite to extremist variants of Islam, which will undermine a culture of freedom in the long run.

I have now presented my analysis of a text from the Qur'an. My conclusion is that it seems difficult to deny that in the holy scripture of Islam there are passages that incite violence. My second example is from the Bible. We have seen, also in Ramadan's criticism of Hirsi Ali, that there are violent passages in holy books other than the Qur'an. And although this was a weak argument to counter the claims of Hirsi Ali, because she focused on actual violence against contemporary Islamic women, the statement in itself is true. There is a plethora of violent texts in the Bible, above all in the Old Testament. Because these texts are not the basis for the actual stoning, flogging, and decapitation of people, they are less discussed by social reformers. But for the sake of a good understanding of how scriptural authority works, and what might be the answer to it, I will dwell on some problematic passages from the Old Testament as well. For the general argument developed in *The Secular Outlook* it is important to understand the whole structure of reasoning connected to religious ethics, that is: ethics based on religious foundations.

The Bible on Apostasy

A good place to start our argument on the scriptural foundations of violence in the Bible is with Deuteronomy 13:1–3 ("a warning against idolatry," as the English Standard Version euphemistically puts it). There we find the following passage:

> If a prophet or a dreamer of dreams arises among you and gives you a sign or a wonder, and the sign or wonder that he tells you comes to pass, and if he says, "let us go after other gods," which you have not known, "and let us serve them," you shall not listen to the words of that prophet or that dreamer of dreams.

[125] Tibi, Bassam, *Europa ohne Identität? Leitkultur oder Wertebeliebigkeit* [Europe without Identity? Leading Culture or Arbitrariness in Values], 2nd ed., Siedler, München 2001 (1998).
[126] Tibi, Bassam, *Euro-Islam: Die Lösung eines Zivilisationskonfliktes* [Euro-Islam: The Solution to a Conflict of Civilizations], Primus Verlag, Darmstadt 2009.

The attitude exemplified in this passage cannot come as a shock to a well-informed reader. Every faith will discourage its devotees from going after other gods. Every religion tries to keep its community together, and so does the Jewish religion. As Rosemary Radford Ruether (1936–) writes in an analysis of the concept of God in the Christian tradition:

> Central to Jewish understanding of its national God, Yahweh, was that this God has chosen them to be his people and had given them the laws of life. They should worship him alone. Infidelity to their God brought stern punishment.[127]

The Bible says: "You shall walk after the Lord your God and fear him and keep his commandments and obey his voice, and you shall serve him and hold fast to him" (Deuteronomy 13:4–5).

The theory of ethics that is implicit in this passage is what has been called the "divine command theory" of ethics.[128] I will analyze that theory more extensively in Chapter 4, but the gist of the theory can be stated now. It holds that the believer is supposed to follow the ethical injunctions that are revealed by God, manifested in Scripture. As philosopher and classicist John E. Hare (1949–) writes: "Morality and religion are connected in the Hebrew Bible primarily by the category of God's command."[129]

There is a problem though. Doing this can imply tensions with what we consider morally appropriate or what is legally required or forbidden by civil law or "human law" (as contrasted with "divine law"). This is, for example, the problem that Abraham faces when ordered from above to sacrifice his son. The story of Abraham and its significance for the secular outlook will be dealt with in the fifth section of Chapter 4.

So far, Deuteronomy has suggested nothing that can be considered problematic in the sense of violating the moral or civil law, but in Deuteronomy 13:5 there is a turn. After the turn, we read: "But that prophet or that dreamer of dreams shall be put to death, because he has taught rebellion against the Lord your God, who brought you out of the land of Egypt and redeemed you out of the house of slavery, to make you leave the way in which the Lord your God commanded you to walk. So you shall purge the evil from your midst" (Deuteronomy 13:5–6).

So the prophet or the dreamer of dreams "shall be put to death."

---

[127] Reuther, Rosemary Radford, "The Politics of God in the Christian Tradition," *Feminist Theology*, 17 no. 3 2009, pp. 329–338, p. 330.

[128] See on this: Idziak, Janine Marie, "Divine Command Morality: A Guide to the Literature," in: Janine Marie Idziak, *Divine Command Morality: Historical and Contemporary Readings*, The Edwin Mellen Press, New York 1979, pp. 1–38.

[129] Hare, John E., "Religion and Morality," in: *Stanford Encyclopedia of Philosophy*, http://plato.stanford, edu, 2006, pp. 1–31, p. 6.

If this is interpreted as a description of what will happen after death, this text may still be compatible with contemporary civil and penal law, for these are only applicable to the situation here on earth. It is not very polite perhaps to tell other people that they will burn in hell for what they believe or do not believe, but as long as the furnace is not ignited *in this life* these visions about what happens in the hereafter do not have to cause us great worry. It appears from the context, however, that the Bible is not simply making a factual statement about what will happen to our souls in a future life, but admonishes believers *in this world* to execute the false prophet or the "dreamer of dreams." That means: the individual believer is exhorted – in contemporary jargon – to "take the law into his own hands" and purge the community of false prophets.

That the Bible takes this point seriously is clear from further commentary on the way this prescript should be interpreted. There it appears that this injunction is not restricted to unknown people but should also be applied to those most intimate and dear to us. Our brother, our son, daughter, wife or friend – they should all be put to death if they preach rebellion against the Lord. In Deuteronomy 13:6–12 we read:

> If your brother, the son of your mother, or your son or your daughter or the wife you embrace or your friend who is as your own soul entices you secretly, saying, "let us go and serve other gods," which neither you nor your fathers have known, some of the gods or the peoples who are around you, whether near you or far off from you, from one end of the earth to the other, you shall not yield to him or listen to him, nor shall your eye pity him, nor shall you spare him, nor shall you conceal him. But you shall kill him. Your hand shall be first against him to put him to death, and afterwards the hand of all the people.
>
> You shall stone him to death with stones, because he sought to draw you away from the Lord your God, who brought you out of the land of Egypt, out of the house of slavery. And all Israel shall hear and fear and never again do any such wickedness as this among you.

"Warning against idolatry" is an unduly euphemistic description of what we find here, so it appears. It is a warning to idolaters, false prophets, and dreamers of dreams, but the text also spells out in no uncertain terms what has to be done with them. They deserve the death penalty. And the execution of this death penalty is not reserved for God in the hereafter; the text proclaims it to be the specific duty of all members of the Jewish tribe to carry it out.

Furthermore, we should not be distracted from our religious duties when the false prophet is our son, our daughter, brother or wife. In particular when it comes to those dear to us, we should be the first to throw the stone, the rest of the community has to follow.

In modern terminology we should describe this as a prohibition of apostasy.[130] When we compare this provision in the Bible with modern constitutions and modern textbooks of penal law there is a manifest contradiction. Modern constitutions and treaties on human rights proclaim the freedom of religion. That freedom also comprises the freedom to reject one specific religion or relinquish all religions. This is stated clearly in article 18 of the Universal Declaration of Human Rights (1948): "Everyone has the right to freedom of thought, conscience and religion; *this right includes freedom to change his religion* or belief, and freedom, either alone or in community with others and in public or private, to manifest his religion or belief in teaching, practice, worship, and observance" (italics added). So here we have a manifest contradiction between modern constitutional texts like The Universal Declaration of Human Rights and "Holy Scripture" as handed down by the ancient religions of the book.

That contradiction is not restricted to the matter of apostasy. Deuteronomy generally has a completely different opinion about taking the law into your own hands than the modern state. It presents no rules to guide an earthbound government in dealing with the matter of apostasy; it does not even refer to God. It is the individual member of the community who is assigned to be officer of the law and executioner. We all have to stone the apostates and those inciting others to embrace the false gods ourselves.

Obviously, this would be detrimental to civil order and to the principle of free speech. And this would not only be detrimental to the *modern* civil order, by the way, but it would also have undermined *ancient* states and communities. No state, whether ancient or modern, can condone violence perpetrated by citizens themselves.[131] A clear example of what this would imply we find in the biblical story of Phinehas.

Biblical Terrorism: The Story of Phinehas

The story of Phinehas is told in the book of Numbers (25:1–18). Numbers 25 is dedicated to Ba'al worship at Peor. As the feminist theologian Rosemary Radford Ruether (1936–) writes: "In the Hebrew Scriptures the

---

[130] In several European countries there is a debate about apostasy in Islam. See on this: Zwemer, Samuel M., *The Law of Apostasy in Islam*, Marshall Brothers, London 1924; Warraq, Ibn, ed., *Leaving Islam. Apostates Speak Out*, Prometheus Books, Amherst, NY 2003.

[131] See: Weber, Max, *Staatssoziologie. Soziologie der rationalen Staatsanstalt und der modernen politischen Parteien und Parlamente* [Sociology of the State. Sociology of the Rational Institution of the State and Modern Political Parties and Parliaments], ed. Johannes Winckelmann, Duncker & Humblot, Berlin 1966, p. 27 and Baldwin, Thomas, "The Territorial State," in: Hyman Gross and Ross Harrison, eds., *Jurisprudence. Cambridge Essays*, Clarendon Press, Oxford 1992, pp. 207–231.

chief rival of Yaweh is Ba'al. Yaweh seeks to supplant the worship of Ba'al, taking over from Ba'al the functions of providing rain and fertility."[132] While Israel lived in Shittim, the people of Israel began "to whore with the daughters of Moab," the Bible informs us. They invited the Israelites to the sacrifices of their gods, and those "daughters of Moab" apparently had considerable success with their invitations because the Israelites "bowed down to their gods" (Numbers 25:2). The Bible spells out what this means: "So Israel yoked himself to Ba'al of Peor."

This made the Lord angry. He addressed himself to Moses and said: "Take all the chiefs of the people and hang them in the sun before the Lord, that the fierce anger of the Lord may turn away from Israel."

Moses took action and said to the judges of Israel: "Each of you kill those of the men who have yoked themselves to Ba'al of Peor."[133]

It is not so clear whether Moses' last command is identical to what the Lord commanded. The Lord seemed to exact the killing and punishment of *all the chiefs*. Moses, though, seems to have built in a proviso: he ordered the killing only of those who had actually yielded to the temptation of the daughters of Moab. So for Moses a precondition for punishment was personal guilt (*mens rea*).[134] From a modern perspective this seems almost self-evident, but not everybody in the community was satisfied with the way Moses handled the matter. There was a certain Phinehas who defied Moses' authority and took the law into his own hands. The immediate occasion for this was the following.

Phinehas saw how one of the men of Israel brought a Midianite woman to his tent (Numbers 25:6). When Phinehas saw this, he rose and left the congregation and took a spear. He "went after the man of Israel into the chamber and pierced both of them, the man of Israel and the woman through her belly" (Numbers 25:8).

So far, we only have an exciting, although gruesome, story. What makes the story interesting, however, is the Lord's reaction. What did God say about Phinehas slaying the people who, according to modern standards, were perfectly justified in revering the gods of their own choosing (protected by the freedom of religion, after all)? The Lord sided with Phinehas and Moses' authority was clearly defied on the basis of the subsequent events. The Lord said to Moses: "Phinehas the son of Eleazar, son of Aaron the

---

[132]   Ruether, "The Politics of God in the Christian Tradition," p. 331.

[133]   Apparently there were other gods as well. Valentin Nikiprowetzky writes: "Moses' religion cannot be considered as anything other than monolatry, or the cult of a national god. But it was a monolatry that was remarkable in certain ways, for Yahweh was not a narrow, tribal god in the fashion of the god of the Patriarchs." "Ethical Monotheism," *Daedalus*, 104, no. 2 1975, pp. 69–89, p. 78

[134]   Slapper, Gary, and Kelly, David, *The English Legal System*, 7th ed., Cavendish, London 2004 (1994), p. 206.

priest, has turned back my wrath from the people of Israel" (Numbers 25:10). Phinehas was even rewarded for the man and woman's public execution without trial. The Lord said: "Behold, I give to him my covenant of peace, and it shall be to him and to his descendants after him the covenant of a perpetual priesthood, because he was jealous for his God and made atonement for the people of Israel" (Numbers 25:13).

So those who flout the legitimate authority of the temporal leaders of the people (Moses) are rewarded by God. Apparently, Phinehas' religious zeal is more appreciated by God than Moses' cautious way of dealing with the matter.

This stance can have (and is likely to have) grave consequences. It can be seen as substantial encouragement to those who claim special knowledge of God's will and are prepared to perpetrate violence in defiance of the traditional political leaders of the state. Why is this so important? The answer is: Phinehas can be seen as the archetypical religious terrorist.[135] Phinehas is prepared, on religious grounds ("I know what God wants") to use violence against citizens of the state, thereby violating the law of the state and defying legitimate authority. That is the essence of the religious terrorist. As terrorism expert Amos Guiora (1957–) rightly states: "terrorism is the conflict between nation-states and non-state entities."[136] Phinehas was such a non-state entity. Yigal Amir (1970–) was another. When Yigal Amir killed Yitzak Rabin in 1995 on the basis of religious considerations or when contemporary Islamist terrorists kill or intimidate people because their victims are accused of "blasphemy" (cf. the Danish cartoonists or the Dutch writer Theo van Gogh) this all adheres to the same pattern. The religious terrorist wants to "punish" or intimidate the blasphemer and instill fear into the hearts of the citizenry.

What makes the story both interesting and disconcerting at the same time is the fact that Phinehas' ruthless behavior wins the Lord's approval in a way that Moses' handling of the matter does not. After all, Phinehas brought the people of Israel back on the right track, the Bible tells us. The people of Israel are expected to serve one God and one God only: the Lord. In the Ten Commandments this is put thus: "You shall have no other gods before me" (Exodus 20:3).

It is clear that this attitude and the whole worldview connected with it is hard to reconcile with modern freedom of religion, freedom of worship, freedom of speech, freedom of conscience, free inquiry and other fundamental rights ingrained in the concept of liberal democracy. It is, of course,

---

[135] See on this: Selengut, *Sacred Fury*; Juergensmeyer, *Terror in the Mind of God*; and Griffith, Lee, *The War on Terrorism and the Terror of God*, William B. Eerdmans Publishing Company, Grand Rapids, MI 2002;
[136] Guiora, Amos N., *Fundamentals of Counterterrorism*, Wolters Kluwer, Austin, TX 2008, p. 4.

possible to acknowledge the prohibition on venerating strange gods as a private religious command (as a modern interpretation would perhaps advocate), but the state cannot act upon this political morality without violating modern human rights.

The story of Phinehas teaches us another lesson though. Since the 1960s and 1970s there has been a tendency to regard *organized religion* as a danger to civil liberties and freedom in general. Prominent philosopher and public intellectual Richard Rorty (1931–2007), for instance, calls himself an "anticlericalist" because he sees religion in its institutionalized forms as a menace to liberal democratic society.[137] Ecclesiastical institutions, he says, "despite all the good they do – despite all the comfort they provide to those in need or in despair – are dangerous to the health of democratic societies, so dangerous that it would be best for them eventually to wither away."[138]

What the story of Phinehas and the contemporary manifestations of religious terrorism teach us is that not only organized but also *un*organized religion poses challenges we have to meet.

Biblical Violence and Modern Legal Practice

What is the conclusion we have to draw from the previous section? Theologian Raymond Hammer (1920–1994) cites the words that are used when the Bible is presented to the British monarch in the course of the coronation ceremony: "Here is Wisdom; this is the royal Law; these are the lively oracles of God."[139] They illustrate, so Hammer argues, the value "ascribed to the Bible and indicate that its authority is ultimately the authority attributed to God": "Because God was held to be holy, the Bible too is described as holy, and terms like 'holy scriptures' and 'sacred writings' become commonplace."[140] As Origen (*c.* 185–254 CE) put it: "The sacred books are not the works of human beings; they were written by the

---

[137] See: Rorty, Richard, "Religion as Conversation-Stopper," 1994, in: Richard Rorty, *Philosophy and Social Hope*, Penguin Books, London 1999, pp. 168–174. For Rorty's views on religion, see also: Rorty, Richard, and Vattimo, Gianni, *The Future of Religion*, ed. Santiago Zabala, Columbia University Press, New York 2005.

[138] See: Rorty, "Religion as a Conversation-Stopper", and also: Rorty, Richard, "Religion in the Public Sphere: A Reconsideration," *Journal of Religious Ethics*, 31, no. 1 2003, pp. 141–149; and Wolterstorff, Nicholas, "An Engagement with Rorty," *Journal of Religious Ethics*, 31, no. 1 2003, pp. 129–139, p. 131.

[139] Hammer, Raymond, "Authority of the Bible," in: Bruce M. Metzger and Michael D. Coogan, *The Oxford Guide to Ideas and Issues of the Bible*, Oxford University Press, Oxford 2001, pp. 51–54, p. 51.

[140] Ibid., p. 51.

inspiration of the Holy Spirit at the will of the Father of all through Jesus Christ."[141]

Now this is all very well as long as we have to deal with precepts such as: "You shall love your neighbor as yourself" (Matthew 22:36). But what if the Bible tells stories like those of Phinehas? What if the Qur'an says: "The adulterer and the adulteress shall each be given a hundred lashes" (24:2)? What if the Bible says that the dreamer of dreams "shall be put to death" (Deuteronomy 13:5–6). Can we then say that these are "just stories"? Or that "most people" do not take these passages and stories seriously? But even if that were the case (that *most people* do not take those stories seriously) do we not have a problem on our hands as long as the authority of some scriptures, based on their "holiness," is left intact?

That brings me to the question to be found at the opening of this paragraph: what should our conclusion be? A reasonable conclusion, so it seems to me, is that the problem with the idea of a "Holy Scripture" (used as a comprehensive term for the Qur'an and the Bible as well) is that there is always a danger that it fails to educate responsible citizens. There are many passages in Holy Scripture that define people exclusively as members of a religious community. It tells them that their highest moral commitments are those formulated by their own god. As long as the moral injunctions of the religious community are the same as the laws and morals of the national community, the inherently problematic nature of this point of view is obscured. But once they diverge, a problem arises. What should the sincere believer do? What precepts should he follow? Here we have the essence of the religious believer's problem. This problem is clearly described and also furnished with a solution (although it may not be a good solution) in the biblical and Qur'anic stories. The primary moral responsibility of man is towards his religious community or – what amounts to the same – his God.[142]

Although contemporary states in the Western world are not directly based on religious Scripture they have been developed against the background of theistic culture.[143] And that makes them susceptible to a type of logic that inheres in the great theistic creeds. Not only is Sura 24:2 influential in contemporary Saudi Arabia but Deuteronomy 13 also has some bearing on the actual course of events in the Western world. However, the passage from Deuteronomy probably has less influence in a Western country

---

[141]   Origen, *De principiis* 4.9, quoted ibid., p. 52.

[142]   A meticulous analysis of what is implied when murder is seen as a religious duty we find in Jansen's analysis of the theological justification of the murder of Anwar Sadat in October 1981. See: Jansen, Johannes J.G., *The Neglected Duty: The Creed of Sadat's Assassins and Islamic Resurgence in the Middle East*, Macmillan, London 1986.

[143]   See for an overview: Freeman, Charles, *The Closing of the Western Mind: The Rise of Faith and the Fall of Reason*, William Heinemann, London 2002.

such as Great Britain than Sura 24:2 has in Saudi Arabia. There are no Christian states (the United States of America, for instance) or Jewish states (Israel, for instance) where the freedom of religion is directly curtailed on the basis of Deuteronomy 13.[144] But let us phrase the question in a slightly different way: is it likely that Deuteronomy 13 still has a degree of *influence* on our penal law, for instance in clauses about blasphemy? If we phrase the question in this way, the answer is probably affirmative. The Dutch penal code, for example, still has a provision for blasphemy in article 147. This article is almost a dead letter because the Central Prosecutor's Office does not bring blasphemy cases before the courts. But the possibility still exists and this has something to do with Europe's religious past. So Deuteronomy 13 (and other passages) certainly exerted an influence in suppressing freedom of speech and freedom of religion in the Christian world, although that influence was much more pervasive in the sixteenth and seventeenth centuries than it is now. From 1559 until 1966 the Catholic Church maintained an *Index librorum prohibitorum*.[145] Until 1820 the Inquisition was active and deterred many dissidents from heterodoxy and heresy, as we saw in Chapter 1.[146] Should we say that those practices were not in any way related to Christian Holy Scripture? Is there no relationship between passages such as Deuteronomy 13 and the Inquisition? That is hardly credible. Jesus says: "And if your right hand causes you to sin, cut it off and throw it away. For it is better that you lose one of your members than that your whole body go into hell" (Matthew 5:30).[147] Once we identify society with the "body" and the individual with the "hand" the suggestion arises that the heretic should be eliminated from society in order to forestall the perdition of the whole community, precisely as was advocated in Deuteronomy 13.

---

[144]   This point is forcefully made by Robert Spencer in: Spencer, Robert, *Religion of Peace? Why Christianity Is and Islam Isn't*, Regnery Publishing, Inc., Washington DC 2007. For a critique of the thesis that the Christian religion is tolerant see: Assmann, Jan, *The Price of Monotheism*, Stanford University Press, Stanford, CA 2009.

[145]   See: Putnam, George Haven, *The Censorship of the Church of Rome and Its Influence upon the Production and Distribution of Literature: A Study of the History of the Prohibitory and Expurgatory Indexes, together with Some Consideration of the Effects of Protestant Censorship and of Censorship by the State*, Kessinger Publishing, Whitefish, MT 2003 [1906–1907].

[146]   See on heresy in general: Evans, G.R., *A Brief History of Heresy*, Blackwell, Oxford 2003; Bradlaugh Bonner, Hypatia, *Penalties Upon Opinion: Some Records of the Laws of Heresy and Blasphemy*, third edition, Watts & Co., London 1934. For a sociological analysis: Kurtz, Lester R., "The Politics of Heresy," *American Journal of Sociology*, 88, no. 6 (May, 1983), pp. 1085–115. For heresy in the ancient world: Demant, V.A., "Ancient Heresy and Modern Unbelief," *The Journal of Religion*, 27, no. 2, (April, 1947), pp. 79–90.

[147]   The Islamic counterpart is here: "Those that deny Our revelations We will burn in Hellfire" (Qur'an 4:56).

Of course, other interpretations are possible. But that is not the point. The point is that an interpretation of the kind that I have presented here is not ludicrous, and this is the way this passage has been interpreted in the past. We may feel more comfortable forgetting this, but that is not a sensible course to follow. In a time when radicalism is on the rise we have to be prepared to accept that some religious believers envisage such radical interpretations.

The same relationship as between the flogging of women in Saudi Arabia and Sura 24:2 is probably also at work here. Again, religion does not exist "per se" (Ramadan) or "en tant que tel" (Meddeb).[148] Religion is not a metaphysical entity in a transcendent realm of ideas, but is a social force that acts on the morals, politics, and judicial system of its believers. Yet, many apologists of religion vehemently deny this. Their reaction is similar to Ramadan's. Any supposed relationship between the actual suppression of freedom of conscience and the scriptural passages enjoining that course of action (e.g. Deuteronomy 13) is flatly denied. Those practices are "cultural," and have nothing to do with "religion per se," most people say. The French author and public intellectual Guy Sorman (1944–) is probably right when he writes that the contemporary, almost entirely atheistic, West has great difficulties in comprehending a worldview that is almost completely based on religion.[149] But we may wonder whether the apologists of religion are not simply fooling us and, in the first place, themselves. If some believers declare their Scripture to be "holy" it is likely that they *really mean* what they say: "holy." And one of the consequences of this is that they consider the content of their Holy Scripture as relevant to their ethical convictions.

Although that insight is not very popular, this should not scare us off. The only thing that should guide us is the truth. The British Germanist, lawyer and mathematician Karl Pearson (1857–1936) once described freethought as "the single-minded devotion to the pursuit of truth."[150] Whether this is a fruitful definition of "freethought" may be doubted (it is much too broad for one thing), but as the formulation of a noble ideal it may be more convincing.

That ideal should be pursued not only because of the loftiness of the ideal in itself but because an effective reformation of religious thought can only be accomplished on the basis of a realistic estimate of what the problems are.

---

[148]   Meddeb, "En terre d'islam," p. 134.
[149]   Sorman, Guy, *Les Enfants de Rifaa: Musulmans et modernes* [The Children of Rifaa: Muslim and Modern], Fayard, Paris 2003, p. 58.
[150]   Pearson, Karl, *The Ethics of Freethought and Other Addresses and Essays*, Abraham and Charles Black, London 1901, p. 107.

The Book of History

In the previous pages we have been concerned with revealed Scripture as a source of information about the characteristics of a religion. But, as I have said before, a religion is not only what is "in the books." It is also as it manifests itself in history. That is why we should not only read from the "book of revelation" but also from the "book of history." In other words, we have to read Joseph Hoffmann on *The Just War and Jihad* (2006) if we want to be informed about "violence in Judaism, Christianity & Islam,"[151] as the subtitle of his book reads. Or we must consult Efraim Karsh (1953–) on "Islamic Imperialism" (2006).[152] Or we should read the classic books by Lecky (1838–1903) on the history and the rise of rationalism in Europe to inform us about the history of Christianity (1865).[153]

It is only these books that can give us an idea of the connection between religion and violence. The major problem, however, is not that these books are contested, but that they are ignored by many people. The vast majority of people reading about religion prefer to read literature that places religion in the most favorable light, such as the books by Karen Armstrong.

To assess the violent aspects of religion is not, of course, to overlook the fact that religion has stimulated many positive developments in world history. The American Declaration of Independence starts with the ringing words: "We hold these truths to be self-evident, that all men are *created equal*, that they are endowed *by their Creator* with certain inalienable rights" (italics mine). Here we find the basis for the American system of law: all men are *created* equal. Because of their status as creatures of God, the drafters of the Declaration state, human beings are in possession of inalienable rights. This is a great idea! Every single human being is the bearer of certain fundamental rights that cannot be denied by the government.[154] This idea changed the whole course of history and, we can safely say, this was a change for the better. Pragmatists might say: "You see? The idea of God as a creator is extremely useful. It brought us the idea of inalienable rights." This pragmatist is right, to a certain extent. But we can, of course, also consider the question of whether it would be possible to defend the idea of inalienable rights *without* the idea of a Creator. Is that possible too? If the people in 1776 accepted inalienable rights as a gift of God, does that imply that we, living in the twenty-first century, still have to believe in

[151]   Hoffmann, Joseph R., ed., *The Just War and Jihad: Violence in Judaism, Christianity, and Islam*, Prometheus Books, Amherst, NY 2006.
[152]   Karsh, Efraim, *Islamic Imperialism. A History*, Yale University Press, New Haven 2006.
[153]   Lecky, *History of the Rise and Influence of Rationalism in Europe*.
[154]   See Grayling, A.C., *Towards the Light: The Story of the Struggles for Liberty and Rights that Made the Modern West*, Bloomsbury Publishing, London 2007.

the same connection to sustain the notion of human rights for the future? Or can we adopt inalienable rights and proclaim our own non-theistic foundation? This is a question I will try to answer in Chapter 4, where we will be dealing with moral autonomy: the attempt to develop a theory of ethics that is not based on religion. As we will see in the latter part of that chapter, there is a long and impressive tradition in European thought that is based on the presumption that autonomous ethics are perfectly possible and desirable. As I said in the preface to this book, the great Dutch scholar of international law Hugo Grotius was one of the first thinkers to proclaim that natural law does not rest on a divine foundation, which, at least from the perspective of moral secularism, allows us to claim him as "the true father of modern ethics."[155]

This is important, because, as we have seen in this chapter, religion has an evil side that ought to be criticized. The attempt to argue that the evil sides of religion are simply "not religious," as Herbert Spencer and many others have done, is not convincing. Religion has to be subjected to criticism because only when this is accomplished can religion be purified of its nastier features.

Religious criticism should be fair (as all criticism should), but straight-forward. Limiting religious criticism within the confines of what liberal interpretation is prepared to acknowledge is too restrictive. If we maintain the myth of authoritative scripture, as "moderate" or "liberal" believers also do, we will make little progress.

Now, the frame of mind that is essential for religious criticism to be effective has been described only partially. It is certainly not necessary to subscribe to the atheist position, as I have made clear in Chapter 1 (although atheism is more consistent than agnosticism).

In Chapter 2 I have made clear what could be seen as the most important challenge in the confrontation with religious violence. This is the challenge of religious terrorism: people perpetrating terrorist crimes and claiming to be religiously motivated. This phenomenon forces us to understand the specific connection between violence and religion. And if we want to take religious terrorism seriously, we must engage in an analysis not only of terrorism, but of religion as well. The great scholar of Middle Eastern studies, Bernard Lewis (1916–), formulates this ambition in his book *The Crisis of Islam* (2003) in the following words: "Terrorism requires only a few. Obviously, the West must defend itself by whatever means will be effective. But in devising means to fight the terrorists, it would surely be useful to understand the forces that drive them."[156] Although Lewis goes

---

[155] See: Larmore, Charles, "Beyond Religion and Enlightenment," *San Diego Law Review*, 30 (1993), pp. 799–815, p. 808.

[156] Lewis, Bernard, *The Crisis of Islam. Holy War and Unholy Terror*, Weidenfeld & Nicolson, London 2003, p. xxviii. The same idea is to be found in: Guiora, Amos N.,

too far in saying that we may use all means in the fight against terrorism,[157] his last words can hardly be challenged: we need to understand the forces that drive the terrorists. The effectiveness of all our policies to combat terrorism is dependent on whether we succeed or fail to understand these forces. If we fail here, we will fail in our counter-terrorist strategies.

It will now be clear why Spencer's attitude toward religion is not only unjustified from a scholarly point of view, but disadvantageous for social policy as well. The reluctance of liberals or moderates to acknowledge anything wrong in religion is not only incoherent but inimical to an effective counter-strategy to the forces that undermine our society as well. The persistent attempts by the advocates of religion to cover up the religious roots of contemporary religious terrorism can have serious consequences. Religious terrorism can only be conquered if we understand how and why violence receives religious sanction.

This approach is rejected by the "true believer," of course. But what is more surprising is that it is not only rejected by the "true believer," the orthodox believer, or the fundamentalist; it is also rejected by those who are called "the moderates." "Moderates" and fundamentalists have one thing in common. That is that they are determined to ignore and deny the dark side of religion.[158] For the fundamentalist those dark sides have to be accepted because they are justified within a wider framework that transcends our capacity to understand. By the moderate those dark sides are construed as something that has nothing to do with real religion, religion "per se," which will remain a precious and pristine phenomenon no matter what believers do "in the name of religion."

Fundamentals of Counterterrorism, Wolters Kluwer, Austin TX 2008, p. 2: "What motivates individuals to commit acts of terrorism? Theories abound, some predicated on research, others on anecdotal evidence. 'Know thy enemy' must be the guiding light for any nation-state in developing operational counterterrorism policy." Guiora also states "that religion is certainly a primary motivator for modern day terrorists." Another author who does not underestimate the religious factor is Christopher Catherwood. See: Catherwood, Christopher, *Making War in the Name of God*, Citadel Press, Kensington Publishing Corp., New York 2007, p. 163: "If we are to deal effectively with the threat of terrorism, we need to understand that millions of people around the world think in an entirely different way from us."

[157]   See on this question: Guiora, *Fundamentals of Counterterrorism* and Ignatieff, Michael, *The Lesser Evil: Political Ethics in an Age of Terror*, The Gifford Lectures, Princeton and Oxford 2004; Grayling, A.C., *Liberty in the Age of Terror: A Defence of Civil Liberties and Enlightenment Values*, Bloomsbury, London 2009; Holmes, Stephen, *The Matador's Cape: America's Reckless Response to Terror*, Cambridge University Press, Cambridge 2007; Wilson, Richard Ashby, ed., *Human Rights in the "War on Terror,"* Cambridge University Press, Cambridge 2005.

[158]   That seems to me the case also in: Abou El Fadl, Khaled, *The Great Theft: Wrestling Islam from the Extremists*, Harper, San Francisco 2007, a plea for a "moderate Islam" and: Esposito, John L., and Mogahed, Dalia, *Who Speaks for Islam? What a Billion Muslims Really Think*, Gallup Press, New York 2007.

Some Objections

This chapter on religious criticism as the second pillar of freethought would not be complete without a discussion of some objections to what has been argued. The aim of Chapter 2 was to show that freethinkers are right to contend that religion deserves to be criticized. One of the most important reasons for religious criticism nowadays is that there appears to be a relationship between religion and violence. With regard to "religion" I have to make a *caveat* though. This is that, strictly speaking, I am not talking about religion in general or even about all religions in general, but about one specific type of religion, *viz.* theism.[159]

Theism has already been analyzed provisionally in Chapter 1 because such an analysis was necessary to the understanding of the nature of "atheism," or rather "non-theism," as we have seen. Atheism, in the sense that I have defined the concept, is intimately linked with theism. It is not simply a critique of religion in general; it is a-theism, so a denial of theism. The nature of theism will be further discussed in the opening section of Chapter 4, where some of its elements will be delineated by reference to an important Christian document: the Apostles' Creed.[160] Nevertheless, we already have a rough idea of theism on the basis of what has been said in Chapters 1 and 2.

One of the things that make theism problematic is that it is easily interpreted as the doctrine that a personal god exists who has revealed his will in Holy Scripture, which must be followed no matter what the consequences may be. I have illustrated this by referring to some examples derived from two important Holy Scriptures: the Qur'an and the Bible. The first example was Qur'an 24:2 stating that an adulterer and an adulteress should each be punished by whipping (the subject of debate between Ramadan and Hirsi Ali). A second example was a text from Deuteronomy 13:5-6, indicating that a prophet who seduced the people of Israel to adore strange gods should be put to death.

The example from the Bible was backed up by another passage from the Bible, but this time a "story": the story of Phinehas, as told in Chapter 25

---

[159] See on Indian fundamentalism for instance: Fernandes, Edna, *Holy Warriors: A Journey into the Heart of Indian Fundamentalism*, Portobello Books, London 2007. And on terrorism in other religious traditions than the theistic: Rapoport, David C., "Fear and Trembling: Terrorism in Three Religious Traditions," *The American Political Science Review*, 78, no. 3 1984, pp. 658–677; Rapoport, David C., "Messianic Sanctions for Terror," *Comparative Politics*, 20, no. 2 1988, pp. 195–213.

[160] Other creeds that are referred to are: the Nicene Creed, framed in 325, and the Athanasian Creed. See: Martin, Michael, *The Case Against Christianity*, Temple University Press, Philadelphia 1991, pp. 7–8; Freeman, Charles, *A New History of Early Christianity*, Yale University Press, New Haven 2009, p. 238 ff.

of the book of Numbers. Phinehas is an interesting figure, because he murdered two people (one of his fellow Israelite men and a woman from a different tribe) whom he deemed guilty of adoring false gods (i.e. not the god of Israel). The legitimate authority, Moses, did not act in the manner that Phinehas thought appropriate, i.e. did not carry out a swift execution without legal process. So Phinehas took the law into his own hands and did precisely that, killing those who had violated the law of God. We have also seen that the Lord, according to the story, did not disapprove of what Phinehas had done but had even rewarded him.

By referring to the story of Phinehas I have not only tried to demonstrate that Holy Scripture sometimes advocates atrocious acts (this point could be illustrated by other examples as well),[161] but to give an idea of the sort of person who could be called a "religious terrorist." A religious terrorist is someone who defies the legitimate state authorities, does not acknowledge the law of the state, and, based on Scripture or some other religious source, draws his own conclusions, even if these are radical indeed.[162]

So far, I have simply given a summary of the argument developed in Chapter 2. Now, there are three more or less common reactions to my argument, and we have to discuss those reactions before we can proceed to the next chapter.

Those reactions are: *first*, "I am convinced because your argument is flawless"; *second*, "I am not convinced because you overestimate the role of religion"; and *third*, "I am not convinced because you underestimate the difference between Islam and Christianity."

Let me start with the reaction that I myself would favor most. It is possible that someone takes cognizance of my arguments and is really convinced. He or she perhaps says: "I had not canvassed the matter thoroughly, so I was inclined to go along with the common prejudice that all the evil that is done in the name of religion is in reality external to it. Now, however, I am convinced that religion has a part in evil. There is something in the theistic religion that stimulates or invites some immoral acts. We had better acknowledge this, because only when we do, will we be able to purify religion of those elements. If, on the contrary, we turn a blind eye to these elements and stubbornly refuse to take notice of them, we will find that we have religious terrorists in our midst who perpetrate terrible acts that we

---

[161]   Other examples are to be found in: Nelson-Pallmeyer, *Is Religion Killing Us?*; and Harris, *The End of Faith*.

[162]   For instance killing the head of state, see: Faraj, Mohammad 'Abdus Salam, "Jihad: The Absent Obligation," in: Laqueur, Walter, ed., *Voices of Terror: Manifestos, Writings, and Manuals of Al-Qaeda, Hamas and Other Terrorists from around the World and throughout the Ages*, Reed Press, New York 2004, pp. 401–403 and Jansen, *The Neglected Duty*, p. 38 ff.

can only consider with utter amazement, while we should have been warned by what we had seen before."

Such a reaction would be wonderful, of course, because it would testify to the fact that my arguments have been convincing. There is no greater compliment one can pay to a philosopher. People who have this reaction will doubtless be curious to see what solutions I will present for the precarious predicament we are in.

Yet it is perhaps not very realistic to expect this to be the reaction of the majority of the people who read this book. What I expect is that many people will have one of the two other reactions I have suggested, because they are common reactions and, I fear, perhaps *more* common than I consider justified and fair.

The second reaction my book may elicit is that of those people who think religion has *no real influence* on what happens in the world. They will say that it is not a problem that old books sometimes tell strange stories or advocate some highly dubious behavior because no sensible person would take these stories seriously anyway. This group is composed of believers and unbelievers alike. Why unbelievers tend to think along these lines is clear: unbelievers tend to underestimate the importance of Holy Scripture. They are unbelievers, after all. They find it difficult to understand that people are seriously convinced that mingling should be punished by lashes simply because this is prescribed in an old book. And that people should be killed because they have changed their religion ("Take all the chiefs of the people and hang them in the sun before the Lord," Numbers 25) will be considered by many people as utterly repulsive. Similarly, taking the law into your own hands and carrying out these cruel prescripts, as Phinehas did, is something that most moral agents would never dream of doing. But here comes my point: this is in fact *so far* beyond the wildest dreams of ordinary people that they tend to think that *nobody takes Scripture seriously if it prescribes immoral conduct*. And so they are not in the least worried by the draconian measures prescribed in Scripture. They belittle the significance of this cruelty by telling us that it is only a "matter of interpretation." The overwhelming majority of believers, so they will tell us, are *not* inclined to perpetrate immoral acts on the basis of Scripture.[163] The conclusion they draw from this fact is that because *numerically* the extremists are such a small group we should not worry too much about those stories, which are considered to be "just stories" or "just texts."

What should we say to this second group of readers? In fact, they have already been answered. I have shown that Sura 24:2 certainly has a modicum

---

[163] This is emphasized by Esposito and Mogahed in *Who Speaks for Islam?* and Karen Armstrong in *The Case for God.*

of influence in some places of the world (to put it cautiously). There are places in the world, for instance, where Sura 24:2 is even more important than the law of the land. That is because the law of the land has always to be interpreted in light of Sura 24:2 and, if it contradicts Sura 24:2, is considered illegitimate.

That brings me to a third group of readers. Like the members of the second group, they are not convinced by my argument – but for different reasons. The members of this third group have not been answered yet, and will more or less argue as follows. They will say: "All right, you made your point with Sura 24:2, but with the biblical passage from Deuteronomy and the story of Phinehas you were less convincing." This group will point out that there is a "great difference" between the Qur'an and the Bible. They are both called "holy books" and at a superficial level there are some similarities, but the differences are greater than the similarities. And these differences are especially important for the matter of religious violence.

There is a host of differences that one can refer to, and my list of these disparities will not be exhaustive, but sufficient to understand what the matter is all about.

It may be possible to say: "The Bible is not one book, but two. And the second book, the New Testament, has mitigated the stern passages from the first book, the Old Testament."

It is clear that Christians (though not orthodox Jews) are likely to refer to the "two-books-argument." So in response to the story of Phinehas from the Old Testament it would be possible to point to Romans 13:1–8 from the New Testament. It is an important passage so I will quote it at length:

> Let every person be subject to the governing authorities. For there is no authority except from God, and those that exist have been instituted by God. Therefore whoever resists the authorities resists what God has appointed, and those who resist will incur judgment. For rulers are not a terror to good conduct, but to bad. Would you have no fear of the one who is in authority? Then do what is good, and you will receive his approval, for he is God's servant for your good. But if you do wrong, be afraid, for he does not bear the sword in vain. For he is the servant of God, an avenger who carries out God's wrath on the wrongdoer. Therefore one must be in subjection, not only to avoid God's wrath but also for the sake of conscience. For because of this you also pay taxes, for the authorities are ministers of God, attending to this very thing. Pay to all what is owed to them: taxes to whom taxes are owed, revenue to whom revenue is owed, respect to whom respect is owed, honor to whom honor is owed.

This seems a good answer to the "anarchistic" story of Phinehas who rebelled against the legitimate authority of Moses. If Phinehas had read

Romans 13, he could have known that he should not have resisted the authority of Moses who was governing him.

It would also be possible perhaps to point to the well-known passage on Caesar and God. Matthew 22:21 formulates it as follows: "Therefore render to Caesar the things that are Caesar's, and to God the things that are God's." In taking this passage as our point of departure and not Romans 13, it might be possible to argue, perhaps, that Phinehas was a kind of "spiritual authority" and that Moses was the worldly leader. Phinehas should not have become involved in anything as worldly as the administration of earthly justice. That was the province of Moses. Phinehas should only have proclaimed that the Israelites who prayed to the wrong gods forfeited their place in heaven or became liable for punishment in the world hereafter. But by claiming worldly power he violated the principle of the separation of church and state that Jesus Christ had so famously inaugurated.

A second difference between the Bible and the Qur'an that is often referred to is that the Bible does not speak directly to people in our time. Its message is, so to speak, more indirect. To substantiate that contention one can, again, refer to the story of Phinehas. This is a *story*. And stories have to be interpreted. The Bible does not tell contemporary Christians or contemporary Jews that they should now kill all the apostates or those who want to change from one religion to another. The story from Deuteronomy tells us something about Jewish history. And perhaps not even that.

The same could be said about the story of Abraham, which will be analyzed in Chapter 4 of this book. This is nothing more than a story. God did not address every reader but only Abraham, just this specific person in a specific situation. It is impossible to draw general conclusions from this.

Is this a convincing argument?

I do not think so. The story of Abraham has an unmistakable moral purpose and so – I am afraid – does the story of Phinehas.

"Why is the willingness to sacrifice one's child *the* quintessential model of faith, why not the passionate protection of the child?" Carol Delaney asks us in her book *Abraham on Trial* (1998).[164] She is not satisfied with the "just a story" argument.[165] Nor is she convinced by the explanation that child sacrifice was an accepted practice in the ancient Near East and that Abraham put an end to it. Such interpretations fail to recognize that Abraham is revered not for putting an end to the practice but for his "willingness to go through with it."[166]

---

[164] Delaney, Carol, *Abraham on Trial: The Social Legacy of Biblical Myth*, Princeton University Press, Princeton 1998, p. 5.
[165] Ibid., p. 6.
[166] Ibid.

That is what establishes him as the father of faith. *That* is what I find so terrifying. The story is not about substitution, symbolic or otherwise, but about a new morality; it represents not the end of the practice of child sacrifice but the beginning of a new order.[167]

The foundational story of Abraham is central to the belief systems of Judaism, Christianity, and Islam.[168] Why didn't Abraham argue with God as he did when Ishmael was to be banished, or as he did to try to save Sodom and Gomorrah from destruction (this subject will be discussed further on in Chapter 4)?

A third difference between the Bible and the Qur'an that some people put forward is that we have to take the attitude of believers into account as well. There may have been one Yigal Amir killing one Yitzak Rabin whilst referring to a divine mission.[169] But if that is the Jewish counterpart of the Islamist suicide bomber, the example of Amir dwindles into insignificance compared with the examples from the Islamist tradition.

A fourth response from this third group will be to point out that the Bible is mitigated by many other books and commentaries. If we want to understand the Torah, we have to read the Talmud as well. And the Talmud will teach us how to interpret the Torah. Once we engage in this type of study it will be clear why Jewish terrorism pales in comparison with Islamist terrorism.

What should our reaction be? Isn't this type of criticism fairly convincing?

I beg to differ. Actually, those who think along these lines have missed the gist of the argumentation that has been developed here. I am not engaged in a kind of empirical study of the dangers of Islamist, Jewish, and Christian terrorism respectively. What I am trying to understand is *religious terrorism as an important manifestation of religious or rather theistic evil.* That the actual danger this religious terrorism poses in some varieties of theism is much greater than in others is true, but at the same time it is irrelevant. I side with Bernard Lewis (1916–) and other commentators[170] in contending that the similarities between the three theistic faiths on a

---

[167]   Ibid., p. 6.

[168]   Ibid., p. 8.

[169]   See on this: Laqueur, Walter, *No End to War. Terrorism in the Twenty-First Century*, Continuum International Publishing, London 2003.

[170]   See e.g. McInerney, Peter K., "God," in: *Introduction to Philosophy*, HarperCollins, New York 1992, pp. 9–22, p. 21: "The main traditions of Judaism, Christianity, and Islam share the conception that there is only one God, who is self-existent, eternal, the creator of all things, transcendent, all-powerful, all-knowing, personal, all-good, and holy."

doctrinal level are important for our analysis, even if the actual manifestations of vulnerability to terrorist influences differ significantly.[171]

A last point that is often alleged is that the story of Phinehas is just a "story." That may be true, but, like the story of Abraham, it is a story with an unmistakably clear message, as has been emphasized by Carol Delaney whom I quoted before. So I do not agree with Robert Spencer (1962–) who writes that the traditional understanding of the Qur'an is "far beyond the biblical idea that God inspired human authors. Allah dictated every word of the Qur'an to the Prophet Muhammad through the Angel Gabriel. Allah himself is the only speaker throughout the Qur'an, and most often he addresses Muhammad, frequently telling him what to say to various adversaries."[172] In my view Spencer underestimates the similarities between the three theistic faiths.[173]

The problem is that if Holy Scriptures are, indeed, considered "holy," even though they contain only a small number of passages that incite violence,[174] they can still cause much harm. I have already quoted Bernard Lewis's dictum: "terrorism requires only a few."[175] He referred to the fact that we only need a few firm believers who are prepared to do the dirty work. But we can also say: "terrorism requires only a few passages in the holy book." If the holy book contains only a small number of passages inciting violence, they still pose a problem if the *whole book* is considered to be holy and the word of God.

[171] See: Lewis, Bernard, *The Crisis of Islam: Holy War and Unholy Terror*, Weidenfeld & Nicolson, London 2003, p. 4; Murray, Douglas, "Studying Islam has made me an atheist," at: *Spectator.co.uk*, Monday, December 29, 2008. See also: Sultan, Wafa, *A God who Hates*, p. 193 who somewhat mitigates the similarities between the three theistic faiths when she points out: "Jews and Christians, according to Islam, believe in the same God as Muslims do, but this does not work in their favor. Islam defines its relationship with them by their attitude to Muhammad, not by their attitude towards God."

[172] Spencer, Robert, *Onward Muslim Soldiers: How Jihad Still Threatens America and the West*, Regnery Publishing, Inc., Washington 2003, p. 127.

[173] See also: Ali, Daniel, and Spencer, Robert, *Inside Islam: A Guide for Catholics*, Ascension Press, West Chester, Pennsylvania 2003; Spencer, Robert, *Religion of Peace? Why Christianity Is and Islam Isn't*, Regnery Publishing, Inc., Washington DC 2007.

[174] Something that is always emphasized by the adherents of "liberal Islam." See e.g. Gresh, Alain, *L'Islam, la République et le Monde* [Islam, the Republic and the World], Fayard, Paris 2006, p. 73 who, with reference to Alfred Morabia, tells us that the term "jihad" appears in 35 verses of the Qur'an. In 22 verses it is in a non-military context, in 10 in a military context, in 3 in a spiritual sense.

[175] Lewis, *The Crisis of Islam*, p. xxviii.

3

Freethought II: Freedom of Expression

Freedom of expression "is applicable not only to 'information' or 'ideas' that are favorably received or regarded as inoffensive or as a matter of indifference, but also to those that offend, shock or disturb the State or any sector of the population." (European Court of Human Rights, Judgment in the Handyside case, 1976)[1]

So far I have elaborated on the first pillar of freethought: religion is not only a source of good things but of some unfortunate developments as well. I referred to verses in the Bible that constitute a denial of freedom of worship and the penalties for sexual misconduct prescribed by the Qur'an. These are still influential in the modern world, although less so in Western countries than in the Middle East. We have also seen that there seems to be a revival of religious feeling, or perhaps we should say of religious "self-confidence." Religious groups revolt against the secular state and secular morals.[2] That revolt sometimes manifests itself through democratic channels: proposals to revitalize blasphemy laws or otherwise curb freedom of speech. But there are violent manifestations of the new religious revival as well. The most extreme manifestation is religious terrorism: the use of violence to intimidate the state and the people or to force the secular state to accept religious rules and values as its basis. Contemporary societies are confronted by a new figure, the religious terrorist, who operates in a way that is remarkably similar to what is shown to us in the biblical story of Phinehas.

---

[1] The Handyside case is quoted in: Janis, Mark W., Kay, Richard S., and Bradley, Anthony W., *European Human Rights Law. Texts and Materials*, Clarendon Press, Oxford 1995, p. 165.
[2] Juergensmeyer, Mark, *Global Rebellion: Religious Challenges to the Secular State, from Christian Militias to Al Qaeda*, University of California Press, Berkeley 2008.

What should the reaction of open or liberal societies be to this assault on the principles on which they are based? Should they compromise on free speech and secular values? Or should they reassert the significance of those values? These are some of the pertinent questions we have to answer. In Chapter 3 I want to deal with freedom of speech as the second pillar of freethought – a freedom that has become the focal point of vehement discussions in the past decades, in particular as a result of the terrorist threat. The Danish cartoons affair, the publication of films and plays critical of elements of one of the world religions, the murder of the iconoclastic Dutch filmmaker Theo van Gogh in 2004 – these occurrences have all contributed to a sometimes vehement dispute on the meaning of free speech.[3] In Chapter 3 I want to evaluate the meaning of free speech against the backdrop of this new discussion about how to deal with terrorists who explicitly target this fundamental value of liberal democracies.

The two pillars of freethought (religious criticism and freedom of speech) are not necessarily connected. One and the same person can subscribe to one pillar and deny the other. It is possible that someone is convinced that religions are a blight and an illusion but nevertheless has no high expectations of free speech as a purifying factor. It is also possible that someone holds religion in high regard and at the same time is committed to free speech as a fundamental right. But both positions individually are not those of the freethinker. Characteristic of freethought is a peculiar *combination* of criticism of religion and trust in freedom of expression to emancipate mankind from one of the evils that besets it.[4]

Let us try to inquire into the reasons for this predilection for freedom of expression. And are these reasons convincing? Is it warranted to believe that free speech can deliver us from the evil sides of religion, or can at least be a step in the right direction? How important is free speech? And for what?

Mill on Liberty

Perhaps it is good to start with a widespread misunderstanding about freethought and freethinkers. Freethinkers do *not* necessarily have to proclaim

[3] See: Warburton, Nigel, *Free Speech: A Very Short Introduction*, Oxford University Press, Oxford 2009, pp. 42–59; Arthur, John, "Sticks and Stones," in: Hugh La Folette, ed., *Ethics in Practice: An Anthology*, second edition, Blackwell Publishers, Oxford 2002 (1997), pp. 364–376; Neu, Jerome, *Sticks and Stones: The Philosophy of Insults*, Oxford University Press, Oxford 2008; Pannick, David, "A curb on free speech that should offend us all, whatever our religion," *The Times*, January 11, 2005; Fish, Stanley, "There's No Such Thing As Free Speech and It's a Good Thing, Too," in: Paul Berman, ed., *Debating P.C. The Controversy over Political Correctness on College Campuses*, Bantam, New York 1992, 231–245.
[4] "One of the evils." I am not so naïve as to think that the removal of religious terrorism will create a utopia in this world. I mean what I say: "one of the evils."

free speech as something absolute. Almost everyone – freethinkers included – can imagine circumstances under which it seems justified to impose restraints on free speech. Even John Stuart Mill (1806–1873), who in 1859 presented the most radical vindication of free speech that had ever appeared in the tradition of Western political thought with his book *On Liberty*,[5] acknowledged certain limitations on the free expression of ideas and opinions. Nobody has the moral right to shout "fire" in an overcrowded hall if there is no actual fire.

Freedom of speech is also subjected to all kinds of *legal* limitations. Anyone who works for the secret service is not free to publish material relating to state security, as everyone will understand.

Mill wanted to inquire into the nature of civil or social liberty.[6] That is: "the nature and limits of the power which can be legitimately exercised by society over the individual."[7] His answer is this:

> The object of this Essay is to assert one very simple principle, as entitled to govern absolutely the dealings of society with the individual in the way of compulsion and control, whether the means used be physical force in the form of legal penalties, or the moral coercion of public opinion. That principle is that the sole end for which mankind is warranted, individually or collectively, in interfering with the liberty of action of any of their number, is self-protection.[8]

This brings Mill to the introduction of his "harm principle." "The only purpose for which power can be rightfully exercised over any member of a civilized community, against its will, is to prevent harm to others."[9] That implies that harm to self is not a legitimate reason for interfering with the freedom of the individual.

Applied to the freedom of expression this means that "opinions lose their immunity, when the circumstances in which they are expressed are such as to constitute their expression a positive instigation to some mischievous act."[10] As an example Mill refers to the "corn-dealers."[11] Anyone who wants to criticize them is allowed to, but there is a limitation. One should

---

[5]   See on this: Reeves, Richard, *John Stuart Mill: Victorian Firebrand*, Atlantic Books, London 2007, pp. 262–307.
[6]   Mill, John Stuart, *Three Essays. On Liberty* (1859), *Representative Government* (1861), *The Subjection of Women* (1869), Oxford University Press, Oxford 1975, p. 5.
[7]   Mill, *On Liberty*, p. 7.
[8]   Ibid., p. 15.
[9]   Ibid.
[10] Ibid., p. 69.
[11] See on this: Cohen-Almagor, Raphael, *The Boundaries of Liberty and Tolerance: The Struggle Against Kahanism in Israel*, University Press of Florida, Gainesville 1994, p. 124.

not invoke *violence* against them. Free speech is limited where there is an incitement to "molesting others."[12] According to Mill, free expression should be curbed if there is – what would later be called – a "clear and present danger" of physical violence.[13]

The example of the corn dealers would now be a bit outdated, but the general problem behind it certainly is not. On the contrary, we might say. In the contemporary world too we are presented – alas – with many examples of people advocating violence against others. A more contemporary example is the "fatwa," issued by the Iranian spiritual and political leader Ayatollah Khomeini (1902–1989) against the British author Salman Rushdie (1947–).

Khomeini v. Rushdie

On February 19, 1989 Ayatollah Khomeini watched the evening news on Iranian television. He saw an angry Muslim crowd in Pakistan, protesting against the publication of a blasphemous book: *The Satanic Verses* by Salman Rushdie. What could he do to help? Khomeini was touched – according to sources around the Iranian politician – by this spontaneous religious upsurge.

To put things into a historical perspective we have to remind ourselves that Khomeini may also have learned, two years before, how easy it was to intimidate Western governments. On April 23, 1987 the Dutch Broadcasting Corporation VARA was about to air a scene taken over from German television in which Ayatollah Khomeini was mocked.[14] The Dutch minister Hans van den Broek (1934–) called the anchorman of the program, Paul Witteman (1946–), and encouraged him *not* to broadcast that specific scene. During the program in a live telephone call the minister made a case for what might be called self-censorship, and the Broadcasting Corporation yielded to the advice of the minister, because otherwise the safety of Dutch citizens in Iran might not be guaranteed.

Two years later Ayatollah Khomeini made an even more intimidating move: threatening a British writer in Great Britain.

He called for a secretary and pronounced the following verdict (*fatwa*)[15] on Rushdie, his publisher, and his book:

---

[12]   Mill, *On Liberty*, p. 69.
[13]   See: Fraleigh, Douglas M. and Tuman, Joseph S., *Freedom of Speech: In the Marketplace of Ideas*, St. Martin's Press, New York 1997, p. 106 ff.
[14]   "Aufgewärmte Slips" [Heated Panties], *Der Spiegel*, no. 44, 27 October, 2007, p. 144.
[15]   See on fatwas: Mozaffari, Mehdi, *Fatwa: Violence and Discourtesy*, Aarhus University Press, Aarhus 1998.

In the name of Him, the Highest. There is only one God, to whom we shall return. I inform all zealous Muslims of the world that the author of the book entitled *The Satanic Verses* – which has been compiled, printed, and published in opposition to Islam, the Prophet, and the Qur'an – and all those involved in its publication who were aware of its content, are sentenced to death. I call on all zealous Muslims to execute them quickly, wherever they may be found, so that no one else will dare to insult the Muslim sanctities. God willing, whoever is killed on this path is a martyr.

In addition, anyone who has access to the author of this book, but does not possess the power to execute him, should report him to the people so that he may be punished for his actions. May peace and the mercy of God and His blessings be with you.[16]

Beneath the fatwa we find a name and a year. The name is: Ruhollah al-Musavi al-Khomeini. The year is: 1367. What strikes the modern reader in this encouragement of a "bribed assassination scheme" (Hitchens)[17] is that in the year 1989 CE such an action by an official religious and political leader was still possible.[18] I say "still possible," because it is reminiscent of similar declarations in the European context long ago. In 1570 Pope Pius V (1504–1572) issued the Bull *Regnans in excelsis* declaring the English queen Elizabeth I (1533–1603) illegitimate and her reign ripe for a takeover by Catholic insurgents.[19]

This papal bull is based on the idea of the superiority of papal over secular authority or of the Church over the State. The theoretical foundation of this approach is to be found in another bull issued by Boniface VIII (1235–1303): *Unam Sanctam* (1302).[20] *Unam Sanctam* lays down the following principles.

In the power of the Roman Church there are two swords, the temporal and the spiritual. The spiritual is to be wielded *by* the Church, the temporal

---

[16]   Quoted in: Pipes, Daniel, *The Rushdie Affair. The Novel, the Ayatollah, and the West*, second edition, Transaction Publishers, New Brunswick 2003, p. 27. For the British context see: Ruthven, Malise, *A Satanic Affair: Salman Rushdie and the Rage of Islam*, Chatto & Windus, London 1990, pp. 1–10.

[17]   Hitchens, Christopher, *god is not Great*, p. 28.

[18]   Baubérot, Jean, "Cultural Transfer and National Identity in French Laicity," in: *Diogenes*, 55 2008, pp. 17–25, p. 22: 1989 seems to be an important year: "The stakes generally changed in the 1980s, and especially in 1989, the year of the collapse of the Berlin Wall, the Ayatollah Khomeini's *fatwa* against Salman Rushdie and, in France, the first 'headscarf affair.'"

[19]   See on this: Petriburg, M., "The Excommunication of Queen Elizabeth," *The English Historical Review*, 7, no. 25 1892, pp. 81–88; Shires, Henry M., "The Conflict between Queen Elizabeth and Roman Catholicism," *Church History*, 16, no. 4 1947, pp. 221–233.

[20]   Preceded by the decree *Sicut universitatis conditor* (1198) by Innocent III in which he set out the principle of the subordination of the State to the Church. See on this: McGrath, Alister E., *Christianity's Dangerous Idea: The Protestant Revolution. A History from the Sixteenth Century to the Twenty-First*, SPCK, London 2007, p. 18.

for the Church. The former is in the hand of the priest, the latter is in the hand of kings and soldiers. The temporal power must be subject to the spiritual. So the spiritual power has to institute the secular power and to judge its "holiness." "Therefore," so the historian J.B. Bury (1861–1927) writes in his important work *History of the Papacy in the 19th Century* (1930), "if the secular power strays from the right way it will be judged by the spiritual power, whence if the highest spiritual power deviates from the right way it will be judged by God alone."[21]

The implication of this doctrine is clear. It implied that the secular power was entrusted to princes simply as servants of the Church. So when Elizabeth I deviated from the path of Rome, the Pope considered himself perfectly justified in inciting her subjects to throw off their queen. Needless to say, this doctrine can cause a lot of trouble if taken seriously. Much later the British philosopher T.D. Weldon (1896–1958) wrote: "One of the many troubles about Hitler was that he claimed to control Germans outside Germany, in other words he extended the definition of the German Community to cover people of German origin anywhere in the world and acted on this hypothesis."[22] That is true. But what is equally true is that this pretension also slumbers within the great religious traditions in various stages of their development. The pope in the sixteenth century had the same ambitions: he wanted to legislate for all Catholics all over the world, superseding local political leaders.[23]

From the perspective of a modern nation-state these pretensions by the pope, Ayatollah Khomeini, or any other religious leader, would be consid-

---

[21] Bury, J.B., *History of the Papacy in the 19th Century*, McMillan and Co. Ltd, London 1930, p. 139. At least this was the Church's interpretation. See also: Blackham, H.J., *Religion in a Modern Society*, Constable, London 1966, p. 33: "The question was whether, as in the theory of the emperor Henry IV, there were 'two swords,' one in the hands of the king who should be obeyed for God's sake, and this should be taught by the Church, the other in the hands of the Church which the king should protect from external enemies of Christ and compel his subjects to obey; or whether, as sealed and celebrated in the famous bull of Boniface VIII *Unam Sanctam* (1302), both swords had been given by God to the Church, which left the exercise of temporal power to princes but kept the right of control over it. This famous declaration at the height of Papal triumph was followed by a contest with the King of France and the exemption of the Gallican Church from *Unam Sanctam*."

[22] Weldon, T.D., *States and Morals: A Study in Political Conflicts*, John Murray, London 1946, p. 29.

[23] See on this: d'Holbach, Paul Henri Dietrich, Baron, *Le Christianisme Dévoilé ou Examen des Principes et des Effets de la Religion Chrétienne* [Christianity Unveiled or an Examination of the Principles and Effects of the Christian Religion], 1761, in: D'Holbach, *Premières Œuvres* [Early Works], Préface et notes Paulette Charbonnel, Éditions Sociales, Paris 1971, pp. 94–138, p. 105. D'Holbach writes that everywhere where religion (read: Christianity) gets a firm hold over the minds of the people and its rulers there arises the problem of the two powers: civil and religious. That same argument was also used by some of the founding fathers in America. See: Glenn, Gary D., and Stack, John, "Is American Democracy Safe for Catholicism?" *The Review of Politics*, 62, no. 1, Winter 2000, pp. 5–29, p. 5.

ered an outright violation of national sovereignty.[24] But the Catholic Church operated on a completely different worldview (at least before 1570). [25] Even in modern times this pretension has still not died out. T.S. Eliot (1888–1965) wrote in his *The Idea of a Christian Society* (1939): "There would always remain a dual allegiance, to the State and to the Church, to one's countrymen and to one's fellow-Christians everywhere, and the latter would always have the primacy. There would always be a tension; and this tension is essential to the idea of a Christian society, and is a distinguishing mark between a Christian and a pagan society."[26]

The Church acts on the basis of what it sees as universal jurisdiction. The result was that for centuries Roman Catholics were subject to disabilities in England. "They were not permitted, for instance, to sit in Parliament. In the seventeenth century they were regarded as a fifth column in the service of England's enemies, Spain and France. James II, a Catholic king, was deposed. Nor did opinion change after the Napoleonic Wars. England remained solidly Protestant."[27]

Actually, it is a worldview that is remarkably similar to the one that we meet in Khomeini's declaration that a British author who violated holy Islamic law by mocking the Prophet should be killed. This worldview completely overturns the modern system of international relations based on the sovereignty of the nation-state as we have known it since the Peace of Westphalia (1648).[28] As a perceptive commentator remarked about Khomeini's claim:

> His concept of the Islamic world order basically rejects the validity of the very notion of the territorial state which is the principal subject of the modern law of nations.[29]

---

[24]   See: *Charter of the United Nations,* article 2.4: "All Members shall refrain in their international relations from the threat or use of force against the territorial integrity or political independence of any state, or in any other manner inconsistent with the Purposes of the United Nations."

[25]   See for contemporary perspectives: Murphy, Francis X., "Vatican Politics: Structure and Function," *World Politics,* 26, no. 4 1974, pp. 542–559 and for Islam: Tibi, Bassam, *Political Islam, World Politics and Europe: Democratic Peace and Euro-Islam versus Global Jihad,* Routledge, London 2008.

[26]   Eliot, T.S., *The Idea of a Christian Society,* Faber and Faber, London 1939, p. 55.

[27]   Annan, Noel, *The Dons: Mentors, Eccentrics and Geniuses,* HarperCollins, London 2000 (1999), p. 45.

[28]   See on this: Philpott, Daniel, "The Challenge of September 11 to Secularism in International Relations," *World Politics,* 55 2002, pp. 66–95; Philpott, Daniel, "The Religious Roots of Modern International Relations," *World Politics,* 52 2000, pp. 206–245.

[29]   Ramazani, R.K., *Revolutionary Islam: Challenge and Response in the Middle East,* Johns Hopkins University Press, Baltimore 1988, pp. 24 and 25.

Khomeini's fatwa also reminds us of another conflict between the spiritual authority of the Church and secular authority. In 1633 the Catholic Inquisition issued a condemnation of the astronomer Galileo Galilei (1564–1642), sentencing him not to the stake, fortunately, but to house arrest and the abjuration of his "errors" and "heresies."[30]

Khomeini's edict on Rushdie was broadcast on the evening news, and to encourage the murder of the writer of the *Satanic Verses* an Iranian organization offered a one million dollar reward for his head.[31]

These outrageous acts occurred in the year 1367 of the Islamic Era, but, as the examples of Galileo (1633) and the Bulls *Regnans in excelsis* (1570) and *Unam Sanctam* (1302) make clear, they were also not uncommon in the history of Christianity between the fourteenth and sixteenth centuries. The "Phinehastic" device of simply killing people who do not subscribe to your own religious ideas (or letting them be killed, see Chapter 2, Biblical Terrorism) was much more common than in times when the state was based on exclusively secular law.

Another famous example is the burning at the stake of Giordano Bruno (born in 1548) in 1600 at the Campo dei Fiori in Rome.[32] Actually the Bull *Unam Sanctam,* introducing the dogma of the superiority of the spiritual to the temporal power dated from 1302 CE, which is quite close to 1367 (Islamic Era).

That brings us to the question: is there a "natural timetable" for religions to be purified of their more violent tendencies? Do they necessarily require hundreds of years to distance themselves from ideas and types of behavior such as those described above?

Sometimes this suggestion is ventilated by those who advocate "modesty" with regard to criticizing Islam or the Muslim world. Can we expect Muslims to skip some phases in the historical process, they ask us? Why hurry them if it took ages for the Western world to eradicate ecclesiastical intolerance? The *Index librorum prohibitorum* was only abolished in 1966.[33] The Inquisition in 1820.[34] Should we not give the Khomeinis of this world a little time to come to their senses?

---

[30] See Russell, Bertrand, *The Scientific Outlook*, Routledge, London 2001 (1931), p. 18.

[31] Pipes, *The Rushdie Affair*, p. 28.

[32] Kirchhoff, Jochen, *Giordano Bruno*, Rowohlt, Hamburg 2003 (1980); Rowland, Ingrid D., *Giordano Bruno: Philosopher/Heretic*, Farrar, Straus and Giroux, New York 2008.

[33] See: Putnam, George Haven, *The Censorship of the Church of Rome and its Influence upon the Production and Distribution of Literature: A Study of the History of the prohibitory and expurgatory indexes, together with some consideration of the Effects of Protestant Censorship and of censorship by the State*, 2 Vols., New York 1906–1907.

[34] See the introduction to: Tollebeek, Jo, *Writing the Inquisition in Europe and America: The Correspondence between Henry Charles Lea and Paul Fredericq (1888–1908)*, Koninklijke Academie van België, Brussel 2004.

Perhaps. Or perhaps not. Although the fact is not widely recognized, this point of view is heavily indebted to a metaphysical outlook. The name for this point of view is "historicism": the idea that we cannot pass over phases in history. This kind of "folk-Hegelianism" was made popular by the American political philosopher Francis Fukuyama (1952–) who in 1989 proclaimed "the End of History," a proclamation that is now generally considered to have been premature.[35] But premature or not, many people are still under the spell of this historicism when they tell us that for the Arabic world is it "too early" to expect liberal democracy.[36]

The consequences of this *prima facie* innocent "folk-Hegelianism" might also be hard to swallow. It would imply that we have to wait for a long time for freedom of speech to flourish in the Middle East, for instance. In the year 622 CE the "Hegira" or "flight" of Mohammed took place. Mohammed fled from Mecca to Medina as a result of the persecutions to which he was subjected. The Muslims date their time reckoning from that year. If it took the Catholic world 1,966 years to get rid of their fear of books, and 1,820 years to see that the Inquisition was not such a good idea after all,[37] and we allow Islamism or political Islam the same amount of time (and why should we not, would anything else not be a violation of the principle of equality?), then there would be violent suppression of heretics until the year 2442 (1820 + 622) and a list of forbidden books until the year 2788 (1966 + 622) in the Muslim world. Depressing as this idea may be, it seems to be the more or less inevitable conclusion that a once so optimistic-sounding writer like Fukuyama must come to.

Fukuyama Giving Up on the Arabic World

In 1989 Francis Fukuyama (1952–) proclaimed the spread of democracy and human rights, in short, modernization, in his widely read essay *The End of History*.[38] But in 2007 he wrote: "the problem of jihadist terrorism

---

[35]   Fukuyama, Francis, "The End of History?" *The National Interest*, no. 16, Summer 1989, pp. 3–18, elaborated in: Fukuyama, Francis, *The End of History and the Last Man*, The Free Press/Macmillan, New York 1992.

[36]   See also: Zakaria, Fareed, "The Islamic Exception," in: Fareed Zakaria, *The Future of Freedom: Illiberal Democracy at Home and Abroad*, W.W. Norton & Company, New York 2003, pp. 119–159.

[37]   It may be a bit simplistic to start the Catholic tradition of suppressing free speech with the beginning of our common era. Perhaps we should consider other data that mark the beginning of the Church's preoccupation with suppressing free speech, but I leave that to historians.

[38]   Fukuyama, Francis, "The End of History?" also in: Paul Schumaker, Dwight C. Kiel, Thomas W. Heilke, eds., *Ideological Voices. An Anthology in Modern Political Ideas*, The McGraw-Hill Companies, Inc., New York 1997, pp. 409–417.

will not be solved by bringing modernization and democracy to the Middle East. Modernization and democracy are good things in their own right, but in the Muslim world they are likely to increase, not dampen, the terror problem in the short run."[39]

The question is an old one, of course.[40] Basically, it is the question of whether democratic values are ripe for export. There have always been skeptics on this question, the most notorious being the late Samuel Huntington (1927–2008).[41] But there are many others besides him. For instance T.D. Weldon (1896–1958) writes: "To my mind it makes no sense to conclude that all men ought to be democratically governed if experience convinces me (as it does) that large groups of human beings are, for whatever reason, so made that they do not want a constitution of this kind and could not work it if they had it."[42]

That seems to me an unacceptable sort of resignation. We should be careful not to juxtapose a reified system of basic Western beliefs and values against another reified but incompatible system of equally basic Muslim beliefs and values. As Sadik J. Al-Azm (1934–) puts it:

> This means that such values as liberalism, secularism, democracy, human rights, religious toleration, freedom of expression, etc. are to be regarded as the West's deepest values, from which the contemporary Muslim World is permanently excluded on account of its own mostly deeply cherished values – theocracy, theonomy and theonomism, scripturalism, literalism, fundamentalism, communalism, totalitarianism, sexism, absolutism, and dogmatism – which are antithetical to the core to liberalism, secularism, democracy, and the rest.[43]

Let us consider what the consequences of Weldon's idea would be for the matter of free speech. The implications for free speech are clear: because it is an integral part of liberal democracy and modernization, rejecting modernization and democracy for the Middle East would also imply portraying the dispersion of freedom of speech as an impossible ideal (at least in the short term). And that brings us to a catch 22. The only way to *change* a situation is to have the opportunity to *criticize* a current state of affairs. If that opportunity is frustrated, there is no prospect of change.

---

[39]   Fukuyama, Francis, "A Question of Identity," *Weekend Australian*, February 3, 2007.
[40]   A similar analysis is to be found in: Wilson, James Q., "Islam and Freedom," *Commentary*, December 2004, pp. 23–28.
[41]   Huntington, Samuel P., *The Clash of Civilizations and the Remaking of World Order*, Simon and Schuster, New York 1996.
[42]   Weldon, T.D., *States and Morals: A Study in Political Values*, John Murray, London 1946, p. 17.
[43]   Al-Azm, Sadik J., "Time Out of Joint," *Boston Review: A Political and Literary Forum*, October/November 2004, pp. 1–8, p. 7.

It may be possible that we have to subscribe to Fukuyama's pessimistic diagnosis, but we should not do this lightly and we must be aware of the consequences of this "give-them-some-time argument."[44] In fact, it is a sort of fatalism. Using this argument implies that we not only condemn a considerable part of the world to backwardness, but – and this is even more serious – we also deny citizens in that part of the world the means to improve their condition, because every improvement in the world starts with criticism and free speech.

There is another element in the quote from Fukuyama that requires our attention. He writes about democracy and modernization *in the Muslim world*. And he suggests that we should not be too optimistic about prospects for a change in that context. But what does that mean for *our world*?

Does that mean that we have to learn to live with fatwas condemning writers to death in our part of the world? Is that simply part of the new dispensation that we are living under? If that were true, some parts of the world would not only be stifling their own development, but their mores would be dragging down the Western world as well. We are living in a globalized world. In earlier times we could perhaps say that this was a problem "in the Muslim world" that did not affect our situation. This no longer holds true. The reason is that *from their world* people like Ayatollah Khomeini send messages *right into our world*.

Another problem is that multicultural societies comprise ethnic and religious minorities who consider the words of a foreign spiritual leader to be – to say the least – something that competes with national law in the struggle for their loyalty.[45] So withdrawing troops from Afghanistan and Iraq is easy enough, but that does not solve the problems we are discussing here. Religious terrorists not only demand the withdrawal of troops from what they consider to be Islamic territory, they also want to change the democratic order in Western countries, as appears from the conviction of three terrorists in Denmark.

On November, 24, 2007 three militant Muslims were sentenced by a Danish court of law on the charge of preparing a terrorist attack.[46] Their

---

[44] See on this the critique of historicism by Hegel's rival Arthur Schopenhauer in: Schopenhauer, Arthur, "On History," in: *The World as Will and Representation*, Vol. II, Dover Publications, New York 1967 (1818), pp. 439–446.

[45] For the situation in the Netherlands see: General Intelligence and Security Service, *From Dawa to Jihad: The Various Threats from Radical Islam to the Democratic Legal Order*, AIVD, The Hague, December 2004. For the situation in Great Britain: Mirza, Munira, Senthilkumaran, Abi, and Ja'far, Zein, *Living Apart Together: British Muslims and the Paradox of Multiculturalism*, Policy Exchange, London 2007; Selbourne, David, *The Losing Battle with Islam*, Prometheus Books, Amherst, NY 2005; Gove, Michael, *Celsius 7/7*, Weidenfeld and Nicolson, London 2006; McRoy, Anthony, *From Rushdie to 7/7: The Radicalisation of Islam in Britain*, The Social Affairs Unit, London 2006.

[46] "Deense moslims cel in na beramen aanslag" [Danish Muslims Imprisoned after Plotting Attack], *NRC Handelsblad*, 24/25 November, 2007.

attack was presented as a protest against two phenomena: first, Denmark's military presence in Iraq, second, the publication of cartoons satirizing the Prophet in the Danish newspaper *Jyllands Posten* (for the sequence of events see Freedom of Speech and Philosophers on the Index below).[47]

The first point is repeatedly emphasized by people who want to create understanding for the terrorist cause, but we should also take cognizance of the second point: the intended terrorist attack was intended to be in retaliation for the publication of some cartoons in a newspaper. That newspaper was not in the hands of the government, but in the hands of private actors. That implies that, in a liberal democracy, it is very difficult for the government to negotiate with potential terrorists. The government of a dictatorship can promise everything because everything is in its power. A democratic government, though, cannot "give away" what is not theirs to give. And what is particularly non-negotiable in a democracy, is the set of limits to its own jurisdiction that the government has acknowledged. This set of limits is defined by the declaration of civil rights and freedoms enshrined in the national constitution or in treaties that are binding on the territory of the national state (i.e. by constitutionalism). Civil rights and freedoms limit the power of the state. So the last thing a democratic government can do is to give away those freedoms to people who want them abrogated (i.e. the terrorists). Yet that is exactly what some contemporary religious terrorists demand (and some democratic governments are inclined to give in to, as appears from the incident on the Dutch television in 1987).

John Stuart Mill wrote: "If all mankind minus one, were of one opinion, and only one person were of the contrary opinion, mankind would be no more justified in silencing that one person, than he, if he had the power, would be justified in silencing mankind."[48] The situation we are familiar with nowadays is that a few religious fanatics are trying to silence mankind, and they have been remarkably successful in that undertaking. In that sense the affair of the Danish cartoons is more relevant than the more or less random attacks by terrorists on the public transport systems in London and Madrid, or on symbols of capitalism like the Twin Towers. In the Danish cartoons affair and in the murder of Theo van Gogh (1957–2004) the terrorist attacks were directed at a principle that is held dear in democracies and that distinguishes them from dictatorships: the principle of free criticism, even when this annoys the defenders of the status quo. What we see happening now in contemporary democracies, *viz.* more limitations on free speech to protect the sensibilities of radical religious groups,[49] is *de facto* a concession to religious terrorism. It looks as if we are in a downward spiral:

---

[47] See on this: Klausen, Jytte, *The Cartoons that Shook the World*, Yale University Press, New Haven and London 2009.
[48] Mill, *On Liberty*, p. 20.
[49] See on this process: Appignanesi, Lisa, ed., *Free Expression is No Offence*, Penguin Books, London 2005.

the limits of free speech are not drawn by the state or the national community, but by religious groups prepared to use violence to substantiate their claims. And in this aim the terrorists have been fairly successful.[50]

I introduced this excursion on the fatwa on Salman Rushdie to make a point about free speech. Let us return now to the problem of free speech and its limitations.

The Limits of Free Speech

I believe that in Khomeini's fatwa on Rushdie we encounter the limits of free speech. Khomeini may say "I do not like Rushdie's book." He may say: "Do not buy Rushdie's book." As Salman Rushdie wrote in 2005: "Democracy is not a tea party where people sit around making polite conversation. In democracies people get extremely upset with each other. They argue vehemently against each other's position."[51] Rushdie also said that you "can be savagely rude" about what a person thinks, and so Khomeini may disagree vehemently with Rushdie. But he may not say: "Kill the writer of the book." That distinction is essential. In a democracy, says Rushdie, you can argue vehemently against each others positions, but you don't shoot.[52]

But now suppose someone else retorts: "Listen, this is a matter of free speech. Khomeini is free to say whatever he likes. You may not like what he says, but he is free to say it."

What ought the answer to be?

Undoubtedly that free speech is not a holy principle and has its limitations. The "clear and present danger test" that was developed in American legal thought in the wake of Mill's approach to free speech seems relevant here. Khomeini's fatwa creates a clear and present danger that the writer will be killed as a result of this pronouncement (which has not happened, fortunately, although Hitoshi Igarashi (1947–1991), the novel's Japanese translator, was stabbed to death in 1991 and Ettore Capriolo (1926–), its Italian translator, was seriously wounded).[53] This underlines the significance

---

[50]   See: Dershowitz, Alan, *Why Terrorism Works: Understanding the Threat, Responding to the Challenge*, Yale University Press, New Haven 2002; and Guiora, *Fundamentals of Counterterrorism*, p. 8 where he states that "in many cases, terrorism works."

[51]   Rushdie, Salman, "Do We Have to Fight the Battle for the Enlightenment all Over Again?" *The Independent*, 22 January, 2005.

[52]   Ibid.

[53]   See also: Ruthven, Malise, *A Satanic Affair: Salman Rushdie and the Rage of Islam*, Chatto & Windus, London 1990, p. 25: "At least twenty-one people were to die in the anti-Rushdie agitation, nineteen of them in the Indian subcontinent, two in Belgium."

of Khomeini's words that not only "the author of the book entitled *The Satanic Verses*" was "sentenced to death" but that this verdict also applied to "those involved in its publication who were aware of its content." A translator's job is far from harmless nowadays, at least with regard to certain books. This is particularly true if we realize that Rushdie was protected by the British authorities, whereas translators were more or less soft targets.

It is important that we see the difference between the "clear and present danger test" and other criteria for limiting free speech. The problem with Khomeini's fatwa is *not* that it shows no "respect" for a British novelist, nor that it fails to stimulate "dialogue." The problem is *not* that his words fissure society. These may be fashionable concepts nowadays, but they are unsuitable as criteria for restricting freedom of speech, although, judging from the frequency with which they are referred to, many people seem to think otherwise. Khomeini's fatwa is a problem, because it incites murder, that is, "physical harm" in Mill's terminology. And the possibility or likelihood of physical harm seems a good justification for limiting free speech. Or, in the words of Mill: "The only purpose for which power can be rightfully exercised over any member of a civilized community, against its will, is to prevent harm to others."[54] This also has implications for the limits on free speech:

> opinions lose their immunity, when the circumstances in which they are expressed are such as to constitute their expression a positive instigation to some mischievous act.[55]

This approach to free speech was further developed by Oliver Wendell Holmes (1809–1894) in *Schenck v. United States* (1919).[56] This was a case in which the defendants were accused of violating the Espionage Act. They had mailed circulars advising potential conscripts not to join the army. They were convicted for this and appealed. The Supreme Court, however, confirmed the verdict. According to Holmes, who wrote the opinion, the conviction did not violate the American Constitution because freedom of speech is not absolute. The most stringent protection of free speech would for instance not protect a man falsely shouting "fire" in the theater. The question is, said Holmes:

---

[54] Mill, *On Liberty*, p. 15.
[55] Ibid. p. 69.
[56] See on this: Friedman, Lawrence M., *American Law in the 20th Century*, Yale University Press, New Haven 2002, p. 142; Rabban, David M., "Clear and Present Danger Test," in: Kermit L. Hall, ed., *The Oxford Companion to The Supreme Court of The United States*, Oxford University Press, New York 1992, p. 158.

> Whether the words used are used in such circumstances and are of such a nature as to create a clear and present danger that they will bring about the substantive evils that Congress has a right to prevent.

In wartime it was a substantive evil that people should be discouraged from fulfilling their duty to do military service, so here the "clear and present danger test" led to a curtailment of the right to freedom of speech.

The subsequent development of the test, however, led to a further protection of free speech rather than to other criteria by which to assess its limits. That became clear in *Abrahams v. United States* (1919) where the defendants were accused of furthering the Bolshevik Revolution in the United States of America. They were convicted, also by a majority of the Supreme Court, but Holmes dissented because the pamphlets distributed by the defendants did not pose a threat to the security of the United States.[57] Holmes characterized the defendants as "poor and puny anonymities" and although he found their creed ignorant and immature they had their right to believe in it. Holmes ended his plea for free speech with a passionate espousal of the "free trade in ideas .... It is an experiment, as all life is an experiment."[58]

It is clear that limiting free speech on the basis of the "clear and present danger" clause is justified if, and only if, the form of words that is under scrutiny contains some instigation to harm others. So "Kill Rushdie" is not protected under the First Amendment of the American constitution nor should it be protected under the freedom of speech clauses in European human rights law. But it is perhaps worth considering the following – rather twisted – interpretation of the "clear and present danger" clause: "Any utterance that puts someone in danger, including the person who actually makes that utterance, ought not to be protected by legislation guaranteeing freedom of speech." In this – I repeat: twisted – interpretation *The Satanic Verses* would not be protected, because writing and publishing the book caused – in a world where there are terrorists around – a "clear and present danger" that the writer would get hurt.

The reason why I emphasize the possibility of such a twisted interpretation is because after the Rushdie affair, the Danish cartoons affair, and the murder of Theo van Gogh, many people flirted with an interpretation of that kind. In their view, a person who publishes books whose content is controversial puts himself or herself in danger. This leads them to ponder

---

[57]   Holmes had also, by reading Harold Laski's *Authority in the Modern State* (1919) and Locke's *Two Treatises on Government* (1689), two classic apologies for freedom of speech, changed his ideas somewhat with regard to free speech. See on this: Lewis, Anthony, *Make No Law: The Sullivan Case and the First Amendment*, Vintage Books, Random House, Inc., New York 1992, p. 81.

[58]   Quoted in Friedman, *American Law*, p. 143.

the question of whether a person who deliberately does this thereby forfeits the right to be protected by "free speech" legislation.

One only has to consider what the consequences of such an interpretation would be to realize its absurdity. It would mean that nothing could be said or published if there were people prepared to use violence against the writer. Martin Luther (1483–1546) could not have published his ideas because by doing so he ran the risk of becoming the victim of violence (in his case at the hands of the Vatican). Giordano Bruno (1548–1600) and Galileo Galilei (1564–1642) could also not have published their ideas for the same reason. In this interpretation the clear and present danger test would be transformed into an encouragement to threaten violence or actually commit violence. We therefore have to distinguish carefully between the above-mentioned interpretation and the classic Millian or Holmesian formulation.

For a long time Mill's criterion was dominant and it left a broad margin of freedom for the expression of ideas, including unpopular ones. Article 10 of the European Convention on Human Rights and Fundamental Freedoms formulates what is the core of free speech. "Everyone has the right to freedom of expression." In an important interpretation of this article the European Court in Strasbourg indicated in 1976 (in the Handyside case) that this "freedom of expression" should be construed as follows. It "is applicable not only to 'information' or 'ideas' that are favorably received or regarded as inoffensive or as a matter of indifference, but also to those that offend, shock or disturb the State or any sector of the population."[59]

These are important words. Freedom of speech, according to the European Court, also protects speech and writing that "offends, shocks or disturbs." And the parties that could be offended, shocked or disturbed are not only the state, but also "any sector of the population."

This is a radical judgment. I do not think it very likely that we would find such a radical affirmation of the principle of free speech being delivered at the beginning of the twenty-first century. Most politicians, confronted with violence perpetrated by fanatics, react in the following way: "Why should you allow people to 'hurt the feelings' of other people? Why be so divisive?"

These complaints are common enough. There are few defenders of "the classical conception of free speech," associated with great minds like John Stuart Mill,[60] W.K. Clifford,[61] T.H. Huxley,[62] Leslie Stephen[63] and other

---

[59] Janis and Bradley, *European Human Rights Law*, p. 165.
[60] Mill, *On Liberty.*
[61] Clifford, "The Ethics of Belief."
[62] Huxley, "Agnosticism and Christianity."
[63] Stephen, *Essays on Freethinking and Plainspeaking.*

Victorian freethinkers. That conception has been abandoned, giving way, so it seems, to what we might call a "multicultural conception of free speech." That multicultural conception pays lip service to the principle of free speech ("don't misunderstand me, free speech is an important ideal, but ..."), but at the same time draws a line around it at the point where some religious minority decides to complain that certain expressions are offensive to its religious feelings.

In the "clear and present danger test" of free speech (or freedom of speech only restricted by the risk of physical harm), we encounter echoes from a time that is apparently now behind us. For fear of a "Clash of Civilizations," the Western world increasingly backs down on what were once considered to be its greatest cultural achievements: human rights as codified in the Universal Declaration of Human Rights and other documents, the right to free expression in particular.

The question is whether this "new approach" to human rights, and freedom of speech in particular, is an improvement by comparison with the older, more robust conception of free speech or a deterioration. A.C. Grayling (1949–) has some doubts. On the question "Does religion deserve respect?" Grayling writes: "I argue that it deserves no more respect than any other viewpoint, and not as much as most."[64] Rushdie formulated a similar point of view:

> At Cambridge I was taught a laudable method of argument: you never personalize, but you have absolutely no respect for people's opinions. You are never rude to the person, but you can be savagely rude about what the person thinks. That seems to be a crucial distinction: people must be protected from discrimination by virtue of their race, but you cannot ring-fence their ideas. The moment you say that any idea system is sacred, whether it's a belief system or a secular ideology, the moment you declare a set of ideas to be immune from criticism, satire, derision, or contempt, freedom of thought becomes impossible.[65]

In order to judge whether this is a correct approach we have to delve into the justification for free speech.

The Deontological and Utilitarian Justifications for Free Speech

The justification for free speech is twofold: it takes an individual and a collective form.

---

[64]   Grayling, *Against all Gods*, p. 7.
[65]   Rushdie, "Do We Have to Fight the Battle for the Enlightenment all Over Again?"

The first (or individual) justification for free speech is that the human individual has an inalienable right to express his or her thoughts and feelings, even if others disagree. The free development of the human personality would be unduly frustrated if others could prescribe to me (or to you) what to think and what to say. If every expression that might cause offence could be suppressed by those who take offence, there would be hardly any room left to express our ideas at all. Put differently, there is a "human right to contradict," but no "human right not to be contradicted." There is a human right to criticize, not a human right not to be criticized.

Again, it was John Stuart Mill who gave us perhaps the most eloquent phrasing of this ideal. It is rooted in a conception of human nature, as we can gather from the third part of *On Liberty*. "Human nature is not a machine to be built after a model, and set to do exactly the work prescribed for it, but a tree, which requires to grow and develop itself on all sides, according to the tendency of the inward forces which make it a living thing."[66]

The third part of *On Liberty* is one long panegyric on individuality and non-conformism. A person with individuality of character expresses his own nature. The great mass of mankind has no character of its own. Society should encourage the individual to form his (and her)[67] own character. Mill advocates "strong natures."

In the early phases of human development individuality was always suppressed, Mill tells us. The individual was always subservient to the collective whole. This tendency was looming again in Mill's own time. "Society has now fairly got the better of individuality."[68] Mill feared "hostile and dreaded censorship."[69]

Calvinism in particular teaches us the wrong virtues. The greatest sin, according to Calvin (1509–1564), is "self-will." The complete opposite of the Calvinist mentality was "pagan self-assertion" as an ideal.[70] "There is a Greek ideal of self-development, which the Platonic and Christian ideal of self-government blends with, but does not supersede. It may be better to be a John Knox than an Alcibiades, but it is better to be a Pericles than

---

[66] Mill, *On Liberty*, p. 73.

[67] Mill was also a great advocate of women's rights. See: Mill, J.S., *The Subjection of Women*, 1869, in: J.S. Mill, *On Liberty with The Subjection of Women and Chapters on Socialism*, ed., Stefan Collini, Cambridge University Press, Cambridge 2004 (1989), pp. 117–219.

[68] Mill, *On Liberty*, p. 75. See for the background of Mill's ideas on individuality: Megill, Allan D., "J.S. Mill's Religion of Humanity and the Second Justification for the Writing of On Liberty," *The Journal of Politics*, 34, no. 2 1972, pp. 612–629.

[69] Mill, *On Liberty*, p. 75.

[70] See on this: Carr, Robert, "The Religious Thought of John Stuart Mill: A Study in Reluctant Scepticism," *Journal of the History of Ideas*, 23, no. 4 1962, pp. 475–495.

either; nor would a Pericles, if we had one in these days, be without anything good which belonged to John Knox."[71]

Genius can only flourish on fertile soil. "Genius can only breathe freely in an *atmosphere* of freedom. Persons of genius are, *ex vi termini,* more individual than any other people – less capable, consequently, of fitting themselves, without hurtful compression, into any of the small number of moulds which society provides in order to save its members the trouble of forming their own character."[72]

The second justification of free speech is to be sought in the fruitful consequences of the development of science, culture and also religion (being a part of culture). Whereas the first justification of free speech could be called "deontological," the second justification is "utilitarian." Both dimensions of the defense of free speech are to be found in Mill's classic work.

All new ideas were, in a way, won over hurt feelings, offended personalities, shattered worldviews – all new ideas generated resistance and opposition. The idea that a person by the name of Jesus Christ was the Son of God was once a blasphemous idea. One author has remarked: "Muslims deny Jesus' divinity, Jews deny Muslim and Christian revelation. If religions find each other's beliefs blasphemous and blaspheme each other, how can a statute of blasphemy be framed that will protect all religions equally?"[73] A good point indeed. And besides that: cultural, scientific and social development would come to a complete standstill if we were to make those "hurt feelings" our guiding principle.

One of the problems with the discussion on free speech that has been conducted of late in many European countries is that too much stress is placed on the *right to free speech*. Consequently the idea took hold that those advocating free speech were motivated by some sort of narcissism, gratifying their own urge to hurt others' feelings. This is unfortunate for there is not only a "right" to free speech and a "right" to criticize religions and worldviews but a certain "duty" as well. This is a duty based on the idea that we all have to make our contribution to the quest for truth and the furtherance of human culture.

That duty was underscored by an author who is now almost forgotten perhaps, but who has important things to say about such a topical subject as the moral and intellectual foundations of free speech. William Kingdon Clifford (1845–1879) was a great mathematician, philosopher, and polyhistor who died of tuberculosis when only 34 years of age.

---

[71]   Mill, *On Liberty*, p. 77.
[72]   Ibid., p. 80.
[73]   Lawton, quoted in: Cohn, Haim H., "The Law of Religious Dissidents: A Comparative Historical Survey," *Israel Law Review*, 34, no. 1 2001, pp. 39–100, p. 93.

Clifford on the Duty to Critique

Clifford's contribution to the debate on free speech was an essay published under the title *The Ethics of Belief* (1877).[74] He unfolded an argument about free speech that, in my view, can best be presented as the *duty to criticize*. What were his views?

First: a belief is never something that is only relevant to the believer himself.[75] "No man's belief is in any case a private matter which concerns himself alone," Clifford writes.[76] Our lives are intimately connected with one another. What is believed by one, in particular when it concerns a deep conviction, has its bearings on the other. Clifford assures us: "Our words, our phrases, our forms and processes and modes of thought, are common property, fashioned and perfected from ages to ages."[77] The totality of our ideas is a kind of heritage that is passed on from generation to generation, from age to age: "an heirloom which every succeeding generation inherits as a precious deposit and a sacred trust to be handed on to the next one, not unchanged but enlarged and purified, with some clear marks of its proper handiwork."[78] Our own ideas and convictions are part of that heritage. So this is collective property. It is the property of mankind. "Belief, that sacred faculty which prompts the decisions of our will, and knits into harmonious working all the compacted energies or our being, is ours not for ourselves, but for humanity."[79]

So far this could also have been written by Edmund Burke (1729–1797) or by Catholic authors[80] who underscore that ideas are intimately connected with each other. But then Clifford continues his line of reasoning in a

---

[74] Clifford, W.K., "The Ethics of Belief," 1877, in: W.K. Clifford, *The Ethics of Belief and Other Essays*, Introduction by Timothy J. Madigan, Prometheus Books, Amherst, NY 1999, pp. 70–96.

[75] This is also to be found in John Stuart Mill, but in his case hidden in convoluted sentences such as the following: "On religion in particular the time appears to have come, when it is the duty of all who being qualified in point of knowledge, have on mature consideration satisfied themselves that the current opinions are not only false but hurtful to make their dissent known." (Mill, John Stuart, *Autobiography of John Stuart Mill*. Published from the original manuscript in the Columbia University Library, with a preface by John Jacob Coss, Columbia University Press, New York 1924 (1873), p. 31).

[76] Clifford, "The Ethics of Belief," p. 73.

[77] Ibid.

[78] Ibid., p. 74.

[79] Ibid.

[80] For instance Lamennais in his first stage of development. See: Lamennais, Félicité de, *Défense de l'essai sur l'indifférence en matière de religion* [Defense of the Essay on Indifference in the Matter of Religion], Deuxième édition, Chez Méquignon fils aîné Libraire, Chez Périsse Frères, Libraires, Paris/Lyon 1821.

completely different direction than Burke would have done or Catholic authors are accustomed to do. He emphasizes that, being the guardians of the collective heritage, we have the responsibility to develop it further – and that implies, to subject this heritage to criticism. Testing the collective heritage of mankind, analyzing it, criticizing it – that is our moral duty. It is an "awful privilege" and an "awful responsibility" that we all work together to build a world that we and posterity would like to live in.[81] Accepting this heritage simply on the basis of "belief" or "authority" is a grave abandonment of our duty to criticize. And then Clifford presents the phrase that, in slightly different formulations, reappears in his work time and again and for which he is still known.[82] What he rejects is: "to believe on insufficient evidence, or to nourish belief by suppressing doubt and avoiding investigation."[83] In short: "It is wrong always, everywhere, and for anyone, to believe anything upon insufficient evidence."[84] This puts a heavy burden on the shoulders of the individual. Clifford emphasizes that this duty to criticize has significance not only for our leaders. "It is not only the leader of men, statesman, philosopher, or poet, that owes this bounden duty to mankind."[85] Everyone, including the pensioner sitting in his garden and enjoying the benefits of old age, "may help to kill or keep alive the fatal superstitions which clog the race."[86] Every housewife can bequeath to her children a belief that either keeps society together or will tear society apart. Nobody can disown this responsibility to question the common beliefs of mankind. We have to guard ourselves against the uncritical forms of belief that are "as from a pestilence, which may shortly master our own body and then spread to the rest of the town."[87] Every time we accept something on the basis of insufficient evidence we debilitate our self-control.

Suppose there is someone who, from his youth onwards, has believed something and simply goes on believing this as a matter of custom instead of on conscious reflection. He has not read books on the subject of his conviction. Views that contradict his ideas he has refused to take into consideration. People who consider the matter from a different angle he has avoided in order not to be forced to reconsider his opinions. What should we think of this man? Clifford answers: "The life of that man is one long sin against mankind."[88]

---

[81]   Clifford, "The Ethics of Belief," p. 74.
[82]   Although mainly because his views were criticized by William James in: James, William, "The Will to Believe," 1897, in: William James, *Writings 1878–1899*, The Library of America 1984, pp. 457–479.
[83]   Clifford, "The Ethics of Belief," p. 74.
[84]   Ibid., p. 77.
[85]   Ibid., p. 75.
[86]   Ibid.
[87]   Ibid., p. 76.
[88]   Ibid., p. 77.

It requires no elaborate argumentation to show that the attitude advocated by Clifford not only has relevance for the development of science, but also for the development of culture and of religion. Is not religion involved in the same process of development as science? In 1409 the Synod of Canterbury issued a ban on the English translation of the Bible.[89] In 1525 William Tyndale's (1494–1536) translation of the New Testament was banned. In 1535 Tyndale was arrested on the orders of King Henry VIII and jailed in the castle of Vilvoorde outside Brussels. Afterwards he was tried for heresy and burned at the stake, together with his Bible.[90] Also, in 1624 the Bible translation by Luther (1483–1546) was banned by the pope.

Interestingly for Ayatollah Khomeini, the Qur'an was also banned. In 1542 the Qur'an was confiscated by the Protestant authorities of Basel and the ban was only lifted after an intervention by Martin Luther.

Against the background of John Stuart Mill's *On Liberty* and W.K. Clifford's *The Ethics of Belief* these are all very unfortunate events. It is especially in the *combination* of Mill's and Clifford's perspective that we find an important legitimation for the freedom to think freely, criticize freely, and write freely.

Freedom of Speech and Philosophers on the Index

Although freedom of speech is the real motor behind all change and all cultural, political and scientific improvement, we always have to remind ourselves that freedom of speech was once a highly contested principle (and still is in many parts of the world). Countless books now considered as classic and indispensable works of the Western tradition[91] were for a long time (1559–1966) suppressed by the Catholic Church and placed on the *Index auctorum et librorum probihitorum*. This list was instigated by Pope Paul IV (1476–1559) in 1559.[92] On the Index we find works by Calvin, Erasmus, Boccaccio, Dante, and many others.

Much more well-known, of course, are the scientific works that were included on the list of papal censure. Galileo's *Dialogues on the Two World*

---

[89] See on these examples: Appignanesi, *Free Expression is No Offence*, p. 247 ff.

[90] Fishburn, Matthew, *Burning Books*, Palgrave, MacMillan, Basingstoke 2008, p. 7; McGrath, *Christianity's Dangerous Idea*, p. 214 ff.; see on the context: Zagorin, Perez, *How the Idea of Religious Toleration Came to the West*, Princeton University Press, Princeton 2003, pp. 68–69.

[91] Roughly the works associated with the core curriculum or with a liberal education. See: Schall, James, S.J., *A Student's Guide to Liberal Learning*, ISI Books, Wilmington, Delaware 2000; Henrie, Mark C., *A Student's Guide to the Core Curriculum*, ISI Books, Wilmington, Delaware 2001 (2000).

[92] MacCulloch, Diarmaid, *Reformation: Europe's House Divided, 1490–1700*, Penguin Books, London 2004 (2003), p. 406.

Systems (1632) was notoriously struck with a papal condemnation by Pope Urbanus VIII (1568–1644) in 1633.

On the list of prohibited books we also find a considerable part of the philosophical canon of the Western tradition. The *Méditations Metaphysiques* by Descartes (1673), the *Essais* by Montaigne (1676), the *Tractatus Theologico-Politicus* by Spinoza (1670), the *Essay Concerning Human Understanding* by John Locke (1734), the French *Encylopédie* by Diderot and D'Alembert (1753), the *Pensées* of Pascal (1789), the *Rights of Man* by Paine (1792), the Italian translation of Kant's *Critique of Pure Reason* (1827). And to these examples several more could be added.

It is important to exemplify what kind of prohibition is at work here. It is a prohibition issued by a spiritual organization with great political power. The secular power of the Catholic Church in the twenty-first century is a mere shadow of what it was in 1600 or 1633, of course, when scholars like Giordano Bruno were burned or scientists like Galileo Galilei had to fear for their lives.[93]

Would that imply that freethought only has historical significance? Unfortunately not. Religious intolerance is still a major factor in contemporary society and one can even say that an upsurge of it has manifested itself in recent years.[94] Criticizing the Islamic God or his Prophet entails serious security risks nowadays, as we know from the verdict of Ayatollah Khomeini referred to above. But there are other examples. In 1959 the Egyptian novelist Naguib Mahfouz (1911–2006), who received the Nobel Prize for his book *The Children of Gebelawi,* had to deal with a fatwa for apostasy, issued by Omar Abdul Rahman (1938–).[95] Ever since that happened, Mahfouz' works have been banned in the Middle East. In 1994 he was stabbed in the neck by extremists.

The most well-known case of religious extremism among the general public is, of course, the Ayatollah Khomeini's fatwa on Salman Rushdie. At the moment Rushdie seems to be able to move about a little bit more freely, but if we consider that Mahfouz was attacked thirty five years after his fatwa, this relative freedom of movement for Rushdie can hardly be seen as reassuring.

More or less the same happened to the female Bengali writer and human rights activist Taslima Nasreen (1962–), who got a fatwa in 1993 for her

---

[93]   Shea, William R., and Artigas, Mariano, *Galileo in Rome. The Rise and Fall of a Troublesome Genius*, Oxford University Press, Oxford 2003.
[94]   See: Jahangir, Asma, *Promotion and Protection of all Human Rights, Civil, Political, Economic, Social and Cultural Rights, including the Right to Development*, Report by the Special Rapporteur on Freedom of Religion or Belief, A/HRC/6/5, 20 July 2007.
[95]   See Najjar, Fauzi M., "Islamic Fundamentalism and the Intellectuals: The Case of Naguib Mahfouz," *British Journal of Middle Eastern Studies*, 25, no. 1 1998, pp. 139–168; Darwish, *Cruel and Unusual*, p. 105; Sorman, *Les Enfants de Rifaa*, p. 38.

novel *Shame*. She fled to Sweden, and has since lived in exile. The latest news is that the mayor of Paris, Bertrand Delanoë (1950–), has given her sanctuary. "You have been chased from your house because you dared to raise your voice against inhuman fanaticism," the mayor said. "Feel at home in Paris, a city where people are born free, live as equals and nobody is denounced for his opinion."[96]

These examples are derived from the Muslim world because there the cases are rampant. We could add the Danish cartoons affair, the row over Pope Benedict XVI's (1927–) lecture in Regensburg on 12 September 2006,[97] and many other examples. But they are not restricted to Islam and Middle Eastern culture. Barely one month after the brutal killing of Theo van Gogh (1957–2004) by a home-grown Dutch Islamist terrorist, on November 2, 2004, in England all performances of the play "Behzti" were cancelled. On December 19, 2004, after the theatre in Birmingham was assaulted by an angry mob of Sikhs, the playwright, Gurpreet Kaur Bhatti, a Sikh herself, went into hiding.[98] The reason why the Sikhs felt offended was that Bhatti's comedy aimed to stimulate a discussion on homosexuality, rape, and suicide within the Sikh community. The result was not discussion, but intimidation. The theatre was stormed, all performances were cancelled and that was the end of it.[99]

A similar row occurred around *Jerry Springer: The Opera* (2003), a British musical by Stewart Lee (1968–) and Richard Thomas (1964–) that was severely criticized for its irreverent handling of Judeo-Christian themes. Its main character was cast to resemble the real Jerry Springer (1944–), the host of one of the most popular TV talk shows in America (since 1991). In *Jerry Springer: The Opera* we see a parade of misfits, sexual deviants, and crooks, mixed with religious themes. Controversy arose when the BBC decided to broadcast the production on television (BBC Two) in 2005. The BBC got 55,000 complaints; Christian groups organized street protests and announced that they were going to bring blasphemy charges.

---

[96]   "Paris bietet Taslima Nasreen Asyl an" [Paris offers Taslima Nasreen Asylum], *St. Galler Tagblatt*, January 5, 2009; "Parijs neemt schrijfster Taslima Nasreen in bescherming" [Paris Takes Writer Taslima Nasreen under its Protection], *De Standaard*, January 9, 2009.

[97]   Lemm, Robert, *Paus Benedictus XVI en de opkomst van Eurabia* [Pope Benedict XVI and the Rise of Eurabia], Uitgeverij Aspekt, Soesterberg 2007; Welzel, Knut, ed., *Die Religionen und die Vernunft: Die Debatte um die Regensburger Vorlesung des Papstes* [Religions and Reason: The Debate about the Pope's Regensburg Lecture], Herder, Freiburg im Breisgau 2007.

[98]   Bhatti, Gurpreet Kaur, *Behzti (Dishonour)*, First Performed at Birmingham Repertory Theatre, Birmingham on December 19, 2004.

[99]   See: Pyke, Nicholas, "Sikhs Storm Theatre in Attempt to Halt Play," *Independent on Sunday*, December 19, 2004. For commentary: Dromgoole, Dominic, "Comment: Drama's Role is to Challenge Religion," *The Guardian*, 20 December 2004; Alibhai-Brown, Yasmin, "No Religion Is immune from Criticism," *The Independent*, December 20, 2004.

Obviously, resorts to violence are not restricted to the Muslim world. Violence is also perpetrated by fanatical Sikhs and, we could add, by Christians. Paul Hill (1954–2003), a Presbyterian, murdered an abortion physician and his assistants. Hill conveyed "the inner joy and peace" that had flooded his soul after he had cast off "the state's tyranny."[100] He declared that he was completely at peace with his incarceration and also with his execution, which took place in 2003. He appeared to accept Christian martyrdom.

What seems to distinguish the violence perpetrated by Sikhs and Muslims from that carried out by Christians is that Islamist violence enjoys a wider popularity among Muslim youth (especially in European countries)[101] and is directed against freedom of speech as an important principle of democratic culture.

The Danish cartoons affair and its aftermath constitute an underestimated sequence of events in this respect. On 30 September, 2005 a Danish newspaper, *Jyllands Posten,* published caricatures or cartoons of the prophet Mohammed. This caused a worldwide controversy lasting for some months, with reverberations continuing up to the present day. On October 20, Islamic ambassadors complained to the Danish Prime Minister, Anders Fogh Rasmussen (1953–). On November 8, Pakistan condemned the pictures. On November 10 some Nordic newspapers decided to publish the cartoons too. On January 26, 2006 Saudi-Arabia withdrew its ambassadors from Denmark. On January, 20 armed men broke into the office of the EU on the Gaza Strip and demanded an apology. This shows close similarities with the Rushdie affair. Indignation seemed to leap from one country to the other, as if carried by some contagious virus.[102] On January 31 *Jyllands Posten* presented something of an apology.

The reaction of the West was the usual political correctness about "dialogue" and "respect," while it was, so Bawer (1956–) contends, "political correctness that has gotten Europe into its current mess,"[103] but there were also voices that vindicated free speech and open debate – including the

---

[100]   Quoted in: Selengut, Charles, *Sacred Fury,* p. 37.

[101]   See: Mekhennet, Souad, Sautter, Claudia, and Hanfeld, Michael, *Die Kinder des Dschihad: Die neue Generation des islamistischen Terrors in Europa* [The Children of Jihad: The New Generation of Islamist Terror in Europe], Piper, Munich 2008.

[102]   The idea of religious indignation as a "virus" that can spread from person to person, from society to society, is developed in the work of: Dennett, Daniel C., *Breaking the Spell. Religion as a Natural Phenomenon,* Allen Lane, Penguin Books, New York 2006 and long before by Baron d'Holbach in *La Contagion Sacrée* [Sacred Contagion] (1768), in: D'Holbach, Paul Henri Dietrich, Baron, *Premières Œuvres,* Éditions Sociales, Paris 1971, pp. 139–175.

[103]   Bawer, Bruce, *While Europe Slept: How Radical Islam Is Destroying the West From Within,* Doubleday, New York 2006, p. 6. See also: Minow, Martha, "Tolerance in an Age of Terror," *Southern California Interdisciplinary Law Journal,* 16 2007, pp. 453–494, p. 479.

freedom to make cartoons on religious themes. In the name of the liberty of the press several European newspapers republished the cartoons.

Apart from this, there was also the economic side to the affair. In many Muslim countries there was a call to boycott Danish products. On February 3, 4, and 5, 2006 several embassies and consulates in Indonesia, Jordan, and Lebanon were stormed and wrecked. On January 1, 2010 Kurt Westergaard (1935–), one of the Danish cartoonists, was attacked in his house by a Somali intruder armed with an axe and a knife yelling "revenge." Westergaard survived the attack.

Intolerance not Restricted to Islam

What should be the state and society's reaction to these assaults on the principle of freedom of speech by religiously motivated zealots? Should religious criticism be more restrained? Should we have more respect for the religious feelings of minorities? Has the Western world gone too far in freely discussing religious ideas? Is the Enlightenment project untenable perhaps, or should it be slowed down? Or should we advocate a new Enlightenment?[104]

If we take some of the commentaries paraphrased above seriously, the question is rather whether we are allowed to speak about the matter *at all*. Many people feel that we should not address religious terrorism (at least not as "religious") because this could lead to stigmatization of the religious minorities from which the radicals are recruited. And perhaps even this formulation is contested because, as many people say, someone like Van Gogh's murderer does not simply "emerge" from the Muslim community. The analogy with the Presbyterians may be illustrative. Paul Hill (1954– 2003) was a Presbyterian cleric. But should we be suspicious of the Presbyterian brand of Christianity merely because one of its adherents committed a murder? The analogy with the Catholics in the sixteenth century may be illustrative as well. We cannot say that because Balthasar Gérard (1557–1584) murdered William of Orange (1533–1584) we must suspect all Catholics of murderous intentions.[105] And the fact that Yigal Amir shot the Israeli president Yitzak Rabin in 1995 does not make all Jews potential

---

[104] See: Amis, Martin, *The Second Plane: September 11: Terror and Boredom*, Alfred A. Knopf, New York and Toronto 2008, p. 13, and p. 91. See also: Rushdie, Salman, "Do We Have to Fight the Battle for the Enlightenment Over Again?" and Kurtz, Paul, *The Courage to Become: The Virtues of Humanism*, Praeger, Westport, CT 1997, p. 11: "The Enlightenment project still needs to be fulfilled: to create a better world based on reason and the ideals of freedom and progress."

[105] See on this: Jardine, Lisa, *The Awful End of Prince William the Silent. The First Assassination of a Head of State with a Handgun*, HarperCollins, London 2005.

murderers. So why should we suspect all Muslims? Is that not a selective sort of interest? Is it, under those circumstances, not much more sensible to prevent "stigmatization" and "polarization" and leave the matter alone?

This may seem an attractive approach, but presupposed in the rationality of this course of action is the notion that radicalization and religious terrorism will fade away if we do not pay attention to them. Another presupposition is that the most pertinent problems we have to deal with are racism, xenophobia, and the unjust targeting of ethnic and religious minorities. Undeniably, these are important problems, but are they the only or even the most important problems we have to deal with? Is not terrorism, the threat to the nation-state's security and the intimidation of writers, cartoonists, and social activists a much greater burden?[106]

Those who answer the last question in the affirmative will say: "We simply cannot afford to be ostriches and keep our head in the sand; we have to face the problems we are dealing with openly and think about strategies to overcome them." One of the most important elements of that strategy would be to candidly acknowledge that there is a religious element involved in religious terrorism. It is easily said that the terrorist problem has "nothing to do with religion," but can we really believe that e.g. Ayatollah Khomeini's fatwa has "nothing to do with Islam"? Or is it in any way convincing to say "Khomeini is not a real Muslim?" You can *say* that, of course, but isn't that the same as saying that the Pope has nothing to do with Catholicism?[107]

Francis Fukuyama (1952–), one of the most prominent authors to have underestimated the significance of the religious upsurge in the contemporary world, writes: "It makes no more sense to see today's radical Islamism as the inevitable outgrowth of Islam than to see fascism as the culmination of centuries of European Christianity."[108]

This is a convoluted sentence containing a mixture of fact and fiction. Fukuyama may be right in stating that radical Islam is not an *inevitable* outgrowth of Islam. This is correct because stressing such inevitability would commit us to a theory of historical determinism. It would mean that

[106] See on this: Phares, Walid, *Future Jihad: Terrorist Strategies against the West*, Palgrave, Macmillan, New York 2005; Phares, Walid, *The War of Ideas: Jihadism against Democracy*, Palgrave, MacMillan, New York 2007.
[107] There is a long discussion, as one might expect, on the question of whether movements such as Al Qaeda should be considered exclusively "criminal," or "political" or also as "religious." I side with those authors who see this as religio-political. See on this: Gelvin, James L., "Al-Qaeda and Anarchism: A Historian's Reply to Terrorology," *Terrorism and Political Violence*, 20, no. 4 2008, pp. 563–581; Kelsay, John, "Al-Qaida as a Muslim (Religio-Political) Movement. Remarks on James L. Gelvin's 'Al-Qaeda and Anarchism: A Historian's Reply to Terrology,' " *Terrorism and Political Violence*, 20, no. 4 2008, pp. 601–605.
[108] Fukuyama, Francis, "A question of identity." On the difference between Islam and Islamism see: Gresh, Alain, *L'Islam, la République et le Monde*, p. 90.

every step in the development of a doctrine is necessitated by previous steps. It would imply that the whole subsequent history of humanity lay hidden in the womb of Eve or that – to take an example from the history of metaphysics – that inherent in the essence of "Caesar" was that he would one day cross the Rubicon. Radical Islam is not the only variety of Islam that can be developed, as is clear from the fact that there are many Islamic sects, such as the Sufis, with completely different ideas from those of the jihadists.[109]

Nevertheless, recognizing this does *not* mean that radical Islam and Islam have no relationship whatsoever. It does *not* mean that political Islam, radical Islam, Islamism, or Jihadism cannot find moorings in Islamic doctrine, as Fukuyama seems hastily to suppose (and many other commentators do as well).[110] Fukuyama is inclined to this unwarranted assumption on the basis of reading the books by the French Islam-scholar Olivier Roy (1949–),[111] so it seems, but his ideas are open to challenge as will be clear once we take cognizance of the work of Bassam Tibi (1944–), for example.[112]

That implies that Fukuyama's comparison with fascism as the culmination of European Christianity and political Islam as related to Islam is not well chosen. Again: portraying fascism as the "culmination" of European Christianity would be a bit strange, but that does not exclude the fact that scholars have seriously pondered the relationship between Christianity and one element of fascism in the broad sense: anti-Semitism.[113]

I say "in the broad sense," because the term "fascism" can refer to the Italian totalitarian movement of Benito Mussolini (fascism in the restricted sense), but also to a more general idea comprising National Socialism as well. In that last (broad) sense the term fascism was used in the 1970s. And in this broad sense anti-Semitism is part of the fascist mind.

Now, where does anti-Semitism come from? Does it have religious roots in the Christian tradition in which the Jews were discriminated against

---

[109] See: Demant, Peter R., *Islam and Islamism. The Dilemma of the Muslim World*, Praeger, Westport, CT 2006; Ismail, Salwa, *Rethinking Islamist Politics: Culture, the State and Islamism*, I.B. Tauris, New York 2006.

[110] E.g. Tony Blair. See his: Blair, Tony, "A Battle for Global Values," *Foreign Affairs*, 86, no. 1 2007, pp. 79–90.

[111] See for the ideas of Roy: Roy, Olivier, *Globalised Islam: The Search for a New Ummah*, C. Hurst & Co., London 2004; Roy, Oliver, *The Failure of Political Islam*, Translated by Carel Volk, Harvard University Press, Harvard 1996.

[112] See for instance: Tibi, Bassam, "Islamic Law/Shari'a, Human Rights, Universal Morality and International Relations," *Human Rights Quarterly*, 16 1994, pp. 277–299; Tibi, Bassam, *Im Schatten Allahs. Der Islam und die Menschenrechte* [In Allah's Shadow. Islam and Human Rights], Ullstein, Düsseldorf 2003; Arjomand, Said Amir, *The Turban and the Crown: The Islamic Revolution in Iran*, Oxford University Press, New York 1988.

[113] See: Poliakov, Léon, *The Aryan Myth: A History of Racist and Nationalist Ideas in Europe*, New American Library, New York 1974 (1971).

because they were regarded as the killers of Christ?[114] This has been, and still is, an object for historical research.

Giniewski v. France

The question of whether that kind of research should be allowed was the focus of a verdict by the European Court of Human Rights in Strasbourg in *Giniewski v. France* (2006).

On January 4, 1994 the Paris newspaper *Le Quotidien* published an article by an Austrian historian named Paul Giniewski (1926–). The title of the article was "The Obscurity of Error." The article contained an analysis of the papal encyclical *Veritatis Splendor* ("The Splendor of Truth" 1993). In his article Giniewski contended that "many Christians have recognized that scriptural anti-Judaism and the doctrine of 'fulfillment' of the Old Covenant in the New led to anti-Semitism and prepared the ground in which the idea and implementation of Auschwitz took seed."

This analysis was contested by an organization with the name (and this name is revealing in itself): *Alliance générale contre le racisme et pour le respect de l'identité française et chrétienne* [General Alliance against Racism and for Respect of the French and Christian Identity]. This organization, we can safely assume, is one that tries to defend the French identity. French identity is apparently sought in (or considered to be synonymous with) Christianity. The organization also seeks to conduct its defense by judicial means, because it brought proceedings against the newspaper and against the author of the article. This was done on the charge that the article by Giniewski contained racially defamatory statements about the Christian community. Domestic courts convicted Giniewski, but the European Court of Human Rights in Strasbourg did not. The Court ruled unanimously that, by his conviction on this charge, Giniewski's freedom of expression had been unduly violated.

In its motivation the Court indicated that it did not think that Giniewski's words amounted to accusing Christians and Catholics in general of being responsible for the Nazi massacres. And therefore Christians were not victims of defamation on account of their religious beliefs. The Court also affirmed that Giniewski had tried to develop an argument about a specific doctrine and its possible links with the Holocaust. Doing this could be considered as a contribution to an ongoing debate. And "it is an integral part of freedom of expression to seek historical truth." Besides, Giniewski's article did not incite hatred or disrespect, nor did it cast doubt in any way on clearly established historical facts.

[114]   Cohn-Sherbok, Dan, *Anti-Semitism*, Sutton Publishing, Phoenix Mill 2002.

Not everything the Court states in its motivation is equally impressive, but the outcome of the case surely is. If every religious community could file suit when its beliefs are criticized, religions would be completely immunized against criticism. Also the construction that religious criticism amounts to a kind of "racism" is – although clever – far from convincing. This kind of criticism has nothing to do with "race."[115] All scientific views, and likewise all worldviews, including religious ones, should be subject to criticism (see what was said by Clifford in an earlier section of this chapter, Clifford on the Duty to Critique). It is therefore somewhat strange that the Court seems to indict casting doubt on "clearly established historical facts." Why should we not challenge "clearly established historical facts"?[116] Is not casting doubt on "clearly established facts" what makes a great historian? And if those facts are so well established, why can they not take care of themselves? Do those facts have to be protected by legal means? "I am an established fact and want to remain an established fact, so please don't contradict me!" Besides, what is "clearly established" in one period may be contested in another. In Chapter 1, I presented Bertrand Russell's "Liberal Decalogue." His fifth "commandment" was: "Have no respect for the authority of others, for there are always contrary authorities to be found." His seventh: "Do not fear to be eccentric in opinion, for every opinion now accepted was once eccentric." The European Court of Human Rights seems to have incorporated part of the spirit of Russell's Liberal Decalogue but not all of it. Had the Court done so, it would have realized that scientific progress is nothing if not the continuous challenging of established facts and hypotheses, as W.K. Clifford and Karl Popper (1902–1994) have advocated.[117] This is no different for a discipline like historical science than for the natural sciences. Books by the British historian A.J.P. Taylor (1906–1990), for instance, were not well-known for their respect of well-established historical facts. Of Taylor's *Origins of the Second World War* (1961) Stefan Collini (1947–) writes: "The book, with its emphasis on the accidental nature of the events leading up to war in September 1939 and its apparent refusal to regard Hitler as anything more than one partly incompetent statesman among others, provoked a storm of criticism."[118] It

---

[115] See: Ternisien, Xavier, *État et Religions* [State and Religions], Odile Jacob, Paris 2007, p. 132.

[116] In relation to denying the holocaust this issue is treated in: Shermer, Michael, and Grobman, Alex, *Denying History: Who Says the Holocaust Never Happened and Why Do They Say It?*, University of California Press, Berkeley 2000.

[117] In: Popper, "Science: conjecture and refutations." For Clifford, see his "The Ethics of Belief."

[118] Collini, Stefan, *Absent Minds: Intellectuals in Britain*, Oxford University Press, Oxford 2006, p. 381. See also: Taylor, A.J.P., *The Origins of the Second World War*, Penguin, London 1991 (1961); Taylor, A.J.P., *The First World War: An Illustrated History*, Penguin Books, Harmondsworth 1978 (1967).

is only when this culture of freedom is maintained (and even encouraged, as it is by Bertrand Russell, see Chapter 1) that critical books about religious movements and institutions can be published.[119]

In the same way as this is possible in the case of Christianity,[120] it should be possible to do research on the roots of violence, in particular of terrorist violence, in political Islam or Islamism. And is the politico-religious ideology of Islamism completely separated from Islam as a religion?[121] That may be the politically correct attitude, but this is not likely. It cannot come as a surprise that some scholars reject this thesis as unfounded. However intricate or difficult these relationships may be, we should not, therefore, refrain from studying them – but we perhaps ought to stop proclaiming that these things "have nothing to do with each other."

Freethought under Fire

Here I want to close my exposition of the ideals of freethought. Freethought has been characterized by two things; *first,* the conviction that religions do not have an exclusively positive nature; *second,* the principle of free speech that freethinkers favor. In the combination of those two ideas we find the specific character of freethought.

In what follows, I want to address some of the criticism that has been leveled at freethought and assess whether – and to what extent – that criticism is justified.

Criticism of freethought used to be directed at its first pillar: the contention that religion has its dark side. The second element (its predilection for free speech) used to be more popular. But that seems to have changed.

In the 1960s and 1970s many people seemed inclined to think that freedom of speech was vitally important. Freedom of speech was not only recognized as a fundamental civil right in almost all constitutions all over the world and in human rights treaties, but also held in high esteem by the intellectual and political elite in liberal democracies.

---

[119]   E.g. about the Catholic Church. See: Verhofstadt, Dirk, *Pius XII en de vernietiging van de Joden* [Pius XII and the Destruction of the Jews], Houtekiet/Atlas, Antwerp 2008. See on unpopular books in general: Karolides, Nicholas J., Bald, Margaret, and Sova, Dawn B., *100 Banned Books: Censorship Histories of World Literature*, Checkmark Books, New York 1999; Fishburn, Matthew, *Burning Books*, Palgrave, MacMillan, Basingstoke 2008.

[120]   Lewy even writes: "it is generally recognized that Nazism's ferocious assault upon European Jewry took place in a climate of opinion conditioned for such an outrage by centuries of Christian hostility to the Jewish religion and people." See: Lewy, Guenter, "If God is Dead, Everything is Permitted?," Transaction Publishers, New Brunswick 2008, p. 65.

[121]   See on this: Podhoretz, Norman, *World War IV: The Long Struggle Against Islamofascism,* Doubleday, New York 2007 and, on the similarities between Khomeinism and fascism, Taheri, Amir, *The Persian Night: Iran under the Khomeinist Revolution*, Encounter Books, New York 2009, pp. 76–105.

Nowadays, freedom of speech seems much less popular than it used to be. A common reaction we hear is this: "Why be so crude? Why be so divisive? Why offend people in their most sacred beliefs?" Or someone will say: "Oh, listen, don't misunderstand me, I am in favor of free speech, but ...." And subsequently he will tell you that freedom of speech is accompanied by "responsibilities." When asked what those "responsibilities" are people are usually less eager to tell you. But, if pressed, they will say that you should not "insult" people.[122] When asked if this means that we are not to publish cartoons, plays, novels, and even operas that some people claim to be insulted by, the adherent of the new speech codes usually responds with evasion and the contention that this is not what he means. But what *does* he mean exactly?

There also seems an enormous proliferation of what I would like to call sympathy for people who claim to have been offended in their deepest religious beliefs.

How to explain this? Have people become weaker and more vulnerable in their deepest beliefs? Do they feel more insecure? Have they grown less tolerant toward other people than they were in earlier times? Another remarkable thing is the spectacular growth of a new discourse regarding religion and free speech that seems *prima facie* innocuous or even fruitful. It refers to concepts such as "respect" and "dialogue." In the end, however, it turns out to be suppressive of free speech and, what I am inclined to call, *real* dialogue. Those pious demands for "dialogue" are usually voiced only to silence unpopular ideas.

This new discourse is not only a break with the 1960s and 1970s but also a change from ideas held in previous centuries. In the time of Luther, Spinoza, Galileo, or Voltaire people did not complain because they were "offended" or "insulted" by the ideas these men put forward.[123] New ideas were suppressed, to be sure, and even more brutally than nowadays, but not because people said they felt "offended." The Inquisition was not "insulted" by the heretics, atheists, and secularists they brought to the stake. Where does this contemporary preoccupation with being "offended" and "insulted" come from? Why do people feel victimized if contradicted? What is the origin of those frequent calls for "respect" and "dialogue," as if there were people who advocated "disrespect" or would favor stopping the dialogue? Let me give the following imaginary example of a dialogue.

- I think that Jesus is the Son of God.
- Sorry, I don't believe that.
- You don't believe that? Why are you insulting me? Why are you so disrespectful?

---

[122] See on this: Neu, *Sticks and Stones: The Philosophy of Insults.*
[123] See: Ruffini, Francesco, *Religious Liberty*, translated by J. Parker Heyes, Williams and Norgate, London 1912, p. 342 ff.

- – I am not; I honor you as a human being by disagreeing with your contentions. Do the same with me: honor me by contradicting my statements. Argue with me, I would love that. And please, criticize my spiritual mentors. I am an adherent of John Stuart Mill and Bertrand Russell. You do not like them, fine, but provide me the reasons why you disagree with them and I will take notice of your criticism. Let's have a fruitful conversation; let's enter into *real* dialogue. Dialogue means taking each other's opinions seriously, does it not?
- – Sorry, this is senseless. As long as you continue to shout and trample on my holiest convictions any dialogue is fruitless.

Do I exaggerate? A little perhaps, but not much. Much contemporary dialogue on sensitive religious topics develops along these lines. My point is that people like Salman Rushdie, Gurpreet Kaur Bhatti, Ayaan Hirsi, and Taslima Nasreen *do engage in dialogue*. The problem is that, because the content of their ideas is not appreciated by fanatics, their work is decried as "disrespectful."[124] This is an unfortunate situation and the tactics of the intolerant should be seen for what they are: intolerant. Philosopher A.C. Grayling writes:

> Those who claim to be 'hurt' or 'offended' by the criticisms or ridicule of people who do not share their views, yet who seek to silence others by law or by threats of violence, are trebly in the wrong: they undermine the central and fundamental value of free speech, without which no other civil liberties are possible; they claim, on no justifiable ground, a right to special status and special treatment on the sole ground that they have chosen to believe a set of propositions; and they demand that people who do not accept their beliefs and practices should treat these latter in ways that implicitly accept their holder's evaluation of them.[125]

Another criticism (the second point) that is launched against freethinkers and other advocates of free speech is that they take an "absolute" stance on freedom of speech. For them free speech knows no boundaries. Freethinkers are free speech junkies of some kind.[126]

I do not think this criticism is justified. We have indicated that John Stuart Mill and other protagonists of free speech usually acknowledge limits to the free flow of ideas in the form of the "clear and present danger test." If there is a danger that certain expressions increase the risk of physical

---

[124] Ignatieff, Michael, "Respect and the Rules of the Road," in: Lisa Appignanesi, ed., *Free Expression is No Offence*, Penguin Books, London 2005, pp. 127–136, p. 128: "The hard part is how to reconcile freedom of expression with respect."
[125] Grayling, A.C., *Against all Gods*, p. 19.
[126] See on why this is not true: Jacoby, Susan, "A First Amendment Junkie," in: Sylvan Barnet and Hugo Bedau, eds., *Current Issues and Enduring Questions. Methods and Models of Argument*, Bedford Books of St. Martin's Press, Boston 1990, pp. 8–13.

harm to others, we should acknowledge a limit to the freedom of speech. An absolute right to free speech is defended by nobody, so it seems.[127]

There are people, though, who go a very long way in defending free speech. One of those people was US Supreme Court Justice Hugo Black (1886–1971). Black wrote: "My view is, without deviation, without exception, without any ifs, buts, or whereases, that freedom of speech means that government shall not do anything to people, or, in the words of the Magna Charta, move against people, either for the views they have or the views they express or the words they speak or write."[128] Black did not believe that there was a "halfway ground for protecting freedom of speech and press."[129] He called the principle of free speech "the lifeblood" of every representative democracy. But Black's position was not representative of the general position. Many people favor a more limited conception of free speech and they will qualify a proscription like the one issued by Philip II of Spain (1527–1598) against William of Orange (1533–1584) as not protected by freedom of speech.[130] Nor will they consider Khomeini's fatwa on Rushdie as within the ambit of freedom of expression.

People Are Not Being Insulted for Having a Religion

Let me summarize. Freethinkers are not (1) motivated by the wish to offend people, nor do they (2) take an absolute stance on free speech. That should be clear by now. A third misunderstanding that must be cleared up has to do with the supposed ambition of freethinkers to insult other people *on account of what they believe*. This misunderstanding is voiced by the politician and scholar Michael Ignatieff (1947–). Ignatieff writes: "Since millions of people identify themselves by their religious faith, it is as wrong to insult a person for their religion, as it is to insult them for their race."[131]

Those kinds of commentaries are rampant nowadays. This is how Jack Straw (1946–), Secretary of State for Justice in the UK, commented in a reaction to the Danish cartoons: "There is freedom of speech, we all respect that, but there is not any obligation to insult or be gratuitously inflammatory." He continued with: "I believe that the republication of these cartoons has been unnecessary, it has been insensitive, it has been disrespectful and it has been wrong."[132]

[127]   See: Lewis, Anthony, *Make No Law, The Sullivan Case and the First Amendment*, Vintage Books, Random House, Inc., New York 1992.
[128]   Black, Hugo LaFayette, *A Constitutional Faith*, Alfred Knopf, New York 1969, p. 45.
[129]   Ibid., p. 47.
[130]   Jardine, Lisa, *The Awful End of Prince William the Silent*.
[131]   Ignatieff, "Respect and the Rules of the Road," p. 129.
[132]   Quoted in: Phillips, *Londonistan*, p. 17.

What can be wrong with such seemingly innocuous remarks as those made by Ignatieff and Jack Straw? More than we might think. Let us focus on what Ignatieff writes.

Michael Ignatieff is an important scholar and politician. He was a former BBC commentator and Harvard professor and is now a member of the Canadian Parliament. He rose to prominence by analyses of the war in Yugoslavia, and Christopher Catherwood (1955–) calls Ignatieff's book *Blood and Belonging* (1993) "an excellent account" of the new kind of savage nationalism that re-emerged in the post-1989 world.[133] Ignatieff has one problem, though: he does not understand religion. He was the most prominent among the "politically correct commentators" who disliked the idea that the war in Yugoslavia was really about religion. As Catherwood points out (following Michael Sells in his book *The Bridge Betrayed: Religion and Genocide in Bosnia*) the only real differences among the Serbs, Croats, and Bosnians are in fact religious, since they are in all other respects the same.[134] So the term *ethnic cleansing* is in fact incorrect. It is *religious cleansing,* "since religious differences alone determined whether or not someone was murdered in the death camps, such as the infamous one that the Serbs established at Moerska, which gained international notoriety when television journalists discovered it in 1992."[135]

Yet Ignatieff writes: "Since millions of people identify themselves by their religious faith, it is as wrong to insult a person for their religion, as it is to insult them for their race."[136] I have already said that in a literal sense this is right: it is impolite or wrong to deliberately insult a person for no other reason than personal gratification (whether it is more impolite or wrong to insult a person for his religion than for his ancestral background, sexual orientation, or taste in music, I will pass over without comment here). But the hidden meaning in sentences like this is that we are not allowed to criticize religions, because once we do this we can be accused of "insulting" the believer. So when we analyze the violent passages in Holy Scripture and warn that these can ignite violence we are accused of "insulting" believers for what they believe. This hampers all objective and candid research into the religious roots of violence. Books with titles such as *The Just War and*

---

[133]   Catherwood, Christopher, *Making War in the Name of God*, Citadel Press, Kensington Publishing Corp., New York 2007, p. 149; Ignatieff, Michael, *Blood and Belonging: Journeys into the New Nationalism*, BBC Books, London 1993. See also: Ignatieff, Michael, *Empire Lite: Nation-building in Bosnia, Kosovo and Afghanistan*, Vintage, London 2003; Ignatieff, Michael, *Virtual War: Kosovo and Beyond*, Chatto & Windus, London 2000; Ignatieff, Michael, *The Warrior's Honour: Ethnic War and the Modern Conscience*, Chatto & Windus, London 1998.
[134]   Sells, Michael A., *The Bridge Betrayed: Religion and Genocide in Bosnia*, University of California Press, Berkeley, CA 1998.
[135]   Catherwood, *Making War in the Name of God*, p. 149.
[136]   Ignatieff, "Respect and the Rules of the Road," p. 129.

Jihad: Violence in Judaism, Christianity and Islam (2006)[137] are insulting. Great philosophers and scientists like Nietzsche, Spinoza, and Sigmund Freud, who see religion as a source of violence, could be accused of spewing out insulting commentaries. The upshot of all this would be the reinstatement of blasphemy laws on the basis of political correctness. Usually this is done not under the banner of blasphemy laws, but under laws that criminalize "defamation of religion."

Scholars like John Esposito (1940–) and Michael Ignatieff do not seem to be bothered about the consequences of their political correctness because they know (or think they know) that religion cannot be the cause of violence. People who think religions have a violent core are simply wrong, so what is all the fuss about? This conviction is not based on scholarly research that they have done, because they have not done any empirical research on the subject. It is their *starting point,* and in giving vent to admonitions to others they also inhibit research by serious colleagues who have different ideas. This is unfortunate and unjustified.

But there is something else that is conspicuous, because the situation is even more complicated than described above. Is it not strange that, although Ignatieff underestimates the role of religion in his explanation of the conflict in the Balkan, he at the same time proclaims that "millions of people" identify themselves by their religious faith?

Think about this: identify themselves by their religious faith. If that is true (as I think it is), would that not imply that religion could be a potent factor in explaining behavior? And would this not also necessitate inquiring into the religious causes of violent behavior? In other words: should we not give free inquiry free rein? Or is Ignatieff perhaps dimly aware that religion plays a much greater role than he is prepared to acknowledge officially? Could it be the case that, subconsciously, he is worried about the role that religion plays because he does not know how to deal with this problem? And if this speculation makes sense, is Ignatieff right perhaps? Is he one of those people who warn that we cannot "declare war" on 1.3 billion Muslims and is this part of his motivation in turning a blind eye to religion as a factor in this conflict?[138] And is the approach of what I would like to call "strategic ignorance" likely to have beneficial effects?

Or is Ignatieff right that there are a great many people who indeed insult others for their religion nowadays? Do we have a problem, perhaps, with our rough commentators, our cartoonists, our playwrights?

His remark presupposes that *there are* people who insult other people *for their religion.* But who would do such a silly and malicious thing? Do

---

[137] Hoffmann, Joseph R., ed., *The Just War and Jihad: Violence in Judaism, Christianity, and Islam,* Prometheus Books, Amherst, NY 2006.

[138] A similar position we find in: Esposito, John L., and Mogahed, Dalia, *Who Speaks for Islam? What a Billion Muslims Really Think,* Gallup Press, New York 2007.

those people exist at all? Can Ignatieff provide us with names of those nasty characters? Did, for instance, Voltaire "insult" people for their religion? Or Friedrich Nietzsche? Are those the thinkers he has in mind? Probably not. When Voltaire signed his letters with *Écrasez l'Infâme* he was surely not motivated by an ambition to insult the Catholic Church.[139] He was convinced that the Catholic Church had certain ideas that were pernicious, and he thought the Church and its leaders should be held responsible for those ideas and be criticized. Nietzsche also had no ambition to "insult" people when he made his "mad man" proclaim the "Death of God," although this was undoubtedly a passage in the *Gay Science* (1882) that worried many of his contemporaries.[140] Nor was it the ambition of Galileo Galilei to "insult" his fellow Catholics "for their religion." The aim of Galileo was to publish a scientific thesis. This he considered to be so important that he took hurt feelings for granted.

And what about the new freethinkers? Did Salman Rushdie set out to insult people for having a religion? Or Taslima Nasreen? Or Gurpreet Kaur Bhatti? That would be a grotesque contention.

Now, certainly, there must be *some* people whose sole ambition is to insult other people because of their religion, because otherwise that remark by Ignatieff would be pointless. Would Richard Dawkins qualify? Or Christopher Hitchens? Or perhaps Theo van Gogh, because if his murderer was prepared to spend the rest of his life in prison, his victim must have said something terribly wrong, must he not?

I do not think so. What Richard Dawkins wants, is to free people from a "delusion." His book, *The God Delusion*,[141] is in the tradition of Sigmund Freud who also considered religion to be an illusion.[142] And when Christopher Hitchens claims to know that *god is not great* he is motivated by the same wish to free his fellow-men from some dangerous ideas.[143]

The most difficult case I have to make is perhaps that of Theo van Gogh (1957–2004). That has to do with the fact that van Gogh was indeed very proficient in insulting people, apparently for no other reason than that insulting them gave him pleasure.[144] Yet I do not think that even van Gogh would qualify for the role that someone like Ignatieff might have in mind

---

[139] See on this: Herrick, Jim, "Voltaire: 'Écrasez l'Infâme,'" in: Jim Herrick, *Against the Faith. Essays on Deists, Skeptics, and Atheists*, Prometheus Books, Amherst, NY 1985, pp. 56–71.

[140] Nietzsche, Friedrich, *The Gay Science: With a Prelude in Rhymes and an Appendix in Songs*, translated by Walter Kaufman, Vintage, New York 1974.

[141] Dawkins, *The God Delusion*.

[142] Freud, *The Future of an Illusion*.

[143] Hitchens, *god is not Great*.

[144] See: Gogh, Theo van, *Allah weet het beter* [Allah knows better], Xtra Producties, Amsterdam 2003.

for him. Not even van Gogh insulted people *for no other reason than that those people had a religion.* The only problem is that in the last phase of his brutally interrupted life he was focused on what he considered to be a very serious threat for the future of Europe: the growth of a fundamentalist variety of a particular world religion.[145] He was sincere in this and he saw some things that other people neglected or deliberately chose not to see (including the Dutch government, which underestimated the danger that proved to be fatal to van Gogh himself). As A.C. Grayling notes: the debate about religion has become an acerbic one "and worse: some contributors to it have their say with bombs."[146]

So the culprit talked about everywhere, the man or woman (many of them may be women, by the way) who deliberately insults other people on account of their beliefs, is a terribly elusive figure. Nevertheless, he or she is high on the wanted list. There is a great urge in the Western world to hunt down the imp of mischief who has no other aim in life than to cause trouble by insulting others "for the sake of their religion." Once this figure has been identified, we can get rid of a serious problem, of course: the problem of the religious terrorists in our midst. If we can identify those people who, purely for personal gratification, senselessly insult other people, and, by doing so, provoke violent behavior in true believers, then the solution to the problem is simple. We address those who cause offence by their cartoons, columns, films, and other means of expression and tell them that their behavior is irresponsible. We tell them that it endangers social cohesion. It is pointless. They should restrain themselves from pursuing their seemingly innocuous but in reality extremely dangerous hobby, and social peace will be secured.

If it were all that simple, we would not have to make difficult calculations weighing the significance of free speech in the balance with the spiritual harm done to believers. And because we are prone to deceive ourselves that it really is that simple, we are ready to invent the culprit even if he does not exist, as Voltaire was prepared to do with God.

I think this whole approach is mistaken. All the controversial cases presented in this chapter were *not meant as insults.* The writer Gurpreet Kaur Bhatti, who had to go into hiding after her play was cancelled and was threatened with death by indignant Sikhs, said of the incident: "I certainly did not write *Behzti* to offend."[147] The same applies to the controversial *The Satanic Verses* by Salman Rushdie. What the writer aimed to do was to *write a novel.* And in this novel things are said that some people might

---

[145]   Van Gogh detected the same process as: Bawer, Bruce, *While Europe Slept. How Radical Islam Is Destroying the West From Within,* Doubleday, New York 2006.
[146]   Grayling, *Against all Gods,* p. 9.
[147]   Bhatti, Gurpreet Kaur, "A Letter," in: Lisa Appignanesi, ed., *Free Expression is No Offence,* Penguin Books, London 2005, pp. 27–32, p. 28.

consider offensive. Sixteen years after publication Rushdie himself tried to set the matter straight and wrote: "Must it really still be explained, sixteen and a half years after the publication of this novel, that the prophet in the books is not called Muhammad, the religion is not called Islam, the city in which the action occurs is not called Mecca, that the whole sequence takes place inside the dreams of a man who is losing his mind, and that this is what we call fiction?"[148] The problem seems to be that many people, and certainly not only Muslims, concluded that the *motives* of the writer must have been extravagant on account of the *extravagant reactions* that the novel provoked. So they tell him: "You should have foreseen these reactions." People seem to think: "These reactions are so extreme; the writer himself must have extreme ideas." Where there's smoke, there must be fire. Rushdie's fellow-writer Roald Dahl (1916–1990) was one of those commentators. Not long after the publication of *The Satanic Verses* he wrote about Rushdie:

> Clearly he has profound knowledge of the Muslim religion and its people, and he must have been totally aware of the deep and violent feelings his book would stir up among devout Muslims. In other words he knew exactly what he was doing and he cannot plead otherwise. This kind of sensationalism does indeed get an indifferent book on the top of the best-seller list ... but to my mind it is a cheap way of doing this.[149]

This reaction seems to me to be the rock bottom that we can come to in the history of protest against religious terrorism. Dahl makes Rushdie himself responsible for the atrocious acts perpetrated against his person. In 1993, after having lived for four years under a death sentence, Rushdie gave us an insight into what was oppressing him most. Everywhere the Rushdie affair was seen as being about freedom of speech and terrorism. But in England it was seen as a case of a man who wanted to be saved from the trouble he had gotten himself into. "To know this is to carry a wound that does not heal. It takes away my strength. I do not know if anyone cares that it does, but it does."[150] Of the contested passages in *The Satanic Verses* Malise Ruthven (1942–) writes: "by a preposterous form of retribution, Rushdie has been given a life sentence for writing them."[151]

This is the first thing to be said about Rushdie, Bhatti, and other writers who have been accused of being insulting or divisive. It was not their aim

---

[148]   Rushdie, Salman, "Coming After Us," in: Lisa Appignanesi, ed., *Free Expression is No Offence*, Penguin Books, London 2005, pp. 21–29, p. 25.

[149]   *The Times*, 28 February 1989. See also: Pipes, *The Rushdie Affair*, p. 70.

[150]   Rushdie, Salman, "A 4-year Death Sentence," *The New York Times*, February 7, 1993.

[151]   Ruthven, *A Satanic Affair*, p. 28.

to insult or to offend. Insult or offence is, to a considerable extent, in the eye of the beholder.

What should we conclude from this? My point is that we should carefully distinguish between two dimensions of the concept of an "insult" or "insulting": (1) an objectified dimension, (2) the motive.

The (first) objectified dimension refers to the feelings of the person offended. He (or she) has the feeling of being insulted. The second dimension refers to the attitude of the person who made the remark deemed to be insulting. He *deliberately aimed* to be insulting. What appears to be common practice nowadays, is that the second dimension (the intention of insulting) is simply deduced from the first (an experienced insult). Someone *feels* offended, so there was someone *deliberately aiming* to give offence.

Implicitly it is also often supposed that there must be a kind of proportionality. If the person who was offended claims to be *very hurt* then the offender must have been *very deliberate* and *very malicious* in voicing his senseless criticism.

Unwittingly, Ignatieff contributes to this common mistake.

Racism without Race

But there is something else. By his remark that "it is as wrong to insult a person for their religion, as it is to insult them for their race,"[152] Ignatieff feeds another misunderstanding. He identifies a critical remark about "religion" with a critical remark on "race." This insinuation is even more dangerous than the first because, for obvious reasons, the incriminating effect on people who supposedly criticize others for their race is enormous. The logical conclusion of this view is that writers who criticize someone's religion are no better than "racists." And who wants to be a racist? No decent person can afford to be called a "racist," so the effect of this fatal insinuation is to silence all criticism of religion by decent people.

For the apologists of religion this is a fortunate outcome, of course, because in their view criticism of religion is wrong and serves no social or moral purpose whatsoever. But for people who advocate the progressive amendment of opinions and ideas, including religious ideas, stimulated by critique (the freethinkers), this outcome is nothing less than disastrous. It would inhibit all religious and cultural development. Of "truth" John Milton (1608–1674) wrote in *Areopagitica: A Speech for the Liberty of Unlicensed Printing to the Parliament of England* (1644): "let her and falsehood grapple." Only in a "free and open encounter" can truth flourish.

---

[152] Ignatieff, "Respect and the Rules of the Road," p. 129.

The Reformation, the Enlightenment, and Romanticism – many cultural movements start with criticism, including criticism of religion.[153] If, under the mantle of "decency," "respect," "dialogue," "pragmatism," and other elements from the lexicon of political correctness, it were possible to dispose of religious criticism, the social costs would be enormous. It is not without justification that the Dutch analytical philosopher René Marres quotes the political theorist Meindert Fennema (1946–) calling this concept of racism without race "dangerous nonsense."[154] The reason is clear: religious beliefs are based on a choice; race or ethnic background is not. For the moral, religious, and political choices people make they should be open to criticism.

Yet this point of view is controversial nowadays. On March, 26, 2009 the Human Rights Council of the United Nations adopted a non-binding resolution on what is called "the defamation of religion."[155] The HRC can make resolutions on matters that, according to the HRC, can be seen as "human rights abuses." It also makes recommendations to the General Assembly. The resolution on "defamation of religion" was proposed by Pakistan and backed by the Organization of the Islamic Conference. The resolution defines any intellectual or moral criticism of religion as a human rights violation. According to the resolution, since 9/11 the world has seen an "intensification of the overall campaign of defamation of religions and incitement to religious hatred in general." The resolution expresses concern that "extremist organizations and groups" seek to create and perpetuate "stereotypes about certain religions." The resolution wants to make an end of all that. It wants governments to ensure that religious symbols "are fully respected and protected."

The whole tenor of the resolution is deeply misguided and a violation of the human rights tradition as interpreted so far. The central misconception, on which this resolution is based, is that beliefs, opinions, and symbols should not be "defamed." From a legal and also a moral point of view this is a highly dubious contention to make. Only human individuals can be "defamed," but ideas, worldviews, religions, scientific theories can be (and

---

[153] See on the Hegelian Left who initiated a systematic criticism of religion: Löwith, Karl, *From Hegel to Nietzsche: The Revolution in Nineteenth-Century Thought*, translated by David E. Green, Constable, London 1964.

[154] See on this: Marres, René, *De verdediging van het vrije woord: de kwestie Wilders en de demonisering van het debat* [The Defense of Free Speech: The Wilders Question and the Demonizing of Debate], Uitgeverij Aspect, Soesterberg 2008, p. 155; Fennema, Meindert, "Noot bij de uitspraak van het Gerechtshof te Amsterdam van 21 januari 2009 waarin het strafvervolging van Geert Wilders beveelt" [Note on the Pronouncement by the Court in Amsterdam of 21 January, 2009 Ordering the Prosecution of Geert Wilders], *Strafblad*, 7, no. 19 June 2009, pp. 198–208.

[155] See on this: Ibn Warraq and Michael Weiss, "Inhuman Rights," *City Journal*, 19, no. 2 2009, pp. 1–6.

should be) freely criticized. Whether those criticisms are "stereotypical," "convincing," "necessary," and "justified" is for the participants in the debate to decide, but there should be no endorsement of censorship. And that is basically what this resolution entails.

Fortunately, international reaction was swift and condemnatory. The outgoing UN High Commissioner for Human Rights, Louise Arbour (1947–) of Canada, said: "It is very concerning in a Council which should be ... the guardian of freedom of expression, to see constraints or taboos, or subjects that become taboo for discussion."[156]

Social Criticism not Identical with the Urge to Provoke

That brings me to a fourth and last point of criticism against freethought. This final point is a variant of the third, but it has a slightly different dimension and therefore I want to treat it separately. It is that freethinkers are not sincere critics, but are motivated by the sole aim of being provocative. They may not be motivated solely by a wish to *insult* other people, but freethinkers voice their criticism in such a way that they know (or may suppose) that it will call forth a tumultuous reaction.

Those who follow this line of reasoning may claim that religious criticism is not the problem; it is the *way in which* this criticism is voiced. This is an old controversy. Hypatia Bradlaugh Bonner (1858–1943) wrote:

> The history of the common law of blasphemy, even as inadequately outlined in these pages, shows that it varies with the temper of the age in which it is administered and the Judge who has to administer it. Lord Hale, in 1676, said it was the *opinion* which was criminal; so did Mr. Justice North in 1883. Lord Coleridge said it was not the opinion; it was the *manner* in which it was expressed.[157]

An important case in this regard is that of the Danish cartoonists who drew pictures of Mohammed. The cartoonists (or the newspaper that published the cartoons) surely expected tumult to arise, did they not? A possible claim that the row was unexpected and unintended would not be credible. Was provocation here not the precise *aim* of the publication?

This indictment has been voiced by many people, including the Dutch Princess Mabel of Orange (1968–). In an interview she confided that she considered it inappropriate to publish cartoons simply "to teach the Muslims

---

[156] Arbour quoted in Ibn Warraq and Weiss, Ibid.
[157] Bradlaugh Bonner, Hypatia, *Penalties upon Opinion: Some Records of the Laws of Heresy and Blasphemy*, third edition, revised and enlarged by F.W. Read, Watts & Co., London 1934, p. 138.

a lesson." She continued: "the intention is very important" and "deliberately publishing something simply to insult, hurt, and humiliate" is wrong.[158]

It is true, of course, that someone who publishes something with no other aim than to insult, hurt, and humiliate another person perpetrates a despicable act. But the underlying suggestion of the Princess's remark is that there *really are* people who do such things. And against the backdrop of the discussion about the Danish cartoons it is hard to see how this could be interpreted as anything other than an allusion to the Danish cartoonists and the paper that published their drawings. Why does the Princess think that the publications aimed to insult?

Of course, the case of the Danish cartoonists is different from that of Rushdie and Kaur Bhatti (the Sikh playwright who had to hide after the theater in Birmingham was stormed by angry Sikhs). Nevertheless there are important similarities as well. Taking the chance that people might be provoked does not necessarily make the publication of something morally objectionable.

Flemming Rose on Why He Published the Danish Cartoons

Perhaps nobody has been more maligned in the recent history of free speech than the Danish journalist Flemming Rose (1958–), best known for commissioning the drawings of Mohammed in the *Jyllands Posten*. In an article in *The Washington Post* he disclosed his motives for publishing those cartoons.[159] From that article it appears that Rose is no "free-speech junkie."[160] He makes clear that he certainly would not publish any thing and everything. He would not publish pornographic images or graphic details of dead bodies. Likewise, swear words rarely make it into the pages of his newspaper, he contends: "So we are not fundamentalists in our support for freedom of expression."

Why then did he publish the cartoons?

He commissioned the cartoons "in response to several incidents of self-censorship in Europe caused by widening fears and feelings of intimidation in dealing with issues related to Islam." The idea was not to provoke gra-

[158] Albrecht, Yoeri, and Broertjes, Pieter, "Ik kan niet tegen onrecht. Het veelkoppige monster van de onvrije democratie" [I Cannot Accept Injustice. The Many-Headed Monster of Unfree Democracy], *De Volkskrant*, March 10, 2007.
[159] Rose, Flemming, "Why I Published Those Cartoons," at: Washingtonpost.com, Sunday, February 19, 2006. See also: Khader, Naser, and Rose, Flemming, "Reflections on the Danish Cartoon Controversy," *Middle East Quarterly*, Fall 2007, pp. 59–66; Ammitzboll, Pernille, and Vidono, Lorenzo, "After the Danish Cartoon Controversy," *Middle East Quarterly*, Winter 2007, pp. 3–11.
[160] See on this: Jacoby, "A First Amendment Junkie" and Barnet and Bedau, *Current Issues and Enduring Questions*.

tuitously, Rose writes. And he certainly had no intention of triggering violent demonstrations throughout the Muslim world. "Our goal was simply to push back self-imposed limits on expression that seemed to be closing in tighter."

The whole affair started when a Danish writer of children's books had trouble finding an illustrator for a book about the life of Mohammed. Nobody wanted to accept the job for fear of the consequences. When finally someone was found who accepted the commission this was on the precondition of anonymity. Not only were cartoonists who would tackle sensitive issues hard to find, it appeared also to be difficult to find translators for books relating to Islam. The translators did not want their names on the cover of the book.

This implied that there was an unequal treatment of religions, Rose contends. The cartoonists treated Islam the same way they treat Christianity, Buddhism, Hinduism, and other religions. The message of the cartoons on Mohammed was the complete opposite of what the critics contended: "By treating Muslims in Denmark as equals they made a point: We are integrating you into the Danish tradition of satire because you are part of our society, not strangers. The cartoons are inclusive, rather than exclusive, of Muslims."

From Rose's article it also appears that he does not have an exceptionally negative view of Islam. The cartoon that drew the harshest criticism (the one depicting the prophet with a bomb for a turban) can also be read as: "Some individuals have taken the religion of Islam hostage by committing terrorist acts in the name of the prophet. They are the ones who have given the religion a bad name."

Rose also makes an interesting point about the notion of respect in relation to the public sphere. When he visits a mosque, Rose tells us, he shows his respect by taking off his shoes. He follows the customs, just as he does in a church, a synagogue, or any other holy place. "But if a believer demands that I, as a nonbeliever, observe his taboos in the public domain, he is not asking my respect, but my submission. And that is incompatible with a secular democracy." This is an important point that brings us to the heart of the matter.

Rose also discloses something about his motives that is rarely revealed in the popular comments on the cartoons affair. His attitude towards free speech was deeply influenced by his work as a correspondent in totalitarian countries. He is a former correspondent in the Soviet Union and he is aware of the popular trick used by totalitarian governments. They labeled every critique or call for debate an "insult" and punished the offenders. That is what happened to Andrei Sakharov (1921–1989), Vladimir Bukowsky (1942–), Alexander Solzhenitsyn (1918–2008), Nathan Sharansky (1948–) and Boris Pasternak (1890–1960). The lesson from the Cold War is: "If you give in to totalitarian impulses once, new demands follow. The West prevailed in the Cold War because we stood by our fundamental values and did not appease totalitarian tyrants."

In the case of the publication of the cartoons in *Jyllands Posten*, the editor of the newspaper and all those involved in its publication wanted to make a point about free speech. They considered it to be outrageous that it appeared to be impossible to make cartoons on holy figures from the Islamic tradition. That kind of self-censure was pernicious and should ignite protest. The makers of the cartoons and those who solicited them did not aim at giving offence, but the fact that people might feel insulted was considered to be of less importance than making an important point about free speech.

One of the problems with the debate on free speech (Mill) and the moral and social duty to criticize (Clifford) is that commentators seldom picture the intents and purposes of other writers in the right context. This is true with regard to all the three theistic faiths but particularly with Islam nowadays, so it seems. Let me illustrate this by referring to a passage in Christopher Catherwood's book *A Brief History of the Middle East* (2006).[161]

Catherwood (1955–) rightly notes in his in many ways excellent book that discussion on Islam has become embroiled in the culture wars in the USA. This is "particularly unhelpful," he continues, "since civilized discussion is highly desirable in a era in which religious terrorism has become a major issue of our time. Mutual understanding is surely preferable to trading insults."[162]

So far, so good. But then Catherwood continues with an illustration of what he has written:

> A classic example of this is the success of a recent book, *The Politically Incorrect Guide to Islam [and the Crusades]*, whose title reveals a great deal. Such polemics only increase heat between Muslims and the rest of the world, with the unfortunate consequences that are all around us.[163]

In this passage there are many hidden presuppositions. Apparently Catherwood does not consider *The Politically Incorrect Guide to Islam and the Crusades* (2005) by Robert Spencer (1962–)[164] "civilized discussion." It does not help "mutual understanding" and is therefore "particularly unhelpful." Another contention that is being insinuated is that the title of

---

[161]   Catherwood, Christopher, *A Brief History of the Middle East: From Abraham to Arafat*, Robinson, London 2006.

[162]   Ibid., p. 79.

[163]   Ibid.

[164]   Spencer, Robert, *The Politically Incorrect Guide to Islam and the Crusades*, Regnery Publishing, Inc., Washington 2005.

this book, "politically incorrect," already "reveals a great deal." Catherwood interprets this as a "polemic" with the "unfortunate consequences that are all around us."

The last statement is important because it contains nothing less than a theory to explain "religious terrorism." Religious terrorism is explained by "polemics." Therefore books like the one written by Spencer are not seen as the *result* of the threat of "religious terrorism" (a term used by Catherwood, by the way, although considered "politically incorrect" in some circles) but as the *cause* of it (or at least as a contributing factor). This theory is widely accepted, but we should ask ourselves whether it is true.

What our final judgment on this undoubtedly complex question will be partly depends on how we interpret the aims and purposes of the writers of the "politically incorrect guides" series. There are two opinions.

The *first* is that this is a provocative series that, for no other reason than provocation or fun, depicts the subjects it discusses in a most unfavorable light. The aim is fun, not the disclosure of unwelcome truths that are being neglected for political reasons or out of religious piety.

The *second* is different, however. It holds that what the writers in this series try to do, *is* to shed light on uncomfortable truths. What guides them is an attempt to reveal objective information, even if that information is unwelcome to specific groups or vested interests.

If we follow the first interpretation we may ask what the consequences of Catherwood's criticism of Spencer's book might be. Ought we not to abolish the whole series then? If we take the first interpretation of the aims of the series, then *The Politically Incorrect Guide to Islam* is not alone in being not "particularly helpful" (because not a contribution to "civilized discussion"). The same can be said about the politically incorrect guide to Western civilization,[165] or the American constitution,[166] or the Bible,[167] or Darwinism,[168] or any other title in the series.

The central question seems to be this: is there a good reason to write and publish "politically incorrect guides" about Christianity, the Jewish religion, Buddhism, Hinduism, Capitalism, Socialism, etc., and exclude one religion (Islam) because publishing such a book would be "particularly unhelpful," "trading insults," and not a contribution to "civilized discussion"?

---

[165] Esolen, Anthony, *The Politically Incorrect Guide to Western Civilization*, Regnery Publishing, Inc., Washington DC 2008.
[166] Gutzman, Kevin R.C., *The Politically Incorrect Guide to the Constitution*, Regnery Publishing, Inc., Washington DC 2007.
[167] Hutchinson, Robert J., *The Politically Incorrect Guide to the Bible*, Regnery Publishing, Inc., Washington DC 2007.
[168] Wells, Jonathan, *The Politically Incorrect Guide to Darwinism and Intelligent Design*, Regnery Publishing, Inc., Washington DC 2006.

It may be the case that there *is* such a reason, but, again, then we have also to take into account that it is not unthinkable that we might make exactly the wrong choice in saving one religion from criticism while encouraging criticism of others. This might help the most conservative, violent, and fanatical leaders within the religion that is considered to be exempt from criticism to disseminate their views. We at least have to ask ourselves whether such preferential treatment is indeed "helpful" in attaining a result that probably Catherwood, Spencer, and most other writers share: a world where people live together peacefully, each revering his own god (or no god), while respecting the choices of others. The contention that some participants in this discussion have dishonorable motives is often voiced, but should require more evidence, I am inclined to think.

That element of balancing two evils against each other (the chance that people might get hurt; the chance that free speech might be eroded) is characteristic of the new situation we are living in. This situation is not dissimilar from the considerations of the great scientists when they were pondering the question of whether they should publish their ideas in full cognizance that this would cause massive upheaval.

We find a similar balancing in the tradition of science, where free inquiry often clashed with religious orthodoxy, sometimes with dramatic consequences for the innovators of scientific ideas.[169]

The Theory of Evolution: Too Controversial to Defend?

A classic example of this is the publication of Darwin's *The Origin of Species* in 1859.[170] Darwin was well aware that once he published his material an outcry would be the result, not only in the scholarly world, but also in the world of religious people. The reason is clear. If the Darwinian thesis of evolution held, the story about the origin of man as told in Genesis could not be literally true. And this would upset the whole history of Christianity that had lasted almost two thousand years. "I have read your book with more pain than pleasure," the Reverend Adam Sedgwick (1785–1873) wrote to Darwin on November 24, 1859, after having read his *Origin*.[171] Sedgwick had read parts of the book "with absolute sorrow" and he con-

---

[169]   See the classical study by: White, A.D., *A History of the Warfare of Science with Theology in Christendom*, Dover Publications, New York 1960 (1896).

[170]   Darwin, Charles, *The Origin of Species by Means of Natural Selection, Or the Preservation of Favored Races in the Struggle for Life*, Penguin Books, Harmondsworth 1981 (1959).

[171]   White, Michael, and Gribbin, John, *Darwin. A Life in Science*, Simon & Schuster, London 1995, p. 219.

fessed: "I think them utterly false and grievously mischievous." Nobody would, however, defend the idea that Darwin should not have published the *Origin* because it is wrong to cause "sorrow" or "pain" or "hurt the feelings" of other people. We all think – at least most of us – that Darwin had to publish his book *in spite of the sorrow* it caused to the poor reverend.

Perhaps it is difficult for us, now, living in the twenty-first century, to gauge exactly how provocative, saddening, and insulting the theory of evolution was to the pride of the Victorians. The theory of evolution really had to fight its way into the scientific world. The evolutionist who had a character perfectly matched to the task was "Darwin's bulldog": T.H. Huxley. Huxley, whom we have already encountered in Chapter 1 as the coiner of the concept of "agnosticism," made no concessions to the religious feelings of the orthodox. On the contrary, *Man's Place in Nature* (1862) was considered to be a bombshell.[172] It was, so Darwin's biographers White and Gribbin wrote, "the first and the most confrontational of the books by British Darwinians."[173]

To estimate the intense and heartfelt feelings of the British Victorians who opposed Darwin, we have to take into account that Darwin's contemporaries had only just gotten a glimpse of the gorilla that had been caught in the jungles of Africa and brought to England. Everybody was now in a position to look the gorilla right in the eyes and monitor the similarities between ape and man. Huxley reveled in making this clear. Darwin, though, felt reluctant to do this and lived as a recluse. He had to spell out some of the more unpopular conclusions drawn on the basis of the theory of evolution, of course, but he never enjoyed it. Huxley, however, wrote to Darwin with great enthusiasm: "By next Friday evening they will all be convinced that they are monkeys."[174]

In the meantime the theologians cried "blasphemy." It is against this background that the wife of the Bishop of Worcester commented: "Descended from the apes! My dear, let us hope that it is not true, but if it is, let us pray that it will not become generally known."[175]

It is clear that those who have no high opinion of the theory of evolution will experience the publications of Huxley and other Darwinians as "needless provocations." How can you advocate disseminating views that are so manifestly untrue, they must have thought.

---

[172] Huxley, Thomas H., *Man's Place in Nature*, Introduction by Ashley Montagu, The University of Michigan Press, Ann Arbor 1959 (1862).
[173] White and Gribbin, *Darwin: A Life in Science*, p. 227.
[174] Ibid.
[175] Quoted in: Montagu, Ashley "Introduction," in: Huxley, *Man's Place in Nature*, p. 3.

Is There Another Way to Discover the Truth than by Free Discussion?

That brings me to the last element of what could be called "the closed mind."[176] Presupposed in the worldview of those who do not feel at ease with religious criticism, of course, is that we already *know* what is true. Truth is manifested to us in divine revelation. We *already know* that man is not descended from the apes, because God told us so. We *already know* that Mohammed's character and behavior are immaculate, because we have been informed of this in the hadith and the Qur'an. There simply is no need for further research. *We already know* – this is the motto of all the censors, inquisitors, and other people eager to kill the free flow of ideas and intellectual debate. The only thing that counts is the dissemination of a message of which the content is clear and unassailable, because it has been "revealed" to us, and the suppression or elimination of all obstacles (in the heyday of suppression including "persons") that stand in the way of the truth that has already been found.

Intimately connected with this worldview is a concept of free speech. Free speech, according to some, means the freedom to disseminate views that are "true." Freedom to spread false views can never be brought under the banner of "real" free speech. What the advocates of false ideas refer to as "free speech" is really a perversion of that principle.

This vision of free speech is highly questionable. Richard Robinson (1902–1996) commented on Pope Leo XIII's (1810–1903) encyclical letter of June 20, 1888 in which the pope declared that the public authorities ought diligently to repress the publication of "lying opinions."

Robinson indicated that there are two good reasons for free speech. First, freedom is a great good and any suppression of freedom is consequently an evil. Second, toleration[177] of free speech is far more likely to produce a general spread of true opinion than the suppression of it.

Both reasons are relevant here, but the second needs more emphasis perhaps because it is likely to be overlooked. That has to do with the fact that many people (and the Pope among them) think that if speech is left free, false views will generally be more easily adopted than true ones. The Pope said: "If unbridled license of speech and writing be granted to all, nothing will remain sacred and inviolate; even the highest and truest man-

---

[176]   Freeman, *The Closing of the Western Mind.*
[177]   Toleration in the classic sense, not in the sense of giving no offence to religious feelings. What Robinson advocates is toleration in the sense used by Leslie Stephen. See: Stephen, Leslie, "Poisonous Opinions," in: Stephen, Leslie *An Agnostic's Apology and Other Essays*, Smith, Elder & Co., London 1893 (republished 1969), pp. 242–338, p. 288: "Toleration implies that each man must have a right to say what he pleases."

dates of nature, justly held to be the common and noblest heritage of the human race, will not be spared."[178] Robinson does not agree. He objects: "When moral rules are not allowed to be criticized, bad ones creep in, and good ones are held in a stupid and immoral way."[179] This is all in the tradition of John Stuart Mill's *On Liberty*.

An impressive vindication of free speech was also recently formulated by A.C. Grayling (1949–) in his book *Liberty in the Age of Terror* (2009) when he writes:

> it is clear that the effort to censor the Danish cartoons by riots and violence, and by threats against the lives of cartoonists and editors, is infinitely the greater offence. It represents a crucial point of difference between the value of free speech and all that turns upon it, and the retrogressive, reactionary, static, punitive and mind-numbingly limited view that monolithic ideologies, spectacularly among them the more fundamentalist religions or versions of religions, seek to impose.[180]

The freethinker starts from a different basis than the "true believer." According to the freethinker what is true must be established by a painful process of discovery.[181] Religion is not excluded from that process.[182] Inhibiting this process will make it impossible to find out what the nature of reality is. So what orthodox people, who frustrate the process of the free development of religion and science, do is to beg the question. We do not know what is true. What is true and what is just have to be found out. And therefore we need to canvass all the options that are available to us, all the theories that are being proposed – even if those theories seem *prima facie* absurd, insulting or offensive. We still have to test them (i.e. publish them, discuss them) in order to corroborate what counts as the truth.

---

[178]   Pope Leo XIII, quoted in: Robinson, Richard, *An Atheist's Values*, The Clarendon Press, Oxford 1964, p. 205.

[179]   Ibid., p. 206.

[180]   Grayling, A.C., *Liberty in the Age of Terror: A Defense of Civil Liberties and Enlightenment Values*, Bloomsbury, London 2009, p. 68.

[181]   This is especially emphasized by a modern freethinker, Karl Popper. See: Popper, Karl R., "Science: Conjecture and Refutations."

[182]   See on this: Wijnberg, Rob, "Mill en de vrijheid van meningsuiting" [Mill and Freedom of Expression], in: Dirk Verhofstadt, ed., *John Stuart Mill: 150 jaar over vrijheid* [John Stuart Mill: 150 Years on Liberty], Houtekiet/Atlas, Antwerpen 2009, pp. 31–41, p. 37 who proclaims that religious worldviews should be treated like every other worldview and therefore not be exempted from criticism.

4

Moral and Political Secularism

Consider this: Is the pious being loved by the gods because it is pious, or is it pious because it is being loved by the gods? (Socrates in Plato's Euthyphro)[1]

Genuine morals and morality are not dependent on any religion, although every religion sanctions them and thereby affords them support. (Arthur Schopenhauer)[2]

In Chapters 2 and 3 I dealt with freethought. My claim is that the secular outlook manifests itself primarily in the attitude of the freethinker. In contrast to atheism, freethought is a public doctrine. It has great significance for the furtherance of culture. Characteristic of the freethinker is: (a) the conviction (or at least acknowledgment) that religions also have darker sides and (b) that freedom of speech is an important principle in questioning and criticizing those darker sides.

As one of the most prominent manifestations of the evil side of religion, we have analyzed lack of sympathy for important civil rights and civil freedoms. In the theistic traditions there are several manifestations of the aim to suppress freedom of speech, freedom of conscience, sexual freedom, and many other values held dear by many people nowadays. There even seems to be a revolt, in a violent form, against modernity whose freedom is interpreted by fanatics as licentiousness:[3] religious terrorism. In Europe

[1] *Euthyphro* 10d, Plato, *Complete Works*, ed. John M. Cooper, Hackett Publishing Company, Indianapolis 1997, p. 9.
[2] Schopenhauer, Arthur, *Parerga and Paralipomena. Short Philosophical Essays*, Vol. II, translated by E.F.J. Payne, Clarendon Press, Oxford 1974, p. 392.
[3] See on this: Rorty, Richard, "Religion in the Public Sphere: A Reconsideration," *Journal of Religious Ethics*, 31, no. 1 2003, pp. 141–149.

religious terrorism has also manifested itself as an assault on one of the core principles of the secular outlook: the principle of expressing your own view of life, even if this view of life is radically different from the view of religious orthodoxy or religious fundamentalism.[4]

One way to understand the secular outlook is to see it as the worldview that is diametrically opposed to the worldview of religious fanaticism. The secular outlook is based on the individual right to freedom of conscience, but also on the freedom to express our ideas in a public context.

That last principle is well known under the name of freedom of speech or freedom of expression and closely connected to freedom of religion in the broad sense of the word. By "broad" I mean that freedom of religion also comprises the freedom to *reject* religion or the freedom to *change* from one religion to another. This is acknowledged in article 18 of the Universal Declaration of Human Rights: "Everyone has the right to freedom of thought, conscience and religion; *this right includes freedom to change his religion or belief,* and freedom, either alone or in community with others and in public or private, to manifest his religion or belief in teaching, practice, worship and observance" (italics mine).[5]

In the present chapter I will engage in a further analysis of the presuppositions of this attitude. This is necessary because religious criticism is based on presuppositions that are not self-evident. One of those preconditions is the institution of free speech as analyzed in Chapter 3. But religious criticism is also premised on the condition that the human mind can, as a matter of fact, free itself from religious tutelage. In other words: the critic must be able to place himself or herself over against the religious tradition ("ought implies can"). That presupposes what may be called *moral autonomy.*

Here we touch upon a new feature of the secular outlook, *viz.* the capacity to justify moral ideals without reference to religion. The adherent of moral autonomy claims that it is possible to live a morally just life without religion.

The movement or mode of thinking that favors moral autonomy may be provided with a separate label. The label I propose is "moral secularism."[6] Moral secularism is intimately connected to the growth of secularist ideals in the modern world. The philosopher Paul Kurtz (1925–) writes: "The modern world has witnessed the widespread secularization of life. This

---

[4] See on this: Bawer, Bruce, *Surrender: Appeasing Islam, Sacrificing Freedom*, Doubleday, New York 2009.

[5] See for a critique of this stance: Sapir, Gidon, and Statman, Daniel, "Why Freedom of Religion Does not Include Freedom from Religion," *Law and Philosophy* 24, no. 5 2005, pp. 467–508.

[6] For the vocabulary used in Chapter 4 I am indebted to my colleague Floris van den Berg, director of the Center for Inquiry, the Netherlands.

means, first, that morality could be freed from religious authorities."[7] Moral secularism manifests itself also in Samuel Porter Putnam's poem, already quoted in Chapter 1. In the first part of the poem the poet comes back to the same question several times: "Why don't he lend a hand"? But suddenly there is a turn: "We look in vain to find him / Upon his throne so grand, / Then turn our vision earthward – 'Tis we must lend a hand." At that moment the focus shifts from criticism of God and religion to man; from theism to humanism. Not God, but man is the centre of attention. This is also made manifest in the poetry of Algernon Charles Swinburne (1837–1909), whose "the supreme evil, God" has already been quoted at the beginning of Chapter 1. Swinburne published poetry that was acclaimed for its style but often criticized as containing many radical ideas. His *Poems and Ballads* (1866) is one long glorification of paganism and a rejection of Christian piety. In his later *Songs before Sunrise* (1871) we find the *Hymn of Man*. The often quoted last line "Glory to Man in the highest! for Man is the master of things" is considered to be one of the most impressive statements of the humanist position in English literature.[8]

> By thy name that in hellfire was written,
> And burned at the point of thy sword,
> Thou art smitten, thou God, thou God, thou art smitten; thy death is upon thee, O Lord.
> And the lovesong of earth as thou diest resounds through the wind of her wings –
> Glory to Man in the highest! for Man is the master of things.

In an earlier poem, *Hymn to Proserpine* (1866), he meditated on the condition of the Roman Empire "after the proclamation in Rome of the Christian Faith." As a nineteenth-century Julian the Apostate (331/332–363), Swinburne deplored the rise of Christianity:

> Thou hast conquered, O pale Galilean; the world has grown grey from thy breath;
> We have drunken of things Lethean, and fed on the fullness of death.[9]

Swinburne was perhaps extreme in his anti-Christian slant, but such a position was not completely uncommon. The historian J.B. Bury (1861–1927)

---

[7]   Kurtz, Paul, *What is Secular Humanism?*, Prometheus Books, Amherst, NY 2006, p. 13. See also: Kurtz, Paul, *The Courage to Become: The Virtues of Humanism*, Praeger, Westport, CT 1997.

[8]   See: Stein, Gordon, *A Second Anthology of Atheism and Rationalism*, Prometheus Books, Buffalo, NY 1987, p. 166.

[9]   Kermode, Frank, and Hollander, John, eds.,*The Oxford Anthology of English Literature*, Vol. II, Oxford University Press, New York 1973, p. 1445.

wrote: "All the great poets of the nineteenth century were more or less unorthodox."[10] Wordsworth (1770–1850) was a pantheist.[11] Shelley (1792–1822) called himself an atheist.[12]

Although many shied away from openly accepting pantheism, atheism, paganism, and other indications of secular thought, the idea of moral autonomy had gained much ground during the nineteenth century. And moral autonomy does not go together easily with theism. Militant theists, like Paul Johnson (1928–), introduced in the first section of Chapter 1 during a discussion of the various definitions of atheism, vehemently deny that morality can stand on its own feet. If there is no God:

> This life then becomes the only one we have, we have no duties or obligations except to ourselves, and we need weigh no other considerations except our own interests and pleasures. There are no commands to follow except what society imposes upon us, and even these we may evade if we can get away with it. In a Godless world, there is no obvious basis for altruism of any kind, moral anarchy takes over and the rule of the self prevails.[13]

Moral secularists claim that the whole worldview implicit in this quote from Johnson is misguided. Nevertheless, Johnson has a point as long as he moves within the framework of the theistic worldview. It may be possible to reconcile moral autonomy with certain interpretations of Christianity, the Jewish religion, and Islam, but there certainly is a tension with the classic orthodox theistic conception of God. To make this clear I have to take up a theme we dealt with Chapter 1, where it was argued that "atheism" can best be understood as "a-theism," *viz.* the denial of the theistic position. In the first four sections of Chapter 1 we saw that this "negative approach" to the concept of atheism was – although well justified – not very common and that brought me to the proposal that the term "atheism" should be relinquished altogether. To avoid misunderstanding it may be better to use the term "non-theism" as an integral element of the secular outlook.

A number of writers have put forward arguments in favor of this "non-theism" (or "atheism" in the restricted sense). Thinkers who subscribe to

---

[10] Bury, *A History of the Freedom of Thought*, p. 208.

[11] See on poetry and freethought: Gordon Stein, *A Second Anthology of Atheism and Rationalism*, Prometheus Books, Buffalo, NY 1987, pp. 345–369; Rosenthal, Peggy, *The Poet's Jesus: Representations at the End of a Millennium*, Oxford University Press, Oxford 2000.

[12] See: Shelley, Percy Bysshe, *The Necessity of Atheism And Other Essays*, Prometheus Books, Buffalo, NY 1993; Shelley, Percy Bysshe, "Essay on Christianity," 1815, in: *Shelley's Literary and Philosophical Criticism*, ed. John Shawcross and Henry Frowde, London 1909, pp. 86–117.

[13] Johnson, *The Quest for God*, p. 1.

the secular outlook usually think non-theism is preferable to theism because it is easier to reconcile with important values. One such value is human freedom. As Jean Paul Sartre and Eduard von Hartmann argued, consistent theism would amount to a complete denial of human freedom. Therefore they rejected theism. It was also rejected by Susan Stebbing and Bertrand Russell, as we saw in Chapter 1, because it conflicts with "spiritual excellencies" (Stebbing) and the "Liberal Decalogue" (Russell).

Chapters 2 and 3 of *The Secular Outlook* can also be understood as criticism of the central claims of theism because this seems hard to reconcile with the two fundamental pillars of freethought, to wit: religious criticism and freedom of speech. The biblical injunction to slay apostates and the story of Phinehas both dealt with in Chapter 2 testified to this.

Chapter 4 continues this line of argument and is dedicated to an important metaethical principle that has great significance for the secular outlook: moral autonomy (and insofar the state as a whole is not based on an official religion: political autonomy). But before I can characterize the aim of moral autonomy as a positive ideal, I first have to explain how this is related to the central claim of theism. That brings me back to the analysis of theism as begun in Chapter 1.

Pope Benedict XVI on the Apostles' Creed

In 1968 Josef Ratzinger (1927–), now Pope Benedict XVI, tried to present a delineation of the essence of the Christian creed. What he wrote here about Christianity is also relevant for theism in general, as we will see. The Pope started his reflections with reference to the Apostles' Creed.[14] This early document (which, in its current form, dates back to *c.* 550 CE) professes to outline the core of the Christian doctrine and reads as follows:

> *I believe in God the Father Almighty, Maker of heaven and earth;*
> *And in Jesus Christ his only Son our Lord,*
> *Who was conceived by the Holy Ghost,*
> *Born of the Virgin Mary,*
> *Suffered under Pontius Pilate,*
> *Was crucified, died and buried,*
> *He descended into hell;*
> *The third day he rose again from the dead,*
> *He ascended into heaven,*
> *And sitteth on the right hand of God the Father Almighty;*

[14]   Ratzinger, Joseph, *Introduction to Christianity*, translated J.R. Forster, Ignatius Press, Fort Collins, CO 1990 (1968); and McGrath, Alister E., *Theology: The Basics*, Blackwell Publishing, Malden, MA 2004.

From thence he shall come to judge the quick and the dead.
I believe in the Holy Ghost;
The holy Catholic Church;
The communion of saints;
The Forgiveness of sins;
The Resurrection of the body,
And the life everlasting. Amen.

Today, The Apostles' Creed may strike some as "too detailed," while others may feel it is "obsolete." Feminist scholar and theologian Rosemary Radford Ruether (1936–) presents a devastating critique of this "official concept of God"[15] as it gradually developed in Hebrew thought indicting it for androcentrism – or male domination over women; anthropocentrism – or human domination over nature; ethnocentrism – or the domination of a "chosen" people over other people; militarism, asceticism, and the dualism of mind and body and the hierarchy of the former over the latter. "Christianity," so Ruether contends, "has a problem with God or rather with its ideas about God."[16] Ruether holds the idea of the oneness of God responsible for much of the trouble with the theistic god. It is hard to untangle universalist monotheism from imperialism, she writes. The idea of the oneness of God is deeply entrenched in the idea of the election of one people and one religion. The notion that one people and their religion have a right to conquer all other people, obliterating their cultures and religions, naturally ensues. This has to be changed and Ruether makes a plea for a different position. She says: "Different religions point in different ways to divine mystery as the source of life and renewal of life. We need to affirm the divine in and through the many gods or even lack of gods, as in Buddhism, of diverse religions traditions, rather than trying to make the ideas of one religion universal by destroying other religious cultures."[17]

One may, of course, sympathize with some elements of this feminist critique of the theistic concept of god without being impressed by what it proposes to put in its place. Ruether proclaims "God must be seen as present in the diverse expressions of life on earth, rather than seeing humans as the unique image of God called to rule over the earth … . God is manifest not just in humans, but in wolves and insects, trees and flowers, the waters that fall from the sky and waters that well up from the earth."[18]

Whatever we may think of this, such a broad concept of god is not the focus of this book.

[15] Ruether, Rosemary Radford, "The Politics of God in the Christian Tradition," *Feminist Theology*, 17 no. 3 2009, pp. 329–338, p. 330.
[16] Ibid., p. 329.
[17] Ibid., p. 336.
[18] Ibid., p. 337.

Here is another characterization of "God," this time by the American philosopher Charles Larmore (1950–). Larmore writes: "God is so great, he does not have to exist. This is the essence of the process of secularization that has so profoundly shaped modern society."[19] Larmore contends that a "respect for God's transcendence" and a "repudiation of idols" has led to "relieving God from the task of being the ultimate explanation for the order of nature and the course of history."[20] This also has important implications for the bond between God and morality.

> A similar unburdening of God seems appropriate in the domain of morality. When the validity of a moral imperative is understood in terms of being God's command, the motive of the moral life becomes the desire to please God, as though we could help him or should fear him. Such a conception of God must appear as an all-too-human projection, if we assume that God must transcend such human needs and passions. We respect God as God, when we learn to value the moral life for itself, without appeal to God's purposes (though we may still believe that God loves what is good and right).[21]

The reason why I present these heterodox god-conceptions of Ruether and Larmore is to illustrate that there is an enormous variety of ideas about the concept of god. In Ruether's approach, god is completely immanent in the sense that almost everything is "god." The divine is to be found through the many gods and even "lack of gods," as she says. God is manifest in humans, but also in wolves, insects, flowers, and the waters that fall from the sky. Larmore's God on the other hand evaporates in complete transcendence and all the usual characteristics of god are here removed to leave us with the idea of complete transcendence.

It will be clear that I do not want to contest anybody's good right to project all kinds of god-definitions, but this is not what I am concerned with in this book. I am concerned with what Ruether characterizes as the "official concept of God." We are informed about this official concept in the writings of the Pope on the Apostles' Creed or (as far as Catholicism is concerned) in the *Catechism of the Catholic Church*.[22] The Apostles' Creed is what many Christians see as the core of Christendom, in particular as regards one of its essential elements, *viz.* belief in the existence of God. What is the nature of this Christian god? He has the following characteristics.[23]

---

[19]   Larmore, Charles, "Beyond Religion and Enlightenment," *San Diego Law Review*, 30 1993, pp. 799–815, p. 799.

[20]   Ibid.

[21]   Ibid.

[22]   *Catechism of the Catholic Church*, second edition, revised in accordance with the official Latin text promulgated by Pope John II, Doubleday, New York, 1995.

[23]   On this subject, see the still eminently readable Harnack, Adolf von, *History of Dogma*, Wipf and Stock Publishers, Eugene, OR 2000 (1889). A list and analysis of the characteristics

Unity. God is one. The god of the major theistic religions is one, thereby distinguishing theism from the polytheism of classical antiquity and other global cultures.[24] It is therefore unnecessary (because it is tautological) to refer to "monotheism" (meaning belief in the existence of one god). The theistic god is by definition singular.[25]

Self-existent. Secondly: God exists independently and has not been caused by something else. God is self-caused: *causa sui.*

Eternal. God is outside time. He always has been and always will be. He cannot "die." As such, Nietzsche's famous announcement of the "death of God," also the basis for Fritz Mauthner's monumental history of atheism, cannot therefore be anything other than a metaphor.[26]

Creator. God is the creator of all things and he governs all things by his providence. The theistic god has created the world from nothing (*"ex nihilo,"* which was impossible for the ancient Greeks, since *"ex nihilo nihil fit":* "from nothing comes nothing").

Transcendent. God is distinct from his creation. The world is not identical to God.[27] Eduard Von Hartmann (1842–1906) wrote that we cannot have a religious bond with a purely immanent idea which we know lacks a transcendental–real correlative.[28]

Omnipotent. God is the creator and governor of the universe. God can do anything he wants to do.[29] There has been some discussion as to whether

---

of God are also presented in: McInerney, Peter K., "God," in: *Introduction to Philosophy*, HarperCollins, New York 1992, pp. 9–22; McGrath, *Theology: The Basics*, pp. 16–34; McGrath, Alister E., *Christian Theology: An Introduction*, Blackwell, Oxford 1994, pp. 205–246.

[24] Haeckel, Ernst, *Die Welträtsel. Gemeinverständliche Studien über monistische Philosophie* [The Riddle of the World. Studies in Monistic Philosophy for the Layperson], Akademie-Verlag, Berlin 1961 (1899), p. 354: "Gott und Welt sind zwei verschiedene Wesen. Gott steht der Welt gegenüber als deren Schöpfer, Erhalter und Regierer. Dabei wird Gott stets mehr oder weniger menschenähnlich gedacht, als ein Organismus, welcher dem Menschen ähnlich (wenn auch in höchst volkommener Form) denkt und handelt" [God and the world are two distinct beings. God stands in relation to the world as its creator, upholder, and ruler. In this regard God is thought of as more or less similar to a human being, as an organism that thinks and acts in a human way (if in a highly perfect form].

[25] See: Wainwright, William, "Monotheism," in: *Stanford Encyclopedia of Philosophy*, in: http://plato.stanford.edu, 2005, pp. 1–23, p. 4.

[26] Nietzsche, Friedrich, *The Gay Science*; Mauthner, Fritz, "Gott" [God], in: Fritz Mauthner, *Wörterburch der Philosophie: Neue Beiträge zu einer Kritik der Sprache* [Dictionary of Philosophy; New Contributions to a Critique of Language], Erster Band, Diogenes Verlag, Zürich 1980 (1910/11), pp. 448–458, p. 455: "The old Jewish god is dead."

[27] The Spinozist conception of god as "God or Nature" (*Deus sive Natura*) is heretical.

[28] See Hartmann, Eduard von, *Die Religion des Geistes, Zweiter systematischer Teil der Religionsphilosophie* [The Religion of the Mind. Second Systematic Part of the Philosophy of Religion], Verlag von Wilhelm Friedrich, Leipzig 1882, p. 6.

[29] The object of the religious sentiment, Eduard von Hartmann writes, can "nur ein solches sein das dem Subjekt überlegen ist, und zwar nicht bloss relativ überlegen, wie ein Mensch

God can do something contradictory. Can he square a circle? The philosopher G.W. Leibniz (1646–1716) believed he could not.[30] One could argue, however, that this does not limit God's omnipotence, as omnipotence means being able to do things that are not self-contradictory.

Omniscient. God is also omniscient. He knows all things that have happened and all that will happen. There are no secrets for him. He even knows our innermost thoughts.

Personal. Like human beings, God is a creature with intellect and a will. At the same time, God transcends biological categories, being neither man nor woman (although he is referred to as "father").

Perfectly good. God is perfectly good as well as the source of all morality. People may not always understand his actions, but they are always perfectly good.

Holy. God is holy and worthy of our adoration.[31]

Interventionist. As a rule, theistic religions also claim that God intervenes in history.[32]

Judge and remunerator. Finally, God is a judge and he rewards us for what we do, so some scholars have defined "faith" as "the desire for the approval of supernatural beings."[33]

"Who Are You to Tell Believers What to Believe?"

Presenting a list of characteristics that define the identity of a religious creed is not popular nowadays. The common reaction is: "Who are you to tell the believers what they have to believe?"

---

dem andern, sondern unvergleichlich überlegen, wie ein höheres Wesen einem niederen" [only be something that is superior to the subject, and not simply relatively superior, as one human being to another, but incomparably superior, as a higher being to a lower one] (ibid., p. 4.).

[30] See the discussion of Leibniz's position by: Kolakowski, Leszek, *Religion*, Fontana Paperbacks, Glasgow 1982, p. 20.

[31] For an outline of theism, see the sections "Theism and modern science" and "Theism and values" in: Quinn, Philip L., and Taliaferro, Charles, eds., *A Companion to Philosophy of Religion*, Blackwell, Oxford 1997, pp. 419–525. Also useful are: Mautner, Thomas, *The Penguin Dictionary of Philosophy*, Penguin Books, London 2000 (1996), p. 561; Brightman, Edgar Sheffield, *A Philosophy of Religion*, Prentice-Hall, Inc., New York 1946, p. 157; and the articles on "Theism and Divine Attributes" in: Taliaferro, and Griffiths *Philosophy of Religion*.

[32] Swinburne, Richard, *Faith and Reason*, second edition, Clarendon Press, Oxford 2005 (1981), p. 233: "God has intervened in history to do certain things and to reveal certain truths." See also: Stark, Rodney, *One True God: Historical Consequences of Monotheism*, Princeton University Press, Princeton 2001, 1.

[33] See on this: Amis, *The Second Plane*, p. 49.

There are two misunderstandings inherent in this question. The first mistake is that it is I who am presenting this list of characteristics of Christianity whereas in reality it is the Pope. And in fact it is not even the Pope who is presenting them, because he is describing what has been codified in the Christian tradition as the essence of the Christian creed.[34] What I am doing is merely to *describe* what one prominent Christian (the Pope) and others (Christians) see as the essence of the Christian creed.

The second mistake is that in presenting such a list we have the ambition to tell people what they *should* believe, while in fact the purpose is merely descriptive. What people believe in is entirely up to them. What I try to do in *The Secular Outlook* is to *understand what* they believe.

The ultimate goal of this process of trying to understand what people believe is to make fruitful communication possible. If we do not say what we understand by "Christianity," "religion," "belief," "faith," "theism," and other terms used in this discourse we are likely to have useless conversations, attacking each other's standpoints before we have specified our terms. "If you want to discuss with me, please define your terms" is a request attributed to Voltaire. He is right.[35]

So, whether the Pope is right (or the Apostles' Creed is right) is not my business to judge. I only say that this is one specific example of an attempt to present the essence of the Christian creed.

Now there are many people who would claim that it is impossible to define the essence of a certain belief, since that is entirely up to the individual who claims to be part of this religious tradition. A clear tendency in this direction we find in the work of Karen Armstrong (1944–). In her book *The Case for God* (2009) she writes: "Surely everybody knows what God is: the Supreme Being, a divine Personality, who created the world and everything in it. They look perplexed if you point out that it is inaccurate to call God the Supreme Being because God is not *a* being at all, and that we really don't know what we mean when we say that he is 'good', 'wise' or 'intelligent'."[36] Apparently Armstrong is opposed to clear definitions of the words she uses so profusely in her books. That results in a situation where "God," "religion," "Christianity," and other key concepts are used interchangeably. This is done with an air of superiority and those who ask

---

[34] See for a historical account of the dogmas: von Harnack *History of Dogma*.

[35] The opposite is defended by William James. See: James, William, *The Varieties of Religious Experience. A Study in Human Nature*, ed. Martin E. Marty, Penguin Books, Harmondsworth 1982 (1902), p. 26: "The man who knows governments most completely is he who troubles himself least about a definition which shall give their essence." But a little further James nonetheless presents something of a definition of religion: "the feelings, acts, and experiences of individual men in their solitude, so far as they apprehend themselves to stand in relation to whatever they may consider the divine." Ibid., p. 31.

[36] Armstrong, *The Case for God*, p. 1.

for more precision are censored as narrow-minded (if not "fundamentalist") and asking for the impossible. Armstrong claims that "the world is currently experiencing a religious revival," but to ascertain whether this is true or not, we should be clear about *what* is being revived. Any attempt to represent God with a certain amount of clarity is rejected by Armstrong as "too limited an idea of God."[37]

Now it is very possible that someone claiming to be a Christian might tell us that the idea of God as presented in the Apostles' Creed no longer captures the essence of his belief. But the next question to that person is: "please, give us *your* description of what the position of a Christian encompasses." In that case the person might answer: "That is impossible, this is a very private matter."

But that is something we have to contradict. Although highly popular nowadays, the pretence that the essence of Christianity, Islam, or whatever other creed you may imagine, is entirely in the eye of the beholder seems to me to be false. You may dispute the criteria that some people use to demarcate Christianity from other creeds (for instance, Buddhism), but the claim that there are *no criteria at all* is highly dubious.

Perhaps we can make this clear by presenting an absurd example that is nevertheless enlightening. Suppose someone confides to you: "I do not believe there is a God. And certainly, he has no son. I detest the Bible. I never go to Church. But, of course, I consider myself to be a true Christian, because I think that we should do unto others as we would have others do unto us."

What should we say to this "Christian"? I do not think we would be meddling in his personal affairs if we told him that he is stretching ordinary language much too far by claiming to be a "Christian." He may retort that he takes the Golden Rule as his moral guideline and claim this to be a Christian idea. Isn't this codified in Matthew 7:12? But apart from the question of whether the Golden Rule is a specifically Christian idea (it is not; the Golden Rule is found in almost all moral and religious traditions)[38] subscribing to it is certainly not sufficient to characterize someone as a "Christian."[39] It is possible, of course, to contest the criteria of the Apostles' Creed, but that does not mean that there are no criteria at all. Defining

---

[37]   Ibid., p. 6.
[38]   See for examples of variations on the rule in other cultures: Lewis, C.S., *The Abolition of Man. Or Reflections on Education with Special Reference to the Teaching of English in the Upper Forms of Schools*, Harper, San Francisco 2001 (1944), p. 87. Metzger, Bruce M., & Coogan, Michael D., *The Oxford Guide to Ideas and Issues of the Bible*, Oxford University Press, Oxford 2001, p. 184 cites Rabbi Hillel (first century BCE): "What is hateful to you, do not do to your fellow creature. That is the whole law; the rest is commentary."
[39]   See Westermarck, Edward, *Ethical Relativity*, Kegan Paul, Trench, Trubner & Co., London 1932, p. 90.

something as being of a Christian identity is not only important for Christians themselves but also for other people who want to understand what Christians believe. When Bertrand Russell wanted to explain why he was not a Christian, he first elaborated on the question "What is a Christian?" And subsequently he noted that in his days the word "Christian" was used in a loose way. Many people presented definitions of "Christian" and "Christianity" that would make every moral actor a "Christian." That is not very fruitful, to put it mildly. He wrote: "I think that you must have a certain amount of definite beliefs before you have a right to call yourself a Christian."[40] He presents three points. A "Christian" is someone (1) who believes in the existence of God, (2) in a life after death, (3) and in the special significance of Jesus Christ.[41]

One may discuss the relative importance of each of those criteria and also the relationship between them. The last, emphasis on the importance of Christ, seems the least controversial. The British philosopher Charlie Dunbar Broad (1887–1971) wrote: "The first and most important peculiarity of Christianity is that it is, to a unique degree, a doctrine about its own Founder."[42] The other two criteria Russell mentioned might be more controversial. Can someone be considered a "Christian," for example, who does *not* believe in the existence of God? Or can he be a "Christian" and *not* believe in life after death?[43]

The last element of the Christian heritage leaves some room for diverging views. Some believe in immediate life after death, others in the resurrection of the body at the end of time.

And what is the relationship between these criteria? Is there some logical connection between life after death and the existence of God?

The British Hegelian philosopher John McTaggart Ellis McTaggart (1866–1925) wrote an elegant book in 1906 in which he expounded his religious ideas. What was striking in McTaggart's book was not only the usual philosophical rigor of his argumentation but also the combination of religious ideas he held to be compatible. McTaggart believed in immortality, but *not* in the existence of an all-powerful God.[44]

It is not necessary for the line of argument of *The Secular Outlook* to elaborate on these matters. The only thing I want to emphasize is that

---

[40] Russell, *Why I am not a Christian*, p. 2.

[41] Ibid.

[42] Broad, C.D., "Relations of Science and Religion," in: C.D. Broad, *Religion, Philosophy and Psychical Research: Selected Essays*, Humanities Press, New York 1969, pp. 220–247, p. 221.

[43] See for an anthology of philosophical views on immortality: Edwards, Paul, ed., *Immortality*, Prometheus Books, Buffalo, NY 1997.

[44] See: McTaggart, John M.E., *Human Immortality and Pre-Existence*, Edward Arnold, London 1915; reprint of chapters. 3–4 as *Some Dogmas of Religion*, with an Introduction by C.D. Broad, Thoemmes Press, Bristol 1997 (1906).

Russell was right when he contended that it is only meaningful to discuss the question of whether you are a "Christian" (or not) if it is possible to present some characteristics of the Christian creed. Again, we may agree or disagree with Russell about the question of whether his three criteria are the right choices, but it would be meaningless to defend the notion that there are no criteria at all.

If we could, together with Humpty Dumpty, let words mean what we choose them to mean, communication would be pointless. Yet many discussions, especially about sensitive issues – and religion is such an issue – are flawed because people are reluctant to provide us with clear definitions. Disputants asking for such definitions are dismissively qualified as "dogmatists" or "fundamentalists." It is all a matter of interpretation, can't you see? (Think about what has been said on the debate between Ramadan and Hirsi Ali in Chapter 2.) Philosopher Walter Sinnott-Armstrong discusses a contention, often made by postmodern authors, that religious language should be understood not as making truth-claims but merely as being expressions of hope (or fear). But such constructions of religion simply change the subject by "robbing all religious claims of all content."[45] Once religion becomes "wishy-washy, you can't refute it, but you also have no reason to believe it," so Sinnott-Armstrong tells us.[46]

Now, from Christianity, as expounded by the Pope, let us go over to theism. This is a necessary preliminary to discussing the relationship between theism and moral autonomy.

What Judaism, Christendom, and Islam Have in Common: Theism

Judaism, Christendom, and Islam differ in some aspects. But none of these differences can hide the one major similarity. This similarity concerns the concept of God upheld by Judaism, Christendom, and Islam. The "religions of the book" do not differ in their understanding of God. "At the heart of Islam stands the reality of God, the One, the Absolute and the Infinite, the Infinitely Good and All-Merciful, the One Who is at once transcendent and immanent, greater than all we can conceive or imagine, yet, as the Qur'an, the sacred scripture of Islam, attests, closer to us than our jugular vein."[47]

---

[45] Sinnott-Armstrong, Walter, "Overcoming Christianity," in: Louise M. Antony, ed., *Philosophers Without Gods: Meditations on Atheism and the Secular Life*, Oxford University Press, Oxford 2007, pp. 69–80, p. 74.
[46] Ibid., p. 74.
[47] Hossein Nasr, Seyyed, *The Heart of Islam. Enduring Values for Humanity*, Harper Collins, San Francisco 2004, p. 3.

So far we have, in the eyes of an Islamic writer, some elements that characterize Islam. But these are not unique to Islam. The same may be said of Judaism and Christianity. The idea of God outlined here is that of the *theistic* god.[48]

As we shall see, it is also important for Christianity, Judaism, and Islam to be labeled the "Abrahamic religions." All three recognize Abraham as a forefather.[49] Likewise, Judaism, Christendom and Islam are labeled "theistic religions" because all three subscribe to "theism," the belief in a single god with the characteristics outlined above.

The American historian of the Middle East Bernard Lewis (1916–) is right when he says that Islam, Judaism, and Christianity display quite a few similarities. Islam is much closer to the Judeo-Christian tradition than to Hinduism, Buddhism, or Confucianism. Judaism and Islam share the belief in a divine law thought to regulate all aspects of human life, even down to the food and drink we consume.

British philosopher Anthony Kenny (1931–) stresses the same point. Not only do Jews and Christians share a common heritage, he writes in his book *What I Believe* (2006), but Christianity and Islam, too, have much in common.[50]

> Both religions are monotheistic and universalist. Both traditions recognize the Hebrew Scriptures as inspired texts, bearing a message from God that has been suspended by later, definitive revelation. Members of all three faiths appeal to their own sacred texts to guide or justify their actions of the present day, and within each tradition there are many different methods and procedures by which the ancient sayings are linked to the conditions of modern life.[51]

That similarity is welcomed by many as the basis of a common ethic. In 1908 philosopher L.T. Hobhouse (1864–1929) wrote: "With regard to the standard, as opposed to the basis of morals, all forms of monotheism have

---

[48] A frequently made observation is that Islam is more consistently monotheistic than Christendom, because Islam has no concept of the trinity. On this subject, see: Haeckel, *Die Welträtsel*, p. 363.

[49] Kuschel, Karl-Josef, *Streit um Abraham. Was Juden, Christen und Muslime trennt und was sie eint* [The Dispute about Abraham. What Divides Jews, Christians and Muslims and What Unites Them], Patmos 2001; Feiler, Bruce, *Abraham. A Journey to the Heart of Three Faiths*, William Morrow 2002.

[50] Kenny, *What I Believe*, p. 55.

[51] Ibid., p. 56. There are also authors who emphasize the differences between the three theistic religions. See: Weigel, George, *Faith, Reason, and the War against Jihadism: A Call to Action*, Doubleday, New York 2007, p. 21 referring to the fact that Islam takes a radically supersessionist view of both Judaism and Christianity "claiming that the final revelation to Muhammad de facto trumps, by way of supersession, any prior revelatory value (so to speak) that might be found in the Hebrew Bible or the Christian New Testament."

something in common. God is the father of all. Therefore, all men are brothers, and should be members of one Church."[52] But only a few lines further that commonality seems to evaporate because although this "potential universalism," as Hobhouse called it, is common to Islam and Christianity, he censured the Jewish religion for its "national exclusiveness." And in continuing his analysis Hobhouse had to acknowledge that Christianity "has really more affinity with Buddhism."[53]

Besides, not all that the theistic creeds have in common can be considered to be great contributions to a basis for living together with non-believers. Lewis points out that Christians and Muslims also share some form of "triumphalism," seeing themselves as the chosen standard-bearers of God's one true message, a message they are expected to pass on to the rest of mankind. Christendom and Islam "are in many ways sister civilizations, both drawing on the same shared heritage."[54]

For much of their shared history Christendom and Islam have fought one another, and yet, Lewis writes, "even in struggle and polemic they reveal their essential kinship and the common features that link them to each other and set them apart from the remoter civilizations of Asia."[55]

From a Muslim perspective, Judaism and Christendom are forerunners of Islam. But the scriptures of the Jews and Christians, although based on authentic sources, are incomplete. These scriptures have, as it were, been "overtaken" by Islam. Islam has incorporated the true elements of Christendom and labeled as untrue those elements that have not been incorporated.[56]

British philosopher John Haldane (1954–) writes that theism "is the belief in a single, all-knowing, all-good, all-present, and all-powerful, eter-

---

[52]   Hobhouse, L.T., *Morals in Evolution: A Study in Comparative Ethics*, Part II, Chapman and Hall, London 1908, p. 148.

[53]   Ibid.

[54]   Lewis, Bernard, *The Crisis of Islam. Holy War and Unholy Terror*, Weidenfeld & Nicolson, London 2003, p. 4.

[55]   Ibid., p. 5.

[56]   Lewis, Bernard, *What Went Wrong? The Clash between Islam and Modernity in the Middle East*, Weidenfeld and Nicolson, London 2002, p. 36. Some believe this is why Islam seems disinclined to develop further. See Constant, Benjamin, "De la religion considérée dans la source, ses formes et ses développements" [Of Religion Considered in Its Source, Forms, and Developments] in: Benjamin Constant, *Œuvres*, ed. Alfred Roulin, Éditions Gallimard, Paris 1957, pp. 1365–1395, p. 1373. Constant says of Islam that it is the most static religion. Alexis de Tocqueville is even more critical of Islam. In their correspondence, he reproaches his friend Gobineau, whom he believes to have developed a certain unwarranted sympathy for Islam. See Tocqueville's letter to Gobineau dated October 2, 1843 in: Tocqueville, Alexis de, and Gobineau, Arthur de, *Correspondance entre Alexis de Tocqueville et Arthur de Gobineau*, 1843–1859, Librairie Plon, Paris 1909, p. 24. On Tocqueville and religion: Cliteur, Paul, "A Secular Reading of Tocqueville," in: Raf Geenens and Annelien de Dijn, eds., *Reading Tocqueville: From Oracle to Actor*, Palgrave, Macmillan, Basingstoke 2007, pp. 112–132.

nally existing God who created and sustains the universe."[57] He adds that, more specifically, he has in mind the so-called "Abrahamic faiths" or "religions of the book": Judaism, Christianity, and Islam. These descriptions derive from the account given in the Torah (the first five books of the Hebrew Bible). All three religions recognize the authority of the Hebrew Bible as the word of God to humankind, Haldane writes.[58]

This is in line with other definitions of theism (or monotheism) that were presented in Chapter 1. Yet there is a problem. In Chapter 2, I discussed the story of Phinehas, who punished his fellow Israelites for their worship of the wrong gods. In a previous section of that same chapter we saw that Deuteronomy 13:1–3 gives "a warning against idolatry." Here is the relevant quote again:

> If a prophet or a dreamer of dreams arises among you and gives you a sign or a wonder, and the sign or wonder that he tells you comes to pass, and if he says, "let us go after other gods," which you have not known, "and let us serve them," you shall not listen to the words of that prophet or that dreamer of dreams.

This is only understandable if "going after other gods" was a common practice among the Israelites, so apparently there were *other gods* besides Yahweh. The biblical injunction "You shall walk after the Lord your God and fear him and keep his commandments and obey his voice, and you shall serve him and hold fast to him" (Deuteronomy 13:4–5) only makes sense against the background of a situation where there are also other gods around. As William Wainwright writes:

> Most mainstream Old Testament scholars believe that the religion of the early Israelites was neither monotheistic nor polytheistic but "monolatrous." While the existence of other gods was not denied, Israel was to worship no god but Yahweh.[59]

One can also say that the religion of Israel was "incipiently" monotheistic from its Mosaic beginnings, Wainwright says.[60]

---

[57] Haldane, John, *An Intelligent Person's Guide to Religion*, Duckworth Overlook, London, 2003, p. 17.
[58] Ibid., p. 18.
[59] Wainwright, William, "Monotheism," in: *Stanford Encyclopedia of Philosophy*, in: http://plato.stanford.edu, 2005, pp. 1–23, p. 1.
[60] Ibid., p. 2. See also: Tilghman, B.R., *An Introduction to the Philosophy of Religion*, Blackwell, Oxford 1994, p. 30 and Nikiprowetzky, V., "Ethical Monotheism," in: *Daedalus*, 104, no. 2, Revelation, and Doubt: Perspectives on the First Millenium B.C., (Spring, 1975), pp. 69–89, p. 76.

In the first five books of the Bible there is little suggestion of monotheism. Yahweh issues commands as: "You shall have no other gods besides Me" (Exodus 20:3, Deuteronomy 5:7). Moses is told: "you must not worship any other god, because the Lord, whose name is Impassioned, is an impassioned God" (Exodus 34:14). Here we do not find a denial that there are other gods; the only message is that they are not to be worshipped by the Israelites.

Also in other places of the Bible Yahweh is introduced as "the God of Abraham, the God of Isaac, and the God of Jacob" (Exodus 3:6). As philosopher of religion B.R. Tilghman rightly says: "In all these dealings and introductions there is ... no suggestion of monotheism."[61]

This all changed when the Babylonians conquered the kingdom of Judah in 587 BCE. The religion of Yahweh underwent a crisis. The city of Jerusalem was partly destroyed, and so was the temple of Solomon. Prominent Israelites were taken to Babylon as hostages. This presented a new problem. How could Yahweh be worshipped if his temple no longer existed? When his powers were primarily local, how could he be worshipped in a foreign land? As a result of this, a new conception of Yahweh developed and by the end of the Babylonian captivity Judaism was "unequivocally monotheist."[62] Yahweh was no longer the deity of a local people, but the God of the whole world who can be worshipped anywhere. This new idea of God is to be found in Isaiah 45:5: "I am the Lord, and there is no other, Besides me there is no God."[63] This mature theistic concept of god (or God) is the focus of this book.

Divine Command Theories

The question now is this: what is the effect of theism, which lies at the heart of the three major religions in Europe, on morality? Is theism tied to a certain ethics and if so, which one?

Before answering this question we first have to elucidate that the term "ethics" has at least two different meanings. First, "ethics" can refer to theories on substantive judgments of right and wrong. Substantive judgments on right and wrong are for instance: "Stealing is wrong," "Lying is wrong." The "ethics" of Christianity comprises a whole list of what Christianity considers morally right and wrong.[64] But – and now we shift

---

[61] Tilghman, *Introduction*, p. 29; Nikiprowetzky, "Ethical Monotheism", p. 78.

[62] Tilghman, *Introduction*, p. 30.

[63] Nikiprowetzky, Ibid., p. 82 writes: "Radical monotheism is unambiguously present ... in the doctrine of the Second Isaiah."

[64] See on this: Gill, Robin, ed., *The Cambridge Companion to Christian Ethics*, Cambridge University Press, Cambridge 2001; McCoy, Alban, *An Intelligent Person's Guide to Christian Ethics*, Continuum, London 2004; Geisler, Norman L., *Christian Ethics: Options and Issues*, Apollos, Leicester 1990.

to the second meaning of the term – "ethics" can also refer to questions about the *nature* of moral theories and judgments. Then we focus on questions like: "What is the nature of moral disagreement?" Or: "How can our moral judgments be justified?" That last branch of ethics is also characterized as "metaethics."

In this book I will be mainly concerned with metaethics, but because linguistic terminology is loose here, I will not be consistent in upholding the distinction between "metaethics" and "ethics." This may serve as a *caveat*. If we talk about "ethics" in *The Secular Outlook* this is primarily about what philosophers would indicate as "metaethics." The question that concerns me in this book is: "What do the three theistic religions have to say on the nature of moral obligation?" And strictly speaking this is metaethics.

The metaethics of theism can best be illustrated through a story about the father of the Abrahamic religions: Abraham himself. As will be made clear from what follows, the ethics (or metaethics) that appears to resonate best with the theistic faiths is the theory known as *divine command theory*. This divine command theory assumes that what is morally right is synonymous with what has been commanded, prescribed, or ordered by God. Morally wrong are those actions forbidden by God. In other words, "morally wrong" means: "forbidden by God." "Morally right" means: "commanded by God."[65] Or, as the Victorian theologian John Bernard Dalgairns (1818–1876) formulated it: "If morals are to have a foundation in a real obligation, then there is a God."[66]

It is against the background of the divine command theory that the abhorrence of atheism which I have described in the first chapter becomes understandable. Atheists are so much hated because they are supposed to be immoral. Psalm 14:1 formulates this clearly:

> The fool says in his heart,
> "There is no God."
>
> They are corrupt, they do
> abominable deeds,
> There is none who does good.

---

[65] Blackburn, Pierre, "L'appel au commandement divin et ses critiques," [The Appeal to Divine Command and Its Critics] in: Pierre Blackburn, *L'éthique. Fondements et problématiques contemporaines* [Ethics. Contemporary Foundations and Problematics], Éditions du Renouveau Pédagogique, Saint Laurent 1996, pp. 115–133, p. 116: "Thus, what is good, is what God commands; what is bad, is what God forbids."

[66] Dalgairns, John Bernard, "Is God unknowable?" in: *Contemporary Review*, Vol. XX, 1872, pp. 615–630, also in: Andrew Pyle, ed., *Agnosticism: Contemporary Responses to Spencer and Huxley*, Thoemmes Press, Bristol 1995, pp. 20–38, p. 27.

So anyone who says "there is no God" is suspected of "abominable deeds."

Some ethicists have called the divine command theory "supernatural-ism." "Supernaturalism says that moral judgments describe God's will," logician and ethicist Harry J. Gensler writes. "Calling something 'good' means that God desires it. Ethics is based on religion."[67] A contemporary proponent of the divine command theory, Janine Marie Idziak, puts it as follows: "Generally speaking, a 'divine command moralist' is one who maintains that the content of morality (i.e. what is right and wrong, good and evil, just and unjust, and the like) is directly and solely dependent upon the commands and prohibitions of God."[68] Divine command ethics sees morality as "revealed." According to divine command ethics there is an intimate relationship between theology and ethics.

Theology or the science of God can be divided into two categories. On the one hand there is natural theology. *Natural theology* seeks knowledge of God through human reason. On the other hand there is revealed theol-ogy. *Revealed theology* requires faith in the veracity of divine revelation. According to most Christian theologians (Thomas Aquinas being the most important) the certainty of faith is superior to the certainty that reason can attain; reason is subservient to faith.

The articles of faith are to be found in the Bible as the infallible authority of God that cannot be demonstrated by reason. Although natural theology, according to Aquinas (*c.* 1225–1274) can justify theism, it cannot justify *Christian* theism.[69]

The relationship between "faith" and "reason" is a great theme in the Christian tradition.[70] It even plays a role in the Bible, as we have seen on several occasions. The Bible, like every other holy book, contains a mixture of general rules that could safely be copied and made the basis for our contemporary morals and legislation in combination with the most atro-cious precepts that mirror a world that is definitely not something to aspire to. Here are some good pieces of advice from St. Paul's letter to the Romans.

In Romans 12:9 Paul defines the characteristics of the true Christian and writes: "Abhor what is evil; hold fast to what is good." That is an important passage because it is difficult to see how this can be interpreted otherwise

---

[67]   Gensler, Harry J., "Supernaturalism," in: *Ethics*, Routledge, London 1998, pp. 33–46, p. 34.

[68]   Idziak, Janine Marie, "Divine Command Morality: A Guide to the Literature," in: Janine Marie Idziak, *Divine Command Morality: Historical and Contemporary Readings*, The Edwin Mellen Press, New York 1979, pp. 1–38, p. 1.

[69]   See on the proofs of God's existence: McGrath, Alister E., *Theology: The Basics*, p. 3; Steenbergen, Fernand van, *Le Thomisme* [Thomism], Presses Universitaires de France, Paris 1983, p. 31 ff.

[70]   See on this: Helm, Paul, ed., *Faith and Reason*, Oxford University Press, Oxford 1999; Helm, Paul, *Faith and Understanding*, Edinburgh University Press, Edinburgh 1997.

than as the recognition of an autonomous idea of "good." Paul also gives some other advice that may sound somewhat impractical but is certainly not evil. He says "Let love be genuine" (Romans: 12:9) and "if possible, so far as it depends on you, live peaceably with all" (Romans 12:18). He also tells us: "Beloved, never avenge yourselves, but leave it to the wrath of God, for it is written, 'Vengeance is mine, I will repay, says the Lord'" (Romans 12:19). "It is written," says Paul, and he cites here Deuteronomy 32:35:

> Vengeance is mine, and recompense,
> for the time when their foot shall slip;
> for the day of their calamity is at hand,
> and their doom comes swiftly.

The *motivation* for the dismissal of vigilante justice might be less laudable but, anyhow, religious terrorists will be discouraged from taking the law in their own hands as a result if passages like these are taken seriously. That impression is reinforced by the well-known opening sentences of Romans 13: "Let every person be subject to the governing authorities. For there is no authority except from God, and those that exist have been instituted by God."

Those laudable recommendations go hand in hand with ideas that we can hardly accept nowadays, the most important one, perhaps, the idea that having a different opinion on religious matters has to be punished by God. Paul's Letter to the Romans opens with a diatribe against the unbelievers who have not accepted God's message although they could have understood this by purely rational means. Romans 1:18 says:

> For the wrath of God is revealed from heaven against all ungodliness and unrighteousness of men, who by their unrighteousness suppress the truth. For what can be known about God is plain to them, because God has shown it to them. For his invisible attributes, namely, his eternal power and divine nature, have been clearly perceived, ever since the creation of the world, in the things that have been made. So they are without excuse. For although they knew God, they did not honor him as God or give thanks to him, but they became futile in their thinking, and their foolish hearts were darkened.

Here we encounter one of the most obnoxious elements of the theistic creeds: their tendency to intimidate people into the right sort of faith by threatening punishments for those who think otherwise. Paul draws the speedy and unwarranted conclusion that people who don't believe in the Christian god do so with "unrighteousness." And he tells us – again without good reason – that those who think differently "suppress the truth." This is nonsense, of course. What makes this passage important, though, is that

Paul also reproaches those who have not accepted God's word on the ground that they could have figured out some of the divine attributes for themselves. "What can be known about God is plain to them," he writes. God had shown it to them. How? The answer is that his invisible attributes could be perceived "in the things that have been made."

The idea seems to be that in analyzing the world around us we could have drawn the conclusion that this must have been made by a divine creator. Not concluding that makes us involved in, in Paul's words, "suppressing the truth," something for which we have to be (and will be) punished. This seems to be a confirmation of the position that apart from revelation in Christ and Holy Scripture there is also the opportunity to know God from his creation. The relationship between natural theology and revealed theology, between reason and faith, has been an immensely important theme in the theistic tradition with the most controversial question being: which should have priority?

Here is one quote from a famous Christian philosopher, theologian and scientist who lays heavy stress on the importance of "faith" and subsequently on revealed theology above natural theology. In his *Pensées* Blaise Pascal writes:

> The metaphysical proofs for the existence of God are so remote from human reason and so involved that they make little impact, and, even if they did help some people, it would only be for the moment during which they watched the demonstration, because an hour later they would be afraid they had made a mistake.[71]

So we have to rely on *revealed theology* for the most important truths. That has relevance for morality as well. We cannot discover by reason what the most important moral rules are, we have to rely on revelation. Divine command ethics pays tribute to that fundamental insight of Pascal. The divine command theory, ethicist James Rachels wrote, typically views God as a lawgiver who has issued the rules that we, human beings, must obey.[72]

According to the philosopher Louis Pojman (1935–2005) the divine command theory of morality is based on three assumptions:

1. Morality (i.e. rightness and wrongness) originates with God.
2. Moral rightness simply means "willed by God," and moral wrongness means "against the will of God."

---

[71] Pascal *Pensées*, p. 168.

[72] Rachels, James, "Does Morality Depend on Religion?" in: James Rachels, *The Elements of Moral Philosophy*, fourth edition, McGraw-Hill Inc., New York etc. 2003 (1986), pp. 48–63, p. 50.

3. Since morality essentially is based on divine will, not on independently existing reasons for action, no further reasons for action are necessary.[73]

Divine command theories come in three varieties.

First there is the *mystic* brand. "Mysticism may broadly be defined as the direct apprehension of the divine by a faculty of mind or soul," Owen Chadwick (1916–) writes.[74] We find this in Exodus when God directs himself to Moses: "Then the Lord said to Moses" (Exodus 7:14; 8:20; 9:1). The famous passage containing the Ten Commandmentss (Exodus 20:1) is introduced with: "And God spoke all these words, saying ... ." So God directs himself immediately to the individual believer. The same idea is found in Islam: "The Prophet of Islam is seen as a second Moses, a man who brings the Law to this earth," writes the French scholar of Islam Abdelwahab Meddeb (1946–).[75]

Second, there is a kind of divine command theory that operates on the basis of mediation: the divine will is made known to humanity by God's special representative on earth (a pope, priest, or ayatollah). In a way this is also present in the story of Moses, because the people of Israel only know what God wants because the will of God has been revealed to Moses. Spiritual leaders, like Moses, "interpret" the will of God for the common man. The Catholic Church is based on this principle. The pope is the ultimate interpreter of the divine will. This second theory might be called the *catholic* divine command theory.

A third theory goes back to the Reformation. Luther's theological teaching boils down to the idea of *Sola Scriptura* (only scripture). The Greeks did not have anything like scripture. The closest they had to it, writes philosopher B.R. Tilghman, was poetry. "It was on the great epic poems of Homer, the *Iliad* and *Odyssey*, and works such as Hesiod's *Theogony* that the Greeks relied for their knowledge of the gods."[76] But the *Iliad* and *Odyssey* never attained the status of the Hebrew Bible or the New Testament. What distinguishes Protestantism from Catholicism is that the status of the Bible as scripture was even more strongly emphasized. As Christopher Catherwood (1955–) argues, this "totally overturned hundreds of years of Catholic Church teaching."[77] Luther taught that Christians can have a

---

[73] Louis P. Pojman, *Ethics. Discovering Right and Wrong*, second edition, Wadsworth, Belmont, California 1995, p. 236.

[74] Chadwick, Owen, *The Counter-Reformation*, Penguin Books, Harmondworth 1964, p. 296.

[75] Meddeb, Abdelwahab, "En terre d'islam" [On Islamic Soil], p. 140.

[76] Tilghman, B.R., *An Introduction to the Philosophy of Religion*, Blackwell, Oxford 1994, p. 24.

[77] Catherwood, Christopher, *Making War in the Name of God*, Citadel Press, Kensington Publishing Corp., New York 2007, p. 112.

direct relationship with God, unmediated by any other human being.[78] This meant that individual Christians could interpret the Bible directly, rather than having an infallible Church impose its meaning on them.[79] The conception of the Catholic Church was different. As the British historian Diarmaid McCulloch (1951–) indicates, Pope Paul V (1552–1621) was serious when in 1606 he confronted the Venetian ambassador with the rhetorical question: "Do you not know that so much reading of Scripture ruins the Catholic religion?"[80] Obviously, there is considerable difference between the Catholic and the Protestant divine command theory.

To sum up, there are three versions: the mystic, Catholic and Protestant divine command theories, each theory drawing inspiration from a certain kind of revelation.

Now, let us see what the problems with this theory are. The most dramatic example of the moral dilemmas of divine command theory are to be found with Abraham, the founding father of all the three theistic creeds: the Jewish religion, Christianity, and Islam. The classic example here is the story of Abraham receiving the divine command to sacrifice his son Isaac.[81]

It is an Old Testament story and is therefore important to both Judaism and Christendom. But it also features (with small variations) in the Qur'an.[82] Let me start with the description of what happened according to the narrative in the Bible.

Abraham and Isaac

In Genesis 22 the Bible tells us the story of the "Akedah," the Binding of Isaac, and God's command to Abraham that he must sacrifice his only son.[83] Abraham is about to do so when God's angel intervenes to halt the tragic

---

[78]   Ibid., p. 55.

[79]   Ibid., p. 112.

[80]   MacCulloch, Diarmaid, *Reformation: Europe's House Divided, 1490–1700*, Penguin Books, London 2004 (2003), p. 406.

[81]   The story of Job would be another good example. By approaching Job in the guise of the devil, God puts Job to the test, Jack Miles explains. He tempts Job, as he tempted Abraham. "That is, he tempts him by speaking to him in the tones of merciless power. Job passes the test precisely as Abraham did." See: Miles, Jack, *God. A Biography*, Alfred A. Knopf, New York 1995, p. 322.

[82]   In the Islamic version the would-be victim is Ishmael or Isma'il, Abraham's son with the bondwoman Hager, who lived to become ancestor of the Arabs. See: Ruthven, Malise, *Islam: A Very Short Introduction*, Oxford University Press, Oxford 2000 (1997), p. 30.

[83]   Moberly, R.W.L., "The Earliest Commentary on the Akedah," *Vetus Testamentum*, 28 1988), pp. 302–323, p. 302: "Few stories within the Old Testament have received more commentary than the story of the testing of Abraham – widely known as the Akedah, the Binding of Isaac – in Genesis 22:1–19."

action. The tragic act is aborted, not because the act is reconsidered, but because of an intervening event: Abraham abandons his initial intent because he hears the Angel.[84] It cannot come as a surprise that this story contains many potential elements of tragedy. It remained a popular dramatic subject well into the sixteenth century, when it was interpreted as a tragedy indeed.[85]

Here is the relevant passage in the Bible. God said to Abraham:

> Take your son, your only son Isaac, whom you love and go to the land of Moraiah, and offer him there as a burnt offering on one of the mountains of which I shall tell you." So Abraham rose early in the morning, saddled his donkey, and took two of his young men with him, and his son Isaac. And he cut the wood for the burnt offering and arose and went to the place of which God had told him. On the third day Abraham lifted up his eyes and saw the place from afar. Then Abraham said to his young men, "Stay here with the donkey, I and the boy will go over there and worship and come again to you." And Abraham took the wood of the burnt offering and laid it on Isaac his son. And he took in his hand the fire and the knife. So they went both of them together. And Isaac said to his father Abraham, "My father!" And he said, "Here am I, my son." He said, "Behold the fire and the wood, but where is the lamb for a burnt offering?" Abraham said, "God will provide for himself the lamb for a burnt offering, my son." So they went both of them together.
>
> When they came to the place of which God had told him, Abraham built the altar there and laid the wood in order and bound Isaac his son and laid him on the altar on the top of wood. Then Abraham reached out his hand and took the knife to slaughter his son. But the angel of the Lord called to him from heaven and said, "Abraham, Abraham!" And he said, "Here am I." He said, "Do not lay your hand on the boy or do anything to him, for now I know that you fear God, seeing you have not withheld your son, your only son, from me." And Abraham lifted up his eyes and looked, and behold, behind him was a ram, caught in a thicket by his horns. And Abraham went and took the ram and offered it up as a burnt offering instead of his son. So Abraham called the name of that place, "The Lord will provide," as it is said to this day, "On the mount of the Lord it shall be provided." (Genesis 22:1–13)

Because of this obedience Abraham is praised by the Lord. The angel of the Lord said to Abraham: "By myself I have sworn, declares the Lord, because

---

[84] See: Mleynek, Sherryll, "Abraham, Aristotle, and God: The Poetics of Sacrifice," *Journal of the American Academy of Religion*, 62, no. 1 1994, pp. 107–121, p. 109; Delaney, Carol, *Abraham on Trial: the Social Legacy of Biblical Myth*, Princeton University Press, Princeton 1998, p. 69 ff.

[85] Elliot John R., Jr, "The Sacrifice of Isaac as Comedy and Tragedy," *Studies in Philology*, 66, no. 1 1969, pp. 36–59, p. 39.

you have done this and have not withheld your son, your only son, I will surely bless you, and I will surely multiply your offspring as the stars of heaven and as the sand that is on the seashore. And your offspring shall possess the gate of his enemies and in your offspring shall all the nations of the earth be blessed, because you have obeyed my voice." (Genesis 22:15–18).

As the American legal scholar Alan Dershowitz (1938–) remarked: "Abraham Commits Attempted Murder – and Is Praised."[86] Abraham proves his faith by obeying God's command. He supremely exemplifies the meaning of living by the Torah. "He as an individual demonstrates the quality of response to God that should characterize Israel as whole," as it has been argued.[87]

The story of Abraham and Isaac obliges us to reconsider the relationship between faith and ethics.[88] It also presents us with many theological and hermeneutic questions: how can we explain that Abraham dared to protest and insist that God should not exceed ethical norms in the story of Sodom (the story of Sodom will be treated more extensively in the section Worship in this chapter), but is so compliant in the Akedah?[89]

The Story of Abraham in the Qur'an

The story of the offering of Abraham's son is – with slight variations – also included in the Qur'an. There, Abraham tells his son: "My son, I dreamt that I was sacrificing you. Tell me what you think" (Qur'an 37:91–110). The son is obedient and replies: "Father, do as you are bidden. God willing, you shall find me steadfast."

> And when they had both submitted to God, and Abraham had laid down his son prostrate upon his face, We called out to him, saying: "Abraham, you have fulfilled your vision." Thus do We reward the righteous. That was indeed a bitter test. We ransomed his son with a noble sacrifice and bestowed on him the praise of later generations. "Peace be on Abraham!" (Qur'an, 37:105, translation Dawood)[90]

---

[86] In: Dershowitz, Alan M., *The Genesis of Justice. Ten Stories of Biblical Injustice that Led to the Ten Commandments and Modern Law*, Warner Books, New York 2000.

[87] Moberly, R.W.L., "The Earliest Commentary on the Akedah," *Vetus Testamentum*, 28 1988, pp. 302–323, p. 305.

[88] Boehm, Omri, "The Binding of Isaac: An Inner-Biblical Polemic on the Question of 'Disobeying' a Manifestly Illegal Order," *Vetus Testamentum*, 52 2002, pp. 1–12, p. 1.

[89] See: ibid., p. 12. See also: Sandmel, Samuel, "Abraham's Knowledge of the Existence of God," *The Harvard Theological Review*, 44, no. 3 1955, pp. 137–139.

[90] *The Qur'an*, translated with notes by N.J. Dawood, Penguin Books, London 1999.

This is a surprising story, but even more surprising is the way it is sometimes interpreted. By many believers it is not interpreted as a manifestation of God's irresponsible behavior in requiring this of Abraham, but as a sign of God's goodness for not requiring the making of the actual offering.

In December 2007 an advertisement in the *International Herald Tribune* was published and headed with the words: "A Muslim Message of Thanks and of Christmas and New Year Greetings."[91] The text runs as follows.

> In the Name of God, the Compassionate, the Merciful
> May God bless Muhammed and his kin and bless Abraham and his kin
> Al-Salaamu Aleikum; Peace be upon you; Pax Vobiscum.

So far nothing special. But then the text continues in a more ecumenical way:

> Peace be upon Jesus Christ who says: Peace is upon me the day I was born, the day I die, and the day I am resurrected (Chapter of Mary; the Holy Qur'an, 19:33).

I am particularly interested in the picture of Abraham that is presented in this advertisement. I shall write in italics what is relevant to our theme.

> We pray, during these blessed days, which have coincided with the Muslim feast of the Hajj or Pilgrimage, which commemorates the faith of the Prophet Abraham (peace be upon him), that the New Year may bring healing and peace to our suffering world. *God's refusal to let Abraham (peace be upon him) sacrifice his son – granting him instead a ram – is to this day a Divine warrant and a most powerful social lesson for all the followers of the Abrahamic faiths, to ever do their utmost to save, uphold and treasure every single human life and especially the life of every single child.*

The advertisement is followed by some elaborations on the idea of the sanctity of life and signed by a long list of Islamic academics and other intellectuals.

How is it possible that the story of Abraham prepared to sacrifice his son is here presented as a morally uplifting tale? Evolutionary biologist Nicholas Humphrey (1943–) comments in his Amnesty Lecture 1997 on a remarkable discovery in the high mountains of Peru in 1995.[92] Some

---

[91]   A Muslim Message of Thanks and of Christmas and New Year Greetings December 2007," Advertisement, *International Herald Tribune*, December 31, 2007, January 1, 2008.
[92]   Humphrey, Nicholas, "What Shall We Tell the Children?" in: Nicholas Humphrey, *The Mind Made Flesh: Frontiers of Psychology and Evolution*, Oxford University Press, Oxford 2002, pp. 289–318, p. 305 and Dawkins commentary in: Dawkins, *The God Delusion*, pp. 366–372.

climbers came across the frozen mummified body of a young Inca girl, dressed as a princess, presumably thirteen years old. This little girl had been taken alive up the mountain by a party of priests, and then ritually killed as a sacrifice to the mountain's gods. The discovery was described by anthropologist Johan Reinhard (1943–) in *National Geographic*.[93] Humphrey was appalled by the uncritical tone of the article about this horrendous practice. This was even more evident in a documentary film on this discovery transmitted on American television. Humphrey says: "The message of the television programme was in effect that the practice of human sacrifice was in its own way a glorious cultural invention – another jewel in the crown of multiculturalism, if you like."[94] Humphrey castigates the makers of the documentary with the words:

> How dare they invite us – in our sitting rooms, watching television – to feel uplifted by contemplating an act of ritual murder: the murder of a dependent child by a group of stupid, puffed up, superstitious, ignorant old men?[95]

How, indeed, can we explain this condoning attitude toward barbarous practices? Is the Canadian political writer and cultural critic Mark Steyn (1959–) right when he says that "Europe has all but succumbed to the dull opiate of multiculturalism"?[96] Is it because people have no empathy with things that happened long ago? Are they inclined to think that religious practices are something one should not criticize? Are they under the spell of cultural relativism? Or do they consider the biblical and Qur'anic story of Abraham prepared to sacrifice his son as "just a story" without significance for the behavior of present-day believers?

What strikes us, of course, is the interpretation that is given to the story of Abraham. There is no critical note whatsoever that Abraham was willing to offer his son.[97] Neither is there any critical remark about the fact that God required this. The only thing that is stressed in the advertisement is the happy ending of the story. It is true, Abraham did not kill Isaac (or Ishmael in the Islamic tradition), but he is nonetheless portrayed as *capable* of an intentional violation of the taboo against kindred bloodshed.[98] This is astonishing, because the fact that Abraham was prepared to sacrifice his

---

[93] Reinhard, Johan, and Alvarez, Stephen, "Peru's Ice Maidens," *National Geographic*, June 1996, 189, no. 6, pp. 62–82.

[94] Humphrey, "What Shall We Tell the Children?", p. 305.

[95] Ibid., p. 306.

[96] Steyn, Mark, *America Alone: The End of the World as We Know It*, Regnery Publishing, Inc., Washington, DC 2006, p. xxiv.

[97] See on this: Delaney, Carol, *Abraham on Trial: The Social Legacy of Biblical Myth*, Princeton University Press, Princeton 1998.

[98] See: Mleynek, Sherryll, "Abraham, Aristotle, and God: The Poetics of Sacrifice," *Journal of the American Academy of Religion*, 62, no. 1 1994, pp. 107–121, p. 118.

son can hardly be seen as a laudable manifestation of respect for the principle of the "right to life," as indicated in the advertisement, especially not for the right to life of children. As Christopher Hitchens (1949–) says:

> All three monotheisms, just to take the most salient example, praise Abraham for being willing to hear voices and then to take his son Isaac for a long and rather mad and gloomy walk. And then the caprice by which his murderous hand is finally stayed is written down as divine mercy.[99]

The upshot of all this is that neither in the Islamic, nor in the Jewish or Christian sources is there broad sympathy for a critical stance toward Abraham's fatal choice. This is strange because, as the American philosopher Philip L. Quinn (1940–2004), rightly remarks, there is also the precept of the Decalogue that forbids murder.[100] From the perspective of divine command ethics, however, this is not a serious objection. The reason is that the direct command of God has priority over the Decalogue. St. Thomas Aquinas (*c.* 1225–1274) makes this clear in the following passage:

> when Abraham consented to slay his son, he did not consent to murder, because his son was due to be slain by the command of God, Who is Lord of life and death: for He is Who inflicts the punishment of death on all men, both godly and ungodly, on account of the sin of our first parent, and if a man be the executor of that sentence by Divine authority, he will be no murderer any more than God would.[101]

So Abraham has a duty to obey God's direct command. If he obeys it, he will be no murderer because he will merely be executing a just sentence of death passed by the lord of life and death, as Quinn summarizes Aquinas' point of view.[102] And since he is no murderer, the Decalogue's prohibition of murder does not apply to his case. Abraham simply has no duty not to kill Isaac.

Yet many followers of divine command ethics seem to be ambivalent in their view. We see this also with the signers of the advertisement. They cling to the second angelic voice that keeps Abraham from committing the tragic deed. By doing so, they manage to reinterpret the story as a story that manifests God's goodness: Abraham was *not* required to kill his son. This

---

[99] Hitchens, Christopher, *god is not Great*, p. 53. Hitchens' remarks about what the Ten Commandments do *not* say are also relevant, see, ibid., p. 100: "Is it too modern to notice that there is nothing about the protection of children from cruelty, nothing about rape, nothing about slavery, and nothing about genocide?"

[100] Quinn, Philip L., "Agamemnon and Abraham: the Tragic Dilemma of Kierkegaard's Knight of Faith," *Journal of Literature and Theology*, 4, no. 2, 1990, pp. 181–193, p. 187.

[101] St. Thomas Aquinas, *Summa Theologiae*, 1a2ae, 19, 6 *ad* 3.

[102] Quinn, "Agamemnon and Abraham," p. 188.

is a strange interpretation that the signers give to the story of the offer of Abraham.[103] Is it perhaps the case that their interpretation testifies to the fact that moral autonomy is unavoidable? That they give an interpretation to the story that conforms to ordinary moral sense?

In the second section of Chapter 2, I have treated the problem of evil and how this relates to the idea of an omniscient, omnipotent, and perfectly good god. This is also relevant here. Could the story of Abraham perhaps also be used as a source of inspiration for the *rejection* of the theistic worldview?

Philip Quinn presents the following argument. (1) Suppose God commands Abraham to kill Isaac; (2) If God commands Abraham to kill Isaac, then God commands Abraham to do something wrong; (3) If God commands Abraham to do something wrong, then God himself does wrong; (4) If God himself does wrong, then God is not morally perfect; and so (5) God is not morally perfect.[104]

No less worrying is the fact that St. Paul develops the typology of Isaac as the symbol of Christ. Paul says that Christians, like Isaac, are "children of promise" (Galatians 4:28; Romans 9:7). The German historian and philosopher of religion Hans-Joachim Schoeps (1909–1980) is probably correct when he writes that "The Binding of Isaac" was a Jewish theological concept that must have been familiar to Paul, a former Pharisee, for whom it served as his model when he undertook to develop his soteriology.[105]

> In the case of Isaac as of Jesus, there is a divinely commanded sacrifice of a son, although in the second case the victim is a man aware of being the Messiah and regarded as a Son of God, while in the first case a father (not God) is ready to sacrifice his only son in obedience to a divine command – a son 'on whom'? depends the fate of Israel and the world. Both are central events in sacred history, although Isaac's sacrifice was not completed.[106]

Also according to Augustine (354–430), the sacrifice of the son by the father was a foreshadowing of God's willingness to sacrifice His son for the

---

[103]   See for other interpretations: Simmons, J. Aaron, "What about Isaac? Rereading Fear and Trembling and Rethinking Kierkegaardian Ethics," *Journal of Religious Ethics*, 35, no. 2 2007, pp. 319–345 and Kretzmann, Norman, "Abraham, Isaac, and Euthyphro: God and the Basis of Morality," in: Eleonore Stump and Michael J. Murray, eds., *Philosophy of Religion: The Big Questions*, Blackwell Publishers, Malden, MA 1999, pp. 417–427. This line of argument is elaborated in: Rachels, James, "God and Human Attitudes," *Religious Studies*, 7 (1971), pp. 325–37, also in: James Rachels, *Can Ethics Provide Answers. And other Essays in Moral Philosophy*, Rowman and Littlefield Publishers, Lanham 1997, pp. 109–125.
[104]   Quinn, "Agamemnon and Abraham," p. 191.
[105]   Schoeps, Hans Joachim, "The Sacrifice of Isaac in Paul's Theology," *Journal of Biblical Literature*, 65, no. 4 1946, pp. 385–392, p. 386.
[106]   Ibid., p. 387.

redemption of mankind.[107] Abraham represented God, and Isaac Christ. Therefore the wood carried by Isaac to the sacrificial hill foreshadowed the cross of Calvary, and also the ram caught by his horn in the briers (Genesis 22:3) signified the Christ of the vicarious atonement crowned with thorns.[108] Abraham, as a type of God, necessarily offers his sacrifice willingly, out of faith and love. And Isaac, as a type of Christ, voluntarily endures his suffering out of faith and obedience.

Augustine also dealt with the seeming arbitrariness and immorality of God's command to Abraham. In his *Confessions* (397–398) Augustine wrote (apparently with Abraham in mind) that many things which appear worthy of men's disapproval are approved by God's command. And who will doubt that it should be done, even though it is opposed to the social conventions of men?[109] In *The City of God* (413–426) Augustine declares that not for a moment "could Abraham believe that God took delight in human sacrifices, although he knew that, once God's command rang out, it was his not to reason why, but to obey."[110]

The Story of Jephtha

The story of Job is similar. Job is "tested" by Satan with the knowledge and compliance of God. The most direct similarity with Abraham's offer, however, is to be found in the story of Jephtha. The story of Jephtha (Judges 11:1–40) is interesting because there is no happy ending. In contrast to Abraham, Jephtha does indeed bring the final offer.[111]

Jephtha was a "mighty warrior" (Judges 11:1) and he led Israel in a struggle against the Ammonites. In this struggle he was helped by the Lord. Jephtha made a vow to the Lord and said: "If you will give the Ammonites into my hand, then whatever comes out from the doors of my house to meet me when I return in peace from the Ammonites shall be the Lord's, and I will offer it up for a burnt offering" (Judges 29:30–32).

Jephtha went to war and the Lord gave the Ammonites into Jephtha's hand. The Ammonites "were subdued before the people of Israel" (Judges

---

[107] Augustine, *The City of God*, xvi 32.

[108] Elliott, John, Jr., "The Sacrifice of Isaac as Comedy and Tragedy," *Studies in Philology*, 66, no. 1 1969, pp. 36–59, p. 40.

[109] Augustine, *The Confessions*, iii, 9.

[110] Augustine *The City of God*, xvi, 32.

[111] See on Jephtha: Linton, Anna, "Sacrificed or Spared? The Fate of Jephtha's Daughter in Early Modern Theological and Literary Texts," *German Life and Letters*, 57, no. 3 2004, pp. 237–255; Houtman, Cornelis, "Rewriting a Dramatic Old Testament Story. The Story of Jephtha and his Daughter in some Examples of Christian Devotional Literature," *Biblical Interpretation*, 13, no. 2, 2005, pp. 167–190; Sjöberg, Mikael, "Jephtha's Daughter as Object of Desire or Feminist Icon," *Biblical Interpretation*, 15, 2007, pp. 377–394.

29:33). Then Jephtha came to his home at Mizpah. What came out from the door of his house? "His daughter came out to meet him with tambourines and with dances." Jephtha, so the Bible tells us, "did with her according to his vow that he had made" (Judges 29:39).

What to make of these stories? The similarity between the story of Abraham offering Isaac and that of Jephtha offering his daughter is striking. Both appear prepared to sacrifice their children. In both stories the children willingly comply. There is only one difference though. Abraham did not have to offer Isaac at the last moment, whereas Jephtha's daughter is actually sacrificed.

Another difference is that Abraham did not volunteer a vow to God, whereas Jephtha more or less caused his own unfortunate destiny because he himself sought the help of the Lord in securing his military success. Perhaps this makes Jephtha an even more unlikely candidate for advertisements with exhortations to respect human life than Abraham. Jephtha seems also a bit naïve. Making a vow that you will offer "whatever comes out from the doors" of your house is rather uncommon. What comes out of the doors of your house? Usually your wife, your children – in short: your own family. So it is hard to avoid the conclusion that Jephtha knowingly and willingly jeopardized his own kin for the sake of military success.

The story of Jephtha was a source of inspiration for several artists, as one can understand on the basis of the drama of the story. Handel (1685–1759) based his oratorio *Jephtha* (1751) on the vicissitudes of the unfortunate warrior. But, like so many others, the pious Handel could not live with the patent immorality of the story. The text of the oratorio was written by Reverend Thomas Morell (1703–1784) who made some amendments to the cruel story that make it more palatable to the taste of those who want to maintain the Bible as an important sourcebook for morals. Morell and Handel also introduced more characters. There is a certain Hamor who is betrothed to Jephtha's daughter who gets the name of "Iphis" in the oratorio, presumably suggested by a happy analogy from Agamemnon's daughter Iphigenea, the victim of a similar paternal vow.[112] The happy ending is, as in the story of Abraham, secured by the intervention of an angel. In Act Three of Handel's oratorio, Jephtha is preparing to carry through the sacrifice of his daughter, but at the last moment an angel appears, declaring that it was the Holy Spirit that inspired Jephtha's vow and explaining that its intent can be met if Jephtha's daughter remains for ever a virgin, dedicated to God. General jubilation is the result. Commentator Winton Dean (1916–) is not very satisfied with this *deus ex machina*: "Morell's attempt

---

[112] See: Dean, Winton, "Handel's Farewell to Oratorio," included in: Handel, *Jephtha*, Oratorio in Three Acts, Monteverdi Choir, English Baroque Soloists, Conducted by John Eliot Gardiner 1988, Decca.

to reconcile the Jehovah of the Old Testament with the Christian God betrayed him into an equivocal treatment of the vow and a feeble end, marred by a mixture of Puritanism and sentimentality characteristic of eighteenth century pietism."[113] There is no angel in this story, Dean tells us. After a sojourn in the mountains bewailing her virginity Jephtha's daughter returns and pays the full price, he says. And that is true. The Reverend Morell and the pious Handel apparently could not live with such an immoral ending in a biblical story.

Not only pious people were shocked by the story. Voltaire (1694–1778) was incensed as well. He wrote about the "abominable Jewish people" who complied with human sacrifices. They were barbarians and on the basis of barbaric laws they were prepared to sacrifice their children.[114]

Is this an unduly harsh verdict? Not from the perspective of an autonomous ethic, of course, but from the perspective of divine command ethics it is certainly not barbaric to conform to the commands of a perfect and eternal God who sometimes requires us to do things that, from our own limited point of reference, seem impossible to justify. For the divine command theorist these consequences are "all in the game": "For as the heavens are higher than the earth, so are my ways higher than your ways and my thoughts than your thoughts" (Isaiah 55:8–9). St. Paul formulates a similar idea:

> But who are you, O man, to answer back to God? Will what is moulded say to its moulder, "Why have you made me like this?" Has the potter no right over the clay, to make out of the same lump one vessel for honored use and another for dishonorable use? (Romans 9:20–22)

Texts like those of Isaiah and Romans are often quoted by those who cannot explain how divine goodness and omnipotence can be reconciled with the evident evil in the world. So they take refuge in the "as-the-heavens-are-higher-than-the-earth" argument. But does it hold? Is it true that God cannot be judged by human standards of morality? American author Sam Harris (1967–) is not convinced and answers that human standards of morality are precisely what believers use to establish God's goodness in the first place.[115] Harris is right.

An analysis of the moral theory implicit in the stories of Jephtha and Abraham is all the more pertinent once we realize that their attitude is not

---

[113] Ibid.

[114] Voltaire, *Extrait des sentiments de Jean Meslier* [Memoir of the Thoughts and Sentiments of Jean Meslier], in: Voltaire, *Mélanges* [Miscellaneous Works], Préface par Emmanuel Berl, Texte établi et annoté par Jacques van den Heuvel, Gallimard, Paris 1961, pp. 458–501, p. 487.

[115] Harris, Sam, *Letter to a Christian Nation*, Alfred A. Knopf, New York 2006, p. 55.

something that is to be found only in old books, but in real life as well. The lynchpin is the figure of Phinehas. What the attitude manifested by Abraham and Jephtha can lead to is shown in the intriguing story of Phinehas told in the book of Numbers. As we saw in Chapter 2, it can result in a total rejection of all temporal legal authority and a direct claim to operate as the executor of God's own wishes. For this is what Phinehas is: a priest, judge, and public hangman in one. He knows the will of God. And who can defy the will of God? Should not all moral considerations be swept aside once the will of God can be known? And what does God think of the heretics, unbelievers, seducers of the people who stray away from the path God has indicated? Of course, we should "not listen to the words of that prophet or that dreamer of dreams" (Deuteronomy 13:1–3), as was likewise made clear in Chapter 2. But what should we do if some people *do* listen to the treacherous seducers in our midst? Should we not use all means available to us to stop those false prophets?[116]

This seems especially pertinent when the state as a whole strays from the path of God. In that case we have an "apostate state," as even countries like Saudi Arabia are in the eyes of religious extremists like Bin Laden and Zawahiri. In that case we must – as Phinehas had the courage to – defy the authority of our political leaders.

This is, basically, the worldview that religious extremists subscribe to. And this worldview is based, among other things, on a firm rejection of the notion of moral autonomy. Religious terrorists are firm believers in divine command morality. Not in a metaphoric or poetical, but in a literal sense.[117] But if that is the case, should we not ponder over the question of how to foster moral autonomy among the citizenry? Especially in a historical context of multiculturalism and globalization, when the will of a religious leader in some far away country (Fukuyama's "religious crackpot") has relevance for the way some citizens of Western democracies think, this seems of vital importance.

Adherents of Divine Command Theory

As I have stated before, the theory of ethics, or more precisely of "metaethics," that is implicit in the stories of Abraham and Jephtha is called the

---

[116] See: Collins, John T., "The Zeal of Phinehas: The Bible and the Legitimation of Violence," *Journal of Biblical Literature*, 122, no. 1 2003, pp. 3–21; Spiro, Abram, "The Ascension of Phinehas," *Proceedings of the America Academy for Jewish Research*, 22 1953, pp. 91–114; Veldman, Ilja M., "The Old Testament as a Moral Code: Old Testament Stories as Exempla of the Ten Commandments," *Simiolus: Netherlands Quarterly for the History of Art*, 23, no. 4 1995, pp 215–239; Feldman, Louis H., "The Portrayal of Phinehas by Philo, Pseudo-Philo, and Josephus," *The Jewish Quarterly Review, New Series*, 92, no. 3/4 2002, pp. 315–345.
[117] See on literalism: Gresh, Alain, *L'Islam, la République et le Monde*, p. 84.

"divine command theory" of ethics. According to this theory "morally right" means "ordained by God," and "morally wrong" means "forbidden by God." There is no independent or "autonomous" ethical good, but morality is ultimately founded in the will of God.

We have to distinguish this position from the one that proclaims that religion influences moral behavior, or that people are "inspired" by their religious belief. The Dutch legal philosopher Bart C. Labuschagne (1962–) writes: "Man's morality is rooted in his religiousness. Religion equips man with the motivation and the grounds to be moral ... ."[118] From a psychological point of view this can hardly be denied. Man is "rooted" in religion and "inspired" by his faith. But the philosophical question is: is this necessarily true? Would morality lose all binding force if not backed up by religion? The adherents of divine command ethics answer in the affirmative.

We do not only find adherents of divine command ethics among biblical and Qur'anic religious figures (Moses, Abraham, Mohammed), but also among the great philosophers and theologians. The moral philosopher Janine Marie Idziak presents an impressive list of adherents among the great philosophers of the Western tradition: John Duns Scotus, William of Ockham, Pierre d'Ailly, Jean Gerson, Martin Luther, John Calvin, Karl Barth, Emil Brunner, and many others.[119] Divine command ethics is a well-known current in philosophical metaethics.

But although the intellectual credentials of the theory – see the impressive list of adherents presented by Idziak – cannot be denied, the practical consequences of adopting it seem, under the present circumstance of a multi-religious composition of the population in many societies, far-reaching. Accepting the direct voice of God (Mohammed, Jesus, Moses) or his text[120] (the majority of the believers) as the ultimate foundation of ethics could lead to self-sacrifice and martyrdom.[121] And what is worse: it could lead to the sacrifice of others, as the story of Abraham and Isaac spells out. In an age of international religious terrorism this poses considerable problems for the maintenance of the political order.[122]

---

[118] Labuschagne, Bart C., "Religion and Order: Philosophical Reflections from Augustine to Hegel on the Spiritual Sources of Law and Politics," in: Bart C. Labuschagne and Reinhard W. Sonnenschmidt, eds., *Religion, Politics and Law: Philosophical Reflections on the Sources of Normative Order in Society*, Brill, Leiden 2009, pp. 71–94, p. 72.

[119] See Idziak, *Divine Command Morality: Historical and Contemporary Readings*, pp. vii–ix and Blanshard, Brand, *Reason and Belief*, George Allen & Unwin, London 1974.

[120] Fernández-Armesto, Felipe, "Books of Truth: The Idea of Infallible Holy Scriptures," in: Felipe Fernández-Armesto, *Ideas that changed the World*, Dorling Kindersley, London 2003, pp. 106–107.

[121] See on this: Davis, Joyce M., *Martyrs. Innocence, Vengeance, and Despair in the Middle East*, Palgrave, MacMillan, Basingstoke 2003.

[122] See on this: Esposito, John L., *Unholy War*. Selengut, Charles, *Sacred Fury*.

It is very well comprehensible that these problems have stimulated several commentators and scholars to look for alternatives to divine command morality. Following the will of God, whatever that may lead to, may make us true believers and earn the praise of God, but it does not make us good citizens. Therefore, people have always inquired whether there are other options.

Command Ethics or *Divine* Command Ethics?

Before we discuss the critique of divine command ethics in some detail we first have to consider an objection to my way of interpreting the biblical and Qur'anic stories. I have contended that adopting divine command ethics is problematic. But *what* is the problem? Is it that Abraham seems prepared to kill his son on a *divine* command? Or is the problem rather that he is prepared to kill on *command* (whatever the source of that command may be)? If the source of the command had not been God but a human tyrant (Stalin, Hitler, Pol Pot) Abraham's mentality would be objectionable as well, a critic of my treatment of the story of Abraham might retort. The problem is not that Abraham is so "religious," but that he is so susceptible to authoritarian command. In other words: the problem is more connected to the kind of personality that Abraham appears to be, than to religion or (as part of that religion) divine command ethics.

This line of argumentation may perhaps be substantiated by referring to famous research by the American psychologist Stanley Milgram (1933–1984) from Yale University. In the early 1960s Milgram conducted a series of psychological experiments aimed at determining the degree to which ordinary citizens were obedient to authority. He recruited volunteers from all walks of life to participate in what he called a "study of memory and learning."[123]

In the basic experimental design, two people come to a psychology laboratory to participate in a study of memory and learning. One of them is the "learner" and the other the "teacher." The pretend purpose of the experiment, as conveyed to the teacher, is acquiring information about the effects of punishment on learning. The learner is seated in a kind of miniature electric chair with his arms strapped to prevent excessive movement. An electrode is attached to his wrist so that he can receive electric shocks every time he makes an error. Those shocks are of an increasing intensity as he makes more errors. The learner is to be tested on his ability to remember the second word of a pair when he hears the first one again.

---

[123]   Milgram, Stanley, "The Perils of Obedience," *Harper's Magazine*, December 1973, 62–77; also in: Louis P. Pojman, ed., *The Moral Life. An Introductory Reader in Ethics and Literature*, Oxford University Press, New York 2000, pp. 625–640.

The learner is an actor. He does not get real electric shocks, but he only feigns to receive them by exclamations every time he is "punished" for a wrong answer by the teacher who controls the machine that gives the shock. The teacher is unaware of the fact that the whole experiment is fake. The real focus is on the teacher. How far will he go in administering the shocks if the learner makes errors?

At 75 volts, the learner grunts. At 120 volts, he complains loudly. At 150 volts he tells the teacher that he wants to quit. The general pattern is that as the voltage increases the learner's protests get increasingly more vocal. At 285 the learner only lets out an agonized scream and after that he produces no sound at all.

If the teacher hesitates in administering the shocks the experimenter orders him to continue. The experimenter says: "The experiment requires that you go on until he has learned all the word pairs correctly." If the teacher protests and refers to the heart condition of the learner the experimenter requires that the experiment go on: "It is absolutely essential that we continue."[124] About 60 percent of the teachers were fully obedient in the sense that they administered heavy punishments to the learners when they failed to produce the right answers in the memory game.

The question is, of course, what conclusions are we allowed to draw from the experiment? One conclusion might be that if a person is placed in a situation in which he has complete power over another individual, whom he may punish as he likes, all that is sadistic and bestial in man comes to the fore.[125] Another conclusion might be that man is apparently prepared to go to great lengths in irresponsible behavior as long as there is someone with authority taking the responsibility for this behavior (the experimenter). The last conclusion is drawn by Milgram himself who refers to similar considerations by Hannah Arendt (1906–1975).[126] Milgram writes:

> Indeed, it is highly reminiscent of the issue that arose in connection with Hannah Arendt's 1963 book, *Eichmann in Jerusalem*. Arendt contended that the prosecution's effort to depict Eichmann as a sadistic monster was fundamentally wrong, that he came closer to being an uninspired bureaucrat who simply sat at his desk and did his job. For asserting her views, Arendt became the object of considerable scorn, even calumny. Somehow, it was felt that the monstrous deeds carried out by Eichmann required a brutal, twisted personality, evil incarnate. After witnessing hundreds of ordinary persons submit to

---

[124] Ibid., p. 628.
[125] Ibid., p. 635.
[126] Especially important in this regard is: Arendt, Hannah, *Eichmann in Jerusalem. A Report on the Banality of Evil*, revised and enlarged edition, Penguin Books, Harmondsworth 1992 (1963).

the authority of our own experiments, I must conclude that Arendt's conception of the banality of evil comes closer to the truth than one might dare imagine. The ordinary person who shocked the victim did so out of a sense of obligation – an impression of his duties as a subject – and not from any peculiarly aggressive tendencies.[127]

Milgram's conclusion seems convincing. Nevertheless, we must always remind ourselves that Milgram is a psychologist and the lesson he draws from his experiments is that of a psychologist. He phrases this lesson as follows:

> This is, perhaps, the most fundamental lesson of our study: ordinary people, simply doing their jobs, and without any particular hostility on their part can become agents in a terrible destructive process. Moreover, even when the destructive effects of their work become patently clear and they are asked to carry out actions incompatible with fundamental standards of morality, relatively few people have the resources needed to resist authority.[128]

Now let us return to Abraham (or Jephtha or Phinehas). In a certain way he resembles the teacher in Milgram's experiment. Like the teacher he was ignorant of the fact that in reality the grave consequences that seemed to be looming would not materialize. It was all a "test." God wanted to know (like the teacher in Milgram's experiment) whether Abraham's loyalty was above reproach. He passed the test gloriously.

Now let us suppose somebody would draw the following lesson from Milgram's experiment in combination with the test of Abraham: "See, there is nothing wrong with religion or even with divine command morality. The problem is human nature. Abraham is weak, susceptible to all kind of authoritarian influences. Religion is not the problem, human nature is the problem."

This comment could draw inspiration from what Milgram writes about Eichmann. But would this be convincing? That is the crucial question. To answer that question, let us suppose that someone reflecting on the Eichmann case says this: "See, Nazism is not the problem, it is human nature."

Everyone would immediately feel that there was something terribly wrong there. Human nature may be *part* of the problem, but there was also an ideology that preached extreme discipline: "An order is an order" ("Befehl ist Befehl").[129] Certainly, if human beings were angels this might

---

[127]   Ibid., p. 636.

[128]   Ibid.

[129]   This issue is discussed by legal philosophers in the so-called Hart/Fuller debate: Hart, H.L.A., "Positivism and the Separation of Law and Morals," *Harvard Law Review*, 71 1958, also in: Hart, H.L.A. *Essays in Jurisprudence and Philosophy*, Clarendon Press, Oxford, 1983, pp. 49–87; Fuller, Lon L., "Positivism and Fidelity to Law – A Reply to Professor Hart,"

not have been a problem,[130] but, human nature being what it is, this ideology constituted a pernicious influence, which needs to be studied.

In all explanations there are always more factors to be considered. Death by knife-stroke is also *partially* conditioned by the vulnerability of the human body, but this cannot exculpate the murderer who wielded the knife, as every judge will ascertain. This is also relevant for the interplay between ideology and human personality.

One may also put it thus. What the psychologist teaches us may be true, that evil ideologies only get a chance because human nature is vulnerable in the sense of being prone to follow evil commands, but that does not make those ideologies preaching blind obedience good or even neutral. What makes Nazism, fascism or other ideologies preaching blind obedience problematic is precisely this element.

Now let us go back to theism. It is true, of course, that Abraham should have resisted God's command (as he had done on other occasions). Jephtha should have broken his vow. And wouldn't it be equally just to say that Phinehas was a religious zealot with a despicable character? Several factors contribute to the unfavorable outcome that those biblical figures were willing to perpetrate atrocious acts (in Jephtha's case actual murder). But we should not leave the discussion there. We should continue and ask ourselves: "did they have bases for their attitude in the religious tradition they refer to?" The fact that they could have made a different choice from the one they actually made does not exculpate the tradition itself. Once we have to acknowledge that in the tradition they refer to there are elements for a justification of their behavior we have to censure that tradition as well.

I think it has been made abundantly clear that these justifications are available. That justification has two elements. The first is the ethical exhortation, consisting of manifest scriptural passages with messages such as "kill the unbeliever, the heretic, the false prophet." The second is a metaethical

---

Harvard Law Review, 71 1958, pp. 630–672, also in: Feinberg, Joel, and Gross, Hyman, eds., *Philosophy of Law*, fourth edition, Wadsworth Publishing Company, Belmont, CA 1991, pp. 82–102; Radbruch, Gustav, "Five Minutes of Legal Philosophy, from *Rechtsphilosophie*," in: Feinberg, Joel, and Gross, Hyman, eds., *Philosophy of Law*, pp. 103–105 and other sources mentioned there.

[130] "But what is government itself but the greatest of all reflections on human nature? If men were angels, no government would be necessary. If angels were to govern men, neither external nor internal controls on government would be necessary. In framing a government which is to be administered by men over men, the great difficulty lies in this: you must first enable the government to control the governed; and in the next place oblige it to control itself. A dependence on the people is, no doubt, the primary control on the government; but experience has taught mankind the necessity of auxiliary precautions." See: Madison in: James Madison, Alexander Hamilton, John Jay, *The Federalist Papers*, ed. Isaac Kramnick, Penguin Books 1987, essay no. 51, p. 319–320.

doctrine. This is the doctrine of divine command ethics being in itself a manifestation of moral heteronomy. The alternative for the first element is the rejection of the notion of scriptural authority. The alternative for the second element is the adoption of moral autonomy.

An Assessment of Divine Command Ethics

Before entering into the question of what the alternatives are, let us first delve into the matter of what the advantages of divine command ethics are. What explains its enormous appeal throughout the ages?

The first advantage seems to be that this theory presents us with a stable foundation of ethics. Ethics is not a matter of personal or arbitrary choices. Ethics is based on a secure foundation: absolute divine security.

What many people like in a supernaturalist foundation for ethics is that good and evil are no longer based on the "subjectivist" and "arbitrary" decisions of humans. We encounter this conviction for instance in the great Christian novelist, academic and literary critic Clive Staples Lewis (1898–1963).

Lewis starts his book *Mere Christianity* (1952) with the contention that people may disagree on moral matters, but that disagreement presupposes a yardstick to measure the agreement. This is the Law or Rule about Good and Evil which is called "the natural law."[131] Usually people complain that no agreement whatsoever is possible about that "natural law," but Lewis disagrees. He contends that there is much more consensus on those matters than most people suppose. There is some consensus on some absolute values and those absolute values presuppose the existence of a "controlling power outside the universe." Once we direct our attention to that power we can experience it "inside ourselves as an influence or a command trying to get us to behave in a certain way."[132]

So God addresses us with "commands." We cannot ignore those commands. Man has a free will, so we can defy the commands of God, but if we do, we make a moral mistake. For to do well and abstain from evil, is in accordance with the will and the commands of God.

Nevertheless, the theory has some obvious disadvantages too. Let us consider three of them somewhat more closely.

---

[131]   Lewis, C.S., "The Moral Law Is from God," in: Harry J. Gensler, Earl Spurgin, and James Swindal, eds., *Ethics*. Contemporary Readings, Routledge, New York 2004, pp. 69–76, p. 70. This fragment is derived from: Lewis, C.S., *Mere Christianity*, Harper, San Francisco, 2001 (1952).
[132]   Lewis, "The Moral Law Is from God," p. 74.

(1) *Religious plurality.* The first problem with divine command ethics seems to be practical, but with consequences that appear serious indeed. In contemporary society we have to share the territory of the state with people who have different religions. Contemporary societies are what we call "multicultural" or "multireligious" and this is not likely to change. We are in the same situation as Phinehas and Moses as recounted in the book of Numbers: a situation of various religious options. How could, under those circumstances, one specific religion provide the moral basis for all the citizens? The multireligious composition of contemporary societies in a time of globalization makes divine command theory really problematic. As we have seen in the Danish cartoons controversy and the Rushdie affair, what some cleric proclaims in Afghanistan, Iran, India, or Pakistan can have direct consequences for the security of a cartoonist or a writer in another part of the world. On February 20, 2006 an Islamic court in Lucknow, the capital of the state of Uttar Pradesh, delivered a judgment on the twelve Danish cartoonists. This was done in a "fatwa," a religious opinion. The head of the Court declared that the death penalty was the only appropriate reaction to the sacrilege of the cartoons.[133] The judgment would be binding on all Muslims, the Court declared, wherever they may live.[134]

A week before this ruling a Pakistani Islamic religious scholar had promised a reward of 8,400 dollars for the killing of one cartoonist. Two of his followers increased the reward to 16,800 dollars and a car.[135]

On November 24, 2007 these proved to be no idle threats because in Denmark three militant Muslims were sentenced by a Danish court of law on the charge of preparing a terrorist attack.[136] Their attack was presented as a protest against (1) Denmark's military presence in Iraq, (2) the publication of the cartoons satirizing the Prophet in the Danish newspaper *Jyllands Posten* (for the sequence of events paragraph, see Chapter 3, Freedom of Speech and Philosophers on the Index).

As can be expected, such a threat completely changes the life of people whom it concerns. The situation is comparable to someone who is targeted by a criminal organization.[137]

[133] "Ook Iran wil zaak cartoons kalmeren" [Iran too Wants to Calm Things Down in the Cartoons Case], in: *NRC Handelsblad*, January 21, 2006.
[134] "Islamic court in India issues death sentence to cartoonists," *Agence France Press*, February 20, 2006.
[135] "Ook Iran wil zaak cartoons kalmeren."
[136] "Deense moslims cel in na beramen aanslag" [Danish Muslims in Prison after Plotting Attack] *NRC Handelsblad*, November 24/25, 2007.
[137] As was the case with the writer Saviano, who wrote a book on the Mafia and subsequently had to hide and be placed under police protection because the criminal organization wanted to kill him. See: Arends, Eric, "Maffia jaagt op journalist/schrijver Saviano" [Mafia Hunts Journalist/Writer Saviano], *De Volkskrant*, October 15, 2008.

One of the cartoonists is Kurt Westergaard (1935–). He is the creator of the most controversial cartoon; the one showing a figure generally construed to be Mohammed wearing a bomb as a turban.[138] On February 18, 2006 a Pakistani cleric put a bounty of 1 million dollars on Westergaard's head.[139] After the imbroglio that resulted many of the cartoonists went into hiding, but not Westergaard. He tried to get into contact with the people who were vehemently critical of the cartoons. In spite of warnings by the Security Service he appeared on television and arranged a meeting with Kasem Said Ahmad, the spokesman for the Islamic Community who had traveled to the Middle East to show the cartoons to religious leaders, which ignited the whole affair. During the conversation that Westergaard had with Ahmad the two parties did not come any closer. Westergaard did not apologize for what he had done, neither did Ahmad. And perhaps the parties simply cannot agree as long as the religious leaders see their mission as a God-given order to defend the rights of religion in a secular world. As long as divine command morality remains the point of departure, the followers of Phinehas present a problem.

Now it might be objected, of course, that the rejection of divine command morality is not necessary. The only thing that a follower of divine command morality should understand is that when we speak of morality as the "command of God" this has to be construed in a poetical sense, or metaphorically. It is not the divine command morality *as such* that is problematic; the problem is that some people take it so seriously and literally. So it is the *attitude* of the adherents of moral heteronomy that is the problem, not the theory in itself.

Now we seem to be back in the discussion we had before with regard to the question whether it was the theory of religious theism that caused the problems or the character of Abraham who is so easily inclined to follow orders from an authoritative source. Let me put it this way: is it not unrealistic to expect all people to understand that we have to interpret the theory of divine commands metaphorically? Especially if the social and political context we are living in makes it so abundantly clear that not all people can live with the ambiguities that moderates so easily embrace? Wouldn't it be better to be clear, needlessly clear perhaps for some, but apparently not for all?

(2)   *The arbitrary character of religious morality.* A second problem with the divine command theory concerns its vision of the status of morality. In discussing the views of C.S. Lewis we saw that the adherents of divine

---

[138]   Sjouwerman, Peter, "Cartoonist: geen spijt van profeet met bom" [Cartoonist; No Remorse for Prophet with Bomb], *Trouw*, September 28, 2006.
[139]   "Danish cartoonist: 'No regrets,'" *The Independent*, 19 February 2006.

command ethics usually pretend to have found an objective and stable foundation for morality. Exactly that is what makes the theory so attractive for many people. Only a divine foundation for our morals can save us from relativism, many people assure us. Once we abandon God, the specter of relativism looms. But is that true? Is divine command ethics really the only way to save us from relativism? Or is it rather the other way round, and should we confess that *adopting* divine command ethics brings us into the quagmire of relativism? Canadian philosopher Kai Nielsen (1926–) defends that last position: "We have not derived our moral convictions just from discovering what are the commands of God. No command, God's or anyone else's, can simply, as a command, serve as our ultimate moral standard; and that this is so is purely a matter of logic and not just a result of 'sinful, prideful rebellion' against God's law."[140]

Many people who have been born and raised in a religious environment have great difficulty in understanding that non-religious people can lead morally satisfying lives. In an exchange of views between the Italian author Umberto Eco (1932–) and Cardinal Carlo Maria Martini (1927–) the clerical leader writes about the idea of an autonomous ethics, an idea that he has some problems with: "The question I have in mind for you concerns the layman's ethical foundation. I would so like to think that the men and women of this world have a clear ethical basis for their actions. And I'm convinced that many people do act honestly, at least in certain circumstances, without a religious foundation to fall back on. Yet I cannot understand how they ultimately justify their actions."[141] C.S. Lewis, writing in a similar vein, argued that God is the power behind the moral law. He does not deny that people who are not Christians can be good, but they are good because they are "led by God's secret influence," so Lewis thinks. They "belong to Christ without knowing it."[142]

Divine command ethics has the reputation of being objective, universal and a stable basis for morality. The curious thing is that even among unbelievers this reputation is seldom contested. Unbelievers see themselves as "relativists" (Richard Rorty is a case in point),[143] and the adherents of divine command morality as "universalists." But is that right? That divine command ethics can be charged with relativism as well appears from the following argument. What we have neglected so far is to inquire into the question of *why* God proclaimed certain values superior to others. Wouldn't

---

[140] Nielsen, Kai, "Some Remarks on the Independence of Morality from Religion," *Mind*, New Series, 70, no. 278 1961, pp. 175–186, p. 176.

[141] Eco, Umberto, and Martini, Cardinal Carlo Maria, *Belief or Nonbelief: A Confrontation*, translated by Minna Proctor, Arcade Publishing, New York 1997, p. 69.

[142] Lewis, C.S., *Mere Christianity*, p. 162.

[143] See: Rorty, "Religion as Conversation-stopper" and "The Priority of Democracy to Philosophy."

that be because those values *are* superior? In other words does not God choose those values for us on the basis of some intrinsic property?

Once we have accepted that intrinsic property we have rejected divine command ethics. And we can reject divine command ethics on the ground that this would make morality a matter of arbitrariness – divine arbitrariness, yet arbitrariness nonetheless. According to divine command ethics, God chose the Ten Commandments in the form in which they have been bequeathed to us by Moses, but he could have presented us with a completely different list. For instance: "Steal as much as you can," "Do not honor your parents," "Cheat your neighbor if you can," etc.

The Polish philosopher and historian of ideas Leszek Kolakowski (1927–2009) makes a distinction within Christian theology between those favoring natural law theory and those who subscribe to divine command ethics.[144] According to natural law theorists stealing is wrong; rightness and wrongness are inherent properties of certain human acts. In the tradition of late medieval nominalism, however, the moral quality of things results from God's free verdict, which might have been different from – indeed, opposite to – what it actually was.

> God decided that it was wrong to kill one's father; given the irreversibility of God's law, patricide has since been inherently and immutably sinful. Seventeenth century natural law doctrines rejected the "decretalist" theology and instead made a distinction between natural law and divine positive law, arguing that while the latter resulted from God's decree alone, natural law was inherent in the nature of things and could not be changed, even by the Creator himself.[145]

It was against that theory that the nominalists reacted. In doing so they eliminated all obstacles to the sovereign will of God and as a result of this morality became an object of divine arbitrariness.

Although completely understandable from the perspective of the logic of theism the nominalist moral theory has odd consequences. It seems justified to say that divine command ethics does not *save us* from relativism but, on the contrary, pulls us right into the relativist quagmire. It is a kind of "divine" relativism, but relativism nevertheless.

Fortunately, most believers do not follow their religious leaders blindly and they reject some of the violent precepts that can be found in holy books. But does that imply not only that C.S. Lewis was wrong, but that the reverse of what he says is right? Many believers follow autonomous morality "without knowing it"?

---

[144]   Kolakowski, Leszek, "Marxism and Human Rights," *Daedalus*, 12, no. 4, Human Rights 1983, pp. 81–92, p. 82.
[145]   Ibid., p. 82.

(3) *The empirical background of divine command ethics.* One may also challenge the empirical basis of divine command ethics. If it is true, as adherents of divine command morality want us to believe, that religion is necessary for the support of morality, then one may wonder why religious times and cultures did not, generally speaking, manifest a more elevated moral standard than less religious times and cultures.

Now the statement that morality needs the support of religion is often meant as a covert way of saying that your own religion is necessary for the support of morals. In Section 176 of the second volume of his short philosophical essays *Parerga und Paralipomena* (1851)[146] Arthur Schopenhauer presents a dialogue between Demopheles and Philalethes, who both voice elements of Schopenhauer's own position towards religion. The religious skeptic Philalethes gives a splendid rebuttal of the claim defended by many religious apologists that religion is the necessary support for morals. This is "as false as it is popular," Philalethes says:

> It is *false* that the State, justice, and the law cannot be upheld without the assistance of religion and its articles of faith, and that justice and the police need religion as their necessary complement for the purpose of carrying out law and order. *False* it is, even if it is repeated a hundred times. For an effective and striking *instantia in contrarium* is afforded by the ancients, especially the Greeks.[147]

Philalethes (and Schopenhauer, we may presume) points out that the Greeks had nothing at all of what we understand by religion. They had no sacred records and no dogma which was taught. There were priests, but the duty of the priests only extended to temple ceremonies, prayers, hymns, sacrifices, processions, lustrations, and the like. The Greeks did not know a "religion" in our sense of the word. But who would dare to say that anarchy and moral chaos prevailed among the ancients?

(4) *Religious terrorism and divine commands.* A fourth problem connected to divine command theory has already been referred to in discussing the first point. It is that divine command ethics is, under the present circumstances, a perfect basis for religious terrorism. The religious terrorist sees himself as driven by a moral force he cannot and ought not to withstand. He must choose between divine law, as expressed in the sharia, and national law, as codified in the national constitutions and ordinary

---

[146] Schopenhauer, Arthur, *Parerga and Paralipomena, Short Philosophical Essays,* Vol. II, translated by E.F.J. Payne, Clarendon Press, Oxford 1974.
[147] Ibid., p. 332.

statutes.[148] If those laws concur there is no problem, but if they contradict each other it is clear what has to be given priority: divine law. The will of God is superior to the will of man, just as Abraham concluded that, when there was a conflict between his religious duties and his moral duties, his religious duties had to be given priority.

This conflict between moral and religious duties is graphically described by a Dutch jihadist: Jason W. (1985–).[149] He was arrested in The Hague (the Netherlands) on November 10, 2004. His farewell letter started with the following words:

> In the name of Allah, the compassionate, the merciful,
> I write you this letter to inform you that I departed for the land of jihad.
> To dispel the unbelievers, and to help to establish the Islamic state.
> I do not do this because I like fighting, but because the Almighty has commanded this: 'Fighting is obligatory for you, much as you dislike it. But you may hate a thing although it is good for you, and love a thing although it is bad for you. God knows, but you know not'.[150]

The last part of this quote is from Sura 2:216, one of the most popular Qur'an quotes among jihadists. We find it reiterated many times in the declarations by Osama Bin Laden (1957–), Ayman al-Zawahiri (1951–) and other representatives of Al Qaeda or other terrorist organizations.[151]

Jason W.'s farewell letter was found after he had been seized by the Dutch police after a prolonged siege in The Hague, during which he threw a hand grenade at police officers. W. was nineteen years old when this took place. In March 2006 he was convicted and sentenced to 15 years' imprisonment.[152]

Reading the farewell letter of Jason W. makes us realize that Leslie Stephen was not writing about abstruse philosophical subjects when, in 1893, he contended: "A religion may command criminal practices, and even practices inconsistent with the very existence of society."[153]

---

[148]   This dilemma is analyzed by: Tibi, Bassam, *Political Islam, World Politics and Europe: Democratic Peace and Euro-Islam versus Global Jihad*, Routledge, London 2008.
[149]   See on W.: Vermaat, Emerson, *Nederlandse Jihad: het Proces tegen de Hofstadgroep* [Dutch Jihad: The Trial of the Hofstad Group], Aspekt, Soesterberg 2006, pp. 31 ff.
[150]   The translation is mine. Quoted in: Groot Koerkamp, Sanne, & Veerman, Marije, *Het slapende leger: een zoektocht naar jonge jihad-sympathisanten in Nederland* [The Sleeping Army: A Search for Young Jihad Sympathizers in the Netherlands], Rothschild and Bach, Amsterdam 2006, p. 7.
[151]   See, for example: Ibrahim, Raymond, ed., *The Al Qaeda Reader*, Broadway Books, New York 2007, p. 59.
[152]   Koerkamp and Veerman, *Het slapende leger*, p. 7.
[153]   Stephen, Leslie, "Poisonous Opinions," in: Leslie Stephen, *An Agnostic's Apology and Other Essays*, Smith, Elder & Co., London 1893 (republished 1969), pp. 242–338, p. 280.

It also reminds us of the wisdom of George Weigel's (1951–) admonition:

> In the war against global jihadism, deterrence strategies are unlikely to be effective, because it is almost impossible to deter those who are committed to their own martyrdom.[154]

Sura 2:216 that Jason W. is referring to is the language of divine command ethics. You may not like to fight, but that is not for fallible human judgment to decide. You may hate a thing although it is good for you, and love a thing although it is bad for you. God knows, but you know not.

As in the Bible, there are many other passages in the Qur'an that do *not* incite to violence. But the problem is: that is irrelevant. It is as irrelevant as it was irrelevant for Abraham that God had many times commanded things that were completely compatible with common sense and human morality. The Sermon on the Mount and the Ten Commandments are also there, sure, but that cannot erase the command to offer your son. *Mutatis mutandis* the same could be argued with regard to the Qur'an. There may be countless admonitions to help the orphans and widows, but what counts is that Sura 2:216 is *also* there.

This is the dilemma that Abraham was facing. Should I substitute my own human judgment for that of God? From the perspective of divine command ethics the answer is clear: "no."

Philosophers like Immanuel Kant (1724–1804) who, every time God commanded something that violated the moral law, simply said "This cannot be the voice of God" take the easy way out. The Danish philosopher Soeren Kierkegaard (1813–1855) realized this. He clearly saw that if Christianity is nothing more than the moral law in parables (as it was for Kant, Fichte, and Hegel) it is nothing at all. Religion requires something from us. In his book *Fear and Trembling* (1843) he appears to have been fascinated by the trial of Abraham.[155] But, as one Kierkegaard scholar writes, "those who persevere with Abraham's story are faced with the question of whether faith might require, too, an act whose justification lies beyond their capacity to understand."[156] For people like Kant, Abraham cannot be the archetype of faith. Kierkegaard thought this was too easy. For the Bible clearly confers that role on Abraham. That leaves us with two options.

---

[154] Weigel, George, *Faith, Reason, and the War against Jihadism: A Call to Action*, Doubleday, New York 2007, p. 95.

[155] Kierkegaard, Soeren, *Fear and Trembling*, translated by Alastair Hannay, Penguin Books, Harmondsworth 1985 (1843).

[156] Rae, Murray, "The Risk of Obedience: A Consideration of Kierkegaard's *Fear and Trembling*," *Journal of Systematic Theology*, 1, no. 3 1999, pp. 308–321, p. 317.

Either we must decide against the Bible and in favor of our very best ethical insights, or we may venture the suggestion that there will be times in the life of faith when the individual must proceed without all reasonable objections having been resolved. Faith proceeds even though doubt has not been absolutely refuted. That is risky. To journey beyond ethics and beyond common sense is to find oneself alone – perhaps even without God, perhaps just alone. People of faith are capable of getting it wrong, and often do. But faith means trusting in God with the hope that one's action is justified, not in the end by our own reason, but by God.[157]

Kierkegaard scholar Murray Rae further writes about Kierkegaard's sympathy for Abraham: "If the command of God is not always fathomable, what safeguards are there against lunacy and evil? What might Kierkegaard have to say about Jonestown and Waco, for instance?"[158] Rae was writing in 1999. Two years later 9/11 took place and more topical examples now force themselves upon us: Mohammed Atta or one of the other highjackers.[159] Governments of Western liberal democracies have not been very successful so far in tackling this new challenge. The core of the problem is succinctly stated by American law scholar Martha Minow (1954–) when she writes:

> The quandary compounds as the risk of home-grown terrorists grows. Terrorists can hide out within a free society and that very freedom constrains efforts to locate them. Those nations that have defeated terrorism, like Argentina and Brazil, did so through domestic deployment of military death squads, torture, surveillance, and internal repression – all forbidden within and contrary to the norms of a democratic society.[160]

Nevertheless, as I hope to make clear in what follows, liberal democracies are not completely powerless in dealing with the problems of religious violence and religious terrorism, in particular. However, this may require a complete reevaluation of their religious traditions, in particular some elements inherent in the theistic conception of god.

Kierkegaard and Mill

"Either we must decide against the Bible and in favor of our very best ethical insights," Rae writes, sketching one horn of the dilemma, or we follow the

---

[157] Ibid., p. 317.
[158] See: Arquilla, John, "True Believers," *The Review of Politics*, 67, no. 1 2005, pp. 188–190, p. 189.
[159] See for an interesting description of the terrorist frame of mind: Amis, Martin, *The Second Plane*. And Desai, Meghnad, *Rethinking Islam: The Ideology of the New Terror*, I.B. Tauris, London 2007.
[160] Minow, Martha, "Tolerance in an Age of Terror," *Southern California Interdisciplinary Law Journal*, 16 2007, pp. 453–494.

divine command and accept all the draconian consequences. What makes Kierkegaard's *Fear and Trembling* such fascinating literature is that he, or his alter ego Johannes de Silentio, understood this. The divine command to offer your son is presented as a *real* dilemma. Many Kierkegaard scholars evade the issue by assuring us that Abraham felt confident that he could both follow God's instructions and retain his son. But that interpretation makes Kierkegaard's book less interesting than it is. It would imply that there *was* no real dilemma. We could have our cake and eat it too. But that is not the case, according to Kierkegaard. He indicted the bourgeois interpretation of Christianity so popular in his time and society and its more elevated manifestations in the idealistic interpretations of Christianity that were so influential in nineteenth-century German theology. One of Kierkegaard's books is entitled *Either/Or* (1843). We may frame Kierkegaard's dilemma in our terminology as: *either* we subscribe to moral autonomy *or* to moral heteronomy. *Either* ethics legislates religion *or* religion legislates ethics. We cannot evade the issue as Kant, Hegel, and Fichte did by identifying the divine with the moral order. That meant a covert acceptance of moral autonomy. We may do this, but then it would be fairer to say so.

Many Hegelians, especially the Hegelian Left, did in fact choose moral autonomy, as Feuerbach (1804–1872) did.[161] And this dealt a severe blow to the classical theistic conception of God.

A similar development is found in the work of the empiricist John Stuart Mill. In his *Autobiography* (1873) Mill presents us with a famous account of his education by his father James Mill. "I was brought up from the first without any religious belief, in the ordinary acceptation of the term."[162] Mill continues with an exposition of the religious, or rather irreligious, ideas of his father and contends that "my father's rejection of all that is called religious belief, was not, as many might suppose, primarily a matter of logic and evidence."[163] What was it then? "The grounds of it were moral, still more than intellectual."[164] James Mill looked upon religion as "the greatest enemy of morality." Religion, at least the Christian religion, was setting up factitious excellencies – beliefs in creeds, devotional feelings, and ceremonies – that had nothing to do with "the good of human kind." But above

---

[161] In Feuerbach, Ludwig, *The Essence of Christianity*, translated by George Eliot, Prometheus Books, Amherst, NY 1989 (1841). See also: Massey, Marilyn Chapin, "Censorship and the Language of Feuerbach's *Essence of Christianity* (1841)," *The Journal of Religion*, 65, no. 2 1985, pp. 173–195 and Lindberg, Carter, "Luther and Feuerbach," *Sixteenth Century Essays and Studies*, 1 1970, pp. 107–118. On the Young Hegelians in general: Löwith, Karl, *From Hegel to Nietzsche: The Revolution in Nineteenth-Century Thought*, translated by David E. Green, Constable, London 1964.

[162] Mill, John Stuart, *Autobiography of John Stuart Mill*, Columbia University Press, New York 1924 (1873), p. 27.

[163] Ibid., p. 28.

[164] Ibid.

all, so John Stuart Mill continued about his father, he opposed what we would now call the theistic "metaethics" that consists of "doing the will of a being, on whom it lavishes indeed all the phrases of adulation, but whom in sober truth it depicts as eminently hateful."[165]

On the basis of these convictions John Stuart Mill acquired his highly peculiar education from his father, completely free from all religious indoctrination and solely oriented on the principles of Bentham. Human good was their only frame of reference, not the transcendent will of a deity.

In contemporary terminology we could say that James Mill gave his son a moral education free from religious bias. His point of departure was the autonomy of morals.

Now, it is all very well to say that man *should* act as a morally autonomous agent, but then the next question is: *can* he? Is what allegedly succeeded with John Stuart Mill also possible with other children? Ought implies can, and do humans have the capacity to be morally autonomous? Can people be educated this way?[166]

This subject is the focus of psychologists active in the field of moral education. Some important names in this respect are Jean Piaget (1896–1980) and Lawrence Kohlberg.

Piaget focused on the moral lives of children; more in particular, he studied the way children play games in order to learn more about their ideas of right and wrong.[167] Piaget was convinced that development emerges from action in the sense of interactions with the environment.

Piaget also interviewed children about such acts as stealing and lying and he concluded that children begin in what he called a "heteronomous" stage of moral reasoning, characterized by a strict adherence to rules and obedience to authority.[168]

---

[165]   Ibid. See on the development of Mill's ideas on religion: Carr, Robert, "The Religious Thought of John Stuart Mill: A Study in Reluctant Scepticism," *Journal of the History of Ideas*, 23, no. 4 1962, pp. 475–495; Megill, Allan D., "J.S. Mill's Religion of Humanity and the Second Justification for the Writing of *On Liberty*," *The Journal of Politics*, 34, no. 2 1972, pp. 612–629.

[166]   Every now and then I consider it fruitful to repeat that I am talking about moral autonomy in the sense of an ethics that is not based on religion. If someone subscribes to the position of moral autonomy, that does *not* mean that he contends that morals are completely subjective or capricious. Moral autonomy only refers to autonomy in relation to religion and should not be confused with subjectivism in ethics.

[167]   See: Piaget, Jean, "Le développement intellectuel chez les jeunes enfants" [Intellectual Development in Young Children], *Mind*, New Series, 40, no. 158 1931, pp. 137–160; Piaget, Jean, *The Moral Judgement of the Child*, Kegan Paul, London 1932; Isaacs, Susan, "Review of *The Moral Judgement of the Child* by Jean Piaget," *Mind*, New Series, 43, no. 169 1934, pp. 85–99.

[168]   The philosopher Patrick Nowell-Smith analyses the consequences of Piaget's approach for ethics and metaethics. See: Nowell-Smith, Patrick, "Morality: Religious and Secular," in:

Piaget's ideas are to be contrasted with the ideas of the well-known sociologist Emile Durkheim. Durkheim (1858–1917) believed, like Piaget, that morality resulted from social interaction or immersion in a group. But he differed from Piaget in seeing moral development as a natural result of attachment to the group. In Piaget's theory individuals define morality individually, through their struggles to arrive at fair solutions. A practical consequence of this theory is that, for instance, an educator must provide students with opportunities for personal discovery through problem-solving instead of indoctrinating the norms of the group or society.

Kohlberg and Moral Education

Piaget's theory was further developed by Lawrence Kohlberg (1927–1987). Kohlberg was dissatisfied with the relativistic orientation of many social scientists and tried to develop a more objective approach to morality.[169] "Central to moral education is the problem of the relativity of values," he tells us: "Are there universal values that children should develop?"[170] On the basis of his studies he claimed that there may be cultural variance, but there is also cultural stability. We all develop our moral thinking in stages, and Kohlberg's approach is characterized as the *cognitive-developmental view*. Young children cannot think about morality other than in terms of obedience and punishment. Morally bad things are simply things that we are punished for. It is only in the later development of man that morality is associated with criticism on the basis of rational principles of justice.

Kohlberg contrasts his own approach with two rival theories. The first is the so called *common-sense theory* behind much of moral education. According to this theory everyone knows what is right and wrong, at least adults do. And those adults who know a set of facts about morality of which children are ignorant ("stealing is wrong," "helping others is good") should simply teach these facts on the basis of the teacher's superior knowledge and authority. Basically, it works in just the same way that arithmetic is taught.

Apart from the common-sense theory there is a second theory that Kohlberg rejects. This is the *relativistic-emotional approach*. This view is

---

Eleonore Stump and Michael J. Murray, eds., *Philosophy of Religion. The Big Questions*, Blackwell, Malden 2001 (1999), pp. 403–412, p. 403.

[169] See: Kohlberg, Lawrence, "The Claim to Moral Adequacy of a Highest State of Moral Judgment," *The Journal of Philosophy*, 70, no. 18 1973, pp. 630–646. For a comment see: Schleifer, Michael, "Moral Education and Indoctrination," *Ethics*, 86. no. 2 1976, pp. 154–163.

[170] Kohlberg, "Moral Education," p. 186.

widespread among child psychologists. In this theory the child is seen as a creature of emotions and needs. "Morality, in turn, is no absolute which the child must be measured against, but represents the relativistic rules and standards of the child's culture. The child must adjust to these rules in a realistic manner as part of his mental health, and will do so if his home and school environment are meeting his inner needs."[171]

Kohlberg tells us that his own *cognitive-developmental view* starts from a different understanding of the nature of morality. He claims that morality represents a set of rational principles of judgment and decisions valid for every culture: the principles of human welfare and justice. The principle central to the development of moral judgment is that of justice. "Justice, the primary regard for the value and equality of all human beings, and for reciprocity in human relations, is a basic and universal standard."[172] Kohlberg gathered considerable evidence that the concept of justice is inherent in human experience, instead of being the product of a particular worldview.

Principles are contrasted with rules.[173] The *rules* drawn up by cultures and schools are more or less arbitrary. And their teaching relies more upon authority than upon reason. Moral *principles* however represent the rational organization of the child's moral experience. Although children are reasonable beings and it is possible to argue with them about morality, they represent a different stage of moral reasoning. Moral education aims to stimulate children to move from one stage of moral development to the next. What are those stages? There are, according to Kohlberg, six stages of moral development to be divided into three groups of two.

1. Orientation to punishment and reward, and to physical and material power.
2. Hedonistic orientation with an instrumental view of human relations ("You scratch my back and I'll scratch yours").
3. "Good boy" orientations; seeking to maintain expectations and win approval of one's immediate group.
4. Orientation to authority, law, and duty, to maintaining a fixed order, whether social or religious, assumed as a primary value.
5. Social-contract orientation, with emphasis on equality and mutual obligation within a democratically established order; for example, the morality of the American Constitution.

---

[171] Kohlberg, Ibid., p. 187.
[172] Kohlberg, Ibid., p. 188.
[173] Here there is some similarity with the work of the legal philosopher Ronald Dworkin. See: Dworkin, Ronald, "The Model of Rules I," in: *Taking Rights Seriously*, Harvard University Press, Cambridge, MA 1978, pp. 14–46.

6. Principles of conscience that have logical comprehensiveness and universality. Highest value placed on human life, equality, and dignity.[174]

The first two stages are typical of young children and delinquents. According to Kohlberg they are "pre-moral." Decisions are made largely on the basis of self-interest. Stages 3 and 4 are "conventional." They are the ones on the basis of which most of the adult population operate. The final stages are the "principled" stages. Those are characteristic of 20 to 25 percent of the adult population. Perhaps only 5 or 10 percent arrive at the sixth and final stage. Only at stage 6 is each life seen as inherently worthwhile, aside from other considerations. According to Kohlberg, one of the most important formulations of moral concern was voiced by the English novelist E.M. Forster (1879–1970) who thought that most of the trouble in the world was due to "the inability to imagine the innerness of other lives."[175]

Kohlberg also reflected on the motivation for moral action. At the lowest stages the individual is only motivated to avoid punishment or to obtain favors. Only in the later stages is the individual emancipated from that narrow view.

As appears from the foregoing, Kohlberg rejects cultural relativism. He said: "The same stages of development are also found in other cultures, although average progress is faster and farther in some than in others."[176] The aim of moral education is to stimulate that moral development. And, like Piaget, Kohlberg teaches that "rather than attempting to inculcate a predetermined and unquestioned set of values, teachers should challenge students with the moral issues faced by the school community as problems to be solved."[177] At present, schools do not have a good record as "moral institutions." Institutional relationships tend to be based more on authority than on ideas of justice. The school atmosphere is a blend of stage 1 and stage 4. If schools wish to foster morality they have to provide an atmosphere in which interpersonal issues are settled on the basis of principle rather than power. They have to take moral questions seriously. And that means providing food for thought rather than conventional right answers.

This sounds all too familiar for those acquainted with the work of Enlightenment authors such as Immanuel Kant[178] and Victorian rationalists

---

[174] Kohlberg, "Moral Education," p. 189.

[175] Ibid., p. 191. This is basically the same as Arthur Schopenhauer teaches in: Schopenhauer, Arthur, *On the Basis of Morality*, translated by E. F. J. Payne, Hackett Publishing Co. Inc., Indianapolis 2000 (1840).

[176] Kohlberg, "Moral Education," p. 190.

[177] Ibid., p. 192.

[178] Kant, Erhard, Hamann, Herder, Lessing, Mendelssohn, Riem, Schiller, Wieland, *Was ist Aufklärung? Thesen und Definitionen* [What Is Enlightenment? Theses and Definitions], ed. Ehrhard Bahr, Philipp Reclam jun., Stuttgart 1974.

such as T.H. Huxley[179] and W.K. Clifford.[180] It is the kind of reasoning that brought philosophers like Immanuel Kant and John Stuart Mill[181] to the view that we cannot accept the moral heteronomy that is inherent in divine command ethics, but should adopt a completely different perspective: moral autonomy. We cannot, or rather should not, do what Abraham did and Kierkegaard defended[182] – suspend our moral duty and rely on the authority of religion. The personality of Abraham is a clear manifestation of what Kohlberg characterized as stage 3 or, at most, stage 4 of moral development.

As might be expected, Kohlberg's work has been placed under critical scrutiny from different angles,[183] but the general idea that it is perfectly possible to base morals on secular considerations has gained confirmation from other scholars. In 2006 Harvard biologist Marc D. Hauser (1959–) published his book *Moral Minds: How Nature Designed Our Universal Sense of Right and Wrong.*[184] Hauser works with moral dilemmas and tries to assess how people experience right and wrong.[185] If religion is that important as a source of morals, one would expect significant differences between people with a religious background and non-believers, but this appears not to be the case. When confronted with certain moral dilemmas, most people come to the same decisions. What drives our moral judgments is a universal moral grammar, a faculty of the mind that evolved over millions of years. In a co-authored article, Hauser and Peter Singer (1946–) arrive at the conclusion that there is no statistically significant difference between believers and unbelievers in making moral judgments.

An interesting question is, of course, whether Kohlberg's model is also relevant for life- and worldviews. Is it applicable to religions in general? Would it be possible, for instance, to determine the stage of development of theistic religion at the time of Abraham? If Abraham was at stage 3 of

---

[179]   Huxley, Thomas Henry, "A Liberal Education; and where to find it," in: Thomas Henry Huxley, *Essays Selected from Law Sermons, Addresses, and Reviews*, Macmillan and Co., London 1871, pp. 20–47.

[180]   Clifford, "The Ethics of Belief."

[181]   See on Mill: Blanshard, *Four Reasonable Men*, p. 99.

[182]   See: Blanshard, Brand, *Reason and Belief*, George Allen and Unwin, London 1974, pp. 187–288.

[183]   See e.g.: Blum, Lawrence A., "Gilligan and Kohlberg: Implications for Moral Theory," *Ethics*, 98, no. 3 1988, pp. 472–491; Flanagan, Owen, and Jackson, Kathryn, "Justice, Care and Gender: The Kohlberg–Gilligan Debate Revisited," *Ethics*, 97, no. 3 1987, pp. 622–637; Abram, Anna, "The Philosophy of Moral Development," *Forum Philosophicum*, 12 2007, pp. 71–86.

[184]   Hauser, Marc D., *Moral Minds: How Nature Designed Our Universal Sense of Right and Wrong*, Little, Brown, London 2006.

[185]   A short introduction to his ideas can be found in: Hauser, Marc, and Singer, Peter, "Morality without Religion," *Free Inquiry*, December 2005/January 2006, pp. 18–19.

moral development, perhaps the whole religion was at that stage as well. This matter was addressed by Nowell-Smith.[186]

Religious and Secular Ethics

British philosopher Patrick Horace Nowell-Smith (1915–2006) is well known as the writer of a hugely successful introduction to ethics, published in 1954, in which he tried to analyze the central concepts of ethics and morality in a succinct and neutral manner.[187] This was all in harmony with the ideals of logical positivism, so much in vogue at that time.[188] As the writer of his obituary rightly remarks, Nowell-Smith will probably be remembered for this successful book on ethics that sold more than 100,000 copies. Nevertheless Nowell-Smith has another claim to fame which derives from the fact that in 1961 he wrote a crystal-clear and thought-provoking essay in *The Rationalist Annual* in which he sharply distinguished religious ethics from secular ethics.[189] In 1967 he elaborated on this distinction in his entry *Religion and Morality* for Paul Edwards' *The Dictionary of Philosophy*.[190]

For our project Nowell-Smith is important because he explicitly connects the ideals of moral autonomy as expounded and defended in the work of Piaget and Kohlberg (discussed in the two previous sections of this chapter) and divine command ethics.

Nowell-Smith, never afraid to confront his readers, formulated the aim of his article in *The Rationalist Annual* as to demonstrate "that religious morality is infantile."[191] He was well aware that most readers would find this statement absurd (who would agree that Aquinas never grew up?). Such a claim is "surely to put oneself out of court as a philosopher to be taken

---

[186]   Another question that could be posed, is the perhaps somewhat heretical question of whether *God* is also subject to moral development? Would it not make sense to say that a God who demands the sacrificial offering of your son is stuck in one of the first stages of Kohlberg's scheme? See on this: Miles, Jack, *God. A Biography*, Alfred A. Knopf, New York 1995.

[187]   Nowell-Smith, Patrick, *Ethics*, Penguin, Harmondsworth 1954.

[188]   Redford, Colin, "Patrick Nowell-Smith," Obituary, *The Guardian*, February 22, 2006. See on logical positivism: Kolakowski, Leszek, *Positivist Philosophy: From Hume to the Vienna Circle*, translated by Norbert Guterman, Penguin Books, Harmondsworth 1972 (1968).

[189]   It is widely anthologized. I quote from: Nowell-Smith, Patrick, "Morality: Religious and Secular," *The Rationalist Annual*, 1961, also in: Eleonore Stump and Michael J. Murray, eds., *Philosophy of Religion*, pp. 403–412.

[190]   Nowell-Smith, Patrick, "Religion and Morality," in: Paul Edwards, ed., *The Encyclopedia of Philosophy*, Vol. VII, Macmillan and The Free Press, New York 1967, pp. 150–158.

[191]   Nowell-Smith, "Morality: Religious and Secular," p. 403.

seriously."[192] Nevertheless, so Nowell-Smith tells us, his thesis should not be taken as so radical. What he wants to show is that in the moralities of adult Christians, there are elements which can be set apart from the rest and which can be called "religious" and "infantile" at the same time.

Nowell-Smith makes clear that he does not oppose the *content* of Christian ethics (love, sympathy, loyalty), but the *form* or *structure*. Although he does not use those terms it might be enlightening to say that Nowell-Smith does not reject Christian "ethics" but Christian "metaethics." Christian metaethics, although false, was hugely successful, Nowell-Smith claims. That appears from the fact that if you tell people that you have moral views but no religious convictions they ask you: "Where do you get your moral ideas from?"[193] The answer "From my father and my mother" usually does not satisfy the person asking that question. But that is strange. In fact, this is a pretty convincing answer as to the source of our moral ideas. Why are people not convinced by this "boring autobiographical answer," Nowell-Smith asks us? It is because people in fact do not want to hear where our moral ideas *come from*, but *on whose authority* they are held. "He did not want to know *from whom* I learnt my moral views; he wanted to know what *authority* I have for holding them."[194] Your parents may have a right to obedience from their children, but this right is always limited. Parents do not have the right "to make the moral law." The whole idea of morality that is binding on the basis of being commanded is false, from the perspective that Nowell-Smith tries to argue for.

> Morality, on this view, is an affair of being commanded to behave in certain ways by some person who has a right to issue such commands; and, once this premise is granted, it is said with some reason that only God has such a right. Morality must be based on religion, and a morality not so based, or one based on the wrong religion, lacks all validity.[195]

From there the whole standard repertoire of – to my mind *successful* – arguments against divine command ethics follows, and here Nowell-Smith reiterates what also has been stated by other authors, like Kai Nielsen (1926–)[196]

[192]   Ibid.
[193]   Ibid.
[194]   Ibid.
[195]   Ibid., p. 404.
[196]   Nielsen, Kai, "Some Remarks on the Independence of Morality from Religion," *Mind*, New Series, 70, no. 278 1961, pp. 175–186; Nielsen, Kai, "Morality and God: Some Questions for Mr. MacIntyre," *The Philosophical Quarterly*, 12, no. 47 1962, pp. 129–137; Nielsen, Kai, "On Being a Secularist All the Way Down," *Philo*, 1, no. 2 1998, pp. 6–21.

and James Rachels (1941–2003).[197] We must be persuaded *independently* of his (God's) goodness before we admit his right to command, Nowell-Smith argues against divine command moralists.[198] This affects the theistic concept of God, of course, because it challenges the idea that omnipotence, omniscience and perfect goodness are all in harmony with each other.

Nowell-Smith distinguishes himself from other critics of divine command ethics, though, by some bold generalizations he makes with regard to the spiritual sources of European culture. He contrasts the Greek tradition with the Jewish–Christian tradition, equating the first, roughly, with autonomous and teleological ethics and the second with heteronomous and deontological morality.

According to the *teleological* morality moral rules are considered to be subordinate to ends. They are rules for achieving ends and consequently to promote those ends. The *deontological* system is different. Here moral rules are thought of as absolute; as categorical imperatives in no way depending for their validity on the good or the bad consequences of obedience. Moral goodness is thought to lie in conformity to these rules for their own sake.[199]

The teleological tradition goes back to the Greeks; the deontological tradition goes back to Jewish sources. So there is a "Greek view of morality" and a "Jewish view of morality."[200] In the Greek tradition morality is regarded as a set of recipes to be followed for the achievement of ends (teleological). In the Jewish (and subsequent Christian) tradition morality is seen as a set of commands to be obeyed (deontological).[201]

Besides the teleologic/deontologic distinction there is the distinction between autonomous and heteronomous ethics. Again the dividing line is that of the Greek tradition and the Jewish-Christian tradition. The Greek tradition is autonomous; the Jewish–Christian tradition heteronomous. Nowell-Smith ends with a clear-cut distinction between two traditions of thought within metaethics: the Greek tradition with its teleological and autonomous direction and the Jewish–Christian tradition with its

---

[197] Rachels, James, "God and Human Attitudes," *Religious Studies*, 7 1971, pp. 325–37, also in: James Rachels, *Can Ethics provide Answers. And Other Essays in Moral Philosophy*, Rowman and Littlefield Publishers, Lanham 1997, pp. 109–125.
[198] Nowell-Smith, "Morality: Religious and Secular," p. 404.
[199] Ibid., p. 405.
[200] Ibid.
[201] Ibid. Similar ideas are developed by Richard Taylor in: Taylor, Richard, *Good and Evil*, Prometheus Books, Buffalo, NY 1984; Taylor, Richard, *Reflective Wisdom: Richard Taylor on Issues That Matter*, ed. John Donnelly, Prometheus Books, Buffalo, NY 1989.

deontological and heteronomous leaning. Obviously, he himself defends the Greek tradition against the Jewish–Christian one.[202]

Another characteristic of Nowell-Smith's bold edifice of moral thought is the way he incorporates the psychology of Jean Piaget in his system. As Kohlberg had done, Nowell-Smith interprets the ideas of "heteronomous" and "autonomous" ethics not only in philosophical terms, but in psychological terms as well. Here he establishes a relationship with the ideas on the development of the child expounded by Piaget.

Piaget distinguished three stages in the development of the child. He made a study of the attitudes of children of different ages to the game of marbles. A very small child (*first* phase) handles the marbles and throws them about as his humor takes him. Although the child is playing he is not "playing a game" in the sense of being subjected to certain rules. Later on the child learns how to obey rules.

The *second* type of attitude is exhibited by children from five to nine. Here the child plays according to rules, but these rules are more or less sacrosanct. Rules are supposed to have emanated from adults and they are regarded as inviolable. Piaget calls this attitude "heteronomous," because the child sees them as imposed from the outside and not allowing for any transgressions or alteration. This is similar to deontology in metaethics, Nowell-Smith contends. The child in this phase does not ask what the rule is *for*. Rules are considered to be absolute commands, in the way that people regarded legal and religious rules in primitive society.[203]

It is only in the *third* stage that the child begins to learn what the rules are for. Now the child also learns to critically evaluate the rules. This type of attitude is called "autonomous" by Piaget and this same attitude conforms to what Nowell-Smith had dubbed "teleological."

The conclusion is clear: religious ethics is similar to the attitude of the child between 5 and 9 years old. It is far too concerned with rules that are experienced as sacrosanct, as deontological commands coming from above, instead of with rules as a product that should be justified and amended if necessary.

Sometimes Nowell-Smith formulates the central core of his ideas somewhat more cautiously, for example, in the words: "the religious attitude retains these characteristics of deontology, heteronomy and realism which are indeed necessary in the development of a child, but not proper to an adult."[204] For Christians the fundamental sin, the fount and origin of all

---

[202]   See on this also: Murray, Gilbert, *Five Stages of Greek Religion*, Watts and Co., London 1935; Murray, Gilbert, *Hellenism and the Modern World*, George Allen and Unwin, London 1953; Murray, Gilbert, *Stoic, Christian and Humanist*, C.A. Watts and Co., George Allen and Unwin, London 1946 (1940).

[203]   Nowell-Smith, "Morality: Religious and Secular," p. 406.

[204]   Ibid., p. 408.

sin, is disobedience to God: "Not as I will, but as thou wilt." What marks the essence of Christian morality is the total surrender of the will that is required. And here Nowell-Smith refers to the story of Abraham.

> Abraham must be prepared to sacrifice Isaac at God's command, and I take this to mean that we must be prepared to sacrifice our most deeply felt moral concerns if God should require us to do so.[205]

Worship

Perhaps Nowell-Smith is a bit too categorical in his insistence on heteronomy and deontology as the defining characteristics of the Jewish–Christian tradition and autonomy and teleology as characteristic of the Greek mind. We know, after all, that Socrates heard a "daimonion" that guarded him against certain moral choices. This may be interpreted as a sort of "divine voice" or special "divine power" that guided his actions, "warning him if he was on the verge of doing something wrong and perhaps also (according to Xenophon) giving positive advice about what he ought to do."[206] We also know that there are passages in the Bible where more emphasis is placed on the ideal of moral autonomy. Abraham may have acted in blind obedience in the story told in Genesis 22, but we know from other places in the Bible that he could be critical as well. This appears from Genesis 18:22 where Abraham argues with the Lord about the plight of the inhabitants of Sodom and Gomorrah.

Rumors reached the Lord about what was done in Sodom and Gomorrah and the Lord decided to go down and see whether what the people had been doing altogether accorded with the reports that had come to him (Genesis 18:21). When a severe punishment is decreed on Sodom and Gomorrah, Abraham asks the Lord whether he would indeed "sweep away the righteous with the wicked" (Genesis 22:23)? Abraham objects and says: "Suppose there are fifty righteous to death within the city. Will you then sweep away the place and not spare it for the fifty righteous who are in it?" (Genesis 22:23). This is a clear manifestation of moral autonomy on the part of Abraham, of course. Why should the righteous suffer for what the wicked have done? It is an elementary feature of every system for administering justice that only those *guilty* of crimes should be punished, not everyone simply because the guilty and the righteous share the same territory, whether a city or a country or another tract of land. Besides, the

---

205 Ibid.
206 See: Wilson, Emily, *The Death of Socrates: Hero, Villain, Chatterbox, Saint*, Profile Books, London 2007, p. 32. Wilson calls Socrates' *daimonion* a "startling innovation in terms of traditional Athenian religion."

separation of people who are guilty from those who are not should be an easy task for an omniscient administrator of justice.[207] So Abraham's objections seem entirely reasonable. The indiscriminate punishment of all, whether guilty or not, is not what we may expect from a perfectly good God.[208] Abraham again:

> Far be it from you to do such a thing, to put the righteous to death with the wicked, so that the righteous fare as the wicked! Far be that from you! Shall not the Judge of all the earth do what is just? (Genesis 22:25)

Now something remarkable happens. We do not hear the "My ways are higher than your ways" argument, but God appears to be open to moral correction. He promises Abraham that if he finds fifty people in Sodom who are righteous, he will spare the city.

Abraham seems surprised by his own courage. He criticized the Lord, did he not? He bargained with the Almighty about an important moral question. He says: "Behold I have undertaken to speak to the Lord, I who am dust and ashes" (Genesis 22:27). But one may ask whether this is relevant here: dust and ashes or not, Abraham is a *man*. And being a man (in contrast to a mere animal) means that one is a moral being. One cannot defer the obligation to make moral decisions, at least not from the perspective or moral autonomy as expounded in the work of all the authors presented in this book.

Although Abraham does not openly endorse moral autonomy as a matter of principle (he is "dust and ashes," after all) he nonetheless acts on the principle of autonomy as we see in his arguing with God. He does that not only once, but several times, because he says: "Suppose five of the fifty righteous are lacking. Will you destroy the whole city for lack of five?" (Genesis 22:28). In other words: if we do not find fifty righteous men but only forty-five, will the city be destroyed? Again, this is an important manifestation of moral autonomy. Abraham is right: destroying forty-five righteous men who happen to live in a city with people who are predominantly guilty is a moral misdeed against those forty-five people. Abraham still objects.

The story goes on and every time Abraham diminishes the amount of righteous people a little further (ultimately to ten). In the end it did not help the cities because both were destroyed (Genesis 19–24). That does not

---

[207] See on this: Sinnott-Armstrong, Walter, "Overcoming Christianity," in: Louise M. Antony, ed., *Philosophers without Gods: Meditations on Atheism and the Secular Life*, Oxford University Press, Oxford 2007, pp. 69–80.

[208] Peter Singer makes a big point of this in: Singer, Peter, "How Can We Prevent Crimes Against Humanity?" in: Nicholas Owen, *Human Rights, Human Wrongs*, The Oxford Amnesty Lectures 2001, Oxford University Press 2002, pp. 92–137.

alter the fact, however, that Abraham courageously exerted moral autonomy and confronted the ultimate fountain of justice with what he considered to be the precepts of justice itself.

What this all amounts to is that Nowell-Smith and others who have
stressed the heteronomous character of the morality of Christianity should
acknowledge that there are some counter-indications as well. That does not
alter the fact, though, that a dominant penchant of the Bible and Christianity
(and, so it seems to me, of theism in general) is that of divine command
morality. It is true, in the story on the destruction of Sodom and Gomorrah
we are confronted with an Abraham who seems to be inspired by the attitude expounded in Immanuel Kant's *What is Enlightenment?* (1784) but
these examples are exceptional, and, what is more important perhaps: they
are hard to reconcile with the concept of "God" as described in some of
the fundamental documents of the Church.

In what Simon Blackburn (1944–) calls "sophisticated circles" there is
an enormous resistance to this contention nowadays. We should see religion, so Blackburn continues, though he himself does not endorse that view,
"in the light of poetry, symbol, myth, practice, emotion, attitude, or, in
general, a *stance* toward the ordinary world, the everyday world around
us."[209] But although this view is overrepresented at universities and among
the people who *write about* religion, the mindset of the ordinary believer
is much more in tune with religious orthodoxy than intellectuals are inclined
to acknowledge.

This last contention is well illustrated by the American philosopher
James Rachels. Rachels also discusses the two stories about Abraham told
in Genesis 22 and Genesis 18 and characterizes the significant differences.
Rachels too seems to consider the story of Abraham and Isaac as more
representative of the general theory of metaethics to be found in the Bible
than the story of Abraham's protests against the destruction of Sodom and
Gomorrah. In an influential essay under the title *God and Human Attitudes*
(1971)[210] Rachels exemplifies the meaning of biblical metaethics with regard
to the notion of worship. His argument can be summarized succinctly as
follows:

1. If any being is God, he must be a fitting object of worship.
2. No being could possibly be a fitting object of worship, since worship
   requires the abandonment of one's role as an autonomous moral agent.
3. Therefore, there cannot be any being who is God.[211]

---

[209] Blackburn, Simon, "Religion and Respect," in: Louise M. Antony, ed., *Philosophers Without Gods: Meditations on Atheism and the Secular Life*, Oxford University Press, Oxford 2007, pp. 179–194, p. 184.
[210] Rachels, "God and Human Attitudes."
[211] Ibid., p. 119.

To substantiate these theses Rachels tries first to determine the nature of worship and contends that God cannot exist, because there could not be a being towards whom we should adopt such an attitude.

What is the nature of worship? *First,* the worshiper believes that certain sorts of things are the case: for example, that the world was created by an all-powerful, all-wise being who knows our every thought and action. He also thinks that this being cares for us and regards us as his children. We are also made by him and in order to return his love we have to live according to his laws. *Second,* these facts have important consequences for our conduct. We must try to discover God's will, for instance, and adapt our behavior to that will. In order to discover this will, we have to consult church authorities and theologians. We can also read scripture and pray for revelations. *Third,* so Rachels argues, the believer thinks that there are certain hardships that befall men and which should be interpreted as "tests" that he should pass. If he does, he will be rewarded. If he fails, he deserves punishment.[212] The philosopher Richard Swinburne (1934–), one of the most prominent theists of our time, writes: "God has the right to allow natural evils to occur (for the same reason as he has the right to allow moral evils to occur – up to a limit.)"[213]

Because worship presumes the superior status of the one worshipped, there can be no reciprocal worship. The worshiper necessarily assumes his own inferiority. He has to act consistently in accordance with his role as God's child. We cannot consistently recognize any being as God and at the same time set ourselves against him, so Rachels argues.

This has to do with the fact that "God" is not a proper name like "Richard Nixon," but a title like "president of the United States" or "king" (see also what has been contended in Chapter 1 of this book about theism). So "Jehovah is God" is not a tautological expression. It merely states that the title "God" is assigned to Jehovah. Statements like "God is perfectly wise," however, are logical truths.[214]

You may also say that to bear the title "God" a being must have certain qualifications. He must be all-powerful and perfectly good in addition to being perfectly wise. And to apply the title of "God" to a certain being is the same as stating that this being has to be obeyed. "That God is not to be judged, challenged, defied, or disobeyed is at bottom a truth of logic. To do any of these things is incompatible with taking him as one to be worshiped."[215]

This all implies that the idea that any being could be worthy of worship is more problematic than we might imagine. The reason is that, once we say a being is worthy of worship, we recognize him as having an unqualified

[212]   Ibid., p. 111.
[213]   Swinburne, Richard, *Is there a God?,* Oxford University Press, Oxford 1996, p. 110.
[214]   Ibid., p. 117.
[215]   Ibid.

claim to our obedience. Can there be such an unqualified claim? Rachels' answer is "no."[216] Such recognition could never be made by a moral agent. To be a moral agent is to be autonomous, or self-directed.[217] So we have a conflict between the role of worshiper and the role of a moral agent.

Patrick Nowell-Smith and James Rachels seem to me proficient defenders of moral autonomy. They draw the ultimate conclusion from the principles of an autonomous ethics that have been developed by Immanuel Kant and other great philosophers,[218] but, writing in a more liberal age, Nowell-Smith and Rachels could go much further than Kant, as I will make clear in the subsequent pages when we deal with the Kantian heritage in nineteenth-century thought.

The work of Nowell-Smith, Rachels, Nielsen and other critics of divine command morality has not eradicated the theory. There even seems to be a revival of divine command ethics (or theories closely related to divine commands ethics) as we can make up from the work of Philip Quinn,[219] Richard Mouw,[220] Robert M. Adams,[221] John Hare,[222] Thomas Carson,[223] Mark Murphy,[224] Linda Zagzebski,[225] Janine Marie Idziak[226] and others.[227] We cannot discuss all the new varieties of divine command ethics though,

---

[216] Ibid., p. 118.

[217] Ibid.

[218] See for the prehistory of the idea of moral autonomy: Schneewind, J.B., *The Invention of Autonomy: A History of Modern Moral Philosophy*, Cambridge University Press, Cambridge 1998. Relevant material from the whole history to our times is to be found in: Edwards, *God and the Philosophers*.

[219] Quinn, P.L., *Divine Commands and Moral Requirements*, Clarendon Press, Oxford 1978; Quinn, P.L., "The Recent Revival of Divine Command Ethics," *Philosophy and Phenomenal Research*, 50 (supplement) 1990, pp. 345–365.

[220] Mouw, R., *The God Who Commands*, University of Notre Dame Press, Notre Dame 1990.

[221] Adams, Robert M., *Finite and Infinite Goods: A Framework for Ethics*, Oxford University Press, Oxford 1999.

[222] Hare, John E., *God and Morality: A Philosophical History*, Blackwell Publishing, Malden 2007.

[223] Carson, Thomas L., *Value and the Good Life*, University of Notre Dame Press, Notre Dame 2000.

[224] Murphy, Mark C., *An Essay on Divine Authority*, Cornell University Press, Ithaca 2002.

[225] Zagzebski, Linda, *Divine Motivation Theory*, Cambridge University Press, Cambridge 2004.

[226] Idziak, J.M., "In Search of 'Good Reasons' for an Ethics of Divine Commands: A Catalogue of Arguments," *Faith and Philosophy*, 8 1991, pp. 47–64; Idziak, Janine Marie, *Divine Command Morality: Historical and Contemporary Readings*, The Edwin Mellen Press, New York 1979, pp. 1–38; Idziak, Janine Marie, "Is Morality Based on God's Commands?" in: Michael L. Peterson and Raymond J. VanArragon, eds., *Contemporary Debates in Philosophy of Religion*, Blackwell Publishing, Malden 2004, pp. 290–298.

[227] See for an overview: Hare, John E., "Religion and Morality," in: *Stanford Encyclopedia of Philosophy*, at: http://plato.stanford.edu, 2006, pp. 1–31; Idziak, Janine Marie, "Divine Command Ethics," in: Philip L. Quinn and Charles Taliaferro, eds., *A Companion to the Philosophy of Religion*, Blackwell, Oxford 1997, pp. 453–460.

because that is not necessary for this project. I will conclude this topic with the contention that moral autonomy does not sit easily with divine command ethics, and that therefore the critics of divine command ethics have stronger arguments than the protagonists. This has important practical consequences. Religious terrorists operate on the basis of divine command ethics, so there is a public interest involved in having a more autonomously educated citizenry. In the remaining sections of Chapter 4 I want to illustrate that the recognition of moral autonomy in Western thought was an indirect affair. Only a few authors were as straightforward about recognizing moral autonomy as Nowell-Smith, Rachels, and Nielsen. Most authors accepted moral autonomy only in an indirect manner. It is, again, the cautious and moderate Enlightenment thinker Immanuel Kant who is more representative of the dominant line of Western thought than the radical Spinoza.

It is intriguing that Kant elaborated on this with exactly the same example I introduced before: the story of Abraham offering his son Isaac. In *Die Religion innerhalb der Grenzen der bloßen Vernunft* [Religion within the Limits of Reason Alone] (1793)[228] Kant wrote that it is clear that nobody may deprive a man of his life on the basis of religious considerations.[229] That God himself would have imposed such a norm is always based on documents that are never completely authenticated. Revelation, so Kant told us, is always something that reaches us by human means. And that implies that we always have to leave open the possibility that we may make a mistake in interpreting revelation.[230]

I think that Kant had a point here. But what he did not say – and could not say openly in his time – is that with this argument he seriously undermined the idea of heteronomous ethics that seems to be implied in the theistic notion of God.[231] In Kant's ethic it is human autonomy that is the guiding principle, but this could only be admitted *sotto voce*.

Kant's Struggle with Moral Autonomy and Free Speech

In the first paragraph of Chapter 3 it was demonstrated that Mill, in *On Liberty*, formulated a manifesto for free speech that continues to fascinate each new generation of liberals. British intellectual Noel Annan (1916–

---

[228]   Kant, Immanuel, *Religion innerhalb der Grenzen der bloßen Vernunft* [Religion within the Limits of Reason Alone], 1793, in: Immanuel Kant, *Die Metaphysik der Sitten* [The Metaphysics of Morals], Werkausgabe, Band VIII, ed. Wilhelm Weischedel, Suhrkamp, Frankfurt am Main 1981, pp. 649–879.

[229]   Ibid., p. 861.

[230]   Ibid.

[231]   See on this: Rae, Murray, "The Risk of Obedience: A Consideration of Kierkegaard's *Fear and Trembling*," *Journal of Systematic Theology*, 1, no. 3 1999, pp. 308–321, p. 217.

2000) wrote in 1968: "The Essay burnt itself into the consciousness of each succeeding generation of liberals: whatever else they discarded from mid-Victorian radicalism, they retained the Essay – it troubled the conscience of converted Marxists and mellowed the convictions of British socialists."[232] This is perfectly true, but, as Brand Blanshard reminded us, this could also make us forget that, in most parts of the world, Mill's doctrine would be regarded as radical if not revolutionary. "It would be rejected by all the Communist governments," Blanshard wrote in 1984, "by most of those of the so-called Third World, and by some even in the 'free world'."[233]

We also have to remind ourselves that less than a century before Mill wrote his essay, Kant wrestled with the same problems and could not write what was on his mind openly. Kant was a cautious writer and he certainly did not want to get into trouble with the authorities.

The skeptical or secular strain in his work manifests itself in Kant's contribution to science. He developed what has come to be known as the "Kant–Laplace hypothesis." This is the astronomical theory that explains the origin of the solar system out of a primordial nebula, making use only of physical laws and without calling upon the intervention of God in nature.

Writing God out of science was not without danger in those times, and Kant was read critically by the authorities of his day. Kant scholar Lewis White Beck (1913–1997) wrote: "Perhaps the only real excitement in his otherwise quiet life was provided by the royal prohibition on his teaching and writing on the subject of religion. This censorship ban was applied soon after his chief work on religion was published, though he had been having trouble with the censor during its publication and had had to employ somewhat tricky procedures to have it published."[234]

How could a Prussia where Voltaire had attained the status of a court philosopher now suddenly ban the work of that other great Enlightenment philosopher, Immanuel Kant?

Kant was writing under Frederick William II (1744–1797), King of Prussia from 1786 till 1797. As long as Frederick the Great was alive (1712–1786) there was no official interference with Kant's publications. This changed when Frederick died in 1786 and was succeeded by his nephew, Frederick William II. Frederick William was a bigoted opponent of Enlightenment thought and one of the first things he did was to appoint a culture minister by the name of Wöllner.[235] Wöllner issued two important

---

[232] Annan, Noel, "John Stuart Mill," in: J.B. Schneewind, ed., *Mill: A Collection of Critical Essays*, Macmillan, London 1968, pp. 22–46, p. 40.

[233] Blanshard, *Four Reasonable Men*, p. 93.

[234] Beck, Lewis White, "Kant," in: Lewis White Beck, *Six Secular Philosophers. Religious Themes in the Thought of Spinoza, Hume, Kant, Nietzsche, William James and Santayana*, Thoemmes Press, Bristol 1997, pp. 63–83, p. 65.

[235] See on this: Edwards, *God and the Philosophers*, p. 108.

edicts. The first (the so-called *Religionsedikt*) threatened the dismissal of all civil servants (including university teachers) who deviated from adherence to biblical doctrines. The second (the *Zensuredikt*) had to do with censorship. It required an official *imprimatur* for all publications dealing with religious topics. Despite the edicts, Kant managed to have his *Religion within the Limits of Reason Alone* published in 1793, but in October 1794 he received peremptory notice from the king.

> Our most high person has for a long time observed with great displeasure how you misuse your philosophy to undermine and debase many of the most important and fundamental doctrines of the Holy Scriptures and Christianity; how, namely, you have done this in your book, *Religion within the Limits of Reason Alone*, as well as in other smaller works … . We demand of you immediately a most conscientious answer and expect that in the future, towards the avoidance of our highest disfavor, you will give no such cause for offence … . If you continue to resist, you may certainly expect unpleasant consequences to yourself.[236]

This was no encouragement to Kant to further develop his ideas on moral autonomy, as can be easily understood. Kant decided to cave in. He replied that his books had been misunderstood. He tried to convince the king that he had not aimed to undermine Christianity and wrote: "I hereby, as Your Majesty's most faithful servant, solemnly declare that henceforth I will entirely refrain from all public statements on religion, both natural and revealed, either in lectures or in writings."[237] One may regret this answer, but we should always remind ourselves that Kant was (like Galileo complying with Church authorities) seventy-one, and, as Paul Edwards rightly remarks, had every right to live out his life in peace.[238] Besides, he had done a lot. His philosophy of religion had been published in 1793 and his seminal essay on Enlightenment in 1784. The king could not turn back the clock to a pre-Enlightenment era. What he could do, of course, is slow down the pace of events.

When the king died, Kant again felt free to publish his thoughts on religion, because he felt bound to the king himself, not to his successors. So in the later editions of *Religion within the Limits of Reason Alone* Kant felt more free.

Kant's work always was a curious blend of radicalism and adherence to traditional doctrine.[239] In his previous work, mainly the *Critique of Pure*

---

[236] Quoted ibid.
[237] Ibid.
[238] Ibid., p. 109.
[239] This is well described by: Heine, Heinrich, *On the History of Religion and Philosophy in Germany*, translated by Howard Pollack-Milgate, Cambridge University Press, Cambridge 2007.

Reason, Kant had held that the theoretical proofs of the existence of God are fallacious. Nevertheless he did not say that God did not exist. He denied only that we could know it. In a famous sentence he declared: "I have found it necessary to deny knowledge, in order to make room for faith."[240] In the work of Kant, faith is contrasted with knowledge, not with reason. It is possible to entertain a reasonable form of faith. What binds Kant to Hume (1711–1776) is that both writers undermined the rational theology that was popular in their time,[241] but with Kant there is not a trace of irony in his religious philosophy, as is the case with Hume. Kant took religion seriously, as did Rousseau (1712–1778).[242] Hume did not.

The question is: how could Kant have founded his rational faith if not on the basis of knowledge? The answer is: it was based on morality.[243] Initially, Kant seemed to reject all traces of religion in the edifice of his thought. He rejected the divine command theory of ethics. Kant said that we respect the moral law because it is a law which we, as reasonable beings, legislate for ourselves. So in that sense morality is not dependent upon religion. Nevertheless, the religion that was in a way thrown out of the window by Kant in his theoretical philosophy is smuggled in again through the backdoor of his practical philosophy. Kant was impressed by the fact that the most virtuous people are not always the happiest. And he thought that in a rational world our moral values and expectations could not always be out of concord with what the world is like. There should be some proportioning of punishment and reward in the world. If this proportioning can not take place in this world, then it should be the case in the world after this one, in the hereafter. According to Kant, God is a postulate.

Let us now see how Kant struggles with the question of moral autonomy. How can Kant harmonize moral autonomy with an eternal legislator for this world whom he did not want to abolish – at least not explicitly? To answer these questions we have to go back to the story of Abraham and Isaac, because, as indicated before, Kant also contrasted his own ideas on the source of morality with the divine command theory as manifested in the biblical story of Abraham. In *Religion within the Limits of Reason Alone*, the book that caused him to be censured by the Prussian government for having "misused his philosophy to the detriment of disparagement of many fundamental tenets of Holy Scripture and Christianity,"[244] Kant

---

[240] Quoted in Beck, "Kant," p. 71.

[241] See for Hume: Hume, David, *Dialogues Concerning Natural Religion*, ed. Henry D. Aiken, Hafner Press, New York 1948 (1779).

[242] There is a long discussion among Hume commentators on the question of what exactly Hume's position is on religion. See: Mossner, Ernest C., "The Enigma of Hume," *Mind*, New Series, 45, no. 179 1936, pp. 334–349; Mossner, Ernest C., "The Religion of David Hume," *Journal of the History of Ideas*, 39, no. 4 1970, pp. 653–663.

[243] Hare, *God and Morality*.

[244] Beck, *Six Secular Philosophers*, p. 77.

started from the presupposition that nobody is free to take anybody else's life on the basis of religious convictions.[245] If God seems to have issued a command as horrific as the one we encounter in the story of Abraham, we should be skeptical about its content.

Kant was a very cautious thinker who tried his best not to give offence to the authorities or the clergy of his time. Nevertheless, implicitly, his comment on the story of Abraham implies a radical critique of the concept of revelation, as the censor was not slow to figure out.

It is illuminating to compare the cautious way of dealing with this topic by Kant with the more straightforward and heretical position of the British freethinker Thomas Paine (1737–1809), who was Kant's contemporary. In his controversial book *The Age of Reason* (1794), published one year after Kant's *Religion within the Limits of Reason Alone*, Paine commented on Moses receiving the Ten Commandments from above. This was a "revelation," so Paine tells us, but he adds: "revelation to that person only."[246] He meant: only a revelation to Moses, not to us.

> When Moses told the children of Israel that he received the two tables of the commandments from the hand of God, they were not obliged to believe him, because they had no other authority for it than his telling them so … .[247]

The same is true, of course, of the revelations to Mohammed. Paine writes:

> When I am told that the Qur'an was written in heaven, and brought to Mahomet by an angel, the account comes to near the same kind of hearsay evidence, and second hand authority, as the former. I did not see the angel myself, and therefore I have a right not to believe it.[248]

What we know about revelation is always mediated by what I have referred to before as "religious leaders." So anyone who believes the Ten Commandment to be true does not do this on account of God's authority but on the basis of the authority of Moses.[249]

Kant's position does not fundamentally differ from that of Paine, but he was at pains to put it far less bluntly than Paine did.[250] What both writers

---

[245]   Kant, *Die Religion innerhalb der Grenzen der bloßen Vernunft*, p. 861.
[246]   Paine, Thomas, *The Age of Reason*, 1794, in: Thomas Paine, *Collected Writings*, The Library of America, New York 1995, pp. 665–885, p. 668.
[247]   Ibid., p. 668.
[248]   Ibid.
[249]   Similar arguments, although more cautiously formulated and represented by the figures in a dialogue, we find in Hume's *Dialogues concerning Natural Religion*.
[250]   Paine's biographer John Keane writes: "Attacks on Christianity were, of course, nothing new, but the plebeian style of Paine's text quickly frightened members of the clergy, who otherwise could live with the mannerly scepticism of a David Hume or an Edward Gibbon or

had in common was a skeptical attitude towards what comes "from above." Even if the command seems to be a command from God – as Abraham appeared to think – we have to leave open the possibility that we ourselves make a mistake in interpreting the command, or that the religious leader makes a mistake.[251]

Now, how would the theoreticians of the divine command theory answer Kant? And, more importantly, do they have an answer?

I think they do. What Abraham and other advocates of divine command morality could answer to the great philosopher from Königsberg is that there is a contradiction between what he claimed to be doing and what he was actually doing. Kant was ostensibly trying to determine the will of God, but, once he decided that he would never accept any injunctions as "divine" (in the sense of coming from God) that violated moral conscience, he was actually establishing moral conscience as his final arbiter, not God. So *de facto* Kant only accepted moral autonomy as his guiding principle.

The mechanism is adequately analyzed by Richard Robinson with regard to Matthew Arnold (1822–1888). Arnold sees religion as nothing other than a picturesque or mythical form of morality. This was his position in *Literature and Dogma* (1887) where he wrote that "religion is ... morality touched by emotion."[252] Arnold pictured God as "the eternal Power, not ourselves, that makes for righteousness." But Robinson comments that at this stage people make no independent effort to communicate with their god or find out his nature; they infer his nature from their own moral views.

It is comprehensible that the theoreticians of the divine command approach object to this. For the final result of Kant's approach (and Arnold's) will be that he simply eradicates all elements from the theological heritage that do not fit in with his Enlightened moral principles.

The dilemma we should confront Kant with is the following. "Is it possible that an interpretation of one of the injunctions of Holy Scripture might lead to something that would horrify us from a moral point of view?" To this question Kant would answer "no." In the *Critique of Practical Reason* he wrote: "Religion is the recognition of all duties as divine commands."[253] This seems to be the language of the divine command theory. But that is only appearance. The reason why there is only a superficial and no real similarity with the divine command theory is because, for Kant, what is a

---

polite deistical speculations in parlors and coffeehouses." See: Keane, John, *Tom Paine. A Political Life*, Bloomsbury, London 1995, p. 393.

[251]   Kant, *Die Religion innerhalb der Grenzen der bloßen Vernunft*, p. 861.

[252]   Arnold, Matthew, *Literature and Dogma: An Essay towards Apprehension of the Bible*, Watts and Co., London 1887, p. 47.

[253]   Kant, Immanuel, *Critique of Practical Reason*, translated L.W. Beck, Macmillan, New York 1956, p. 134.

moral duty cannot be decided by simply listening to the voice of God or reading His Scripture. Our moral duty has to be delineated purely by philosophical reasoning. The starting point of his moral reasoning is, therefore, not God's command, but moral autonomy. But the final outcome of his moral reasoning Kant called "divine." Would it, under those circumstances, not be more appropriate to say that, from Kant's perspective, God is not legislating for man, but man is legislating for God? Or, to put it differently, religion is not the basis for morality but the other way around: morals are the basis for religion. Lewis White Beck sums up Kant's position: "Any religion that requires anything of man other than earnest and conscientious morality is mere superstition and idolatry."[254] This is, basically, no different from John Stuart Mill who in his essay *Theism* wrote: "If the moral character of the doctrines of an alleged Revelation is bad and perverting, we ought to reject it from whomsoever it comes; for it cannot come from a good and wise Being."[255]

This is something the adherents of divine command theory simply cannot accept. They see this as an unacceptable limitation of the divine personality. God is a person. God must have a "choice." If God could not do otherwise than what he actually does, he would not be a person. He would be an automaton, a "Dieu machine" [machine God], a Spinozistic *Deus sive Natura* [God or otherwise Nature], not the theistic personal God that we encounter in the scriptural tradition.[256]

Here the response from the side of divine command moralists appears to be convincing, I would say.

As I said before, Kant always tried to avoid trouble with the authorities. He certainly did not volunteer for martyrdom, like Thomas More (1478–1535). His attitude might be characterized adequately in the words of Montaigne (1533–1592): "I shall support the good side as far as (but, if possible, excluding) the stake."[257] So Kant struggled to reconcile his predilection for moral autonomy with confessional orthodoxy.

Kant addressed the same question five years later in *Der Streit der Fakultäten* [The Conflict of the Faculties] (1798),[258] and here, as he had

---

[254]   Beck, *Six Secular Philosophers*, p. 76.

[255]   Mill, John Stuart, "Theism," in: John Stuart Mill, *Three Essays on Religion*, Prometheus Books, Amherst, NY 1998 (1874), pp. 125–257, p. 216.

[256]   Analogous to La Mettrie's *L'homme machine* [The Machine Man]. See: La Mettrie, *Textes Choisis. L'Homme-Machine, Histoire Naturelle de l'Ame*, e.a. [The Machine Man, Natural History of the Soul], Éditions sociales, Paris 1974.

[257]   Montaigne, Michel de, *The Essays of Michel de Montaigne*, translated and edited by M.A. Screech, Allen Lane, The Penguin Press, London 1991, p. 894.

[258]   Kant, Immanuel, *Der Streit der Fakultäten* [The Conflict of the Faculties], 1798, in: Immanuel Kant, *Schriften zur Anthropologie, Geschichtsphilosophie, Politik und Pädagogik* [Writings on Anthropology, the Philosophy of History, Politics, and Pedagogics], 1, Werkausgabe XI, ed. W. Weischedel, Suhrkamp, Frankfurt am Main 1981, pp. 267–393.

done in *Religion within the Limits of Reason Alone,* he dwelled on the problem of Abraham. In *Der Streit* he assures us that even if God *seems* to speak to humankind, we can never be sure that it is God who is speaking. Kant used what might be called "the agnostic argument": man will never be able to understand an Infinite God with his finite capacities.[259] In some cases it is even possible to contend with absolute certainty that we cannot hear the voice of God, *viz.* if what is commanded flatly violates the moral law. That voice may sound majestic, Kant told us, but it should be considered a fraud.[260]

As an example of this state of affairs Kant referred to Abraham's sacrifice and called this *a myth.* The poor unknowing child brought the wood for the fire himself, Kant wrote. Abraham should have answered: "that I should not kill my son is clear, but that you, appearing to me as God are really God, is far from certain, not even if your voice were to cry aloud from heaven."[261]

It is remarkable that such a "dry" author as Immanuel Kant talked in such emotional terms about the story of Abraham. And what is also remarkable: he called it "a myth."

This is plain language. Kant qualified a central part of Holy Scripture as mythical.

Kant's Legacy in Nineteenth-Century German Theology

We may call the tradition initiated by Kant "the modernist tradition" in religious thought. The term "modernism" covers a variety of movements and tendencies, but I will use it here to designate the attempt to take moral autonomy in religious thought as a starting point while at the same time trying to avoid an open conflict with divine command ethics. Modernism in this sense is an attempt to reconcile modern science and philosophy with religious traditions.[262] When applied to the theory of interpretation, modernism means that the holy text and the holy tradition are interpreted

---

[259] Ibid., p. 333.

[260] Ibid.

[261] Ibid.

[262] See: Livingstone, Elizabeth A., ed., *The Concise Oxford Dictionary of the Christian Church,* Oxford University Press, Oxford 1977, p. 341: "Modernism: a movement within the RC Church which aimed at bringing the tradition of Catholic belief into closer relation with the modern outlook in philosophy, the historical and other sciences, and social ideas." See also: *The Penguin Dictionary of Religions,* ed. John R. Hinnells, Penguin Books, London 1995 (1984), p. 319: "Religions are essentially conservative movements, usually organized to preserve traditions and the status quo. Historically, therefore, religions have always had to come to terms with changes in society and culture, and this has never been more true than in the nineteenth and twentieth centuries, periods normally referred to as 'modern'."

against the background of autonomous morality. Modernism has two important features. *First,* the modernists want to be "modern." That means they, by and large, subscribe to the ideas of moral education as expounded by Kohlberg, reject the religious sternness of the Abrahamic strain in theistic religion, and follow Mill and others in the proclamation of the great importance of free speech. *Second,* modernism defines itself by attempting to narrow the chasm between ancient religion and modern life. As we will see in the pages that follow, modernists made use of a special technique to bridge that gap: that technique is called "interpretation." Applied to the theory of interpretation, modernism means that the holy text and the holy tradition are interpreted against the background of autonomous morality. Sometimes commentators who stand in the modernist tradition belittle the significance of autonomous reasoning, rationalism, and Enlightenment values. They want us to believe that the "true core" of the theistic religions *has always been* respect for moral autonomy and modern values. And because this is their basic conviction, it colors all their interpretations.

In some cases these interpretations are rather weird. An unprejudiced reading of the stories of Abraham, Jephtha, and Job cannot ignore that there is a strong element of heteronomy and divine command ethics in the holy book and the holy tradition. But, according to the more cautious or conciliatory voices among the modernists, the autonomy of ethics is not an idea that germinated in a non-religious context and has gradually gained ground in the religious traditions, but rather an inherent element of the religious traditions themselves. We find this tendency in Immanuel Kant, but, for instance, also – and more surprisingly – in the great French conservative writer, politician, and historian Chateaubriand.

Chateaubriand presented an eloquent apology for Christianity in his book *Génie du Christianisme* [Genius of Christianity] (1802), published nine years after Kant's *Religion within the Limits of Reason Alone*.[263] Contrary to Kant, Chateaubriand presented a scathing critique of the Enlightenment authors. What the French *philosophes* accomplished, Chateaubriand ranted, was nothing. They only brought revolution and havoc upon the country.[264] Their sole aim was destruction.[265] And what did they put in place of what they destroyed? Nothing.

---

[263] Chateaubriand, *Génie du Christianisme ou Beautés de la Religion Chrétienne* [Genius of Christianity or Beauties of the Christian Religion], ed. Maurice Regard, Gallimard, Paris 1978 (1802).

[264] Chateaubriand, *Essai historique, politique et moral sur les révolutions anciennes et modernes, considérées dans leur rapports avec la Révolution française* [Historical, Political and Moral Essay on Ancient and Modern Revolutions Considered in Relation to the French Revolution], ed. Maurice Regard, Gallimard, Paris 1978 (1797), p. 358.

[265] Ibid., p. 259.

When we realize that Kant wrote a superb vindication of the principles of the Enlightenment in his famous essay *What is Enlightenment?*,[266] the difference between him and Chateaubriand could not be greater, it would seem. But that is only superficial,[267] as we will notice as soon as we delve into the matter a little further.

One of the most important elements in Enlightenment thinking was the doctrine of moral autonomy. This is correctly described by the great historian of philosophy, F.C. Copleston (1907–1994), as the main contribution of the Enlightenment to the cultural heritage of mankind. What the Enlightenment authors accomplished, so wrote Copleston, is that they separated ethics from metaphysics and theology.[268] There was certainly a difference in tone between the moral idealism of Diderot (1713–1784) and the utilitarian approach of La Mettrie (1709–1751), so Copleston told us, but what all Enlightenment philosophers had in common is that they wanted "to set morality on its own feet."[269]

If this judgment is right – as I think it is – every criticism of the Enlightenment should address this particular issue: can morality be made to stand on its own feet?

What we see, however, in the tradition of what we may call "moderate theism" or modernism is that it tries to belittle the significance of the Enlightenment, insinuating that moral autonomy is an inherent element of the theistic or religious tradition. This is also what we find in Chateaubriand. What he tried to do in *Génie du Christianisme* is, he told us, "not to prove that Christianity is excellent because it comes from God, but that it comes from God because it is excellent."[270] That means that Chateaubriand's point of departure was, just like Kant, moral autonomy, and not divine command ethics. But what he did not realize (at least he did not address it) is that unknowingly he subscribed to the central tenets of the position he professed to criticize: that of the Enlightenment. Chateaubriand is an adherent of the Enlightenment philosophy *malgré lui*.

It is a paradoxical fact that many apologies of Christianity in the long run work to undermine it. The British idealist philosopher William Ritchie

---

[266] Kant, Immanuel, *Beantwortung der Frage: Was ist Aufklärung?* [An Answer to the Question: What Is Englightenment?] (1784), in: *Schriften zur Anthropologie, Geschichtsphilosophie, Politik und Pädagogik* [Writings on Anthropology, the Philosophy of History, Politics and Pedagogics], 1, ed. Wilhelm Weischedel, Suhrkamp, Frankfurt am Main 1981, pp. 53–61.

[267] As Joseph de Maistre was well aware. See what he writes on Chateaubriand in: Maistre, Joseph de, *Œuvres, suivis d'un Dictionnaire de Joseph de Maistre* [Works, Followed by a Dictionary of Joseph de Maistre], ed. Pierre Glaudes, Robert Laffont, Paris 2007, p. 1147.

[268] Copleston, Frederick, S.J., *A History of Philosophy*, Vol. VI, Part I, *The French Enlightenment to Kant*, Image Books, New York 1960, p. 18.

[269] Ibid.

[270] Chateaubriand, *Génie du Christianisme*, p. 469.

Sorley (1855–1935) makes a comparison between the religious ideas of John Locke (1632–1704) and John Toland (1670–1722). On Locke's *Reasonableness of Christianity* (1695) Sorley gives the following comment: "Locke went to the Scriptures: miracles and prophecy convinced his reason of their authority; the same reason was used for understanding the doctrines they revealed."[271]

Toland's *Christianity not Mysterious* (1696) was influenced by Locke's book but much more radical. The difference was this (still according to Sorley): "Locke's aim was to show that Christianity was reasonable; Toland's, to demonstrate that nothing contrary to reason, and nothing above reason, can be part of Christian doctrine."[272] We may call this the tragedy of all rationalist apologies of religion: they acknowledge the authority of reason. And once that is acknowledged there can be no half-measures in accepting its results. Sometimes, even for the rationalist this comes as a surprise. When *Christianity not Mysterious* was published Toland reckoned himself a member of the Church of England. When his book was burned at the door of the Irish house of parliament, "he may have felt his churchmanship insecure," as Sorley writes.[273]

Schleiermacher as the Father of Modern Hermeneutics

Modernism, or an orientation on Enlightenment thinking, was also at the centre of German theological thought from Immanuel Kant onwards and exerted an overwhelming influence on modern culture. In theological circles it was defended by Friedrich Ernst Daniel Schleiermacher (1768–1834).[274]

Schleiermacher was a professor of theology at the University of Berlin. His first important publication dates from 1799: *On Religion: Speeches to its Cultured Despisers.*[275] He argued that religion is "feeling and intuition of the universe." This liberal and Romantic approach made it possible to reconcile Christianity with the spirit of Enlightenment and thereby with modern times. If religion is a "feeling," why bother about contradictions in the biblical text or about divine commands that order gross violations

---

[271] Sorley, W.R., *A History of British Philosophy to 1900*, Cambridge University Press, London 1965 (1920), p. 145.

[272] Ibid., p. 146.

[273] Ibid., p. 147.

[274] On Schleiermacher, see: Nowak, Kurt, *Schleiermacher: Leben, Werk und Wirkun* [Schleiermacher: Life, Work, and Influence], 2. Auflage, Vandenhoeck & Ruprecht, Göttingen 2001.

[275] Schleiermacher, Friedrich, *On Religion: Speeches to its Cultured Despisers*, Cambridge University Press, Cambridge 1996.

of the moral law? Schleiermacher's liberal theology, attuned to modern culture, set the tone for much Protestant theology. In the nineteenth century his ideas developed into what has been called "liberal Protestantism" or "cultural Protestantism" (*Kulturprotestantismus*). "From its outset, liberal Protestantism was committed to bridging the gap between Christian faith and modern knowledge."[276] What the liberal Protestants did is: "they demanded a degree of freedom in relation to the doctrinal inheritance of Christianity on the one hand, and traditional methods of biblical interpretation on the other."[277] Elements of Christian belief which they regarded as seriously out of line with modern cultural values were treated in the following way, according to Alister McGrath. Either, they were abandoned (as happened with the doctrine of original sin), or they were reinterpreted in a manner more conducive to the spirit of the age.[278] One of the main representatives of the movement, Albrecht Benjamin Ritschl (1822–1889), saw history as a divinely guided process toward perfection. In the course of history some people are bearers of special divine insights. Jesus Christ was such a person.[279]

The most representative figures of the movement were, apart from Ritschl, Wilhelm Herrmann (1846–1922), Adolf von Harnack (1851–1930) and (in a certain sense) Ernest Troeltsch (1865–1923). A representative from closer to our own time is Paul Tillich (1886–1965).

Mark Lilla (1956–), in his overview of the tradition of political theology, calls those liberal Protestants "immensely learned scholars whose greater theological-political ambitions were usually clearer than the reasoning they used to achieve them."[280] This is a devastating observation.

What is the background to their thinking? According to the liberal Protestants there was no contradiction between Christianity and modern German life. Now, they might have been right in this – although we should never forget to mention how this lack of contradiction came about. It did so because they simply, first, *ignored* all the problematical texts I have quoted before or, second, *"interpreted"* those texts in such a way that all contradictions with modern thought simply evaporated. Only thanks to their own interventions and interpretative work could they contend that, in the words of Mark Lilla, "there was an organic connection between

---

[276] McGrath, Alister E., *Christian Theology: An Introduction*, p. 93.
[277] Ibid., p. 93.
[278] Ibid.
[279] See: Ritschl, Albrecht, Instruction in the Christian Religion, translated by Alice Mead Swing in: *The Theology of Albrecht Ritschl together with Instruction in the Christian Religion*, ed. Albert Temple Swing, Kessinger Publishing, Whitefish, MT 2006.
[280] Lilla, Mark, *The Stillborn God: Religion, Politics, and the Modern West*, Alfred A. Knopf, New York 2007, p. 230.

Protestantism and modernity, a shared conception of the values of individuality, moral universalism, reason, and progress."[281] As Harnack put it in *What is Christianity* (1900): "Law or ordinances or injunctions bidding us forcibly to alter the conditions of the age in which we happen to be living are not to be found in the Gospels."[282]

German cultural Protestantism is a manifestation of what William James (1842–1910) called the "healthy-mindedness" of liberal theology. He wrote:

> The advance of liberalism, so-called, in Christianity, during the past fifty years, may fairly be called a victory of healthy-mindedness within the church over the morbidness with which the old hell-fire theology was more harmoniously related.[283]

Modernist movements not only gained ground within Protestant Christianity but within the Jewish tradition as well. An important figure was Hermann Cohen (1842–1918), professor in Marburg and together with Natorp the founder of the Marburg School of Neo-Kantianism. In his posthumously published treatise *Religion of Reason out of the Sources of Judaism* (1919) he argued that Judaism is both the source and quintessence of all ethical monotheism.[284] It was Kant again who was helpful in establishing this conviction. Cohen followed Kant in accepting that the core of religion was following the moral law and "that religious practice can be justified only so long as it actualizes that law in social life, without straying beyond reason's bounds."[285] Cohen censured Kant, however, because the great German thinker had overlooked the fact that his convictions about the moral law and moral freedom "had derived" from Judaism. Kant could hear in Judaism only the brute commands of heteronomous laws and he was deaf to the profound modernity of Judaism.

---

[281]   Ibid., p. 231.

[282]   Harnack quoted ibid., p. 231.

[283]   James, William, *The Varieties of Religious Experience. A Study in Human Nature*, ed. Martin E. Marty, Penguin Books, Harmondsworth 1982 (1902), p. 91.

[284]   See: Cohen, Hermann, *Religion der Vernunft aus den Quellen des Judenthums* [Religion of Reason out of the Sources of Judaism], Zweite Auflage, Joseph Melzer Verlag, Darmstadt 1966 (1919), p. 6: "Ein gerader Weg führt uns von dem geschichtlichen Begriffe des Judentums zur Philosophie der Religion" [There is a direct path from the historical concept of Judaism to the philosophy of religion]. This point of view had also been defended a little earlier by the great French scholar Ernest Renan: Renan, Ernest, "Le judaïsme comme race et comme religion" [Judaism as Race and Religion], 1883, in: Ernest Renan, *Discours et Conférences* [Speeches and Lectures], sixième édition, Calmann-Lévy, Paris 1887, pp. 341–374. See on Renan: Bierer, Dora, "Renan and His Interpreters: A Study in French Intellectual Warfare," *The Journal of Modern History*, 25, no. 4 1953, pp. 375–389; Pitt, Alan, "The Cultural Impact of Science in France: Ernest Renan and the *Vie de Jesus*," *The Historical Journal*, 43, no. 1 2000, pp. 79–101; Blanshard, Brand, "Ernest Renan," in: *Four Reasonable Men*, pp. 103–179.

[285]   Quoted in Lilla, *The Stillborn God*, p. 240.

What Cohen did not understand (and this is crucial), is that from an ethical point of view it is irrelevant where our moral precepts *come from* (their historical origin). What counts is *how they can be justified* (the justification of our moral beliefs).[286] And once we have stated the dilemma in these terms, the conclusion is inevitable: they are *either* justified as expressions of the will of God as manifested in revelation *or* they are justified as conforming to the moral law itself. Either religion is the basis for ethics, or ethics is the basis for religion. With "ethics as the basis for religion" I mean that on ethical grounds we try to ascertain what religion we think is preferable. Cohen and other modernists obfuscated the issue by pretending that the religious tradition could never contradict our moral ideas. He said: "There is comfort and hope for us in the fact that the moral ideas of our religion are in full accord with the exemplary ethics of the new era ushered in by the French Revolution."[287] Comforting this certainly was, but was it rational to believe such a thing? It would be nothing short of a miracle if ancient religious texts were to be in "full accord" with e.g. the values and rights exemplified in the French *Déclaration des Droits de l'Homme et du Citoyen* [Declaration of the Rights of Man and the Citizen] (1789). Such a naïve or optimistic conviction could only be held by people who unconsciously or deliberately ignored the passages I have quoted in the sections of Chapter 2 dealing with apostasy and the story of Phinehas.

But in one respect Cohen was right. He was right when he implicitly criticized the liberal Protestants for unjustifiably proclaiming their belief (i.e. Christianity) to be compatible with modern moral ideas while insinuating that this could not be the case for the Jewish religion.[288] For the rest, Cohen and the liberal Protestants shared the same illusions. They defended the notion that there was some kind of pre-established harmony between their religions and modernity and they both obfuscated the fact that the miraculous harmony between their religion and modernism was not a fact of nature but the product of their own blinders (denial of problematic passages in Holy Scripture) and the application of what we might call the "trick of interpretation." Therefore Mark Lilla is right (although for somewhat different reasons than he himself advances) when he calls the convictions of the modernists "extraordinarily naïve." He writes: "Neither Troeltsch nor Cohen thought that the destructive forces within biblical religion, which had surfaced repeatedly in premodern Jewish and Christian history, could ever again pose a threat."[289]

---

[286] See on the justification of ethical beliefs: Brandt, Richard, *Ethical Theory. The Problems of Normative and Critical Ethics*, Prentice-Hall, Engelwood Cliffs, NJ 1959, pp. 241–271.

[287] Cohen quoted in Lilla, *The Stillborn God*, p. 240.

[288] Another scholar combating this view was Ernest Renan in "Le judaïsme comme race et comme religion" [Judaism as Race and Religion].

[289] Lilla, *The Stillborn God*, p. 243.

Calling the modernists "extremely naïve" may sound a bit harsh, for we have to remind ourselves that the modernist strategy of "interpretation" was the only device that enabled enlightened morality to manifest itself. Religious suppression was prevalent and morality explicitly contrasted with Scripture could only prevail in a small part of the world during a very limited space of time (from the second half of the nineteenth century). The only option for religious criticism was to act *as if* enlightened morality was part of Scripture. There simply was no other way out for the believer than to pretend that Holy Scripture is a "living text" sending out different messages to different people in different times. That means the *theory of interpretation*, intimately connected with liberal Protestantism, did not arise as the product of a harmonious scholarly development, but out of a state of emergency: the existence of movements such as the Inquisition, censorship, and other limits on free speech. What motivated the modernists was a heartfelt need for a reconciliation of the religious tradition with modern moral ideas.

It was Kant who was pivotal in this process of adapting religion to the stern demands of modernity, but a great influence on liberal Protestantism's theory of interpretation was Schleiermacher. The tradition of thinking that he initiated is called "hermeneutics."

Let me try to state what the relationship between Kant and Schleiermacher is. Whereas Kant initiated the *moral autonomy* that liberal Protestantism was based upon, Schleiermacher provided the *theory of interpretation* that made it possible for moral autonomy to prevail in the religious context.

Schleiermacher lectured from 1819 onwards on the interpretation of texts and speech. Initially, the theory of hermeneutics supposed that it was possible to grasp the original meaning intended by the authors of a text, but in its subsequent development adherents of the theory became more and more skeptical. The interpreter of a text from a past culture belongs to, and is conditioned by, his own different culture, they said. The interpreter always views the past from a particular "horizon," involving a particular "pre-understanding." Ultimately, this led to a relativist stance towards interpretation: we can never retrieve what the ancient texts meant to the people who created them. And this made it "respectable" to have no qualms about reading texts in such a way that they suit our moral purposes.

Armstrong's Plea for Liberal Interpretation

What is foreshadowed by Kant, more explicitly pronounced in Schleiermacher, and further developed in contemporary hermeneutics is a most intriguing phenomenon of Western culture. That is, that moral autonomy is usually not manifested in a direct way but only indirectly, namely, by means of "interpretation." The dominant tradition in the West is aimed at not confronting religious orthodoxy and its idea of heteronomous ethics *directly*, but only *indirectly*. It is for that very reason that the atheist or radical secularist tradition was always a "counter-narrative" – a "contre-histoire de la philosophie" [counter-history of philosophy], as the French thinker Michel Onfray (1959–) calls it.[290] And this has brought into being all kinds of religious movements that are usually characterized as "liberal" or "moderate." "Liberal Protestantism" is, in short, only one variant of a sheer endless spectrum of possibilities.

I want to illustrate exactly how the modernist approach functions, not by referring to the work of one of the German theologians previously mentioned but by analyzing a modern thinker. It seems legitimate to choose the work of Karen Armstrong (1944–), one of the most widely read authors on religion nowadays. She rose to prominence in 1993 with *A History of God*, a study in comparative religion and the key figures that have shaped the different religions.[291] Armstrong's central thesis is that all religions are equally beautiful and that it is only fundamentalist approaches (occurring in all) that are responsible for the violence connected with religion.[292] Armstrong is also convinced that all religions basically teach the same.[293] They all subscribe to the Golden Rule: do unto others what you would have others do unto you.

This view of religion is all very well, of course, as a profession of faith, but this approach leaves much to be desired as a scholarly orientation because it cannot explain violence. Are there really no bases for violence in the religious traditions themselves? Is violence something that comes from outside and is it completely alien to those traditions themselves? Why does it occur more often in some traditions than others? Why more under some historical conditions than others?

Armstrong's books confirm people in their most sacred beliefs but are, from a scholarly point of view, more problematic, as I hope to substantiate in this paragraph. Particularly after the September 11, 2001 attacks, she was in great demand on the lecture circuit where she pleaded for inter-faith dialogue. In fact, her approach is very much in harmony with the German nineteenth-century theologians who saw no friction between religious ideas

---

[290] Onfray, Michel, *Contre-histoire de la Philosophie* [Counter-History of Philosophy], 5 Vols., Bernard Grasset, Paris 2006–2009.

[291] Armstrong, *A History of God*.

[292] Armstrong, Karen, *The Battle for God: Fundamentalism in Judaism, Christianity and Islam*, HarperCollins, London 2000.

[293] See on this: Antes, Peter, "Sagen alle Religionen dasselbe?" [Do all Religions Say the Same Thing?], *Marburg Journal of Religion*, 12, no. 1 2007, pp. 2–10, who contends that the thesis that all religions say the same cannot be maintained empirically.

and modern life. The contradictions between religion and modern life are explained by focusing on the misguided interpretations that fundamentalists give to their religious tradition. This attitude is clearly manifested in her book on the interpretation of the Bible: *The Bible* (2007).

Her starting point in *The Bible* is sacred books, Holy Writ or Scripture. In nearly all the major faiths, she says, people have regarded certain texts as sacred and ontologically different from other documents. "They have invested those writings with the weight of their highest aspirations, most extravagant hopes and deepest fears, and mysteriously the texts have given them something in return."[294]

Yet Armstrong has also noticed that scriptural authority has acquired a dubious flavor. "Today scripture has a bad name," she writes. "Terrorists use the Qur'an to justify atrocities, and some argue that violence of their scripture makes Muslims chronically aggressive. Christians campaign against the teaching of evolutionary theory because it contradicts the biblical creation story. Jews argue that because God promised Canaan (modern Israel) to the descendants of Abraham, oppressive policies against the Palestinians are legitimate."[295] There has been a scriptural revival that has intruded into public life, Armstrong concludes. And it is against those political manifestations of religion in particular that secularist criticism is directed. "Secularist opponents of religion claim that scripture breeds violence, sectarianism and intolerance; that it prevents people from thinking for themselves, and encourages delusion. If religion preaches compassion, why is there so much hatred in sacred texts?"[296]

That is a very good question indeed. And it undoubtedly makes readers curious to hear her answer. Alas, that answer is not very satisfying. Basically, her answer boils down to the same argument we have discussed before in relation to Tariq Ramadan in Chapter 2 and that was introduced by Schleiermacher into the Western tradition of philosophical theology. Armstrong thinks, just like many "liberal believers," that it is all a matter of interpretation. What she tries to do in her book on the Bible is to make two claims. First, an analytical claim. This is that allegorical reading of scripture is perfectly legitimate. Second, a historical claim. Armstrong argues that an exclusively literal interpretation of the Bible is a "recent phenomenon." Armstrong thinks, for instance, that until the nineteenth century very few people imagined that the first chapter of Genesis was a factual account of the origins of life. For centuries, Jews and Christians relished "highly allegorical and inventive exegesis, insisting that a wholly literal reading of the Bible was neither possible nor desirable."[297]

[294]   Armstrong, Karen, *The Bible: The Biography*, Atlantic Books, London 2007, p. 2.
[295]   Ibid.
[296]   Ibid., p. 3.
[297]   Ibid.

I think both claims are dubious, but for different reasons. As a historical argument, it would be wrong to claim that literalist interpretations were completely unknown in the past and literalism is an invention of modern fundamentalists.[298] The tendency to take Scripture as literally true was much more widely dispersed in earlier times. Historical research can point this out. But that is not the point I want to focus on. I want to concentrate on the analytical claim. What is more important for the line of argument developed in *The Secular Outlook,* is that Armstrong also seems to be an adherent of semantic relativism or the "Humpty Dumpty approach" to meaning (see Chapter 2, Textual Relativism). And how she reconciles this with her claim of the sacredness of the texts remains unclear. All the same, the reason why she believes this is crystal clear: we do not have to take the problematic passages in Scripture seriously, because we can simply focus on what we like. "Interpretation" always provides a way out (the same point Ramadan was hinting at when he asked "Is it difficult to understand that this is a question of interpretation?").[299] What Armstrong wants to demonstrate in her book is that biblical authors felt free to "revise texts they had inherited and give them entirely different meanings."[300] Later exegetes used the Bible as the template for the problems of their time. This somewhat relaxed way of dealing with Scripture seems very attractive to Armstrong. Of the attitude of those "exegetes" with regard to Scripture she writes:

> Sometimes they allowed it to shape their world-view but they also felt free to change it and make it speak to contemporary conditions. They were not usually interested in discovering the original meaning of a biblical passage.

[298] See: White, A.D., *A History of the Warfare of Science with Theology in Christendom,* Vol. II, Dover Publications, New York 1960 (1896), p. 305: "The Reformers, having cast off the authority of the Pope and of the universal Church, fell back all the more upon the infallibility of the sacred books. The attitude of Luther toward this great subject was characteristic. As a rule, he adhered tenaciously to the literal interpretation of the Scriptures." See also the Cambridge theologian Charles E. Raven, in "Religion and Science: A Diagnosis," L.T. Hobhouse Memorial Trust Lecture, No. 16, delivered on May 1, 1946, in: *Hobhouse Memorial Lectures 1941–1950,* Oxford University Press, London 1952, pp. 3–16, p. 10. Raven says: "The earliest Reformers alike in science and in religion were not liberals but conservatives, bent upon recalling mankind to an earlier and truer wisdom rather than upon exploring uncharted seas. Hence comes their reverence for the written word, their insistence upon the infallibility of their authorities." For another testimony along these lines, see Huxley: "From being the slave of the Papacy, the intellect was to become the serf of the Bible." (Huxley, Thomas Henry, "Naturalism and Supernaturalism," 1892, in: Thomas Henry Huxley, *Agnosticism and Christianity. And Other Essays,* Prometheus Books, Buffalo, NY 1992, pp. 92–118, p. 98).

[299] Ramadan, Tariq, "A response to Ayaan Hirsi Ali: A Case of Selective Hearing," *The International Herald Tribune,* December 17, 2007.

[300] Armstrong, *The Bible,* p. 4.

> The Bible "proved" that it was holy because people continually discovered fresh ways to interpret it and found that this difficult, ancient set of documents cast light on situations that their authors could never have imagined. Revelation was an ongoing process; it has not been confined to a distant theophany on Mount Sinai; exegetes continued to make the Word of God audible in each generation.[301]

This is a revealing passage that sums it all up. But there are some pertinent questions to be posed with regard to this approach. Let us look more closely at the passage quoted before.

Those exegetes that Armstrong admires for their relaxed attitude toward Scripture "sometimes" allowed it to shape their worldview but "they also felt free to change it" and "make it speak to contemporary conditions."

An obvious question then is: "In what situations did those exegetes choose to let their worldview be changed by Scripture and in what situations did they resist and decide to change Scripture?" The dilemma seems to be this: either we are changed by Scripture or Scripture is changed by us. The traditional approach seems to be that we have to be changed by Scripture, but according to Armstrong and the liberal exegetes from the past she admires so much, it is also perfectly legitimate to change Scripture. But how do those "exegetes from the past" decide one way or the other? Armstrong does not give us an answer to that pertinent question, at least not explicitly.

A second question that can be posed with regard to the passage quoted from Armstrong's book is: what exactly were those liberal exegetes doing? One thing is sure, according to Armstrong "they were not usually interested in discovering the original meaning of a biblical passage." But if that was not the focus of their interest, what was exactly? From the traditional perspective is it clear what the meaning of Scripture is. Scripture informs us about the divine. It tells us what a personal, omnipotent and perfectly good God wants us to do. In Scripture God "reveals" his will ("Thy will be done, as in heaven, so on earth." Matthew 6:10).

A respectful intercourse with the divine would suppose, so it seems, that the exegete scrupulously tries to ascertain what the meaning of Scripture is, in order to know what God has in mind for mankind. But apparently the exegetes that Armstrong favors are not interested in this type of question. But what is *their* focus of interest?

A New Way to Look at the "Sacredness" of Scripture?

Armstrong also introduces a completely new, and we may say revolutionary, way of looking at the "sacredness" of Scripture. In the traditional view,

---

[301]   Ibid., p. 5.

Scripture is sacred because it informs us about the eternal plans God has for the world. "In its specifically theological usage, the term (Scripture) serves to identify the written and authoritative word of God rather than any specific textual content."[302] Scripture presents us with moral values and rules that have eternal significance. The Bible was held in high esteem, because there we were provided with the moral injunctions that are not the whims of fashion, the human, all too human, ideas about right and wrong, but absolute and universal guidelines. The whole idea of texts that are sacred and, in the words of Armstrong, "ontologically different," is based upon this presumption.

But what does Armstrong do? She tells us that the Bible "proved" that it was holy because people could continually discover "fresh ways to interpret it." So what makes the Bible holy is not its fixed meaning, but exactly the opposite: it has no meaning at all because meaning constantly changes over time. It is merely logical that from here she continues with another disconcerting vision, *viz.* that in this conception of scripture "revelation was an ongoing process." So what has been revealed today as higher wisdom may be obsolete tomorrow. The Ten Commandments revealed on Mount Sinai and one of the most authoritative parts of the Bible, because they were written or at least dictated by God himself,[303] may in the future be abolished by new insights – and this ought not to convince us of the relative character of the text of the Bible but of its sacredness. The sacredness of the text consists precisely in the fact that everything is possible. Or, to put it somewhat more instrumentally, Scripture is sacred because it can be used by the exegete for anything he or she wishes.

Armstrong is very supportive of the exegesis by the rabbis called *midrash.* This is derived from the verb *darash* meaning "to investigate" or "to seek."[304] The meaning of a text is not "self-evident," so Armstrong tells us. "The exegete had to go in search of it, because every time a Jew confronted the Word of God in scripture, it signified something different. Scripture was inexhaustible."[305]

These are revealing words. That the meaning of a text is not self-evident is not very surprising, to be sure, but that *every time* a text is read there exists a new meaning is nothing short of magic. This would make – if it were true – all human communication impossible. Alice (in Wonderland) understood that very well when she was puzzled by the response of Humpty Dumpty quoted in Chapter 2.

---

[302] *The HarperCollins Encyclopedia of Catholicism,* Richard P. McBrien, HarperCollins Publishers, New York, NY 1995, p. 1171.

[303] See on this: Lewis, Joseph, *The Ten Commandments: An Investigation into the Origin and Meaning of the Decalogue and an Analysis of its Ethical and Moral Value as a Code of Conduct in Modern Society,* Freethought Press Association, New York 1946.

[304] Armstrong, *The Bible,* p. 81.

[305] Ibid.

Also the claim that Scripture is "inexhaustible" is a bit strange. How does Armstrong know? History is still not at an end, so theoretically there may be a point in time where Scripture is really "exhausted." Or is the "inexhaustibility of Scripture" all that the religion of Armstrong and the rabbis she quotes amounts to? I mean: they apparently do not believe in an eternal God who reveals his ideas to mankind but in a kind of magic phenomenon called "Scripture." Scripture makes it possible for them to "get revealed" exactly what they want to hear, each time this "Scripture" is consulted. Is the essence of their faith perhaps a kind of *fetishism:* they believe that one specific book that has *in the past* sent out new messages to different people all the time *will continue to do so* till the end of times? If that's the case, fine, but then people who believed such a thing would be the creators of a whole new religion.

Classic Books and Sacred Books

What Armstrong seems to do, is to equate the Bible with what we call a classic work. This was already apparent in the first of her books that gained a worldwide audience: *A History of God* (1993). It is here that she writes about the founder of Islam and states: "It is not surprising that Muhammad found the revelations such an enormous strain: not only was he working through an entirely new political solution for his people, but he was composing one of the great spiritual and literary classics of all time."[306] As one commentator has rightly remarked: "This is high praise for a fellow composer perhaps, but nonetheless reductionist in its familiar repetition of the old cornerstone of Jewish and Christian excising God from the authorship of the Holy Qur'an."[307] Philosopher John Haldane (1954–) refers to some modern liberal theologians and adds that, if the first Christians had taken their view, it is hard to believe that Christianity would have survived the lifetimes of the apostles.[308] That remark is relevant for the work of Armstrong as well, so it seems.

What do we understand by a "classic"?[309] Or, as Armstrong puts it: "a great spiritual and literary classic"? The word "classic" refers to a specific

[306]   Armstrong, Karen, *A History of God*, p. 164.
[307]   Mason, Herbert, "Review of *A History of God* by Karen Armstrong," *The American Historical Review*, 100, no. 2 1995, pp. 481–482, p. 481.
[308]   Haldane, John, *An Intelligent Person's Guide to Religion*, Duckworth Overlook, London 2003, p. 28.
[309]   See on this: Young, R.V., *A Student's Guide to Literature*, ISI Books, Wilmington, DE 2000; Henrie, Mark C., *A Student's Guide to the Core Curriculum*, ISI Books, Wilmington, DE 2000; Barzun, Jacques, "Of What Use the Classics Today?" in: *The Jacques Barzun Reader*, ed. Michael Murray, HarperCollins Publishers, New York 2002, pp. 412–423.

quality of a book, play, or work of art that does not antiquate. Common examples are the plays of Shakespeare or the *Iliad* and *Odyssey* of Homer.[310] Every new generation can read those books or see those plays performed on stage and see new things in them, discover new shades of meaning. That makes those plays interesting, but does it make them "holy" or "sacred"?

In Chapter 2, I analyzed the story of Phinehas, who killed the Israelite man Zemri and the Mideanite woman Cozbi for no other reason than that Zemri and Cozbi (Numbers 25:14–15) had sacrificed to the wrong gods (in the eyes of Phinehas). According to contemporary treaties and constitutions guaranteeing freedom of worship, Cozbi and Zemri had done nothing wrong. Phinehas's deed was cold-blooded murder. There was no excuse for what he did from the perspective of autonomous ethics.

Yet this is different from the perspective of a radical theonomous ethics. Here Phinehas is the hero of the story. Moses, the legitimate authority so to speak, had to act "that the fierce anger of the Lord may turn away from Israel" (Numbers 25:4). And Moses did not – at least he did not act immediately. So Phinehas took the law into his own hands and did the killing. "Thus the plague on the people of Israel was stopped" (Numbers 25:9), the Bible story tells us, apparently approving what Phinehas did.

This is a gruesome story, but does it have any relevance for our contemporary world? I think it has. A contemporary phenomenon like religious terrorism makes perfect sense against the background of this story. What religious terrorists like Yigal Amir, Osama Bin Laden, Ayman al-Zawahiri, and other religiously motivated perpetrators of violence have in common is that they act upon the logic that is inherent in the story of Phinehas. Phinehas commits violence (two murders) because his fellow Israelites act in contradiction of – what he sees as – the commandments of God. Those commandments of God reflect a kind of morality that is superior to the everyday morality we normally act upon. So the "real believer" will follow God's commands, not those of the state.

One can read theoretical books on terrorism from important experts like Amos Guiora,[311] but the "trouble with terror," to quote the title of a book on terrorism by Tamar Meisels,[312] can hardly be explained more succinctly than in this little story. It exemplifies not only the problems with the "mystic variant" of divine command morality (see Divine Command Theories above) but the tension that exists between the nation-state (the legitimate

---

[310] See on Shakespeare: Bloom, Harold, *Shakespeare: The Invention of the Human*, Riverhead Books, New York 1998.

[311] Guiora, Amos N., *Freedom From Religion: Terrorism and Global Justice Series*, Oxford University Press, Oxford 2009; Guiora, Amos N., *Fundamentals of Counterterrorism*, Wolters Kluwer, Austin, TX 2008.

[312] Meisels, Tamar, *The Trouble with Terror: Liberty, Security, and the Response to Terrorism*, Cambridge University Press, Cambridge 2008.

authority) and those challenging the legitimacy of the nation-state on religious grounds. Zemri and Cozbi are the first victims *avant la lettre* of 9/11, 7/7, or rather 2/11 (the murder of Theo van Gogh). Zemri and Cozbi were butchered for no other reason than that they exerted their right to – what we would nowadays call – their "freedom of religion," and what the religious terrorist Phinehas does is to try to topple the state that is too tolerant towards heretics (Zemri in this story).

Now, one might say, what does that imply for our times? Does it imply anything at all? Is this not "just a story" about something that happened long ago or perhaps never even happened at all? The troubling passage is, of course, Numbers 25:10: "And the Lord said to Moses ... ." It is the *Lord himself* who praises Phinehas for his vigilante justice. The troubling factor is that what monotheism *can* mean is not only exemplified in the Sermon on the Mount in Matthew 5, but also in the story of Phinehas in Numbers 25 (Baal Worship at Peor).

I do not say, of course, that many believers are inspired by Numbers 25, nor that here we find the essence of the Bible. On the contrary, people who want to proclaim Matthew 5 as the "essence" of the gospel may be right. But what I do say is that if we want to understand the logic behind religious terrorism the story of Phinehas is interesting, because it perfectly illustrates all the characteristics of contemporary religious terrorists. It is here that we find the unique combination of challenging the nation-state and autonomous ethics on the basis of the execution of the presumed will of God.

Stories like that of Phinehas are illuminating examples of the wisdom we can extract from ancient scriptures, but there are other examples, of course – examples that have nothing to do with "holy scripture" in the usual sense of the word. I referred to the *Iliad* and the *Odyssey,* but we could also refer to fairy tales as sometimes expressing deep philosophical and moral truths. We can illustrate this by referring to a fairy tale by the Danish writer Hans Christian Andersen (1805–1875).

In the story *The Emperor's New Clothes* Andersen tells us about an emperor who cared so much for beautiful clothes that he spent all his money on them.[313] One day two cheats came to visit him. They presented themselves as weavers. They could weave the finest stuff any one could imagine. Those clothes had a special quality: they were invisible to anyone who was unfit for the office he held, or was incorrigibly stupid.

The emperor was impressed. How useful these clothes would be! If he wore them, the emperor thought he would be able to find out which men in his empire were unfit for the positions they occupied. He could distin-

---

[313] Andersen, Hans Christian, "The Emperor's New Clothes," in: Hans Christian Andersen, *The Complete Fairy Tales*, Wordsworth, Ware 1998, pp. 89–95.

guish the clever from the stupid. He therefore gave the two cheats a great deal of cash in hand and they immediately started work.

After a while the emperor wanted to know how far the weavers had got with his (imaginary) clothes, but he felt a bit uncomfortable because the clothes could not be seen by anyone who was unfit for his office. Suppose the *emperor himself* was not fit for his office?

The emperor did not want to take the risk so he preferred to send someone else: his honest oldest minister. This honest old minister went to the weavers, inspected the "clothes," but could not see anything at all. What to do? Should he say openly that he did not see the clothes? That would make him unfit for his office, so he chose to admire what wasn't there: "Oh, it is charming – quite enchanting!" said the old minister. "What a fine pattern, and what colors! Yes, I'll tell the emperor that I am very much pleased with it."[314]

The rest of the story is easy to predict: one person after another was sent to inspect the emperor's new clothes and one after another praised them. No one dared to say that they saw nothing at all. Finally the emperor went in procession showing off his new clothes, and everyone said: "How incomparable are the emperor's new clothes! What a train he has to his mantle! How it fits him!"[315]

But in the end there was a little child. Only the little child said: "But he has nothing on! The emperor is naked!"[316] This caused a turn. "But he has nothing on!" said the whole people at length. The emperor shivered, for it seemed to him that they were right. But he thought within himself: "I must go on with the procession."[317]

Again, this is a beautiful story – just like the story of Phinehas. But we could give this story an interpretation such that its morals were completely different from those of the Phinehas story. In Andersen's tale the old minister is afraid to rely on his own judgment. There are also interests at stake (not losing your position or making a fool of yourselves in the eyes of others). That is why the minister sets a wrong trend and all the others follow – like a flock of sheep.

There is only one – I am inclined to say – "little freethinker": the child at the end. He (or she; the gender is not disclosed in the story) is open-minded and speaks his or her mind frankly. Through being naïve? Through having no official position and thus being free to speak the truth? Through being courageous and willing to stand up for his or her convictions? There are several interpretations, of course, but not all of those interpretations

[314]   Ibid., p. 91.
[315]   Ibid., p. 94.
[316]   Ibid., p. 95.
[317]   Ibid.

are equally good. It does not seem outrageous to read in this story a warning against slavishly following others, parroting what others think, not speaking your mind. We may read here an encouragement for autonomy. Here we have the ideal of W.K. Clifford, J.S. Mill, and Bertrand Russell (see Chapter 1) exemplified.

The upshot of all this is that Western culture (and undoubtedly other cultures as well) is full of stories with interesting lessons.[318] The Bible and other holy books are rich providers of those stories. But being rich sources of meaning does not make the Qur'an or the Bible "holy books" in the sense that *The Iliad* or the fairy tales of Andersen are not holy. The argument made by Armstrong that the Bible and probably also the Qur'an contain many important "myths" may be a good reason to put them on the Great Books Program, and if that is her purpose we would all willingly comply. But isn't that something crucially different from pretending that Scripture is "sacred"?[319] Isn't what Armstrong does *abolishing* the pretence of the sacredness of Scripture in a polite way? But if so, why doesn't she tell us openly?

As might be expected, Armstrong's view of biblical interpretation is intimately connected with her view of what religion should be and what she considers a perversion of religion. Religion, so Armstrong tells us, "is a practical discipline that teaches us to discover new capacities of mind and heart."[320] She also calls religion "a skill" that requires perseverance, hard work, and discipline. "Some people will be better at it than others, some appallingly inept, and others will miss the point entirely."[321]

It is clear that, with this definition of religion, any criticism of religion can easily be discarded as "missing the point" or "appallingly inept." Actually, it immunizes religion entirely from any type of critique. Any justified criticism of religion is always criticism of something that aspires to be religion but should be carefully distinguished from it: fundamentalism. "Fundamentalism" Armstrong sees as the "perversion of religion." It is something that we encounter in all religions. She writes:

---

[318]   See: Bennett, William J., *The Book of Virtues: A Treasury of Great Moral Stories*, Simon & Schuster, New York 1993; Rosenstand, Nina, *The Moral of the Story: An Introduction to Ethics*, second edition, Mayfield Publishing Company, Mountain View 1997; Singer, Peter, and Singer, Renate, *The Moral of the Story: An Anthology of Ethics Through Literature*, Blackwell Publishing, Malden 2005.

[319]   Although there are some similarities between classical books and holy books. See: Amis, *The Second Plane*, p. 17, who writes about the Leavisites whom you could always identify by the sorry dilapidation of their bookshelves. Left to itself, Leavisism might have ended with a single text; "and that sacred book would have been the collected works of an obvious sociopath – D.H. Lawrence."

[320]   Armstrong, *The Case for God*, p. 1.

[321]   Ibid., p. 4.

The Western media often give the impression that the embattled and occasionally violent form of religiosity known as "fundamentalism" is a purely Islamic phenomenon. This is not the case. Fundamentalism is a global fact and has surfaced in every major faith in response to the problems of our modernity. There is fundamentalist Judaism, fundamentalist Christianity, fundamentalist Hinduism, fundamentalist Buddhism, fundamentalist Sikhism and even fundamentalist Confucianism.[322]

Then the question is: how do we discern true religion from fundamentalism? In her book on fundamentalism she develops an analysis in which fundamentalism is seen as the attempt in various religions to turn *mythos* into *logos*. That means that religion in its pristine state is, according to Armstrong, *mythos*.[323] But what serious believer could go along with that? This definition of "fundamentalism" would make the overwhelming majority of serious believers "fundamentalists." Only those who, like Armstrong, are prepared to let their religious convictions evaporate into myths would be considered believers in the positive sense of the word – the rest are all dubbed "fundamentalists."

This view, often presented as "moderate," is in fact extreme and something no serious believer could embrace. But also from a non-religious analytical or scholarly point of view it is not very satisfying. It misses the things that believers consider important in their religion.

Liberal believers usually react to criticism along the lines outlined above with an accusation. They say: "You argue just like the fundamentalists. Why shouldn't it be permissible to modernize religious traditions? You want to relegate religious texts to the dustbin of history, don't you?" But these are all *ad hominem* arguments, that is to say: fallacies and evasions of the issue. That someone argues "just like the fundamentalists" is irrelevant. The question is: are the fundamentalists right with regard to the issue that is under consideration? And it may well be that the fundamentalists are *wrong* in so far as they are prepared to use violence, *wrong* in that they do not want to discuss their presuppositions, but *right* in the sense that their view of what distinguishes sacred texts from classic books is much more convincing than the view expounded by liberal believers. It is also an unfounded allegation that critics of the liberal approach to belief are motivated by the urge not to modernize religious traditions. The issue at stake

---

[322] Armstrong, Karen, *Islam: A Short History*, Random House, Toronto 2002, p. 164.

[323] See on this: Thomas, Scott M., "Review of *The Battle for God: Fundamentalism in Judaism, Christianity and Islam*," *International Affairs*, 77, no. 1 2001, pp. 194–196. Armstrong's ideas about myths are elaborated in: Armstrong, Karen, *A Short History of Myth*, Canongate, Edinburgh 2005. "Human beings have always been mythmakers," she writes (p. 1), and this will always remain so, her book gives us to understand. She deplores the fact that since the Greeks there has been a rift between mythos and logos (p. 102). See also: Armstrong, *The Case for God*, p. 1.

is: *how* are we going to do that? The critics of religious traditions I have in mind advocate the open acceptance of moral autonomy. The moral secularists' view of scriptural interpretation is that we accept or reject biblical values and norms on the basis of *moral* criteria, not *religious* criteria. The yardstick with which we measure the moral value of scriptural passages is itself not a principle derived from Scripture. And it is a principle of scholarly and moral integrity to make that clear.

Richard Robinson (1902–1996), the British philosopher introduced in Chapter 1, had some very pertinent advice for the interpreters of Scripture. "To interpret the gospels correctly you must read them with what may be called interpreter's piety, that is, the will to receive into your mind the exact meaning the author intended, however strange or repellent or boring it may turn out to be."[324]

It requires no elaborate argumentation to show that this is the exact opposite of what Karen Armstrong requires an interpreter to do. What Robinson calls "interpreter's piety" means that you should try to ascertain as objectively as possible what is *in the text* (texualism) and/or what the *intentions* were of the person, group of persons or institution that made the text (intentionalism). Armstrong has no patience for such an exercise. She (and the rabbis she admires so much) are not busy with the text but with *their own* moral ideas. But exactly that, so Robinson would argue, makes them violators of "interpreter's piety." If you want to know what a "Christian ethics" looks like then you have to gauge what Christ said and what he meant, not what you, the interpreter, hope he has said. "I urge you to do this, or at least not to use the phrase 'Christian values' until you have done it."[325]

To further illustrate this point, let us pay some attention to what Armstrong finds so refreshing in the Jewish tradition of interpreting Scripture. She refers to the tradition of *midrash* and says: "Above all, midrash must be guided by the principle of compassion."[326] On the basis of this guideline Armstrong says, referring to the great Jewish religious leader Hillel (*c.* 60 BCE–10 CE): "The essence of Torah was the disciplined refusal to inflict pain on another human being. Everything else in the scriptures was merely 'commentary,' a gloss on the Golden Rule."[327] Hillel also had a clear vision of the way the Torah should be studied by the exegetes: "When they studied Torah, rabbis should attempt to reveal the

---

[324]   Robinson, *An Atheist's Values*, p. 142.

[325]   Ibid.

[326]   Armstrong, *The Bible*, p. 82.

[327]   Ibid., p. 83. See also: White, *A History of the Warfare of Science with Theology in Christendom*, p. 293: "It can not be forgotten that Rabbi Hillel formulated the golden rule, which has before him been given to the extreme Orient by Confucius, and which afterward received a yet more beautiful and positive emphasis from Jesus of Nazareth."

core of compassion that lay at the heart of all the legislation and narratives in the scriptures – even if this meant twisting the original meaning of the text."[328] R. Akiba (*c.* 50–135 CE), the leading sage of the later Yavneh period, declared that the greatest principle of the Torah was the command-ment of Leviticus: "Thou shalt love thy neighbor as thyself'" (Leviticus 19:18).

Many people will read this with approval. But the relevant question is: *what* do we like in those words? What we like in those words, so it seems, are the *moral guidelines* that are being proclaimed, but that is crucially different from the *theory of interpretation* that is presented (if we are kind enough to call this a "theory" at all). The moral principles presented here are:

- compassion;[329]
- with as consequence refusal to inflict pain;
- the golden rule.

The German philosopher Arthur Schopenhauer, who made "compassion" the cornerstone of his ethics, would have been satisfied.[330] And his British colleague Jeremy Bentham (1748–1832) would have been happy with the consequence drawn from this principle: "Never inflict pain." This means the rabbis were true followers of Schopenhauer and (on the basis of the second inference) utilitarians.[331] And finally they were Kantians as well: they advocated the golden rule.[332] So apparently the Torah is a commentary on Schopenhauer, Bentham, and Kant.

Now, Hillel knew that there are things in the Torah that do *not* accord with Schopenhauer, Bentham, and Kant. What to do with those passages? Well, the rabbis should *attempt* to reveal the core of compassion that lies at the heart of Scripture, according to Armstrong. But what if that appears

---

[328] Armstrong, *The Bible*, p. 83.
[329] See also ibid., p. 84: "R. Johanan had shown that, as Hillel claimed, charity was indeed central to scripture: it was the exegete's job to elucidate this hidden principle and bring it to light."
[330] See: Schopenhauer, Arthur, *On the Basis of Morality*, translated by E.F.J.Payne, Hackett Publishing Co., Indianapolis 2000.
[331] See on the ethics of Bentham: Bentham, Jeremy, *An Introduction to the Principles of Morals and Legislation*, ed. J.H. Burns and H.L.A. Hart, Methuen, London 1982 (1789).
[332] Kant, Immanuel, *Grundlegung zur Metaphysik der Sitten* [Groundwork of the Metaphysics of Morals], (1785), in: *Werkausgabe*, Band VII, ed. W. Weischedel, Suhrkamp, Frankfurt am Main 1981, pp. 11–102, p. 51: "Der categorische Imperativ ist also nur ein einziger, und zwar dieser: handle nur nach derjenigen Maxime, durch die du zugleich wollen kannst, daß sie ein allgemeines Gesetz werde" [The categorical imperative is, therefore, a single one, namely this: act only in accordance with that maxim which you can at the same time wish to see become a general law].

to be impossible? In that case "twisting the original meaning of the text" is allowed, Armstrong approvingly remarks.

What is the conclusion we have to infer from this "theory" of interpretation? The only conclusion seems to be that in case of conflict between some passages of the Torah on the one hand and Schopenhauer, Bentham, and Kant on the other, it is those philosophers who have the final word. The value of compassion, the principle never to inflict pain and the golden rule are the final word, not Scripture. Scripture is molded according to those values and principles; the principles are not derived from Scripture and neither can they be abolished on the basis of Scripture.[333] Leslie Stephen (1832–1904) put it as follows:

> The Deity whom good men revere to-day is not the savage, jealous tyrant of ancient times, nor the cruel persecutor of error and protector of favorites who is now accepted by the most ignorant and belated minds.[334]

This way of expressing yourself would be much too blunt for those standing in Armstrong's tradition: the liberal Protestants, the followers of Schleiermacher. They want us to believe that they derive their values from Scripture itself. But if we carefully observe what they advocate, we see that they really do not derive their morality from that source. Richard Dawkins (1941–) makes the following point when he summarizes his treatment of this issue:

> My main purpose here has not been to show that we *shouldn't* get our morals from scripture (although that is my opinion). My purpose has been to demonstrate that we (and that includes most religious people) as a matter of fact *don't* get our morals from scripture.[335]

Violating the Integrity of the Text

There are some, although only a few, passages where it seems to dawn upon Armstrong that this "theory" is no theory at all. Of the liberal interpretation of the rabbis so much admired by her she tells us: "To a modern scholar, this seems to violate the integrity of the text, and seek meaning at

---

[333] Richard Dawkins comes to a similar conclusion when he writes in *The God Delusion*, p. 275: "we pick and choose among the scriptures for the nice bits and reject the nasty. But then we must have some independent criterion for deciding which are the moral bits: a criterion which, wherever it comes from, cannot come from scripture itself and is presumably available to all of us whether we are religious or not."

[334] Stephen, "The Scepticism of Believers," p. 66.

[335] Dawkins, *The God Delusion*, p. 283. See also ibid., p. 298: "the holy books do not supply any rules for distinguishing the good principles from the bad."

the expense of the original."[336] But that conscientious objection (reminiscent of Robinson's "interpreter's piety") is silenced immediately in the sentence following the passage just quoted: "But the rabbis believed that because scripture was the word of God, it was infinite. Any meaning that they discovered in a text had been intended by God if it yielded fresh insight and benefited the community."[337]

This seems to me a kind of wordplay with the word "infinity." Because, according to the classical definitions (the Apostles' Creed), God is considered to be "infinite," Armstrong contends that "his Scripture" is also supposed to be "infinite." Subsequently that "infinity" of Scripture gets a whole new meaning because it is interpreted as a license to the caste of interpreters to project into the text whatever benefits the community (or rather whatever *they think* benefits the community). This is not very convincing. If Scripture is always interpreted against the background of the three principles mentioned before (show compassion; never inflict pain; apply the golden rule) it is far from "infinite." It is highly restricted. If Scripture commands the destruction of another people (see for instance Numbers 31) the enlightened interpreters will tell us that this could not be the intention of the maker of the text. This is all fine, but it proves that the range of interpretations is restricted.

There is another conclusion we have to draw from the passages quoted from Armstrong. That is that not only the *rabbis* who are a combination of utilitarians, Kantians, and followers of Schopenhauer, but that *God himself* is as well. If Armstrong or the rabbis read something in Holy Scripture that contradicts the principles expounded by the philosophers mentioned, this will not be accepted as "divine." So, for liberal believers, what is authoritative is not a free divine will; "the benefit of the community" is the real guideline for interpretation. The principle of interpretation upon which Armstrong and the rabbis are operating is that, if the text reveals something that seems to violate the benefit of the community, they take a second look and the "hidden meaning" of the text will be "revealed" to them. They call that the "infinite meaning" of the text. But the only "infinity" that is in play here, so it seems, is that liberal believers will endlessly go back to the text until it "reveals" what they want to hear.[338] "By altering the text in this way, they sometimes introduced into scripture a note of compassion that had been absent from the original,"[339] Armstrong even writes openly about the rabbis. And that sentence does not worry her

---

[336] Armstrong, *The Bible*, p. 86.
[337] Ibid.
[338] See for a similar criticism of this type of interpretation: Richard Taylor, "Law and Morality," *New York University Law Review*, 43, no. 4 1968, pp. 611–650 and Taylor, Richard, *Good and Evil*, Prometheus Books, Buffalo, NY 1984, in particular, Chapter 12.
[339] Armstrong, *The Bible*, p. 86.

is the least ("There could be no definitive interpretation of scripture")[340] – but that is what we would expect from what we have seen before. It does not come as much of a surprise either to find Armstrong saying about the rabbis: "When they studied the Torah, the rabbis felt as though they were standing beside Moses on Sinai. Revelation continued to unfold and the insights of all Jews past, present and to come derived from God as surely as the written Torah given to Moses."[341] Nor, finally, is it in any way unexpected that Armstrong quotes approvingly a certain Bavli who, to the question of what the Torah is, answered: "It is: the interpretation of the Torah."[342] This is the theological equivalent of Chief Justice Hughes' quip: "The Constitution is what the judges say it is."

Charles Evans Hughes (1862–1948) became chief justice in the American Supreme Court in 1930 and his vision of judicial interpretation was indicative for a whole new school of "realists" who treated constitutional texts as malleable material on which every new generation of judges could leave its mark.[343] And why restrict this to "a generation"? Why not simply go ahead and say that the Constitution is in the eye of the beholder? Any individual beholder!

That leads to the conclusion that the liberal theory of interpretation is, from a rational point of view, rather unsatisfactory. We have to make a distinction, though. It may very well be that, in the time of Immanuel Kant, liberal interpretation according to the hermeneutics developed by Schleiermacher and liberal Protestantism in theology and advocated by Armstrong in her book on the Bible was the only possible way to freely criticize certain unfortunate developments and ideas. Kant simply did not have the freedom to say "Abraham makes a terrible mistake in listening to God," or "God should never have required Abraham to kill his son," or "Jephtha's daughter should never have been sacrificed." Kant was writing under censorship. Open religious criticism would have caused great difficulties for him – as it had brought so many other people into difficulties: Thomas Paine (1737–1809), for example, who wrote critically about revealed religion in Kant's time.[344] Why great historical thinkers like

---

[340]   Ibid., p. 87.

[341]   Ibid., p. 96.

[342]   Ibid., p. 100.

[343]   For a powerful critique of this point of view, see: Scalia, Antonin, "Common-Law Courts in a Civil-Law System: The Role of United States Federal Courts in Interpreting the Constitution and Laws," in: Antonin Scalia, *A Matter of Interpretation. Federal Courts and the Law, An Essay by Antonin Scalia with commentary by Amy Gutmann, Gordon S. Wood, Laurence H. Tribe, Mary Ann Glendon, Ronald Dworkin*, Princeton University Press, Princeton, New Jersey 1997, pp. 3–47.

[344]   See: Paine, Thomas, The Age of Reason, 1794, in: Thomas Paine, *Collected Writings*, The Library of America, New York 1995, pp. 665–885, published one year after Kant published his *Religion within the Limits of Reason Alone* (1793).

Immanuel Kant were obliged to compromise is clear. In their time this was simply inevitable if you wanted to survive (literally, or in your chair as professor of philosophy).

Thomas Paine is one of the few authors who acknowledged this. He wrote about Montesquieu (1689–1755). Montesquieu is often somewhat obscure, but, so Paine argued, he "went as far as a writer under a despotic government could well proceed."[345] Or: "His mind often appeared under a veil, and we ought to give him credit for more than he has expressed."[346]

It is also clear that reformers of Islam in countries in the Middle East, where there is no freedom of expression, can only bring reform by pretending that the new directions are derived from the Qur'an. But that does not mean that *in the West* we have to adopt the same disingenuous strategies. We can say: "I am fascinated by the biblical stories. They are a constant source of inspiration to me. But I am perfectly aware that Scripture can never force me or anyone else to do something that the moral law forbids. So, ultimately, when Scripture and the moral law are in conflict, it is Scripture that has to be put aside, not the moral law."

That, of course, would be the answer of a consistent – what I would like to call – "moral autonomist." That is the position that Lawrence Kohlberg and Jean Piaget want us to focus on in the education of children. This is what "the war for children's minds" is all about.[347] Children should have the courage of the little child in Andersen's fairy tale. *Noblesse oblige*: if you live in a time and under circumstances in which you *can* criticize things that ought to be criticized, do it. If you don't, you will undermine the freedom that you have. This is the "duty to criticize" that W.K. Clifford stressed, as we saw in Chapter 3. Or, to put it slightly differently and still the same: not using the freedom to think will undermine the tradition of freethought in the long run.

Perhaps there are people who will object: "But that is, basically, what Armstrong is saying. Read between the lines." In that case my answer would be: "Fine, but let's make it explicit. If that is her position I have no problem with her views." But what I fear is that it is essential for her position *not* to say this. Her position *presupposes* moral autonomy but does not help to foster it, or further develop it. Her whole approach is predicated on a certain amount of moral autonomy, but this can never be said openly, because once this happens there is no room left for the books to be "holy" in the ordinary sense of the word. She and the rabbis she refers to would simply be Kantians, utilitarians, and adherents of the philosophy of

---

[345]   Paine, Thomas, *Rights of Man. Being an Answer to Mr. Burke's Attack on the French Revolution, 1791/92*, in: Thomas Paine, *Collected Writings*, The Library of America, New York 1995, p. 433–661, p. 490.

[346]   The same applies to Voltaire and Rousseau. See: ibid., p. 490.

[347]   See: Law, Stephen, *The War for Children's Minds*, Routledge, London 2006.

Schopenhauer, as I have indicated. It would be philosophy, not religion, that is the basis for morals.

Is Hermeneutics the Only Way to Modernize Traditions?

As I said, although in former times and in some parts of the world the only way to modernize religious traditions was by means of "interpretation," this is no longer the case in the liberal democracies and open societies of the twenty-first century where freedom of speech is protected by law. In those countries it is possible to advocate moral autonomy as the most honest and appropriate way to evaluate religious traditions. But can such an approach ever be acceptable for religious believers? Do we not in fact require them to become atheists?

This is always the bugbear for the "moderate" or "liberal" believers: what you require of people is to relinquish their faith. We all have to become "atheists"; and is it not a bit unrealistic to expect that?

My answer is that the adoption of moral autonomy and the rejection of the authority of Scripture does not make us all atheists. Moral autonomy and the rejection of divine command ethics are possible within the framework of a religious worldview. Or rather: we can reject some elements of the theistic worldview (whether in its Jewish, Christian, or Islamic variant) and retain others.

Let us first look at Islam. What makes a Muslim? One possible answer would be: a Muslim is someone who subscribes to the Five Pillars of Islam. The Five Pillars of Islam is the term given to the five duties incumbent on every Muslim. These duties are Shahadah (profession of faith), Salah (ritual prayer), Zakat (almsgiving), Sawm (fasting during Ramadan) and Hajj (pilgrimage to Mecca).[348] Analytical philosopher René Marres correctly states that whoever is critical of some elements of the Islamic tradition does not necessarily have to oppose *all the five pillars of Islam*.[349] Most people who are e.g. critical of sharia law or some elements of Islamic tradition do not oppose almsgiving or fasting during Ramadan. Politically correct commentators usually react with disproportional vehemence when even the slightest criticism of some element of Islamic doctrine is voiced.[350] They

---

[348]   Lewis, Bernard, and Churchill, Buntzie Ellis, *Islam: The Religion and the People*, Wharton School Publishing, Upper Saddle River, New Jersey 2009, pp. 13–25.

[349]   Marres, *De verdediging van het vrije woord*, p. 22.

[350]   Esposito and Mogahed, *Who Speaks for Islam?*, p. 136: "We live in a world in which two of the greatest world religions with Semitic origins are often under siege." Those religions are the Jewish religion and Islam, so Esposito and Mogahed continue. They say: "The term *Islamophobia* was coined to describe a two-stranded form of racism – rooted in both the 'different' physical appearance of Muslims and also in an intolerance of their religious and

want to make us believe that "Islam is under Siege"[351] when the slightest criticism is voiced or Muslims are "discriminated against" if they are contradicted. In fact, it is possible to criticize elements of a religious tradition without rejecting everything. The main criticism of theism that is voiced in *The Secular Outlook* concerns the metaethical foundation of the theistic religions. I have worked this out with particular reference to Christianity. But that does not mean, as I hope to make clear in the following pages, that all the teachings of Christ or all the social work of the church must be rejected. One can even be critical about divine command ethics (the metaethical doctrine of theism) and still consider oneself a Christian. We find this, for instance, in the work of the Most Reverend Richard F. Holloway (1933–), a Scottish writer, broadcaster and retired Bishop of Edinburgh in the Scottish Episcopal Church.

In 1999 Holloway published a book under the title *Godless Morality: Keeping Religion out of Ethics,* in which he advocated what is, in *The Secular Outlook,* presented as the secularist position. Holloway writes: "One of the intentions behind this book is to ... explore the possibility of a new moral ecumenism that would unite people on the basis of an agreed human ethic."[352] As I have shown in this chapter, such an agreed-upon human ethic is unlikely to flourish on a specific religious basis, at least not in a pluralistic or religiously divided society. So Holloway advises us not to treat the Bible as a book of law for all generations and he sides with moral philosopher John Harris (1945–) who said that for a moral judgment to be respectable it must have something to say about exactly why a supposed wrong action is wrongful. "If it fails to meet this test it is a preference and not a moral judgment at all."[353]

Holloway also rejects the divine command morality. "We no longer live in command societies in which we instinctively obey orders from above, wherever above is thought to be. For better or for worse, we live in an age in which justifications have to be offered for moral restraints upon individuals."[354] Command moralities may exercise a nostalgic appeal in a

---

cultural beliefs" (p. 136). So Esposito states that there is "racism" against Muslims because of a "different" physical appearance and he apparently also categorizes criticism of religious and cultural beliefs as part of the racist attitude. That would make every critical evaluation of religious and cultural beliefs a kind of racism and a violation of the penal law. If we followed this approach, all development of religions in reaction to critical evaluation would be impossible. This would be the death-blow to Clifford's *The Ethics of Belief* and John Stuart Mill's *On Liberty.*

[351]   Ahmed, Akbar S., *Islam under Siege,* Polity Press, Cambridge 2003.
[352]   Holloway, Richard, *Godless Morality. Keeping Religion out of Ethics,* Canongate, Edinburgh 1999, p. 34.
[353]   Referred to in ibid., p. 62.
[354]   Ibid., p. 33.

time of confusion, but should not guide us any longer, says Holloway, in a way that harmonizes well with the results of the Milgram research and Kohlberg's ideas on moral education, both dealt with earlier in this Chapter.[355]

As can be expected, Holloway's approach has important implications for the justification of morality. "Saying that an act is wrong, because it is forbidden by God, is not sufficient unless we can also justify it on moral grounds."[356] And, like all the other philosophers I have presented in *The Secular Outlook,* Holloway also refers to the example of Abraham. Holloway writes: "there are passages in the Bible where God orders the performance of acts of great wickedness in order to test the obedience of his children. The most extreme test is found in Genesis chapter 22, where Abraham's obedience is tested by God in a particularly cruel way."[357]

It may be true that this narrative is a remnant from a time when human sacrifice was practiced, but, so Holloway contends, "this kind of historical approach dilutes its religious value by trying to account for the offence that is the very point of the story."[358] The story seems to celebrate the type of conscience that wants to be commanded to perform extreme acts of obedience by an absolute authority. This is also what is meant by sinful behavior. Sin is not only committing what is forbidden, but also refusing what is commanded by God. "The power of the concept lies in the unthinking nature of the obedience that is demanded."[359]

What makes Holloway's contribution to the debate important is that here we see an unmistakably religious thinker who nonetheless demonstrates an unequivocal commitment to moral autonomy. What this makes clear is that people who consider themselves serious believers can be moral secularists as well.

Holloway stands in the Christian tradition, of course. But in the other theistic traditions there are also currents and thinkers who have favored moral autonomy within a theistic world picture. An example from the Jewish tradition is Saadia ben Joseph (882–942).

Saadia was born in the village Dilaz in Upper Egypt. After a life of study and travel he was appointed Gaon (an illustrious rabbi) at the academy of Sura (an important institute of learning at that time). He achieved renown as an accomplished Talmudist, commentator, grammarian and educator in all fields of knowledge. He also translated most of the Bible into Arabic.[360]

---

[355]   Ibid.
[356]   Ibid., p. 15.
[357]   Ibid., p. 5.
[358]   Ibid., p. 7.
[359]   Ibid.
[360]   Goldberg, David J., and Rayner, John D., *The Jewish People: Their History and their Religion,* Penguin Books, London 1989 (1987), p. 95.

Saadia's classical work was *The Book of Doctrine and Beliefs*. Here he proves himself to be an expert in the Islamic *kalam* (theology) and *falasifa* (Aristotelian philosophy).

Saadia was a firm believer in the supremacy of reason, which also included the moral sense. God's ways and his revelation, so Saadia teaches his pupils, are in accordance with reason. This is not the case because God *defines* reason and justice, but rather because God, completely free, acts and reveals himself in accordance with absolute standards of reason and justice. As Norman Solomon (1933–), fellow in Modern Jewish Thought at the Oxford Centre for Hebrew and Jewish Studies, remarks in his introduction to Judaism, paraphrasing the ideas of Saadia, "God does what is rational or just because it is a priori rational or just; it is not rational or just *because* God does it."[361]

The most important thinker from the Muslim tradition favoring moral autonomy is Averroes (1126–1198) or in Arabic Ibn Rushd. Although contested during his lifetime, he was important for the formation of Muslim identity.[362] One of the most important questions that Averroes addresses is: in what sense can Muslim philosophy respect the autonomy of ethics? That is: a morality that is not founded in the will of God as manifested in revelation? Are there moorings for the position taken by Socrates in the *Euthyphro* that morally good is not identical with "willed by God"?[363] Contrary to common opinion, the position that the ethical has some independent status apart from the religious has a base in Muslim thought.

As Ernest Renan describes in his well-known treatise *Averroès et l'averroïsme* [Averroes and Averroism] (1852) this topic arose in connection to "les motecallemîn" [the Motecallemin]. This sect was convinced that the good and the right are nothing other than what God wants (the position taken by Euthyphro in *Euthyphro*).[364] And – in harmony with the position of heteronomy – God's will is directed at certain things not because these things are inherently valuable (that would undermine the divine will as the last point of reference for goodness), but solely because he "wills them." In the words of Renan: the Motecallemin contended that the good is what God wants, and God does not want something because of an intrinsic

---

[361] Solomon, Norman, *Judaism: A Very Short Introduction*, Oxford University Press, Oxford 2000 (1996), p. 38.

[362] See: Leaman, Oliver, *Averroes and His Philosophy*, Clarendon Press, Oxford University Press, Oxford 1988; Averroes, *Faith and Reason in Islam. Averroes' Exposition of Religious Arguments*, translated by Ibrahim Najjar, One World, Oxford 2005 (2001).

[363] See on this: Kretzmann, Norman, "Abraham, Isaac, and Euthyphro: God and the Basis of Morality," in: Eleonore Stump and Michael J. Murray, eds., *Philosophy of Religion*, pp. 417–427.

[364] Plato, *Euthyphro*, 4e. ff. See also: Taylor, A.E., *Plato. The Man and his Work*, Methuen, London 1977 (1926), p. 151.

reason that is anterior to his will.[365] The Motecallemin even deemed God as not subject to logical laws.

This system, Renan comments, was very consistent in itself, but for obvious reasons something that Averroes wanted to undermine. For Averroes it was clear that once this perspective was adopted, it would undermine the whole system of ethics and all notions of rightness and fairness.

The fact that these traditions, i.e. those presented in the work of Holloway, Saadi, and Averroes are also present in the history of theism seems to me a promising fact. There is a lot of talk about the revision of religious traditions. Usually the suggestion is made that what distinguishes "fundamentalists" from "moderate" or "liberal" believers is that the first category are "literalists" while those in the latter category know that we cannot take scripture literally. Proponents of that point of view are Tariq Ramadan in Islam and Karen Armstrong in Christianity. But, as we have seen as a result of our discussion of the ideas of Ramadan in Chapter 2 and those of Karen Armstrong in the present chapter, the problem is not "literalism." Scripture contains several passages that clearly incite violence. The idea that only "interpretation" can help us out is a myth. This myth is nonetheless clearly shared and cherished by many people, and both Ramadan and Armstrong are very popular and influential in upholding that myth. Everywhere governments and important politicians try to assure us that there is nothing wrong with believing in the authority of revealed scripture. The only thing that counts is how we *interpret* revelation, so they say. And because revelation can be interpreted in accordance with ordinary law (for instance the penal law), the constitution of the land, and human rights declarations, so many people presuppose unquestioningly, there is nothing wrong with the notion of scriptural authority. The only thing we have to do is: educate semantic relativists, *viz*. people who will proclaim that Scripture can mean what we want it to mean. We all have to become religious Humpty Dumptians. We all have to adhere to the position that there is – in the words of Ramadan – no "religion per se." Or rather: that "religion per se" is anything we want it to be.

But, as my analysis of the work of Ramadan and Armstrong has made clear (at least, this is my sincere hope), this view could well be too optimistic. The arguments of "extremists" or "fundamentalists" – that we cannot manipulate the text in every direction we think desirable – are strong. What the "moderates" fail to see is that what makes "extremists" extreme is *not* their theory of interpretation but something else. It is the so-called

---

[365]   Renan, Ernest "Averroès et l'averroïsme" [Averroes and Averroism], *Essai Historique*, 1852, in: Ernest Renan, *Œuvres Complètes de Ernest Renan*, Tome III, Édition définitive établie par Henriette Psichari, Calmann-Lévy, Paris 1947–1961, pp. 1–323, p. 132.

"moderate" who is theoretically extreme. The claim that scripture can constantly send completely different messages to different times and cultures (the theory of interpretation championed by Armstrong and countless others) is theoretically extreme and misconceived.

What makes "extremists" "extreme" is not their theory of interpretation, but their adherence to the notion of scriptural authority. It is the idea that we can base our conscience and moral evaluation on Scripture that is the source of the problem. What we have to stimulate is moral autonomy, or rather the human capacity to take autonomous moral decisions. That does not make those decisions arbitrary. On the contrary. Those decisions have to be made on the basis of moral principles and rules. But the rules that are being applied are *moral* rules, not *religious* rules derived from Scripture.

That should not necessarily make Scripture meaningless as a "source of inspiration." And, contrary to what is often proclaimed, no moral secularist will contend that religious believers should abandon their religious books as "sources of inspiration." What the moral secularist claims is that ultimately what we derive from Scripture must be based on moral grounds that are in themselves not dependent on Scripture. Morality is the basis for religion, not vice versa.

That does not make moral secularists necessarily "atheists" in the derogatory sense of the word described in Chapter 1. Richard Holloway is not an atheist. Immanuel Kant was no atheist either. Even Voltaire was not an atheist. One can be a committed believer and subscribe to moral secularism. Can one also be a "theist" and subscribe to moral secularism?

I think there is some tension there. The idea of an all-powerful, perfectly good moral legislator for this world seems difficult to reconcile with the notion of moral autonomy, as Eduard von Hartmann and Jean-Paul Sartre have made clear (see Atheist Values in Chapter 1).

In particular with regard to Islam a whole debate has developed around the question of what variety of this important religion should be cherished in order to prevent radicalization and extremism. So there is a debate about what kind of Islam should be developed or stimulated.[366] Bassam Tibi (1944–) spoke of a "European Islam."[367] That debate has gained momentum as a result of some notorious cases such as the murder of Theo van Gogh, the cartoons affair, the fatwa on Salman Rushdie and the reactions

---

[366] Cox, Caroline, and Marks, John, *The West, Islam and Islamism: Is Ideological Islam Compatible with Liberal Democracy?*, Civitas, Institute for the Study of Civil Society, London 2003; Kamrava, Mehran, ed., *The New Voices of Islam: Reforming Politics and Modernity – A Reader*, I.B. Tauris, London 2006; Charfi, Mohamed, *Islam and Liberty: The Historical Misunderstanding*, Zed Books, London 2005; Bennett, Clinton, *Muslims and Modernity: An Introduction to the Issues and Debates*, Continuum, London 2005.

[367] Tibi, Bassam, *Europa ohne Identität?*

to the Pope's speech in Regensburg.[368] This has even raised doubts about the question of whether Islam can be reconciled with democratic values. Should not Islam be revised? And how is that to be done? And no less important: *who* will do this?

Is Islam "Secularization-Resistant"?

There are voices who say that Islam has resisted all attempts at reform. Two of the most authoritative thinkers who have shocked the world with similar views are Bernard Lewis and Ernest Gellner.

Lewis (1916–) wrote in 1996: "In Islam ... there is from the beginning an interpenetration, almost identification, of cult and power, or religion and the state."[369] He refers to the same historical fact as Malise Ruthven (1942–) in his book on the Rushdie affair.[370] Mohammed was not only a prophet, but also a political leader. Islam's position is therefore more similar to that of the Jews in Old Testament times than that of Christianity under the Roman Empire. Even when Christianity became the official religion of the empire under Constantine in the fourth century CE the distinction between "spiritual" and "temporal" power was still honored. Islam does not acknowledge that distinction, Lewis writes. The words "secular" and "secularism" are not originally to be found in the Arabic language. The only hope that Lewis gives us is that the distinction between the secular and the spiritual "has arisen now" and, so Lewis continues, "it may be that Muslims, having contracted a Christian illness, will consider a Christian remedy, that is to say, the separation of religion and the state."[371]

Another important thinker who brought this to the fore is the anthropologist and philosopher Ernest Gellner (1925–1995). In 1991 he wrote: "I think it is fair to say that no secularization has taken place in the world of Islam: that the hold of Islam over its believers is as strong, and in some ways stronger, now than it was 100 years ago." Somehow, Gellner tells us, Islam is "secularization-resistant."[372]

Three years later Gellner reaffirmed his position and declared that Islam had a different position than other world religions.[373] In all other religions

---

[368] Welzel, *Die Religionen und die Vernunft.*
[369] See: Lewis, Bernard, "Islam and Liberal Democracy. A Historical Overview," *Journal of Democracy*, 7. no. 2 1996, pp. 52–63, p. 61.
[370] Ruthven, *A Satanic Affair*, p. 48.
[371] Lewis, *Islam and Liberal Democracy*, p. 62.
[372] Gellner, Ernest, "Islam and Marxism: Some Comparisons," *International Affairs*, 67, no. 1 1991, pp. 1–6, p. 2.
[373] Gellner, Ernest, *Conditions of Liberty. Civil Society and Its Rivals*, Hamish Hamilton, London 1994, p. 15.

industrialization had made the position of religion weaker. Not in Islam. The secularization thesis is roughly correct: "it would be difficult to deny the overall trend towards secularization," Gellner wrote. But the position of Islam is the exception. Islam has not been weakened but made stronger.

> The hold of Islam over the populations of the lands in which it is the main religion has in no way diminished in the course of the last hundred years. In some ways it has been markedly strengthened.[374]

If the rebirth of Islam had been in the form of the resurgence of a kind of "moderate," "liberal," or even better a "secular" Islam,[375] the Islam "per se" of Ramadan or the Islam depicted by Karen Armstrong,[376] this would have been no problem, of course. But, as we noted at the beginning of *The Secular Outlook* with reference to a report by the United Nations,[377] it is radical and violent religion that seems attractive to some people nowadays.[378] With regard to Islam, that means that European youngsters[379] in particular who are disaffected from their countries are receptive to radical varieties of Islam. As Peter R. Neumann, director of the Centre for Defense Studies, King's College London, writes:

> What makes the situation in Europe different from North America is the presence of a large number of second- or third-generation Muslim immigrants – estimated at 15–20 million.[380]

---

[374] Ibid.

[375] See: the "St. Petersburg Declaration," Manifesto and Affirmation of Human Rights and Freedom of Thought for Muslims and non-Muslims in the Muslim World, released March 2007 in St. Petersburg, Florida, during the "Secular Islam Summit," an international forum for secularists of Islamic societies in March 2007.

[376] See: Armstrong, *Islam: A Short History*.

[377] Jahangir, Asma, *Promotion and Protection of all Human Rights, Civil, Political, Economic, Social and Cultural Rights, Including the Right to Development*, Report by the Special Rapporteur on Freedom of Religion or Belief, A/HRC/6/5, 20 July 2007. See also the preface of *The Secular Outlook*.

[378] Desai, Meghnad, Rethinking Islam; Mirza, Senthilkumaran, and Ja'far, *Living Apart Together*.

[379] See, for the situation in the Netherlands: Bessems, Kustaw, *En dat in Nederland! De roerige jaren sinds 11 september* [And in the Netherlands of all Places! The Turbulent Years since September 11], Uitgeverij L.J. Veen, Amsterdam 2006; Groen, Janny, and Kranenburg, Annieke, *Strijdsters van Allah: Radicale moslima's en het Hofstadnetwerk* [Fighters for Allah: Radical Muslims and the Hofstad Network], De Volkskrant / Meulenhoff, Amsterdam 2006; and Ministerie van Binnenlandse Zaken en Koninkrijksrelaties *Van Dawa tot Jihad*. For Germany: Mekhennet, Sautter, and Hanfeld, *Die Kinder des Dschihad*.

[380] Neumann, Peter R., "Europe's Jihadist Dilemma," *Survival*, 48, no. 2, 2006, pp. 71–84, p. 73.

They often find themselves torn between the traditional values of their parents and the demands of Western society. There can be no doubt, so Neumann continues, that the presence of such a large pool of young, alienated Muslims presents Salafi jihadists with "opportunities for recruitment and radicalization which do not exist elsewhere."[381]

It is political Islam, petro-Islam, Wahhabi-Islam,[382] desert-Islam, that seems to be on the march. In its extreme consequences this can lead to a great estrangement of some Muslim youngsters from the secular state and secular morality. And this problem has not yet been adequately countered by European states. It has not even been adequately analyzed. *The Secular Outlook* hopes to make a contribution to that analysis.

I hope that what I write about radical religion will not be mistaken for pessimism. I do not adhere to the deterministic thesis that people who come from the Muslim world (or have affiliations with the Islamic tradition) are necessarily enemies of the secular state.[383] Fortunately, there are many promising developments that show people trying (and also rather successfully) to reform some elements of what might be called Wahhabi-Islam. But the question is: whom do we identify as promising reformers? Is Tariq Ramadan, whose stance on the stoning of women we discussed in Chapter 2, such a reformer? Or should we seek other people, for instance those intellectuals who gathered at the Secular Islam Summit in March 2007 in St. Petersburg, Florida?[384]

Two Kinds of Reformers: Liberal Islam and Secular Islam

There seems to be a rift between two kinds of reformers. The first group we may bring together under the label of "liberal Islam" or "moderate Islam." The second group we could characterize as "secular Islam."[385]

---

[381]　Ibid., p. 73.

[382]　Allen, Charles, *God's Terrorists: The Wahhabi Cult and the Hidden Roots of Modern Jihad*, Little, Brown, London 2006; DeLong-Bas, Natana J., *Wahhabi-Islam: From Revival and Reform to Global Jihad*, I.B. Tauris, London 2007.

[383]　See on this: An-Na'im, Abdullahi, *Islam and the Secular State: Negotiating the Future of Shari'a*, Harvard University Press, Cambridge, MA, London 2008.

[384]　Or female critics of Islamism such as: Ahadi, Mina, (with Sina Vogt), *Ich habe abgeschworen*; Djavann, Chadortt, *À mon corps défendant l'occident* [Reluctantly the West], Flammarion, Paris 2007; Selim, Nahed, *Nehmt den Männern den Koran! Für eine weibliche Interpretation des Islam* [Take the Qur'an Away from Men! For a Female Interpretation of Islam], Piper, München Zürich 2007; Manji, Irshad, *The Trouble with Islam: A Muslim's Call for Reform in Her Faith*, St. Martin's Press, New York 2003.

[385]　See e.g.: Tal, Shlomi, "Necessity and Primacy of Secularism," Institute for the Secularisation of Islamic Society, at: www.secularislam.org, p. 1: "Declare, without apology or faltering, that secularism is the best of systems for mankind; and though it may have its failings, it is better

As the British scholar of comparative religion Anna King writes:

> In the aftermath of 9/11 and the July 2005 London bombings, the UK's political and religious leaders, partly to maintain civic peace, encouraged the assumption that there is a liberal or progressive Islam deriving from the Qur'an which is compatible with modernity, liberal values, and gender equality.[386]

The "moderates" want to propose reforms, but they are most cautious not to offend religious sensibilities. This is all very sympathetic, but a disadvantage of this approach seems to be that the most conservative elements in the community can dictate the pace of reform (even inhibiting all reform). The British writer, lecturer and broadcaster Kenan Malik (1960–) shows us the limitations of this approach in his book *From Fatwa to Jihad* (2009). By the end of the 1980s progressive intellectuals had become disenchanted with Enlightenment ideas of rationalism and humanism. What emerged was a "politics of difference." As the hallmarks of a progressive and anti-racist outlook, multiculturalism was adopted. What was the result?

> Multiculturalism has helped foster a more tribal nation and, within Muslim communities, has undermined progressive trends while strengthening the hand of conservative religious leaders. While it did not create militant Islam, it helped, as we shall see in this book, create for it a space within British Muslim communities that had not existed before.[387]

Another problem with "moderates" who are so afraid to hurt religious sensibilities is that the abolition of some pernicious religious and cultural practices simply cannot be delayed. With regard to atrocious acts, such as

---

in many orders of magnitude than the other systems, and especially more so than those which rest upon the authority of a fictional autocratic God." See also: "Is Islam Compatible With Democracy and Human Rights?" Institute for the Secularisation of Islamic Society, at: www.secularislam.org, pp. 1–35. Also the German professor of international relations Bassam Tibi has always stressed that only a secular society can assert itself against Islamists and secure peaceful cohabitation. See: "Why Europe Needs a 'Leading Culture,'" Interview with Bassam Tibi, at: Spiegel Online, www.spiegel.de, November 26, 2004, pp. 1–8. Richard Kraince makes a distinction between the "skeptics" and the "optimists" on the question of whether Islam is compatible with secular democracy. The "skeptics" are: Bernard Lewis, Martin Kramer, and Daniel Pipes. The "optimists" are: John Esposito, Graham Fuller, and Noah Feldman. See: Kraince, Richard G., "U.S. Perspectives on Islam and Democracy," in: *Liberal Islam Network*, 26/6/2003, at: http://islamlib.com, pp. 1–6. See on secular movements within Islam also: Armstrong, Karen, *Islam: A Short History*, pp. 148 ff.

[386] King, Anna, "Islam, Women and Violence," *Feminist Theology*, 17 no. 3 2009, pp. 292–328, p. 318.

[387] Malik, Kenan, *From Fatwa to Jihad: The Rushdie Affair and Its Legacy*, Atlantic Books, London 2009, p. xx.

stoning as a punishment for "mingling" (see Chapter 2), we cannot say: "take your time about finding a settlement for wholesale abolition" or "try to find a solution that everybody can live with, the religious fundamentalists included" or "search for an interpretation of Holy Scripture that allows you to eradicate this practice."[388] This would only allow atrocious practices to continue and create more innocent victims. It would further compromise the credibility of all the people involved in the act of reforming the religious practice. With regard to those practices "impatience" is more than morally justified: it is imperative. It is quite comprehensible that Nicolas Sarkozy was incensed by Ramadan's evasive answers on the practice of stoning.

It seems to me that the group of thinkers that we can bring together under the label of "secular Islam" is more open to the moral considerations presented above than "moderates" or "liberals."

In March 2007 such a group of "secularists" came together at the "Secular Islam Summit" in Florida and adopted a declaration of their values and approaches under the name of the "St. Petersburg declaration." This is what they agreed upon:

We are secular Muslims, and secular persons of Muslim societies. We are believers, doubters, and unbelievers, brought together by a great struggle, not between the West and Islam, but between the free and the unfree.

We affirm the inviolable freedom of the individual conscience. We believe in the equality of all human persons.

We insist upon the separation of religion from state and the observance of universal human rights.

We find traditions of liberty, rationality, and tolerance in the rich histories of pre-Islamic and Islamic societies. These values do not belong to the West or the East; they are the common moral heritage of humankind.

We see no colonialism, racism, or so-called "Islamophobia" in submitting Islamic practices to criticism or condemnation when they violate human reason or rights.

We call on the governments of the world to

- reject sharia law, fatwa courts, clerical rule, and state-sanctioned religion in all their forms; oppose all penalties for blasphemy and apostasy, in accordance with Article 18 of the Universal Declaration of Human rights;
- eliminate practices, such as female circumcision, honor killing, forced veiling, and forced marriage, that further the oppression of women;
- protect sexual and gender minorities from persecution and violence;
- reform sectarian education that teaches intolerance and bigotry towards non-Muslims;
- and foster an open public sphere in which all matters may be discussed without coercion or intimidation.

---

[388] See on this: Ahadi, *Ich habe abgeschworen*; Darwish, *Cruel and Unsual*.

We demand the release of Islam from its captivity to the totalitarian ambitions of power-hungry men and the rigid strictures of orthodoxy.

We enjoin academics and thinkers everywhere to embark on a fearless examination of the origins and sources of Islam, and to promulgate the ideals of free scientific and spiritual inquiry through cross-cultural translation, publishing, and the mass media.

We say to Muslim believers: there is a noble future for Islam as a personal faith, not a political doctrine; to Christians, Jews, Buddhists, Hindus, Baha'is, and all members of non-Muslim faith communities: we stand with you as free and equal citizens; and to nonbelievers: we defend your unqualified liberty to question and dissent.

Before any of us is a member of the Umma, the Body of Christ, or the Chosen People, we are all members of the community of conscience, the people who must choose for themselves.

There seems to be a clear difference of emphasis between the adherents of what I would like to call "Secular Islam" and "Liberal Islam." The advocates of secular Islam do take the frame of reference of the secular outlook as their point of departure (not necessarily *my* interpretation of this tradition, of course, but a secular outlook nonetheless).[389] They do not exclude Islam from the ordinary way of treating religions in a democratic secular state. Islam has to conform to the principles of human rights, democracy, and the rule of law, like any other religion. In this respect the "liberals" are much vaguer and even evasive. They are inclined to adopt special regulations for Islam as opposed to other religions, thereby caving in to the demands of the most extremist elements.

The question is of course: what approach ("secular Islam" or "liberal Islam") will be most effective in securing the rights of individuals and bringing social harmony? The so called "moderates" and "liberals" reject a declaration such as the one quoted above as much too ambitious, shocking, or divisive. "This will not help," they say. This will only be "counterproductive." They think we cannot reject sharia law out of hand. What we should do is to try, by means of "interpretation," to mitigate the harsh elements of that legal system.

It is difficult to generalize about the most successful strategy of religious reform. What will help in the Netherlands and France may not be effective in Saudi Arabia. Openly adopting a secular outlook in Sudan and, like the child in Andersen's *The Emperor's New Clothes,* saying that scriptural authority is based on a myth would be literally suicidal (prisons are full of those people). Here approaches such as those advocated by the liberal

---

[389] Not all of them assembled at the conference mentioned here, such as Akbar Ganji. See: Ganji, Akbar, *The Road to Democracy in Iran*, A Boston Review Book, MIT Press Cambridge, MA, 2008 and Sorman, *Les Enfants de Rifaa.*

reformers might well be useful. But that does not mean that we have to advocate those myths also for the modernized countries of Europe and the United States of America, as thinkers like Karen Armstrong, John Esposito, and Tariq Ramadan uncritically presuppose.

Characteristic of *The Secular Outlook* is that the focus on liberal inter-pretation for Europe and the United States is bound to be disappointing. The high expectations of the intellectual elite and policymakers for this device are too sanguine. What we should do is to focus on moral autonomy. What we have failed to do is to make citizens of the disaffected youngsters. We have failed in our "moral education." And the most important contri-bution of such a moral education should be fostering moral autonomy. Here the work of Laurence Kohlberg discussed earlier in this chapter is more promising than the contemporary orientation on "liberal" or "moderate" interpretations of religious traditions also expounded in this chapter under Kant's Legacy in Nineteenth-Century German Theology.

As a topical example to make this clear I would like to go back to the Dutch jihadist Jason W., who was introduced earlier in this chapter. Being suspected of planning terrorist attacks W. was arrested by the police in 2004. During the raid he had thrown a hand grenade at the police officers. As I said before, his testament comprised a reference to an important passage in the Qur'an that tells the reader that fighting is "obligatory."[390] The passage is to be found in Sura 2:216, one of the Qur'an quotes most popular with jihadists. It is frequently referred to by Osama Bin Laden, Ayman al-Zawahiri, and others who wage war on the Western "decadent" democracies[391] and apostate states within the Islamic world.[392] Obviously, Jason and his kind present a problem for the state. But what is the remedy?

Should we follow Armstrong and other "moderates" and say: "Jason gives a wrong interpretation to Sura 2:216?" Should we advocate that the "fighting" that is talked about should be construed as a "spiritual fight"? That would be the Ramadan–Armstrong policy. But, on the basis of the perspective advocated in *The Secular Outlook*, it would be false because it is dangerously naïve to say that the problem with radical youngsters is that they are mistaken in their interpretation of Holy Scripture. What should give us reason for concern is that they identify ethics with scriptural inter-

---

[390]   Quoted in: Groot Koerkamp and Veerman, *Het slapende leger*, p. 7.

[391]   Much of the criticism of European democracies by the radical Islamism of today is similar to the critique by the counter-culture of the 1960s and 1970s. See on this: Aron, Raymond, *Plaidoyer pour l'Europe décadente* [Plea for Decadent Europe], Éditions Robert Laffont, Paris 1977; D'Souza, Dinesh, *The Enemy at Home: The Cultural Left and Its Responsibility for 9/11*, Doubleday, New York, Auckland 2007.

[392]   See, for example: Ibrahim, Raymond, ed., *The Al Qaeda Reader*, Broadway Books, New York 2007, p. 59.

pretation and blindly follow the instructions of religious leaders. The problem with youngsters consulting cyber imams with the question of whether it is allowed to slay the unbelievers is *not* that the clerics present them with wrong interpretations, but that they feel the need to consult those religious sources of authority in moral matters at all, and blindly follow what Holy Scripture or the religious leaders seem to dictate. For our shared morality we should not make ourselves dependent on the always partly unpredictable outcome of a theological debate.

Believers, even liberal believers, think that once they depart from the notion of scriptural authority they deprive morals of their firm basis. It is for this reason that liberal or moderate believers are of so little help in fostering real moral autonomy and effective moral education. But the liberals are wrong. Separating morals from scripture does not *undermine* morality, it puts morality *on its own feet*. Under the present circumstances of religious plurality, basing our common ethics on religion implies that morals become capricious.

What contemporary societies with a multicultural composition should aim to accomplish is to educate citizens in moral responsibility. And moral responsibility means that they should be able to place their morals on an autonomous foundation. They should be able to reason about moral questions without reference to their own specific religion. Is that possible? Will we be able to educate those citizens? Or will moral autonomy always remain a chimera?

This is not to say, of course, that the adoption of moral autonomy is sufficient for the realization of a well-functioning liberal democracy. Maoism and Stalinism were not based on moral heteronomy but on moral autonomy in the sense outlined in Chapter 4. Yet Maoism and Stalinism produced brutal dictatorships that warped the minds of the people subjected to them. So adopting the secular outlook is not a recipe for universal harmony. Moral autonomy is, at best, a *necessary ground* for a good political order, not a *sufficient ground*. Nevertheless, in an age of religious extremism that accomplishment should not be underestimated. It is very important to see that youngsters who radicalize in religious extremism are missing something and to know what that is.[393]

Although Bernard Lewis has many important things to say and many lessons can be learned from his sobering commentary on the chances of an easy reform of Islam, in one area he seems to have a blind spot. His explanations underestimate the power and influence of the secular contribution to European culture. He (and Malise Ruthven) may be right in saying that

---

[393] See for an overview of the ideas of young radicals in the Netherlands: Bessems, *En dat in Nederland!*

the founder of Christianity is a completely different figure from the political and religious leader of Islam. It may be correct that the separation of Church and State is easier to reconcile with Christian than with Islamic doctrine. Nevertheless we should not forget that theocracy took a firm hold in the European tradition as well.[394] The fact that this could be countered was due not least to the development of the secular outlook, a tradition and perspective we have to cherish, further develop, and build upon.

---

[394]   See: Frégosi, *Penser l'islam dans la laïcité*, pp. 19 and 27; and Gresh, *L'Islam, la République et le Monde*, p. 35.

Selected Reading

Abou El Fadl, Khaled, *The Great Theft: Wrestling Islam From the Extremists,* Harper, San Francisco, New York 2007.

Ahadi, Mina, (with Sina Vogt), *Ich habe abgeschworen: warum ich für die Freiheit und gegen den Islam kämpfe* [I have Apostatized: Why I Fight for Freedom and against Islam], Heyne, München 2008.

Al-Azm, Sadik J., "Time Out of Joint," *Boston Review: A Political and Literary Forum,* October/November 2004, pp. 1–8.

Amis, Martin, *The Second Plane: September 11: Terror and Boredom,* Alfred A. Knopf, New York 2008.

Andersen, Hans Christian, "The Emperor's New Clothes," in: Hans Christian Andersen, *The Complete Fairy Tales,* Wordsworth, Hertfordshire 1998, pp. 89–95.

An-Na'im, Abdullahi, *Islam and the Secular State: Negotiating the Future of Shari'a,* Harvard University Press, Cambridge, MA, London 2008.

Annan, Noel, *Our Age: The Generation that Made Post-War Britain,* Fontana, London 1990.

Appignanesi, Lisa, ed., *Free Expression is No Offence,* Penguin Books, London 2005.

Armstrong, Karen, *A History of God: From Abraham to the Present: the 4000-Year Quest for God,* Heinemann, London 1993.

Armstrong, Karen, *The Battle for God: Fundamentalism in Judaism, Christianity and Islam,* HarperCollins, London 2000.

Armstrong, Karen, *Islam: A Short History,* Random House, Toronto 2002.

Armstrong, Karen, *A Short History of Myth,* Canongate, Edinburgh 2005.

Armstrong, Karen, *The Bible: The Biography,* Atlantic Books, London 2007.

Armstrong, Karen, *The Case for God: What Religion Really Means,* The Bodley Head, London 2009.

Arnold, Ages, "Voltaire and the Problem of Atheism: the Testimony of the Correspondence," *Neophilologus,* 68 1984, pp. 504–512.

Assman, Jan, *The Price of Monotheism,* Stanford University Press, Stanford, CA 2009.

Augustine, *Confessions,* translated with an introduction by R.S. Pine-Coffin, Penguin Books, Harmondsworth 1961.

Augustine, *Concerning The City of God against the Pagans,* translated by Henry Bettenson with an introduction by David Knowles, Penguin Books, Harmondsworth 1972.

Averroes, *Faith and Reason in Islam: Averroes' Exposition of Religious Arguments,* translated with footnotes, index and bibliography by Ibrahim Najjar, One World, Oxford 2005 (2001).

Baber, H.E., *The Multicultural Mystique: The Liberal Case against Diversity,* Prometheus Books, Amherst, NY 2008.

Baggini, Julian, *Atheism: A Very Short Introduction,* Oxford University Press, Oxford 2003.

Barzun, Jacques, "Of What Use the Classics Today?" in: *The Jacques Barzun Reader: Selections from his Works,* ed. Michael Murray, HarperCollins Publishers, New York 2002, pp. 412–423.

Baubérot, Jean, "Cultural Transfer and National Identity in French Laicity," in: *Diogenes,* 55 2008, pp. 17–25.

Bawer, Bruce, *While Europe Slept: How Radical Islam Is Destroying the West From Within,* Doubleday, New York 2006.

Bawer, Bruce, "Heirs to Fortuyn," in: *The Wall Street Journal,* April 23, 2009.

Bawer, Bruce, *Surrender: Appeasing Islam, Sacrificing Freedom,* Doubleday, New York 2009.

Beck, Lewis White, "Hume," in: Lewis White Beck, *Six Secular Philosophers: Religious Thought of Spinoza, Hume, Kant, Nietzsche, William James and Santayana,* Thoemmes Press, Bristol 1997, pp. 41–63.

Beck, Lewis White, "Kant," in: Lewis White Beck, *Six Secular Philosophers: Religious Thought of Spinoza, Hume, Kant, Nietzsche, William James and Santayana,* Thoemmes Press, Bristol 1997, pp. 63–83.

Bell, Daniel, "The Return of the Sacred," in: Daniel Bell, *The Winding Passage: Essays and Sociological Journeys 1960–1980,* Basic Books, New York 1980, pp. 324–355.

Bennett, William J., *The Book of Virtues: A Treasury of Great Moral Stories,* A Touchstone Book, Simon & Schuster, New York 1993.

Berg, Floris van den, "Zero Tolerance," *Free Inquiry,* January/February 2005.

Berg, Floris van den, *Hoe komen we van religie af? Een ongemakkelijke liberale paradox* [How Do We get Away from religion? An Uncomfortable Liberal Paradox], Houtekiet/Atlas, Antwerp 2009.

Berman, David, *A History of Atheism in Britain: From Hobbes to Russell,* Routledge, London 1988.

Berman, Paul, "Who is afraid of Tariq Ramadan? The Islamist, the Journalist, and the Defense of Liberalism," *The New Republic,* June 4, 2007, pp. 37–62.

Bessems, Kustaw, *En dat in Nederland! De roerige jaren sinds 11 september* [And in the Netherlands of all Places! The Turbulent Years since September 11], Uitgeverij L.J. Veen, Amsterdam/Antwerpen 2006.

Bhatti, Gurpreet Kaur, *Behzti (Dishonour),* First Performed at Birmingham Repertory Theatre, Birmingham on 19 December, 2004. Published by Oberon Books, London 2005.

Bible (Holy), English Standard Version Containing the Old and the New Testaments, HarperCollins, London 2001.

Bierer, Dora, "Renan and His Interpreters: A Study in French Intellectual Warfare," *The Journal of Modern History*, 25 no. 4 1953, pp. 375–389.

Bishop, John, "Can There Be Alternative Concepts of God?" *Noûs*, 32, no. 2 1998, pp. 174–188.

Black, Hugo LaFayette, *A Constitutional Faith*, Alfred Knopf, New York 1969.

Blackburn, Pierre, "L'appel au commandement divin et ses critiques [The Appeal to Divine Command and Its Critics]," in: Pierre Blackburn, *L'éthique. Fondements et problèmatiques contemporaines* [Ethics. Contemporary Foundations and Problematics], Éditions du Renouveau Pédagogique, Saint Laurent 1996, pp. 115–133.

Blackburn, Simon, "Religion and Respect," in: Louise M. Antony, ed., *Philosophers without Gods: Meditations on Atheism and the Secular Life*, Oxford University Press, Oxford 2007, pp. 179–194.

Blackham, H.J., *Religion in a Modern Society*, Constable, London 1966.

Blair, Tony, "A Battle for Global Values," *Foreign Affairs*, 86, no. 1 2007, pp. 79–90.

Blanshard, Brand, *Reason and Belief*, George Allen & Unwin, London 1974, pp. 187–288.

Blanshard, Brand, *Four Reasonable Men: Marcus Aurelius, John Stuart Mill, Ernest Renan, Henry Sidgwick*, Wesleyan University Press, Middletown, CT 1984.

Blanshard, Paul, *The Right to Read: The Battle Against Censorship*, The Beacon Press, Boston 1955.

Bloom, Harold, *Shakespeare: The Invention of the Human*, Riverhead Books, New York 1998.

Boehm, Omri, "The Binding of Isaac: An Inner-Biblical Polemic on the Question of 'Disobeying' a Manifestly Illegal Order," *Vetus Testamentum*, 52 2002, pp. 1–12.

Braaten, Carl E., "Paul Tillich and the Classical Christian Tradition," in: Paul Tillich, *A History of Christian Thought From Its Judaic and Hellenistic Origins to Existentialism*, A Touchstone Book, Simon & Schuster 1967.

Bradlaugh Bonner, Hypatia, *Penalties upon Opinion: Some Records of the Laws of Heresy and Blasphemy*, third edition, revised and enlarged by F.W. Read, Watts & Co., London 1934, pp. 71–75.

Bradlaugh, Charles, "A Plea for Atheism" (1864), at: http://www.infidels.org/library/historical/charles_bradlaugh/plea_for_atheism.html (accessed 2/19/10), also in: *Charles Bradlaugh: Champion of Liberty* (London 1933) and: Stein, Gordon, ed., *An Anthology of Atheism and Rationalism*, Prometheus Books, Buffalo, NY 1980, pp. 9–19.

Brandt, Richard, *Ethical Theory: The Problems of Normative and Critical Ethics*, Prentice-Hall, Engelwood Cliffs, N.J. 1959.

Broad, C.D., "Relations of Science and Religion," in: C.D. Broad, *Religion, Philosophy and Psychical Research: Selected Essays*, Humanities Press, New York 1969, pp. 220–247.

Bury, J.B., *History of the Papacy in the 19th Century*, McMillan and Co. Limited, London 1930.

Bury, J.B., *A History of the Freedom of Thought,* Thornton Butterworth, London 1932 (1913).

Caldwell, Christopher, *Reflections on the Revolution in Europe: Immigration, Islam and the West,* Allen Lane, Penguin Books, London 2009.

Caputo, John D., *On Religion,* Routledge, London 2001.

Carroll, Lewis, *Through the Looking-Glass,* in: Lewis Carroll, *Complete Works,* Vintage Books, Random House, New York 1976, pp. 138–277.

Carson, Thomas L., *Value and the Good Life,* University of Notre Dame Press, Notre Dame 2000.

Catherwood, Christopher, *A Brief History of the Middle East: From Abraham to Arafat,* Robinson, London 2006.

Catherwood, Christopher, *Making War in the Name of God,* Citadel Press, Kensington Publishing Corp., New York 2007.

Cerf, Walter, "Nicolai Hartmann," in: Paul Edwards, ed., *The Encyclopedia of Philosophy,* Vol. 3, Macmillan & The Free Press, New York 1967, pp. 421–426.

Chadwick, Owen, *The Counter-Reformation,* Penguin Books, Harmondworth 1964.

Chateaubriand, *Essai historique, politique et moral sur les révolutions anciennes et modernes, considérées dans leur rapports avec la Révolution française* [Historical, Political and Moral Essay on Ancient and Modern Revolutions Considered in Relation to the French Revolution], ed. Maurice Regard, Gallimard, Paris 1978 (1797).

Chateaubriand, *Génie du Christianisme ou Beautés de la Religion Chrétienne* [Genius of Christianity or Beauties of the Christian religion], ed. Maurice Regard, Gallimard, Paris 1978 (1802).

Chesterton, G.K., "Thomas Carlyle," 1902, in: *The Essential G.K. Chesterton,* introduced by P.J. Kavanagh, Oxford University Press, Oxford 1987, pp. 3–7.

Clifford, W.K., "The Ethics of Belief," 1877, in: W.K. Clifford, *The Ethics of Belief and Other Essays,* Introduction by Timothy J. Madigan, Prometheus Books, Amherst, NY 1999, pp. 70–96.

Cliteur, Paul, "A Secular Reading of Tocqueville," in: Raf Geenens and Annelien de Dijn, eds., *Reading Tocqueville: From Oracle to Actor,* Palgrave, Macmillan, Basingstoke 2007, pp. 112–132.

Coady, C.A.J., "Defining Terrorism," in: Igor Primoratz, ed., *Terrorism: The Philosophical Issues,* Palgrave, Macmillan, Basingstoke 2004, pp. 3–15.

Cohen, Chapman, *A Grammar of Freethought,* The Pioneer Press, London 1921.

Cohen, Hermann, *Religion der Vernunft aus den Quellen des Judenthums* [Religion of Reason out of the Sources of Judaism], Zweite Auflage, Joseph Melzer Verlag, Darmstadt 1966 (1919).

Cohen-Almagor, Raphael, *The Boundaries of Liberty and Tolerance: The Struggle Against Kahanism in Israel,* University Press of Florida, Gainesville 1994.

Cohn, Haim H., "The Law of Religious Dissidents: A Comparative Historical Survey," *Israel Law Review,* 34, no. 1 2001, pp. 39–100.

Collini, Stefan, *Absent Minds: Intellectuals in Britain,* Oxford University Press, Oxford 2006.

Collins, John T., "The Zeal of Phinehas: The Bible and the Legitimation of Violence," *Journal of Biblical Literature*, 122, no. 1 2003, pp. 3–21.

Comte-Sponville, André, *L'esprit de l'athéisme: Introduction à une spiritualité sans Dieu*, Albin Michel, Paris 2006.

Constant, Benjamin, "De la Religion considérée dans la Source, ses Formes et ses Développements [Of Religion Considered in Its Source, Forms and Developments]," in: Benjamin Constant, *Œuvres*, Texte présenté et annoté par Alfred Roulin, Éditions Gallimard, Paris 1957, pp. 1365–1395.

Cooke, Bill, *Dictionary of Atheism, Skepticism, and Humanism*, Prometheus Books, Amherst, NY 2006.

Cooke, Bill, "Samuel Porter Putnam," in: Tom Flynn, ed., *The New Encyclopedia of Unbelief*, Prometheus Books, Amherst, NY 2007, pp. 624–625.

Cox, Caroline, and Marks, John, *The West, Islam and Islamism: Is Ideological Islam Compatible with Liberal Democracy?*, Civitas, Institute for the Study of Civil Society, London 2003.

Dacey, Austin, *The Secular Conscience: Why Belief Belongs in Public Life*, Prometheus Books, Amherst, NY 2008.

Dalrymple, Theodore, *Life at the Bottom: The Worldview That Makes the Underclass*, Ivan R. Dee, Chicago 2001.

Dalrymple, Theodore, "When Islam Breaks Down," in: Theodore Dalrymple, *Our Culture, What's Left of It: The Mandarins and the Masses*, Ivan R. Dee, Chicago 2005, pp. 283–296.

Darwin, Charles, *The Origin of Species by Means of Natural Selection, Or the Preservation of Favored Races in the Struggle for Life*, ed. J.W. Burrow, Penguin Books Harmondsworth 1981 (1959).

Darwish, Nonie, *Cruel and Unusual*, Thomas Nelson, Nashville 2008.

Davison, David, "Turkey, a 'Secular' State? The Challenge of Description," *The South Atlantic Quarterly*, 102, nos. 2/3 2003, pp. 333–350.

Dawkins, Richard, *The God Delusion*, Black Swan, Transworld Publishers, London 2006.

Dean, Winton, "Handel's Farewell to Oratorio," included in: Handel, *Jephtha*, Oratorio in three acts, Monteverdi Choir, English Baroque Soloists, Conducted by John Eliot Gardiner 1988, Decca.

Delaney, Carol, *Abraham on Trial: The Social Legacy of Biblical Myth*, Princeton University Press, Princeton, NJ 1998.

Delcambre, Anne-Marie, *L'Islam des Interdits* [The Islam of the Proscribed], Desclée de Brouwer, Paris 2003.

Demant, Peter R., *Islam and Islamism: The Dilemma of the Muslim World*, Praeger, Westport, CT 2006.

Demant, V.A., "Ancient Heresy and Modern Unbelief," *The Journal of Religion*, 27, no. 2 1947, pp. 79–90.

Dennett, Daniel C., *Breaking the Spell: Religion as a Natural Phenomenon*, Allen Lane, Penguin Books, New York 2006.

Dershowitz, Alan, *The Genesis of Justice: Ten Stories of Biblical Injustice that Led to the Ten Commandments and Modern Law*, Warner Books, New York 2000.

Dershowitz, Alan, *Why Terrorism Works: Understanding the Threat, Responding to the Challenge*, Yale University Press, New Haven, CT 2002.

Desai, Meghnad, *Rethinking Islam: The Ideology of the New Terror,* I.B. Tauris, London 2007.

Desmond, Adrian, *Huxley: From Devil's Disciple to Evolution's High Priest,* Helix Books, Reading, MA 1994

D'Holbach, Paul Henri Dietrich Baron, *Le Christianisme Dévoilé ou Examen des Principes et des Effets de la Religion Chrétienne* [Christianity Unveiled or an Examination of the Principles and Effects of the Christian Religion], 1761, in: D'Holbach, *Premières Œuvres* [Early Works], Préface et notes Paulette Charbonnel, Éditions Sociales, Paris 1971, pp. 94–138.

D'Holbach, Paul Henri Dietrich Baron, *La Contagion Sacrée, ou Histoire Naturelle de la Superstition ou Tableau des Effets que les Opinions Religieuses ont produits sur la Terre* [The Sacred Contagion or Natural History of Superstition and a Table of the Effects that Religious Opinions have produced on Earth] (1768), in: D'Holbach, *Premières Œuvres* [Early Works], Préface et notes Paulette Charbonnel, Éditions Sociales, Paris 1971, pp. 139–175.

D'Holbach, Paul Henri Dietrich Baron, *Histoire Critique de Jésus Christ ou Analyse raisonnée des Evangiles* [Critical History of Jesus Christ or Reasoned Analsis of the Gospels], Edition critique par Andrew Hunswick, Librairie Droz S.A., Genève 1997 (1770).

Donnelly, Jack, "Cultural Relativism and Universal Human Rights," *Human Rights Quarterly,* 6 1984, pp. 400–419.

Drachmann, A.B., *Atheism in Pagan Antiquity,* Kessinger Publishing, Whitefish 2005 (1922).

Drury, Shadia B., *Terror and Civilization: Christianity, Politics, and the Western Psyche,* Palgrave, Macmillan, Basingstoke 2004.

D'Souza, Dinesh, *The Enemy at Home: The Cultural Left and Its Responsibility for 9/11,* Doubleday, New York 2007.

D'Souza, Dinesh, *What's So Great about Christianity,* Regnery Publishing, Inc., Washington, DC 2007.

Eco, Umberto, and Martini, Cardinal Carlo Martini, *Belief or Nonbelief: A Confrontation,* translated by Minna Proctor, Arcade Publishing, New York 1997.

Edwards, Paul, "Atheism," in: *The Encyclopedia of Philosophy,* Paul Edwards, ed., Vol. I, Macmillan & The Free Press, New York, London 1967, pp. 174–189.

Edwards, Paul, "God and the Philosophers. Part I: From Aristotle to Locke," *Free Inquiry,* 18, no. 3, 1998.

Edwards, Paul, "God and the Philosophers. Part II: From Fideism to Pragmatism," *Free Inquiry,* 18, no. 4, 1998.

Edwards, Paul, ed., *Immortality,* Prometheus Books, Buffalo, NY 1997.

Edwards, Paul, *God and the Philosophers,* Introduction by Timothy J. Madigan, Prometheus Books, Amherst, NY 2009.

Eliot, T.S., *The Idea of a Christian Society,* Faber and Faber, London 1939.

Eliot, T.S., *Notes towards the Definition of Culture,* 1948, in: T.S. Eliot, *Christianity and Culture,* A Harvest Book, Harcourt, inc., San Diego 1976, pp. 79–202.

Ellian, Afshin, "Criticism and Islam," *The Wall Street Journal,* March 31, 2008.

Elliott, John, Jr., "The Sacrifice of Isaac as Comedy and Tragedy," *Studies in Philology*, 66, no. 1 1969, pp. 36–59.

Esposito, John L., *Unholy War: Terror in the Name of Islam*, Oxford University Press, New York 2002.

Esposito, John L., and Mogahed, Dalia, *Who Speaks for Islam? What a Billion Muslims Really Think*, Gallup Press, New York 2007.

European Court of Human Rights, *Giniewski v. France*, Chamber Judgment (2006) at: http://cmiskp.echr.coe.int/tkp197/view.asp?item=1&portal=hbkm&action= html&highlight=Giniewski%20%7C%20v%20%7C%20France&sessionid=4 8786781&skin=hudoc-en.

Evans, G.R., *A Brief History of Heresy*, Blackwell, Malden, MA 2003.

Evans, Stephen C., *The Historical Christ and the Jesus of Faith: The Incarnational Narrative as History*, Clarendon Press, Oxford 1996.

Fakhry, Majid, *An Interpretation of the Quran*, New York University Press, Washington, NY 2002.

Faraj, Mohammad 'Abdus Salam, "Jihad: The Absent Obligation," in: Laqueur, Walter, ed., *Voices of Terror: Manifestos, Writings, and Manuals of Al-Qaeda, Hamas and Other Terrorists from around the World and Throughout the Ages*, Reed Press, New York 2004.

Feiler, Bruce, *Abraham: A Journey to the Heart of Three Faiths*, William Morrow, New York 2002.

Feldman, Louis H., "The Portrayal of Phinehas by Philo, Pseudo-Philo, and Josephus," *The Jewish Quarterly Review*, New Series, 92, no. 3/4 2002, pp. 315–345.

Fernández-Armesto, Felipe, "Books of Truth: The Idea of Infallible Holy Scriptures," in: Felipe Fernández-Armesto, *Ideas that changed the World*, Dorling Kindersley, London 2003, pp. 106–107.

Fishburn, Matthew, *Burning Books*, Palgrave, MacMillan, Basingstoke 2008.

Flanagan, Owen, and Jackson, Kathryn, "Justice, Care and Gender: The Kohlberg–Gilligan Debate Revisited," *Ethics*, 97, no. 3 1987, pp. 622–637.

Flew, Antony, ed., *A Dictionary of Philosophy*, Pan Books, Macmillan, London 1979.

Flew, Antony, *The Presumption of Atheism and Other Philosophical Essays on God, Freedom and Immortality*, Elek/Pemberton, London 1976.

Foucault, Michel, *Power/Knowledge: Selected Interviews and Other Writings 1972–1977*, ed. Colin Gordon, Pantheon, New York 1980.

Fourest, Caroline, *Brother Tariq: The Doublespeak of Tariq Ramadan*, Encounter Books, New York 2008.

Frégosi, Franck, *Penser l'islam dans la laïcité* [Thinking Islam in the Secular State], Fayard, Paris 2008.

Freud, Sigmund, *The Future of an Illusion*, W.W. Norton, New York 1989 (1927).

Friedman, Lawrence M., *American Law in the 20th Century*, Yale University Press, New Haven 2002.

Froese, Paul, "Forced Secularization in Soviet Russia: Why an Atheistic Monopoly Failed," *Journal for the Scientific Study of Religion*, 43, no. 1 2004, pp. 35–40.

Fukuyama, Francis, "The End of History?," *The National Interest*, no. 16, Summer 1989, pp. 3–18, also in: Paul Schumaker, Dwight C. Kiel, and Thomas W. Heilke, eds., *Ideological Voices: An Anthology in Modern Political Ideas*, The McGraw-Hill Companies, Inc., New York 1997, pp. 409–417.

Fukuyama, Francis, *The End of History and the Last Man*, The Free Press/Macmillan, New York 1992.

Fukuyama, Francis, "A question of identity," *Weekend Australian*, February 3, 2007.

Gandhi, M.K., *Ethical Religion*, translated by A. Rama Iyer, S. Ganesan Publisher, Triplicane, Madras 1922.

Ganji, Akbar, *The Road to Democracy in Iran*, A Boston Review Book, MIT Press Cambridge MA 2008.

Geisler, Norman L., *Christian Ethics: Options and Issues*, Apollos, Leicester 1990.

Geisler, Norman L., and Turek, Frank, *I Don't Have Enough Faith to Be an Atheist*, Crossway Books, Wheaton, IL 2004.

Gellner, Ernest, "Islam and Marxism: Some Comparisons," *International Affairs*, 67, no. 1 1991, pp. 1–6.

Gellner, Ernest, *Reason and Culture: The Historic Role of Rationality and Rationalism*, Blackwell, Oxford 1992.

Gellner, Ernest, *Conditions of Liberty: Civil Society and Its Rivals*, Hamish Hamilton, London 1994.

Gelvin, James L., "Al-Qaeda and Anarchism: A Historian's Reply to Terrorology," *Terrorism and Political Violence*, 20, no. 4 2008, pp. 563–581.

General Intelligence and Security Service, *From Dawa to Jihad: The Various Threats from Radical Islam to the Democratic Legal Order*, AIVD, The Hague, December 2004.

Gensler, Harry J., "Supernaturalism," in: Harry J. Gensler *Ethics*, Routledge, London 1998, pp. 33–46.

Gill, Robin, ed., *The Cambridge Companion to Christian Ethics*, Cambridge University Press, Cambridge 2001.

Goldberg, David J., and Rayner, John D., *The Jewish People: Their History and their Religion*, Penguin Books, London 1989 (1987).

Gove, Michael, *Celsius 7/7*, Weidenfeld & Nicolson, London 2006.

Graham, Roderick, *The Great Infidel: A Life of David Hume*, John Donald, Edinburgh 2004.

Grayling, A.C., *Against all Gods: Six Polemics on Religion and an Essay on Kindness*, Oberon Books, London 2007.

Grayling, A.C., *Ideas that Matter: A Personal Guide for the 21st Century*, Weidenfeld & Nicholson, London 2009.

Grayling, A.C., *Liberty in the Age of Terror: A Defense of Civil Liberties and Enlightenment Values*, Bloomsbury, London 2009.

Gresh, Alain, *L'Islam, la République et le Monde* [Islam, the Republic and the World], Fayard, Paris 2006.

Groot Koerkamp, Sanne, and Veerman, Marije, *Het slapende leger: een zoektocht naar jonge jihad-sympathisanten in Nederland* [The Sleeping Army: A Search for Young Jihad Sympathizers in the Netherlands], Rothschild & Bach, Amsterdam 2006.

Guiora, Amos N., *Fundamentals of Counterterrorism,* Wolters Kluwer, Austin, TX 2008.

Guiora, Amos N., *Freedom From Religion: Terrorism and Global Justice Series,* Oxford University Press, Oxford 2009

Habermas, Jürgen, and Ratzinger, Joseph, *The Dialectics of Secularization: On Reason and Religion,* Ignatius Press, San Francisco 2005.

Hammer, Raymond, "Authority of the Bible," in: Bruce M. Metzger and Michael D. Coogan, eds., *The Oxford Guide to Ideas and Issues of the Bible,* Oxford University Press, Oxford 2001, pp. 51–54.

Hammond, Nicholas, "Introduction," in: Nicholas Hammond, ed., *The Cambridge Companion to Pascal,* Cambridge University Press, Cambridge 2003, pp. 1–3.

Hare, John E., "Religion and Morality," in: *Stanford Encyclopedia of Philosophy,* at: http://plato.stanford.edu, 2006, pp. 1–31.

Hare, John E., *God and Morality: A Philosophical History,* Blackwell, Oxford 2007.

Hargreaves, H.A., "Swinburne's Greek Plays and God, 'The Supreme Evil,'" *Modern Language Notes,* 76, no. 7 1961, pp. 607–616.

Harnack, Adolf von, *History of Dogma,* Wipf and Stock Publishers, Eugene, OR 2000 (1889).

Harris, Sam, *The End of Faith: Religion, Terror, and the Future of Reason,* The Free Press, London 2005.

Harris, Sam, *Letter to a Christian Nation,* Alfred A. Knopf, New York 2006.

Harrison, Frederic, "The Ghost of Religion," *The Nineteenth Century,* XV, March 1884, pp. 494–506, also in: Andrew Pyle, ed., *Agnosticism: Contemporary Responses to Spencer and Huxley,* Thoemmes Press, Bristol 1995, pp. 109–124.

Hartmann, Eduard von, *Die Selbstzersetzung des Christenthums und die Religion der Zukunft* [The Self-Annihilation of Christianity and the Religion of the Future], Zweite Auflage, Carl Ducker's Verlag, Berlin 1874.

Hartmann, Nicolai, *Moral Phenomena,* Vol. I of *Ethics,* with a new introduction by Andreas A.M. Kinneging, Transaction Publishers, New Brunswick 2002.

Hartmann, Nicolai, *Moral Values,* Vol. II of *Ethics,* with a new introduction by Andreas A.M. Kinneging, Transaction Publishers, New Brunswick 2003.

Hartmann, Nicolai, *Moral Freedom,* Vol. III of *Ethics,* with a new introduction by Andreas M. Kinneging, Transaction Publishers, New Brunswick 2004.

Haught, James A., *Holy Horrors: An Illustrated History of Religious Murder and Madness,* Prometheus Books, Amherst, NY 1990.

Haught, James A., *Holy Hatred: Religious Conflicts of the '90s,* Prometheus Books, Amherst, NY 1995.

Hauser, Marc D., *Moral Minds: How Nature Designed Our Universal Sense of Right and Wrong,* Little, Brown, London 2006.

Hauser, Marc, and Singer, Peter, "Morality without Religion," *Free Inquiry,* December 2005/January 2006, pp. 18–19.

Heine, Heinrich, Heine, Heinrich, *On the History of Religion and Philosophy in Germany,* translated by Howard Pollack-Milgate, Cambridge University Press, Cambridge 2007.

Herrick, Jim, "Voltaire: 'Écrasez l'Infâme,'" in: Jim Herrick, *Against the Faith: Essays on Deists, Skeptics and Atheists,* Prometheus Books, Amherst, NY 1985, pp. 56–71.

Herrick, Jim, "Foote, George William," in: Tom Flynn, ed., *The New Encyclopedia of Unbelief,* Prometheus Books, Amherst, NY 2007, pp. 332–333.

Hick, John, *Philosophy of Religion,* fourth edition, Prentice Hall International, Inc., London 1990 (1963).

Hirsi Ali, Ayaan, *Infidel: My Life,* The Free Press, London 2007.

Hirsi Ali, Ayaan, "Islam's Silent Moderates," *The New York Times,* December 7, 2007.

Hitchens, Christopher, *god is not Great: How Religion Poisons Everything,* Twelve, New York 2007.

Hobhouse, L.T., *Morals in Evolution: A Study in Comparative Ethics,* Part II, Chapman and Hall, London 1908.

Hoffmann, Joseph R., ed., *The Just War and Jihad: Violence in Judaism, Christianity, and Islam,* Prometheus Books, Amherst, NY 2006.

Holyoake, George Jacob, and Bradlaugh, Charles, "Is Secularism Atheism?" in: Gordon Stein, *A Second Anthology of Atheism and Rationalism,* Prometheus Books, Buffalo, NY 1987, pp. 345–369.

Holyoake, George Jacob, *The Principles of Secularism,* third edition, Austin and Company, London 1870.

Horkheimer, Max, *Die Sehnsucht nach dem ganz Anderen* [Longing for the Totally Other, an Interview with Commentary by Helmut Gumnior], Ein Interview mit Kommentar von Helmut Gumnior, Furche Verlag, Hamburg 1975 (1970).

Hossein Nasr, Seyyed, *The Heart of Islam: Enduring Values for Humanity,* Harper Collins, San Francisco 2004.

Houtman, Cornelis, "Rewriting a Dramatic Old Testament Story. The Story of Jephtha and his Daughter in Some Examples of Christian Devotional Literature," in: *Biblical Interpretation,* 13, no. 2 2005, pp. 167–190.

Hume, David, *Dialogues concerning Natural Religion,* ed. Henry D. Aiken, Hafner Press, New York 1948 (1779).

Humphrey, Nicholas, "What Shall We Tell the Children?" in: Nicholas Humphrey, *The Mind Made Flesh: Frontiers of Psychology and Evolution,* Oxford University Press, Oxford 2002, pp. 289–318.

Huntington, Samuel P., *The Clash of Civilizations and the Remaking of World Order,* Simon & Schuster, New York 1996.

Hutchinson, Robert J., *The Politically Incorrect Guide to the Bible,* Regnery Publishing, Inc., Washington DC 2007.

Huxley, Thomas H., *Man's Place in Nature,* The University of Michigan Press, Ann Arbor 1959 (1863).

Huxley, Thomas Henry, "Agnosticism and Christianity," in: Thomas Henry Huxley, *Agnosticism and Christianity. And Other Essays,* Prometheus Books, Buffalo, NY 1992, pp. 193–232.

Huxley, Thomas Henry, "Agnosticism," in: Thomas Henry Huxley, *Agnosticism and Christianity. And Other Essays,* Prometheus Books, Buffalo, NY 1992, pp. 142–167.

Ibn Warraq and Weiss, Michael "Inhuman Rights," *City Journal,* 19, no. 2 2009, pp. 1–6.

Ibrahim, Raymond, ed., *The Al Qaeda Reader,* Broadway Books, New York 2007.

Idziak, Janine Marie, ed., *Divine Command Morality: Historical and Contemporary Readings,* Edwin Mellen, New York 1979.

Idziak, Janine Marie, "Divine Command Ethics," in: Philip L. Quinn and Charles Taliaferro, eds., *A Companion to the Philosophy of Religion,* Blackwell, Oxford 1997, pp. 453–460.

Idziak, Janine Marie, "Is Morality Based on God's Commands?" in: Michael L. Peterson and Raymond J. VanArragon, eds., *Contemporary Debates in Philosophy of Religion,* Blackwell Publishing, Malden, MA 2004, pp. 290–298.

Ignatieff, Michael, "Respect and the Rules of the Road," in: Lisa Appignanesi, ed., *Free Expression is No Offence,* Penguin Books, London 2005, pp. 127–136.

Ingersoll, R.G., "Why Am I an Agnostic?" *North American Review,* December 1889, Part I, pp. 1–14.

Ingersoll, R.G., "Mistakes of Moses," in: R.G. Ingersoll, *Complete Lectures of Col. R.G. Ingersoll,* M.A. Donogue & Company, Chicago 1900, pp. 7–19.

Israel, Jonathan I., *Radical Enlightenment: Philosophy and the Making of Modernity 1650–1750,* Oxford University Press, Oxford 2001.

Israel, Jonathan I., *Enlightenment Contested: Philosophy, Modernity, and the Emancipation of Man 1670–1752,* Oxford University Press, Oxford 2006.

Jacoby, Susan, "A First Amendment Junkie," in: Sylvan Barnet and Hugo Bedau, eds., *Current Issues and Enduring Questions: Methods and Models of Argument,* Bedford Books of St. Martin's Press, Boston 1990, pp. 8–13.

Jahangir, Asma, *Promotion and Protection of all Human Rights, Civil, Political, Economic, Social and Cultural Rights, including the Right to Development,* Report by the Special Rapporteur on Freedom of Religion or Belief, A/HRC/6/5, 20 July 2007.

James, William, *The Varieties of Religious Experience: A Study in Human Nature,* ed. Martin E. Marty, Penguin Books, Harmondsworth 1982 (1902).

Jami, Ehsan, *Het recht om ex-moslim te zijn* [The Right to be an Ex-Muslim], Ten Have, Amsterdam 2007.

Jami, Ehsan, "An Interview With Muhammed," posted on the internet on December 9, 2008.

Jansen, Johannes J.G., *The Neglected Duty: The Creed of Sadat's Assassins and Islamic Resurgence in the Middle East,* Macmillan Publishing Company, London 1986.

Jansen, Johannes J.G., *The Dual Nature of Islamic Fundamentalism,* Cornell University Press, Ithaca, NY 1997.

Jardine, Lisa, *The Awful End of Prince William the Silent: The First Assassination of a Head of State with a Handgun,* HarperCollins, London 2005.

Jespersen, Karen, and Pittelkow, Ralf, *Islamisten en naïvisten. Een aanklacht* [Islamists and Naivists. An Accusation], Nieuw Amsterdam, Amsterdam 2007.

Johnson, Paul, *The Quest for God: A Personal Pilgrimage,* Weidenfeld and Nicolson, London 1996.

Joshi, S.T., ed., *Icons of Unbelief: Atheists, Agnostics, and Secularists*, Greenwood Press, Westport, CT 2008.

Juergensmeyer, Mark, *Global Rebellion: Religious Challenges to the Secular State, from Christian Militias to Al Qaeda*, University of California Press, Berkeley 2008.

Kant, Erhard, Hamann, Herder, Lessing, Mendelssohn, Riem, Schiller, Wieland, *Was ist Aufklärung? Thesen und Definitionen* [What is Englightenment? Theses and Definitions], ed. Ehrhard Bahr, Philipp Reclam jun., Stuttgart 1974.

Kant, Immanuel, *Beantwortung der Frage: Was ist Aufklärung?* [An Answer to the Question: What is Enlightenment?] (1784), in: *Schriften zur Anthropologie, Geschichtsphilosophie, Politik und Pädagogik* [Writings on Anthropology, the Philosophy of History, Politics, and Pedagogics], 1, ed. Wilhelm Weischedel, Suhrkamp, Frankfurt am Main 1981, pp. 53–61.

Kant, Immanuel, *Der Streit der Fakultäten* [The Conflict of the Faculties], 1798, in: Immanuel Kant, *Schriften zur Anthropologie, Geschichtsphilosophie, Politik und Pädagogik* [Writings on Anthropology, the Philosophy of History, Politics, and Pedagogics], 1, Werkausgabe XI, ed. Wilhelm Weischedel, Suhrkamp, Frankfurt am Main 1981, pp. 267–393.

Kant, Immanuel, *Die Religion innerhalb der Grenzen der bloßen Vernunft* [Religion within the Limits of Reason Alone], 1793, in: Immanuel Kant, *Die Metaphysik der Sitten* [The Metaphysics of Morals], Werkausgabe, Band VIII, ed. Wilhelm Weischedel, Suhrkamp, Frankfurt am Main 1981, pp. 649–879.

Kant, Immanuel, *Grundlegung zur Metaphysik der Sitten* [Groundwork of the Metaphysics of Morals], (1785), in: *Werkausgabe, Band VII, ed. Wilhelm Weischedel, Suhrkamp, Frankfurt am Main 1981, pp. 11–102.

Karolides, Nicholas J., Bald, Margaret, and Sova, Dawn B., *100 Banned Books: Censorship Histories of World Literature*, Checkmark Books, New York NY 1999.

Karsh, Efraim, *Islamic Imperialism: A History*, Yale University Press, New Haven, CT 2006.

Kelek, Necla, *Die fremde Braut: Ein Bericht aus dem inneren des türkischen Lebens in Deutschland* [The Foreign Bride: A Report from inside Turkish Life in Germany], Kiepenheuer & Witsch 2005.

Keller, Timothy, *The Reason for God: Belief in an Age of Skepticism*, Riverhead Books, New York 2008.

Kelsay, John, "Al-Qaida as a Muslim (Religio-Political) Movement. Remarks on James L. Gelvin's 'Al-Qaeda and Anarchism: A Historian's Reply to Terrology,'" *Terrorism and Political Violence*, 20, no. 4 2008, pp. 601–605.

Kenny, Anthony, *A Life in Oxford*, John Murray, London 1997.

Kenny, Anthony, *The Unknown God: Agnostic Essays*, Continuum, London and New York 2004.

Kenny, Anthony, *What I Believe*, Continuum, London 2006.

Kepel, Gilles, *La Revanche de Dieu: Chrétiens, juifs et musulmans à la reconquête du monde* [The Revenge of God: Christians, Jews and Muslims Out to Reconquer the World], Le Seuil, Paris 1991.

Khader, Naser, and Rose, Flemming, "Reflections on the Danish Cartoon Controversy," *Middle East Quarterly*, Fall 2007, pp. 59–66.

Kierkegaard, Soeren, *Fear and Trembling,* translated by Alastair Hannay, Penguin Books, Harmondsworth 1985 (1843).

Kimball, Roger, *Tenured Radicals: How Politics Has Corrupted Our Higher Education,* revised edition, Elephant Paperbacks, Ivan R. Dee Publisher, Chicago 1998 (1991).

King, Anna, "Islam, Women and Violence," *Feminist Theology,* 17, no. 3 2009, pp. 292–328.

Kirsch, Jonathan, *A History of the End of the World: How the Most Controversial Book in the Bible Changed the Course of Western Civilization,* HarperCollins, New York 2007.

Klausen, Jytte, *The Cartoons that Shook the World,* Yale University Press, New Haven, CT 2009.

Kohlberg, Lawrence, "Moral Education," in: Harry J. Gensler, Earl Spurgin, and James Swindal, eds., *Ethics: Contemporary Readings,* Routledge, New York 2004, pp. 186–194.

Kohlberg, Lawrence, "The Claim to Moral Adequacy of a Highest State of Moral Judgment," *The Journal of Philosophy,* 70, no. 18 1973, pp. 630–646.

Kretzmann, Norman, "Abraham, Isaac, and Euthyphro: God and the Basis of Morality," in: Eleonore Stump and Michael J. Murray, eds., *Philosophy of Religion: The Big Questions,* Blackwell Publishers, Malden, MA 1999, pp. 417–427.

Kurtz, Lester R., "The Politics of Heresy," *American Journal of Sociology,* 88, no. 6 1983, pp. 1085–1115.

Kurtz, Paul, *Forbidden Fruit: The Ethics of Humanism,* Prometheus Books, Amherst, NY 1988.

Kurtz, Paul, *The New Skepticism: Inquiry and Reliable Knowledge,* Prometheus Books, Amherst, NY 1992.

Kurtz, Paul, *The Courage to Become: The Virtues of Humanism,* Praeger, Westport, CT 1997.

Kurtz, Paul, *Eupraxophy: Living without Religion,* Prometheus Books, Amherst, NY 1998.

Kurtz, Paul, *What is Secular Humanism?,* Center For Inquiry, Prometheus Books, Amherst, NY 2006.

Kuschel, Karl-Josef, *Streit um Abraham: Was Juden, Christen und Muslime trennt und was sie eint* [The Dispute about Abraham: What Divides Jews, Christians, and Muslims and What Unites Them], Patmos, Düsseldorf 2001.

Labuschagne, Bart C., "Religion and Order: Philosophical Reflections from Augustine to Hegel on the Spiritual Sources of Law and Politics," in: Bart C. Labuschagne and Reinhard W. Sonnenschmidt, eds., *Religion, Politics and Law: Philosophical Reflections on the Sources of Normative Order in Society,* Brill, Leiden 2009, pp. 71–94.

Lamont, Corliss, *The Philosophy of Humanism,* eighth edition, Humanist Press, Amherst, NY 1997 (1949).

Landau, Paul, *Le Sabre et le Coran: Tariq Ramadan et les frères musulmans à la conquête de l'Europe* [The Sabre and the Qur'an: Tariq Ramadan and the Muslim Brothers Out to Conquer Europe], Éditions du Rocher, Paris 2005.

Laqueur, Walter, *Krieg dem Westen: Terrorismus im 21. Jahrhundert* [War on the West. Terrorism in the Twenty-First Century], Propyläen, München 2003.

Laqueur, Walter, *The Last Days of Europe: Epitaph for an Old Continent*, Thomas Dunne Books / St. Martin's Griffin, New York 2007.

Larmore, Charles, "Beyond Religion and Enlightenment," *San Diego Law Review*, 30 1993, pp. 799–815.

Larrimore, Mark, ed., *The Problem of Evil: A Reader*, Blackwell Publishing, Malden, MA 2008.

Law, Stephen, *The War for Children's Minds*, Routledge, London 2006.

Lecky, W.E.H., *History of the Rise and Influence of Rationalism in Europe*, Longman, Green, Longman, Roberts, & Green, London 1865.

Lecky, W.E.H., *History of European Morals from Augustus to Charlemagne*, Longman, London 1869.

Levy, Leonard W., *Blasphemy: Verbal Offense against the Sacred from Moses to Salman Rushdie*, The University of North Carolina Press, Chapel Hill 1993.

Lewis, Bernard, "Islam and Liberal Democracy. A Historical Overview," *Journal of Democracy*, 7, no. 2 1996, pp. 52–63.

Lewis, Bernard, *What Went Wrong? The Clash between Islam and Modernity in the Middle East*, Weidenfeld & Nicolson, London 2002.

Lewis, Bernard, *The Crisis of Islam: Holy War and Unholy Terror*, Weidenfeld & Nicolson, London 2003.

Lewis, C.S., *Mere Christianity*, revised edition, Harper, San Francisco, 2001 (1952).

Lewis, C.S., *The Abolition of Man. Or Reflections on Education with Special Reference to the Teaching of English in the Upper Forms of Schools*, Harper, San Francisco 2001 (1944).

Lewis, C.S., "The Moral Law Is from God," in: Harry J. Gensler, Earl Spurgin, and James Swindal, eds., *Ethics: Contemporary Readings*, Routledge, New York 2004, pp. 69–76.

Lewy, Guenter, *"If God is Dead, Everything is Permitted"?*, Transaction Publishers, New Brunswick 2008.

Lilla, Mark, *The Stillborn God: Religion, Politics, and the Modern West*, Alfred A. Knopf, New York 2007.

Linton, Anna, "Sacrificed or Spared? The Fate of Jephtha's Daughter in Early Modern Theological and Literary Texts," *German Life and Letters*, 57, no. 3, 2004, pp. 237–255.

Lipson, Leslie, *The Ethical Crises of Civilization: Moral Meltdown or Advance?*, Sage Publications, London 1993.

Löwith, Karl, *From Hegel to Nietzsche: The Revolution in Nineteenth-Century Thought*, translated by David E. Green, Constable, London 1964.

Luce, J.V., *An Introduction to Greek Philosophy*, Thames and Hudson, London 1992.

MacCulloch, Diarmaid, *Reformation: Europe's House Divided, 1490–1700*, Penguin Books, London 2004.

Madigan, Timothy J., *W.K. Clifford and "The Ethics of Belief,"* Cambridge Scholars Publishing, Cambridge 2009.

Madison, James, *Essay LI: The Same Subject Continued with the Same View and Concluded*, in: James Madison, Alexander Hamilton, John Jay, *The Federalist Papers*, edited by Isaac Kramnick, Penguin Books 1987 (1788), pp. 319–320.

Malik, Kenan, *From Fatwa to Jihad: The Rushdie Affair and Its Legacy,* Atlantic Books, London 2009.

Manji, Irshad, *The Trouble with Islam: A Muslim's Call for Reform in Her Faith,* St. Martin's Press, New York 2003.

Marres, René, *De verdediging van het vrije woord: de kwestie Wilders en de demonisering van het debat* [The Defense of Free Speech: The Wilders Question and the Demonizing of Debate], Uitgeverij Aspect, Soesterberg 2008.

Martin, Michael, "Atheism Defined and Contrasted," in: Michael Martin, *Atheism: A Philosophical Justification,* Temple University Press, Philadelphia 1990, pp. 463–476.

Martin, Michael, *The Case Against Christianity,* Temple University Press, Philadelphia 1991.

Martin, Michael, "Atheism," in: Tom Flynn, ed., *The New Encyclopedia of Unbelief,* Prometheus Books, Amherst, NY 2007, pp. 89–96.

Martin, Michael, ed., *The Cambridge Companion to Atheism,* Cambridge University Press, Cambridge 2007.

Marx, Karl, *Zur Kritik der Hegelschen Rechtsphilosophie* [Critique of Hegel's Philosophy of Right], 1843/44, in: Karl Marx and Friedrich Engels, *Ausgewählte Werke* [Selected Works], Dietz Verlag, Berlin 1977, pp. 9–25.

Mason, Herbert, "Review of A History of God by Karen Armstrong," *The American Historical Review,* 100, no. 2 1995, pp. 481–482.

Masterson, Patrick, *Atheism and Alienation: A Study of the Philosophical Sources of Contemporary Atheism,* Penguin Books, Harmondsworth 1973.

Mauthner, Fritz, "Gott [God]," in: Fritz Mauthner, *Wörterburch der Philosophie: Neue Beiträge zu einer Kritik der Sprache* [Dictionary of Philosophy: New Contributions to a Critique of Language], Erster Band, Diogenes Verlag, Zürich 1980 (1910/11), pp. 448–458.

Mauthner, Fritz, "Gotteswort [The Word of God]," in: Fritz Mauthner, *Wörterburch der Philosophie: Neue Beiträge zu einer Kritik der Sprache* [Dictionary of Philosophy: New Contributions to a Critique of Language], Erster Band, Diogenes Verlag, Zürich 1980 (1910/11), pp. 458–468.

Mavrodes, George I., "Atheism and Agnosticism," in: Ted Honderich, ed., *The Oxford Companion to Philosophy,* Oxford University Press, Oxford 1995, p. 63.

McCabe, Joseph, *The Existence of God,* Watts & Co., London 1933.

McGrath, Alister E., *Christian Theology: An Introduction,* Blackwell, Oxford 1994.

McGrath, Alister E., *A Brief History of Heaven,* Blackwell Publishing, Malden, MA 2003.

McGrath, Alister E., *Theology: The Basics,* Blackwell Publishing, Malden, MA 2004.

McGrath, Alister E., *The Twilight of Atheism: The Rise and Fall of Disbelief in the Modern World,* Doubleday, New York 2004.

McGrath, Alister E., *Christianity's Dangerous Idea: The Protestant Revolution, A History from the Sixteenth Century to the Twenty-First,* SPCK, London 2007.

McInerney, Peter K., "God," in: *Introduction to Philosophy,* HarperCollins, New York 1992, pp. 9–22.

McRoy, Anthony, *From Rushdie to 7/7: The Radicalisation of Islam in Britain*, The Social Affairs Unit, London 2006.

McTaggart, John M.E., *Human Immortality and Pre-Existence*, Edward Arnold, London 1915; reprint of chapters. 3–4 as *Some Dogmas of Religion*, with an Introduction by C.D. Broad, Thoemmes Press, Bristol 1997 (1906).

Meddeb, Abdelwahab, "En terre d'islam [On Islamic Soil]," in: André Glucksmann, Nicole Bacharan, and Abdelwahab Meddeb, *La plus belle histoire de la liberté* [The Most Beautiful History of Liberty], Avec Michka Mindel, Postface de Vaclav Havel, Éditions du Seuil, Paris 2009, pp. 123–167.

Mekhennet, Souad, Sautter, Claudia, and Hanfeld, Michael, *Die Kinder des Dschihad: Die neue Generation des islamistischen Terrors in Europa* [The Children of the Jihad: The New Generation of Islamist Terror in Europe], Piper, München 2008.

Metzger, Bruce M., & Coogan, Michael D., *The Oxford Guide to Ideas & Issues of the Bible*, Oxford University Press, Oxford 2001.

Micklethwait, John, and Wooldridge, Adrian, *God is Back: How the Global Rise of Faith Is Changing the World*, Allen Lane, Penguin Books, London 2009.

Miles, Jack, *God. A Biography*, Alfred A. Knopf, New York 1995.

Milgram, Stanley, "The Perils of Obedience," *Harper's Magazine*, December 1973, pp. 62–77; also in: Louis P. Pojman, ed., *The Moral Life: An Introductory Reader in Ethics and Literature*, Oxford University Press, New York and Oxford 2000, pp. 625–640.

Mill, John Stuart, *Autobiography of John Stuart Mill*, Columbia University Press, New York 1924 (1873).

Mill, John Stuart, *Three Essays. On Liberty (1859), Representative Government (1861), The Subjection of Women (1869)*, Oxford University Press, Oxford 1975.

Mill, John Stuart, *On Liberty with the Subjection of Women and Chapters on Socialism*, edited by Stefan Collini, Cambridge University Press, Cambridge 1989.

Mill, John Stuart, The Subjection of Women, 1869, in: John Stuart Mill, *On Liberty with The Subjection of Women and Chapters on Socialism*, ed., Stefan Collini, Cambridge University Press, Cambridge 1989, pp. 117–219.

Mill, John Stuart, *Three Essays on Religion*, Prometheus Books, Amherst, NY 1998 (1874).

Minow, Martha, "Tolerance in an Age of Terror," *Southern California Interdisciplinary Law Journal*, 16 2007, pp. 453–494.

Mirza, Munira, Senthilkumaran, Abi, and Ja'far, Zein, *Living Apart Together: British Muslims and the Paradox of Multiculturalism*, Policy Exchange, London 2007.

Mleynek, Sherryll, "Abraham, Aristotle, and God: The Poetics of Sacrifice," *Journal of the American Academy of Religion*, 62, no. 1 1994, pp. 107–121.

Moberly, R.W.L., "The Earliest Commentary on the Akedah," *Vetus Testamentum*, 28, July 1988, pp. 302–323.

Montaigne, Michel de, *The Essays of Michel de Montaigne*, translated and edited by M.A. Screech, Allen Lane, The Penguin Press, London 1991.

Montenot, Jean and Garzanti *Encyclopédie de la Philosophie* [Encyclopedia of Philosophy], La Pochothèque, Librairie Générale Française 2002.

Mossner, Ernest C., "The Enigma of Hume," *Mind*, New Series, 45, no. 179 1936, pp. 334–349.

Mossner, Ernest C., "The Religion of David Hume," *Journal of the History of Ideas*, 39, no. 4 1970, pp. 653–663.

Mozaffari, Mehdi, *Fatwa: Violence and Discourtesy*, Aarhus University Press, Aarhus 1998.

Murphy, Francis X., "Vatican Politics: Structure and Function," *World Politics*, 26, no. 4 1974, pp. 542–559.

Murray, Douglas, "Studying Islam has Made Me an Atheist," at: *Spectator.co.uk*, December 29, 2008.

Murray, Douglas, "Think Tank: Betrayal of Muslim Reformers," at: *Timesonline*, November 23, 2008.

Murray, Douglas, and Verwey, Johan Pieter, *Victims of Intimidation: Freedom of Speech within Europe's Muslim Communities*, The Centre for Social Cohesion, London 2008.

Murray, Gilbert, *Five Stages of Greek Religion*, Watts & Co., London 1935.

Nagel, Ernest, "A Defense of Atheism," in: Paul Edwards and Arthur Pap, eds., *A Modern Introduction to Philosophy*, revised edition, The Free Press, Collier-MacMillan, New York 1967 (1957).

Najjar, Fauzi M., "Islamic Fundamentalism and the Intellectuals: The Case of Naguib Mahfouz," *British Journal of Middle Eeastern Studies*, 25, no. 1 1998, pp. 139–168.

Nasreen, Taslima, *Selected Columns*, translated by Debjani Sengupta, Srishti Publishers, New Dehli 2004.

Nelson-Pallmeyer, Jack, *Is Religion Killing Us? Violence in the Bible and the Qur'an*, Trinity Press International, Harrisburg 2003.

Neu, Jerome, *Sticks and Stones: The Philosophy of Insults*, Oxford University Press, Oxford 2008.

Neuhaus, Richard John, *The Naked Public Square: Religion and Democracy in America*, second edition, William B. Eerdmans, Publishing Company, Grand Rapids, Michigan 1997 (1984).

Neumann, Peter R., "Europe's Jihadist Dilemma," *Survival*, 48, no. 2 2006, pp. 71–84.

Nielsen, Kai, "Some Remarks on the Independence of Morality from Religion," *Mind*, New Series, 70, no. 278 1961, pp. 175–186.

Nielsen, Kai, "Morality and God: Some Questions for Mr. MacIntyre," *The Philosophical Quarterly*, 12, no. 47 1962, pp. 129–137.

Nietzsche, Friedrich, *Werke IV, Aus dem Nachlass der Achtzigerjahre, Briefe (1861–1889)* [Works Vol. IV, From the Remains of the Eighties, Letters (1861–1889)], ed. Karl Schlechta, Ullstein, Frankfurt am Main 1969.

Nietzsche, Friedrich, *The Anti-Christ*, 1888–89, translated with an introduction by H.L. Mencken, See Sharp Press, Tucson, AZ 1999.

Nietzsche, Friedrich, *The Gay Science: With a Prelude in Rhymes and an Appendix in Songs*, translated by Walter Kaufman, Vintage, New York 1974 (1882).

Nikiprowetzky, V., "Ethical Monotheism," *Daedalus*, 104, no. 2, Revelation, and Doubt: Perspectives on the First Millenium B.C. (Spring, 1975), pp. 69–89.

Nowell-Smith, Patrick, "Religion and Morality," in: Paul Edwards, ed., *The Encyclopedia of Philosophy*, Vol. 7, Macmillan & The Free Press, New York 1967, pp. 150–158.

Nowell-Smith, Patrick, "Morality: Religious and Secular," in: Eleonore Stump and Michael J. Murray, eds., *Philosophy of Religion: The Big Questions*, Blackwell, Malden, MA 2001 (1999), pp. 403–412.

Paine, Thomas, *The Age of Reason*, 1794, in: Thomas Paine, *Collected Writings*, The Library of America, New York 1995, pp. 665–885.

Pannick, David, "A curb on free speech that should offend us all, whatever our religion," *The Times*, January 11, 2005.

Parekh, Bhikhu, *Rethinking Multiculturalism: Cultural Diversity and Political Theory*, Macmillan Press, Basingstoke 2000.

Parekh, Bhikhu, *A New Politics of Identity: Political Principles for an Interdependent World*, Palgrave Macmillan, Basingstoke 2008.

Parfit, Derek, *Reasons and Persons*, Clarendon Press, Oxford 1984.

Pascal, Blaise, *Pensées*, translated by A.J. Krailsheimer, Penguin Books, London 1966.

Pascal, Blaise, *The Provincial Letters*, 1657, translated by A.J. Krailsheimer, Penguin Books, Harmondsworth 1982 (1967).

Pascal, "The Wager," in: Louis Pojman, ed., *Philosophy of Religion: An Anthology*, Wadworth Publishing Company, Belmont, CA 1994, pp. 420–422.

Pearson, Karl, *The Ethics of Freethought and Other Addresses and Essays*, Abraham and Charles Black, London 1901.

Pessin, Andrew, *The God Question: What Famous Thinkers from Plato to Dawkins Have Said about the Divine*, Oneworld, Oxford 2009.

Petriburg, M., "The Excommunication of Queen Elizabeth," *The English Historical Review*, 7, no. 25 1892, pp. 81–88.

Pettit, Philip, "Analytical Philosophy," in: Robert E. Goodin and Philip Pettit, eds., *A Companion to Contemporary Political Philosophy*, Blackwell, Oxford 1993, pp. 7–39.

Phares, Walid, *Future Jihad: Terrorist Strategies against the West*, Palgrave, Macmillan, New York 2005.

Phares, Walid, *The War of Ideas: Jihadism against Democracy*, Palgrave, Macmillan, New York 2007.

Phillips, Melanie, *Londonistan: How Britain is Creating a Terror State Within*, Gibson Square, London 2006.

Philpott, Daniel, "The Challenge of September 11 to Secularism in International Relations," *World Politics*, 55 (October 2002), pp. 66–95.

Philpott, Daniel, "The Religious Roots of Modern International Relations," *World Politics*, 52 (January, 2000), pp. 206–245.

Piaget, Jean, *The Moral Judgement of the Child*, Kegan Paul, London 1932.

Pipes, Daniel, *Militant Islam Reaches America*, W.W. Norton & Company, New York, London 2002.

Pipes, Daniel, *The Rushdie Affair: The Novel, the Ayatollah, and the West*, second edition, Transaction Publishers, New Brunswick, NJ 2003.

Plato, *Apology*, in: Plato, *Complete Works*, ed. John M. Cooper, Hackett Publishing Company, Indianapolis 1997.

Plato, *Euthyphro,* in: Plato, *Complete Works,* ed. John M. Cooper, Hackett Publishing Company, Indianapolis 1997.

Poidevin, Robin, *Arguing for Atheism: An Introduction to the Philosophy of Religion,* Routledge, London 1996.

Pojman, Louis P., *Ethics: Discovering Right and Wrong,* second edition, Wadsworth, Belmont, CA 1995.

Putnam, Samuel Porter, *Four Hundred Years of Freethought,* The Truthseeker Company, New York 1894.

Pyle, Andrew, ed., *Agnosticism: Contemporary Responses to Spencer and Huxley,* Thoemmes Press, Bristol 1995.

Quinn, Philip L., "Agamenmon and Abraham: The Tragic Dilemma of Kierkegaard's Knight of Faith," *Journal of Literature and Theology,* 4, no. 2 1990, pp. 181–193.

Qur'an, translated with notes by N.J. Dawood, Penguin Books, London 1999.

Rachels, James, "God and Human Attitudes," *Religious Studies,* 7 1971, pp. 325–37, also in: James Rachels, *Can Ethics provide Answers? And other Essays in Moral Philosophy,* Rowman & Littlefield Publishers, Lanham, MA 1997, pp. 109–125.

Rae, Murray, "The Risk of Obedience: A Consideration of Kierkegaard's *Fear and Trembling,*" *Journal of Systematic Theology,* 1, no. 3 1999, pp. 308–321.

Ramadan, Tariq, "A response to Ayaan Hirsi Ali: A Case of Selective Hearing." *International Herald Tribune,* December 17, 2007.

Rapoport, David C., "Fear and Trembling: Terrorism in Three Religious Traditions," *The American Political Science Review,* 78, no. 3 1984, pp. 658–677.

Ratzinger, Joseph, *Introduction to Christianity.* translated J.R. Forster, Ignatius Press, Fort Collins, CO 1990 (1968).

Raven, Charles E., "Religion & Science: A Diagnosis," L.T. Hobhouse Memorial Trust Lecture, No. 16, delivered on May 1, 1946, in: *Hobhouse Memorial Lectures 1941–1950,* Oxford University Press, London 1952, pp. 3–16.

Redford, Colin, "Patrick Nowell-Smith," Obituary, *The Guardian,* February 22, 2006.

Reeves, Richard, *John Stuart Mill: Victorian Firebrand,* Atlantic Books, London 2007.

Reinhard, Johan, and Alvarez, Stephen, "Peru's Ice Maidens," *National Geographic,* 189, no. 6 1996, pp. 62–82.

Renan, Ernest, "Le judaïsme comme race et comme religion [Judaism as Race and Religion]," 1883, in: Ernest Renan, *Discours et Conférences* [Discourses and Lectures], sixième édition, Calmann-Lévy, Paris 1887, pp. 341–374.

Reuther, Rosemary Radford, "The Politics of God in the Christian Tradition," *Feminist Theology,* 17, no. 3 2009, pp. 329–338.

Ritschl, Albrecht, Instruction in the Christian Religion, translated by Alice Mead Swing in: *The Theology of Albrecht Ritschl together with Instruction in the Christian Religion,* ed. Albert Temple Swing, Kessinger Publishing, Whitefish, MT 2006.

Robertson, J.M., *A History of Freethought in the Nineteenth Century,* Vol. I, Watts & Co., London 1929.

Robinson, John A.T., *Honest to God,* The Westminster Press, Philadelphia 1963.

Robinson, Richard, *An Atheist's Values*, The Clarendon Press, Oxford 1964.

Rohls, Jan, *Geschichte der Ethik* [History of Ethics], 2., umgearbeitete und ergänzte Auflage, Mohr Siebeck, Tübingen 1999 (1991).

Rorty, Richard, "The Priority of Democracy to Philosophy," in: Richard Rorty, *Objectivism, Relativism, and Truth: Philosophical Papers*, Vol. 1, Cambridge University Press, Cambridge 1991, pp. 175–197.

Rorty, Richard, "Religion As Conversation-stopper," 1994, in: Richard Rorty, *Philosophy and Social Hope*, Penguin Books, London 1999, pp. 168–174.

Rorty, Richard, "Religion in the Public Sphere: A Reconsideration," *Journal of Religious Ethics*, 31, no. 1 2003, pp. 141–149.

Rorty, Richard, and Vattimo, Gianni, *The Future of Religion*, edited by Santiago Zabala, Columbia University Press, New York 2005.

Rose, Flemming, "Why I Published Those Cartoons," at: *Washingtonpost.com*, Sunday, February 19, 2006.

Ross, J.M., "Introduction," in: Cicero, *The Nature of the Gods*, Translated by Horace C.P. McGregor, with an introduction by J.M. Ross, Penguin Books, London 1972, pp. 7–63.

Roy, Olivier, *Globalised Islam: The Search for a New Ummah*, C. Hurst & Co., London 2004.

Ruether, Rosemary Radford, "The Politics of God in the Christian Tradition," *Feminist Theology*, 17, no. 3 2009, pp. 329–338.

Ruffini, Francesco, *Religious Liberty*, translated by J. Parker Heyes, Williams and Norgate, London 1912.

Rushdie, Salman, "A 4-year Death Sentence," *The New York Times*, February 7, 1993.

Rushdie, Salman, "Do we have to fight the battle for the Enlightenment all Over Again?" *The Independent*, January 22, 2005.

Russell, Bertrand, *History of Western Philosophy and its Connection with Political and Social Circumstances from the Earliest Times to the Present Day*, George Allen & Unwin, London 1974 (1946).

Russell, Bertrand, *The Autobiography of Bertrand Russell*, Unwin Paperbacks, London 1975.

Russell, Bertrand, *Bertrand Russell on God and Religion*, ed. Al Seckel, Prometheus Books, Buffalo, NY 1986.

Russell, Bertrand, *Why I Am Not a Christian: And Other Essays on Religion and Related Subjects*, Routledge, London 2004 (1957).

Ruthven, Malise, *A Satanic Affair: Salman Rushdie and the Rage of Islam*, Chatto and Windus, London 1990.

Ruthven, Malise, *Islam: A Very Short Introduction*, Oxford University Press, Oxford 2000 (1997).

Sandmel, Samuel, "Abraham's Knowledge of the Existence of God," *The Harvard Theological Review*, 44, no. 3 1955, pp. 137–139.

Sarkozy, Nicholas, *La République, les religions, l'espérance. Entretiens avec Thibaud Collin et Philippe Verdin* [The Republic, Religions, Hope. Conversations with Thibaud Collin and Philippe Verdin], Les Éditions du Cerf, Paris 2004.

Sartre, Jean-Paul, *L'existentialisme est un humanisme* [Existentialism is a Humanism], Les Éditions de Nagel, Paris 1970.

Scalia, Antonin, "Common-Law Courts in a Civil-Law System: The Role of United States Federal Courts in Interpreting the Constitution and Laws," in: Antonin Scalia, *A Matter of Interpretation: Federal Courts and the Law,* An Essay by Antonin Scalia with commentary by Amy Gutmann, Gordon S. Wood, Laurence H. Tribe, Mary Ann Glendon, Ronald Dworkin, Princeton University Press, Princeton, NJ 1997, pp. 3–47.

Schleiermacher, Friedrich, *On Religion: Speeches to its Cultured Despisers,* Cambridge University Press, Cambridge 1996 (1799).

Schoeps, Hans Joachim, "The Sacrifice of Isaac in Paul's Theology," *Journal of Biblical Literature,* 65, no. 4 1946, pp. 385–392.

Schopenhauer, Arthur, *The World as Will and Representation,* Dover Publications, New York 1967 (1818).

Schopenhauer, Arthur, *Parerga and Paralipomena,* translated by E.F.J. Payne, Clarendon Press, Oxford 1974.

Scruton, Roger, *Gentle Regrets: Thoughts from a Life,* Continuum, London 2005.

Scruton, Roger, *Culture Counts: Faith and Feeling in a World Besieged,* Encounter Books, New York 2007.

Searle, John R., "Rationality and Realism, What is at stake?" *Daedalus, Journal of the American Academy of Arts and Sciences,* 122, no. 4 1993, pp. 55–83.

Selengut, Charles, *Sacred Fury: Understanding Religious Violence,* Rowman & Littlefield Publishers, Lanham, MA 2003.

Selim, Nahed, *Nehmt den Männern den Koran! Für eine weibliche Interpretation des Islam* [Take the Qur'an Away from Men! For a Female Interpretation of Islam], Piper, München Zürich 2007.

Shelley, Percy Bysshe, *The Necessity of Atheism. And other Essays,* Prometheus Books, Buffalo, NY 1993.

Shires, Henry M., "The Conflict between Queen Elizabeth and Roman Catholicism," *Church History,* 16, no. 4 1947, pp. 221–233.

Simmons, J. Aaron, "What about Isaac? Rereading *Fear and Trembling* and Rethinking Kierkegaardian Ethics," *Journal of Religious Ethics,* 35, no. 2 2007, pp. 319–345.

Singer, Peter, *Practical Ethics,* second edition, Cambridge University Press, Cambridge 1993 (1979).

Singer, Peter, "How Can We Prevent Crimes Against Humanity?" in: Nicholas Owen, *Human Rights, Human Wrongs,* The Oxford Amnesty Lectures 2001, Oxford University Press 2002, pp. 92–137.

Singer, Peter, *The President of Good and Evil: Taking George W. Bush Seriously,* Granta Books, London 2004.

Sinnott-Armstrong, Walter, "Overcoming Christianity," in: Louise M. Antony, ed., *Philosophers Without Gods: Meditations on Atheism and the Secular Life,* Oxford University Press, Oxford 2007, pp. 69–80.

Sjöberg, Mikael, "Jephtha's Daughter as Object of Desire or Feminist Icon," *Biblical Interpretation,* 15 2007, pp. 377–394.

Smith, George H., *Atheism: The Case Against God,* Prometheus Books, Buffalo, NY, 1989 (1979).

Smith, George H., *Why Atheism?,* Prometheus Books, Amherst, NY 2000.

Sokal, Alan and Bricmont, Jean, *Impostures Intellectuelles* [Intellectual Impostures], ed. Odile Jacob, Paris 1997.

Solomon, Norman, *Judaism: A Very Short Introduction,* Oxford University Press, Oxford 2000 (1996).

Sorley, W.R., *A History of British Philosophy to 1900,* Cambridge University Press, London 1965 (1920).

Sorman, Guy, *Les Enfants de Rifaa: Musulmans et modernes* [The Children of Rifaa: Muslims and Moderns], Fayard, Paris 2003.

Spencer, Herbert, "The Reconciliation," in: Andrew Pyle, ed., *Agnosticism: Contemporary Responses to Spencer and Huxley,* Thoemmes Press, Bristol 1995, pp. 1–19.

Spiro, Abram, "The Ascension of Phinehas," *Proceedings of the America Academy for Jewish Research,* 22 1953, pp. 91–114.

Stark, Rodney, *One True God: Historical Consequences of Monotheism,* Princeton University Press, Princeton 2001.

Stark, Rodney, and Finke, Roger, *Acts of Faith,* University of California Press, Berkeley 2000.

Stebbing, L. Susan, *Ideals and Illusions,* Watts & Co., London 1948 (1941).

Stebbing, L. Susan, *Thinking to Some Purpose,* Penguin Books, Harmondsworth 1952 (1939).

Stebbing, L. Susan, "Men and Moral Principles," 1943, in: L. Susan Stebbing, *Hobhouse Memorial Lectures 1941–1950,* Oxford University Press, London 1952, pp. 3–27.

Stebbing, L. Susan, *Philosophy and the Physicists,* Dover Books, New York 1958 (1937).

Stein, Gordon, ed., *An Anthology of Atheism and Rationalism,* Prometheus Books, Buffalo, NY 1980.

Stein, Gordon, *A Second Anthology of Atheism and Rationalism,* Prometheus Books, Buffalo, NY 1987.

Stenger, Victor J., *The New Atheism: Taking a Stand for Science and Reason,* Prometheus Books, Amherst NY 2009.

Stephen, Leslie, "An Agnostic's Apology," *Fortnightly Review,* XXV, 1876, pp. 840–860, also in: Andrew Pyle, ed., *Agnosticism: Contemporary Responses to Spencer and Huxley,* Thoemmes Press, Bristol 1995, pp. 48–72.

Stephen, Leslie, *Essays on Freethinking and Plainspeaking,* Longmans, Green, London 1879 (republished 1969).

Stephen, Leslie, "Poisonous Opinions," in: Leslie Stephen, *An Agnostic's Apology and Other Essays,* Smith, Elder & Co., London 1893 (republished 1969), pp. 242–338.

Stephen, Leslie, "The Religion of All Sensible Men," in: Leslie Stephen, *An Agnostic's Apology and Other Essays,* Smith, Elder & Co., London 1893 (republished 1969), pp. 338–380.

Stephen, Leslie, "The Scepticism of Believers," in: Leslie Stephen, *An Agnostic's Apology and Other Essays,* Smith, Elder & Co., London 1893 (republished 1969), pp. 42–86.

Steyn, Mark, *America Alone: The End of the World as We Know It,* Regnery Publishing, Inc., Washington, DC 2006.

Sultan, Wafa, *A God Who Hates: The Courageous Woman Who Inflamed the Muslim World Speaks Out against the Evils of Islam*, St. Martin's Press, New York 2009.

Sweetman, Brendan, *Why Politics Needs Religion: The Place of Religious Arguments in the Public Square*, Interversity Press, Downers Grove 2006.

Sweetman, Brendan, *Religion*, Continuum, London 2007.

Swinburne, Richard, *Is There a God?*, Oxford University Press, Oxford 1996.

Swinburne, Richard, *Faith and Reason*, second edition, Clarendon Press, Oxford 2005.

Taheri, Amir, *The Persian Night: Iran under the Khomeinist Revolution*, Encounter Books, New York 2009.

Taliaferro, Charles, *Philosophy of Religion*, Oneworld, Oxford 2009.

Taylor, A.E., *Plato: The Man and his Work*, Methuen & Co, London 1977 (1926).

Taylor, A.J.P., *The First World War: An Illustrated History*, Penguin Books, Harmondworth 1978 (1967).

Taylor, A.J.P., *The Origins of the Second World War*, Penguin, London 1991 (1961).

Taylor, Richard, "Law and Morality," *New York University Law Review*, 43, no. 4 1968, pp. 611–650.

Taylor, Richard, *Good and Evil*, Prometheus Books, Buffalo, NY 1984.

Ternisien, Xavier, *État et Religions* [State and Religions], Odile Jacob, Paris 2007.

Thatcher, Adrian, *The Savage Text: The Use and Abuse of the Bible*, Wiley-Blackwell, Malden 2008.

Thiselton, Anthony C., *A Concise Encyclopedia of the Philosophy of Religion*, Oneworld Publications, Oxford 2002.

Thomas, Scott M., "Review of The Battle for God: fundamentalism in Judaism, Christianity and Islam," *International Affairs*, 77, no. 1 2001, pp. 194–196.

Tibi, Bassam, "Islamic Law/Shari'a, Human Rights, Universal Morality and International Relations," *Human Rights Quarterly*, 16 1994, pp. 277–299.

Tibi, Bassam, *Europa ohne Identität? Leitkultur oder Wertebeliebigkeit* [Europe without Identity? Leading Culture or Arbitrariness in Values], 2nd ed., Siedler, München 2001 (1998).

Tibi, Bassam, *Kreuzzug und Djihad: Der Islam und die christliche Welt* [Crusade and Jihad: Islam and the Christian World], Goldman, München 2001 (1999).

Tibi, Bassam, *Im Schatten Allahs: Der Islam und die Menschenrechte* [In the Shadow of Allah: Islam and Human Rights], Ullstein, Düsseldorf 2003.

Tibi, Bassam, *Political Islam, World Politics and Europe: Democratic Peace and Euro-Islam versus Global Jihad*, Routledge, London 2008.

Tibi, Bassam, *Euro-Islam: Die Lösung eines Zivilisationskonfliktes* [Euro-Islam: The Solution to a Conflict of Civilizations], Primus Verlag, Darmstadt 2009.

Tilghman, B.R., *An Introduction to the Philosophy of Religion*, Blackwell, Oxford 1994.

Tillich, Paul, *Dynamics of Faith*, Harper Torchbooks, New York 1958.

Tocqueville, Alexis de, and Gobineau, Arthur de, *Correspondence entre Alexis de Tocqueville et Arthur de Gobineau, 1843–1859* [Correspondence between Alexis de Tocqueville and Arthur de Gobineau, 1843–1859], publiée par L. Schemann, Librairie Plon, Paris 1909.

Vallet, Odon, *Petite lexique des guerres de religion, d'hier et d'aujourdhui* [Small Dictionary of Wars of Religion, Yesterday and Today], Albin Michel, Paris 2004.

Veldman, Ilja M., "The Old Testament as a Moral code: Old Testament Stories as Exempla of the Ten Commandments," *Simiolus: Netherlands Quarterly for the History of Art,* 23, no. 4 1995, pp 215–239.

Verhofstadt, Dirk, *Pius XII en de vernietiging van de Joden* [Pius XII and the Destruction of the Jews], Houtekiet/Atlas, Antwerp 2008.

Voltaire, "Théiste," in: *Dictionnaire Philosophique,* avec introduction, variantes et notes par Julien Benda, texte établi par Raymond Naves, Éditions Garnier Frères, Paris n.d. (1764), pp. 399–400.

Walter, Nicolas, "Obituary: Richard Robinson," *The Independent,* June 14, 1996.

Weigel, George, *Faith, Reason, and the War against Jihadism: A Call to Action,* Doubleday, New York 2007.

Weldon, T.D., *States and Morals: A Study in Political Conflicts,* John Murray, London 1946.

Weldon, T.D. *The Vocabulary of Politics,* Penguin Books, Harmondsworth 1953.

White, A.D., *A History of the Warfare of Science with Theology in Christendom,* Dover Publications, New York 1960 (1896).

Wilkinson, Philip, *Religions,* Dorley Kindersley Limited, London 2008.

Windschuttle, Keith, *The Killing of History: How Literary Criticism and Social Theorists Are Murdering Our Past,* Encounter Books, San Francisco 1996.

Wolterstorff, Nicholas, "An Engagement with Rorty," *Journal of Religious Ethics,* 31, no. 1 2003, pp.129–139.

Wright, Robert, *The Evolution of God,* Little, Brown and Company, New York 2009.

Zakaria, Fareed, "The Islamic Exception," in: Fareed Zakaria, *The Future of Freedom: Illiberal Democracy at Home and Abroad,* W.W. Norton & Company, New York 2003, pp. 119–159.

Zwemer, Samuel M., *The Law of Apostasy in Islam. Answering the Question Why There Are So Few Moslem Converts, and Giving Examples of their Moral Courage and Martyrdom,* Marshall Brothers, London 1924.

Index

Index compiled by Tim Penton